Digital Archa

THE ART AND SCIEI
DIGITAL FORENSICS

Michael W. Graves

♦ Addison-Wesley

Upper Saddle River, NJ • Boston • Indianapolis • San Francisco
New York • Toronto • Montreal • London • Munich • Paris • Madrid
Capetown • Sydney • Tokyo • Singapore • Mexico City

Many of the designations used by manufacturers and sellers to distinguish their products are claimed as trademarks. Where those designations appear in this book, and the publisher was aware of a trademark claim, the designations have been printed with initial capital letters or in all capitals.

The author and publisher have taken care in the preparation of this book, but make no expressed or implied warranty of any kind and assume no responsibility for errors or omissions. No liability is assumed for incidental or consequential damages in connection with or arising out of the use of the information or programs contained herein.

The publisher offers excellent discounts on this book when ordered in quantity for bulk purchases or special sales, which may include electronic versions and/or custom covers and content particular to your business, training goals, marketing focus, and branding interests. For more information, please contact:

U.S. Corporate and Government Sales
(800) 382-3419
corpsales@pearsontechgroup.com

For sales outside the United States, please contact:

International Sales
international@pearsoned.com

Visit us on the Web: informit.com/aw

Library of Congress Cataloging-in-Publication Data
Graves, Michael W.
   Digital archaeology : the art and science of digital forensics / Michael W. Graves, MSDIM.—First Edition.
        pages   cm
   Includes bibliographical references and index.
   ISBN 978-0-321-80390-0 (pbk. : alk. paper)
   1. Computer crimes—Investigation. 2. Forensic sciences—Data processing. I. Title.
   HV8079.C65G7293 2013
   363.250285—dc23

                                                        2013020221

ISBN-13: 978-0-321-80390-0
ISBN-10:   0-321-80390-6
Text printed in the United States on recycled paper at LSC Communications.

Editor-in-Chief
Bernard Goodwin

Development Editor
Michael Thurston

Managing Editor
John Fuller

Project Editor
Elizabeth Ryan

Copy Editor
Teresa Wilson

Indexer
Infodex Indexing, Inc.

Proofreader
Carol Lallier

Editorial Assistant
Michelle Housley

Cover Designer
Chuti Prasertsith

Compositor
Graphic World, Inc.

I guess I'm just a regular guy after all. In spite of the fact that my daughter's assignment to draw a picture of one of her parents consisted of a silhouette of my head against a computer monitor—despite the fact that I learned that my son got a blue ribbon in marksmanship by seeing the award hanging on the wall—even though my wife had to remind me twice of anniversaries and dozens of times about birthdays—my family always stuck with me. This book is for them.

CONTENTS

PREFACE

In performing an investigation that explores the use of computers or digital data, one is basically embarking on an archaeological expedition. To extract useful artifacts (information, in our case), one must be exceedingly careful in how one approaches the site. The similarities between a digital investigation and an archaeological excavation are much closer than you might imagine. Data, like physical artifacts, gets dropped into the oddest places. The effects of time and environment are just as damaging, if not more so, to digital artifacts as they are physical mementos.

WHY THIS BOOK?

Archaeologists are fully aware that, due to the passage of time, there are things they can never recover. The skin that once covered a skeleton long buried in the desert can never be found and analyzed. Likewise, data that was once stored in active memory on a computer can't be recovered once the computer is switched off. However, in each example, it is possible to uncover evidence that both existed. When you first begin a digital investigation, you are undertaking a modern archaeological dig. Just like the shards of broken pots tell the anthropologist a lot about the culture that once used the vessel, the data you dig out of the computer can tell you volumes about the people who used the system.

This book takes the concepts of archaeology and applies them to computer science. It is a tutorial on how to investigate a computer system to find evidence of a crime or other misbehavior, and to make sure that evidence will stand up in court. While there are numerous other books that cover the whys and wherefores of digital forensics, this one will go into some detail on how to accomplish the task.

We've all watched the TV programs where the good guys figure out everything the bad guys did just from examining a piece of hair. (Is this why the bad guys are always called "hairballs"?) In modern-day investigations, the role of the computer plays as big a part as the star witness in many cases. In fact, the computer often *is* the star witness. Many cases have been solved or settled on the basis of what trained professionals were able to discover while examining *electronic evidence* (e-evidence).

However, the courts take a dim view on just anybody digging around in somebody else's computers. They generally insist that legal process be followed, and that only a trained professional attempt the examination. The extraction and analysis of e-evidence is all part of what we call *computer forensics.* So what is forensics? The word itself originated from the Latin word *forum,* which described a place where people could assemble publicly and discuss matters of interest to the community. In that context, the word was derived from the strict rules of presentation applied to such discussions. In the context of this book, the word best means *application of science or technology to the collection of evidence for the purpose of establishing facts.* The vast majority of references specify that forensic science is targeted at criminal investigation. However, in the real world, digital investigations are commonly used in civil cases and within organizations to identify members engaged in illicit activities.

A crime scene investigator might have DNA from samples of hair found at the scene analyzed to prove that a specific individual was on the scene at least once. Chemical analysis of soil can identify a geographical origin. The process of computer forensics is a series of steps by which professionals can prove the following:

- Data exists.
- Data once existed.
- Data originated from a specific source.
- A particular individual either created or had access to the data in question.
- The data is relevant to the case.
- The data has not changed in any way from acquisition to analysis.

While it is not always necessary to prove all of the above statements are true, in order to secure a case it is best if as many as possible can be locked down. Even when all of the above are proven, a slick lawyer can always point out the fact that e-evidence is almost always circumstantial and press for reasons why the investigation team has presented insufficient corroborating evidence to demonstrate relevance or authenticity. (Both of these terms will be discussed in greater detail in the course of this book.) Even if you can prove beyond a shadow of a doubt that Tammy Sue created the letter you found on Billy Bob's computer, can you prove that Billy Bob actually acquired the letter illegally? Probably not—which is why, as an expert witness, you don't even try. You simply collect the evidence and state the facts. The more incriminating evidence that you can find, the better the chances are that your side wins the battle.

WHO WILL BENEFIT FROM THIS BOOK?

This book is primarily targeted at the reader who is preparing for a career as a professional investigator. It will not server as a legal tome for the prosecutor but will provide the background needed to efficiently and accurately collect evidence that a prosecutor can use. It will also prove handy to the IT professional who is occasionally called upon to perform e-investigations.

In addition, while the book's primary goal is not to show people how to hide their tracks, understanding the processes discussed in this book can help an individual or organization prepare for a hostile demand for the delivery of electronic information (*e-discovery*). Properly identifying the bits on your computer can go a long way in preparing a defensible stance. If you know the garbage they are likely to find, you can be ready with an explanation. Foreknowledge also stops you from making the legally indefensible mistake of deliberately destroying evidence in advance of e-discovery. Such bad behavior doesn't just result in a slap on the wrist. It can result in fines ranging into the millions (or even billions) of dollars.

WHO WILL **NOT** BENEFIT FROM THIS BOOK?

Before attempting to fully understand this book, a wise reader will already have fulfilled a few prerequisites. He or she already knows a computer inside and out. Swapping out hard disks is second nature, and she finds it easier to work from the command prompt than a GUI. And he doesn't have to ask what a GUI is. Operating systems and file systems aren't a foreign language. Opening a registry editor doesn't induce spasms of panic, and most of all, exploring new areas of technology is a form of entertainment—not a nightmare.

There will be terms used in this book that I assume the reader already knows from previous experience or learning, because they are more relevant to general computer technology than to digital forensics. While it is not necessary to be a networking guru, it is certainly essential that you have a firm understanding of the concepts of networking, including principles of TCP/IP, network hardware, and communications.

How This Book Is Organized

The book starts out by introducing the reader to various things that must be clear before an investigation is ever initiated. The key differences between civil and criminal investigations are covered. What are the rules of the game? What laws affect us? Tools of the trade and minimum levels of training are a topic of discussion. What are the basic procedures of performing a computer forensic investigation?

From there on, the book describes tools and techniques that the average investigator will use on a day-in, day-out basis. The chapters are set up in approximately the order that the tasks will be accomplished in the real world. Finally, some of the humdrum aspects of the profession are discussed. Documentation, certification, and business aspects of digital forensics aren't that much fun. But they are necessary aspects of the profession.

Understanding the Book's Format

In order to present information in an orderly fashion, this book follows a scheme that will help the reader learn the material more quickly:

- **Bold:** A new term that will appear in the glossary
- *Italics:* A definition
- `Monospace type`: Code or commands to be typed into the computer
- Command Syntax:

  ```
  copy {filename.doc} {PATH:\newfile.doc} is the syntax used in
  the text to represent the command copy novel.doc c:\temp\docs\
  novel.doc. Brackets will not be used at the command prompt.
  ```

- Sidebars: Anecdotes or examples that relate to the current text

The Need for Professionals

Sadly enough, this is a litigious world we live in. If you run a business, chances get better every day that you will find the need to sue someone—or will be on the wrong end of the need. Some people want to retain a rosy outlook on life and go into computer forensics because they think it is a way to bring the bad guys to justice. I'm delighted to report that sometimes, they are actually right. Just don't forget that the other side always has their team of professionals ready to refute everything you say or write. That's why so many computer investigators are needed.

A sign of how strong the field is can be seen in the Great Recession of 2008. When nearly six million people in regular walks of life all lost their jobs, openings couldn't be filled for practitioners in the black arts of digital forensics. To top things off, scanning a listing of job offerings showed the lowest offering salary (that was stated) at $46,000 per year. The vast majority of starting salaries listed ranged from the high fifties to the mid-sixties per year. And this was starting salary.

With recent laws such as Sarbanes-Oxley and the new Federal Rules of Civil Procedure, along with venerable old laws like HIPAA and Gramm-Leach-Bliley, putting more pressure on business, health, and nonprofit organizations, it is a certain bet that the number of investigators needed will only increase. The key to getting one of these jobs is training and certification. And compliance has become a huge issue for many organizations.

CERTIFICATION PROGRAMS FOR FORENSICS PROFESSIONALS

As of this writing, there are several certification programs dedicated specifically to forensic investigation of digital data sources. In order to impress a potential client with your qualifications, it is not only necessary to demonstrate your competence with digital forensic tools, but you must also show that you have a satisfactory knowledge of operating systems, networks, and computer hardware. The following list is by no means comprehensive, but offers a glimpse of what the industry offers. In addition to certification programs, a number of colleges have begun to offer computer forensics as a degree program, including a handful that offers master's degree programs in the subject.

GENERIC FORENSICS CERTIFICATIONS

- Certified Computer Examiner (CCE): International Society of Forensic Computer Examiners
- Certified Electronic Evidence Collection Specialist (CEECS): International Association of Computer Investigative Specialists (offered only to law enforcement officials)
- Certified Forensic Computer Examiner (CFCE): International Association of Computer Investigative Specialists
- Certified Information Systems Security Professional (CISSP): (ISC)[2]
- Global Information Assurance Certification (GIAC) Certified Forensic Analyst
- GIAC Certified Forensic Examiner

VENDOR-SPECIFIC FORENSICS CERTIFICATIONS

- AccessData Certified Examiner (ACE): Certification of proficiency with the AccessData Forensics Toolkit
- EnCase Certified Examiner: Guidance Software
- Paraben: Various certificates of completion

NONFORENSIC CERTIFICATIONS

- Microsoft Certified Systems Engineer (MCSE): Microsoft certification of professional excellence in managing Microsoft servers
- Cisco Certified Network Engineer (CCNE): Proof of mastery of Cisco router and switch management
- A+: Vendor-neutral certification of expertise in computer hardware installation and maintenance offered by the Computing Technology Industry Association (CompTIA)
- Network1: Vendor-neutral certification of expertise in network infrastructure and administration offered by CompTIA

A PERSONAL NOTE ON CERTIFICATION PROGRAMS

Many years ago, I earned my daily bread in a completely different field. I sold computer hardware and systems to businesses and schools. As it was, the company for which I worked was unwilling to hire telephone support staff to assist customers with hardware issues. Instead, they expected the sales staff to field support calls. I got very good at that task. So much so that my boss started dispatching me to perform actual repairs any time the service call was close enough to justify the travel.

I discovered that I liked repairing computers a whole lot more than I did selling them. So I started distributing my resume to a variety of potential employers—and didn't get a single response. On a whim, I self-studied for the A+ certification from CompTIA, took the exams, and passed with flying colors. As soon as I had those letters behind my name, I started circulating my resume again and got three invitations to interview on the first pass. Of those, I was offered a position that paid approximately 35% more than I earned in my best year as a sales rep. For me, that was a very powerful lesson on the value of certification. Getting a master of science in digital investigation management hasn't hurt either.

ACKNOWLEDGMENTS

A book of this nature is not the product of a single individual. I get my name on the cover because it was my idea and I did most of the writing—on the first go-around, anyway. However, there are some people who might go completely unnoticed for their patience, knowledge, skill, and understanding if I don't point them out.

First of all, I would like to thank Robert J. Sherman for his help in mobile phone technology. Okay, to be precise, he didn't just help . . . he wrote the whole chapter on mobile device forensics. He is an expert in this field, and my knowledge pales in comparison. So in the face of a lot of begging and pleading, along with promises of fame and fortune (sorry, bud . . . this is all the fame and fortune you're likely to get out of this deal), he caved and agreed to help me. In the end, he turned out an excellent chapter. So if, after reading that chapter, you wonder why it reads so much better than the rest of the book, now you know.

Next, I'd like to give credit to two amazing reviewers whose comments turned a marginal first draft into a profoundly better final manuscript. Jay Lightfoot and Ruth Watson both provided chapter-by-chapter comments on my first effort, suggesting numerous improvements in both structure and content. Without those reviews, I don't think this book would be as good as it is (however good that may be).

Naturally, I'm saving the best for last. My publisher actually made me *complete* the book! What's with that? Michelle Housley, Michael Thurston, and Bernard Goodwin at Addison-Wesley all refused to give up hope on either me or the project (although I'm sure there were times it was tempting) and got me through that inevitable mid-book crisis where I felt I couldn't possibly write another page without insanity setting in. This book is proof that I was wrong about the former, but I cannot with certainty attest to the latter.

Michael W. Graves
April, 2013

ABOUT THE AUTHOR

Michael W. Graves has worked as an IT professional for more than 15 years—as a network specialist, a security analyst, and most recently as a forensic analyst. He holds a master of science in digital investigation from Champlain College, where he spent several semesters as an adjunct professor of computer science. His publications include a number of certification manuals for several of the CompTIA certifications, as well as two novels. When not poking around in computers or writing books, he carts around an 8x10 view camera and makes black-and-white landscape photographs with a nod toward the F64 school of photography.

THE ANATOMY OF A DIGITAL INVESTIGATION

This chapter will deal with the structural aspects that are common to most, if not all, digital investigations. Most current texts on the subject refer to a common investigation model, although there is some disagreement on how many components make up the model. This book will use a six-part model, which will be covered in more detail later in this chapter.

It is essential to understand at the outset precisely what the scope of the investigation entails. The type of investigation dictates the level of authorization required. Generally, there are three types of investigation. **Internal investigations** are sponsored by an organization. They generally start out as a deep, dark secret that the company doesn't want getting out. Therefore, courts and state and federal agencies are rarely involved at the outset. The other two types—**civil** and **criminal**—both require involvement by the courts, but on different levels.

There will never be an investigation that does not have multiple stakeholders. In all court cases, there is the **plaintiff** and the **defendant.** In civil cases, these are the two litigants asking the courts to settle a dispute. In criminal cases, the defendant is the person accused of a crime and the plaintiff is the one making the accusation, which will always be some level of government authority. In addition to these obvious players, there are those on the sidelines whose interests must be considered. Lawyers will almost always be involved, and in cases that are likely to end up in court, be assured that the judge will take an active interest.

With people's finances, freedom, or even lives at stake, the necessity for accurate and thorough reporting cannot be emphasized enough. It is so critically important that the subject of documentation will be discussed several times and in several places in this book. This chapter will start the reader off with the basics of good documentation.

Please be aware that this chapter deals only with the process of investigation. In Chapters 2 and 3, there will be detailed discussions of the various legal issues that the digital investigator must face on a daily basis. Consider the legal issues to be the glue that binds the model, but not the actual model. You can perform any number of investigations with no regard for the law. The results will be very revealing, but useless. Failure to be aware of legal aspects will cause the most perfectly executed investigation to fall apart the instant the case is picked up by the legal team.

A Basic Model for Investigators

Today's teaching methods require everything to be broken down into a simplified structure that you can put into a diagram. Computer investigations are no different. Even though there will probably never be any two cases that are identical, they should always be processed in accordance with a standard investigative model. Kruse and Heiser (2001) laid out the basic computer investigation model in their book entitled *Computer Forensics: Incident Response Essentials.* Their model was a four-part model with the following steps:

- Assess
- Acquire
- Analyze
- Report

As shown in Figure 1.1, the four steps are further broken down into more granular levels that represent processes that occur within each step. A more thorough study expands the model to six steps, as follows:

- Identification/assessment
- Collection/acquisition
- Preservation
- Examination
- Analysis
- Reporting

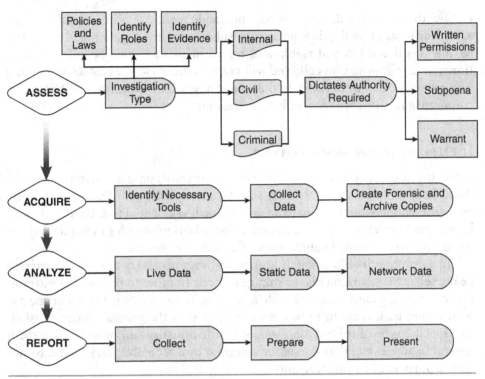

Figure 1.1 The steps of a digital investigation

The six-step model (Casey 2001) as seen in Figure 1.1 emphasizes the importance (and process) of preserving the data. It also distinguishes between the process of examination and analysis, whereas Kruse and Heiser considered them to be two parts of a single process. Experience has shown that acquisition and preservation are not the same, and while it might be an easy enough procedure to extract and examine data, accurate analysis is as much an art as it is a science.

From a management standpoint, each of these steps must be carefully monitored. Through a process of careful documentation of the history of each case, the various processes can be constantly reassessed for efficiency and reliability. When it becomes necessary, knowing what works and what doesn't allows the observant manager to tweak the steps in order to improve organizational effectiveness.

Figure 1.1 emphasizes just how detailed these seemingly simple steps can actually be. The assessment phase alone has a multitude of steps involving people, hardware, environment factors, political implications, and jurisdiction. Acquisition of evidence cannot begin until all potential sources of evidentiary material are identified, collected, inventoried, and catalogued. All of this must be done according to strict legal guidelines, or any subsequent investigation will be a waste of time. Legal and internal regulations regarding privacy must be followed at all times, or any information collected will not be admissible as evidence should the case ever make its way to court. In the case of internal investigations, adherence to corporate guidelines will generally be sufficient.

IDENTIFICATION/ASSESSMENT

Before beginning any investigation, the general rules of engagement must be established in advance and from the very start be strictly followed. Those rules can be very different between criminal and civil cases. It is essential that the investigator know what regulations apply to a specific investigation in order to not damage or destroy a case by failure to abide, either flagrantly or inadvertently.

In a criminal investigation, it is almost always necessary to obtain a warrant before seizing systems, media, or storage devices. In order to obtain that warrant, the investigating entity must provide a judge sufficient evidence that a crime has been committed, is about to be committed, or is in the process of commission. The specific type of information sought by the investigation must be identified; general fishing expeditions are never approved by a reputable judge—at least not for the purpose of issuing warrants.

Civil cases have more lenient guidelines. Internal investigations sponsored by an organization can be even more lenient. Federal guidelines regarding invasion of privacy are not as strictly enforced on civilian investigators looking into civil infractions as they are on agents of a government—state, federal, or local— who are investigating criminal complaints. Internal investigations can be made even easier when employees or members have signed a statement outlining an organization's policies and guidelines.

No case should be accepted by an investigator directly. An executive-level decision, based on a set of predefined guidelines (to be discussed later), must be made on whether to accept or decline each individual case presented to the organization. While it falls upon a law enforcement agency to accept any case assigned that involves violation of state or federal statutes, a private organization can refuse to accept cases for a variety of reasons. The organization's leadership must indentify the criteria for case acceptance and stick to those criteria. It does the company's reputation no good to be associated with a pedophile after publicly stating that its motives are to defend the community.

Make a list of all legal documentation that will be required. Warrants will be required in criminal cases. Court orders or subpoenas will be needed in civil matters. Signed agreements outlining the scope of the investigation should be required in all internal investigations.

Once the ground rules are established, it is time to identify potential sources of evidence. The obvious place to look is on the local system, including hard disk drives, removable media that might be lying about, printers, digital cameras, and so forth. Less obvious sources of information might be PDAs, external hard disks or optical drives, and even system RAM if the data processing systems are still running when the incident is reported. Knowing in advance what must be acquired can prevent the investigator from making critical errors during the process of acquisition.

COLLECTION/ACQUISITION

This is the most technical part of the investigation and can also be the most critical time for making errors. If the case under scrutiny should ever come to trial, the investigator presenting the case must be able to prove the following:

- The data is authentic.
- The copy of the data used for analysis is reliable.
- The data was not modified during acquisition or analysis (chain of custody).
- The tools used to analyze the data are valid tools.
- Sufficient evidence, both **incriminating** and **exculpatory,** has been acquired and analyzed to support the proffered conclusion.
- The conclusions drawn are consistent with the data collected and analyzed.
- People involved in the collection and analysis of the data are properly trained and qualified to do their job.

This doesn't sound easy, and it isn't. Details on how to assure that all of these requirements are met are covered in greater detail in later chapters. For now, suffice it to say that it is essential that they be fulfilled.

PRESERVATION

A cardinal rule of digital investigation is that the original data must *never* be touched. For many years, the standard rule has been that a forensically sound copy of the original be made and that the examination and analysis of data be performed on the forensic copy. In terms of nonvolatile media, such as hard disks, removable media, and optical disks, this is still the rule. Devices should always be mounted as read-only in order to assure that no data is modified or overwritten during the process of mounting the device. Hard disk duplicators are designed specifically for this purpose, and in Windows systems, a simple modification of the registry allows USB devices to mount read-only.

Legal issues might arise if there is any possibility that media used to store images may have been contaminated. Be aware of that possibility and either have new media available for collection or be certain that previously used media has been forensically wiped.

In many cases, it becomes essential that copies of data be acquired through a process of live acquisition. This is the case when it becomes necessary to capture the contents of memory from a running system, to acquire log files from network devices that cannot be brought down, or to archive information from network servers or storage appliances that defy the making of a forensic copy. If it is not possible, for any reason, to create a forensically sound copy, it is essential that the investigator document the reasons such a copy could not be made and record as accurately as possible the state of the evidentiary source before and after acquisition.

Storage of preserved information becomes part of the chain of custody process, and care must be taken that all data and devices collected during this phase are properly documented and tracked. Be able to verify that there was never a possibility for evidence to become tainted through outside tampering, corruption, or improper procedure.

EXAMINATION

The process of examining data increases in scope and complexity every year. Whereas 1.44MB floppy disks were once the repository for stolen and illicit data, investigators these days are presented with flash drives the size of key fobs that hold 64 or more gigabytes of data and hard disks that store in excess of a terabyte. To make matters worse, the data is not likely to sit on a porch swing in plain view for anyone to see. Investigators will find it necessary to look for evidence in **unallocated space** left behind by deleted files. Hidden partitions, **slack space,** and even registry entries are capable of hiding large quantities of data. Steganography can hide documents inside of an image or music file. So essentially, the investigator is given an archive the size of the Chicago Public Library and asked to find a handwritten note on the back of a napkin tucked somewhere inside of a book.

Data carving tools and methods of looking for evidentiary material have evolved, and depending on the nature of the case, the investigator's tool kit will require having several utilities. For criminal cases requiring forensically sound presentation, it is critical that the tools used to examine data be those considered valid by the courts. There are a few commercially available software suites approved for evidentiary use. Among these are Encase by Guidance Software and the Forensics Tool Kit (FTK) from Access Data Corporation. A suite of tools running on Linux that is not "officially" sanctioned but is generally considered acceptable by most courts is The Sleuth Kit, designed by Brian Carrier.

Keeping up with technical innovations in the industry is most critical in this area. As new technology emerges, new tools will be needed to examine the accumulated data it creates. The organization that follows the cutting edge of technology will always be two steps behind those that help develop it. The balancing act comes when management must defend the use of a new tool to which the courts and lawyers have not yet been exposed. Be prepared to defend the tool along with the conclusions it helped you formulate.

ANALYSIS

Here is where the process of digital forensic investigation leaves the realm of technology and enters that of black magic. It is up to the investigator to determine what constitutes evidence and what constitutes digital clutter. A variety of tools exist that assist the investigator in separating OS files from user data files. Others assist in identifying and locating specific types of files.

Technique is as critical as the selection of tools. For example, when searching an e-mail archive for messages related to a specific case, string searches can bring up all those that contain specific keywords. Other utilities can detect steganography or alternate data streams in NTFS file systems. Collecting the data necessary to prove a case becomes as much art as it is science. One thing that the investigator must always keep in mind is that exculpatory evidence must be considered as strongly as incriminating evidence.

REPORTING

Documentation of the project begins the minute an investigator is approached with a potential case. Every step of the process must be thoroughly documented to include what people are involved (who reported what, who might be potential suspects, potential witnesses, or possible sources of help), as well as thorough documentation of the scene, including photographs of the environment and anything that might be showing on computer monitors. Each step taken by the investigator needs to be recorded, defining what was done, why it was done, how it was done, and what results were obtained. **Hash** files of data sources must be generated before and after acquisition. Any differences must be documented and explained. Conclusions drawn by the investigating team must be fully explained. On the witness stand, it is likely that an investigator will be required to prove his or her qualifications to act as an investigator. A meticulously investigated case can be destroyed by inadequate documentation. While commercial forensic suites automate much of the documentation process, there is still much manual attention required of the investigator.

UNDERSTANDING THE SCOPE OF THE INVESTIGATION

As mentioned, there are three basic types of investigation. With each type, the rules get tighter and the consequences of failure to comply get progressively stricter. A good rule of thumb is to pretend that the strictest rules apply to all investigations. However, as you might imagine, there are some role-specific requirements that don't apply to all of them.

INTERNAL INVESTIGATIONS

Internal investigation is the least restrictive of the inquiries you might make. From a standpoint of professional courtesy, internal investigations are more likely to be the least hostile type you'll ever do. You work directly with management, and the target of your inquiries probably won't even be aware of your activities until you are finished. You don't have courts and lawyers combing every word you say or write, hoping to find the smallest mistake.

That is not to say that there aren't laws that apply to internal probes. There most certainly are. State and federal laws regarding privacy apply to even the smallest organization. Also, different states have different laws regarding how companies deal with employment matters, implied privacy issues, and implied contracts. This isn't intended to be a law book, so for the purposes of brevity and clarity, understand this. It is important to review any relevant regulations before you make your first move.

Most corporations have formal guidelines for such matters. In addition to a written employee handbook, it is very likely that a company has documented guidelines regarding issues leading to termination, use of company infrastructure (including computers, e-mail systems, and network services), and so forth. In every step of your process, make sure that you adhere to the law and to corporate policy. If there appears to be a conflict between the two, get legal advice. At the very least, make sure you have written authorization to perform every step you take. Management needs to be aware of your process and every step involved in the course of investigation, and they must sign off, giving approval. Document everything you do, how you did it, and what results you obtained. In digging into the source and impact of any internal security breach, your foremost concern is the protection of your client. However, should your probe uncover deeper issues, such as illegal activity or a national security breach, then it becomes necessary to call in outside authorities.

CIVIL INVESTIGATIONS

Civil cases are likely to be brought to the organization in situations where intellectual property rights are at risk, when a company's network security has been breached, or when a company suspects that an employee or an outsider is making unauthorized use of the network. Marcella and Menendez (2008) identify the following possible attacks:

- Intrusions
- Denial-of-service attacks
- Malicious code
- Malicious communication
- Misuse of resources

An investigator involved in a civil dispute should be cognizant of the Federal Rules of Civil Procedure. Although a legal degree is hardly necessary, a strong background in civil law is invaluable. Additionally, experience in business management is useful, in that a good understanding of standard corporate policy is necessary. Good communications skills are required. Management needs to be able to feel equally comfortable dealing with a CEO or a secretary.

When working with large repositories of data connected to many different users and devices, it becomes more difficult to assess who actually committed an infraction. Proving that a specific user was accessing the network at a specific time (and possibly from a particular machine) can be critical to winning a case. Anson and Bunting (2007) point out the difficulties of generating an accurate **timeline** and recommend some good tools for simplifying the matter. A good manager will keep abreast of changing technology and make sure that the organization is equipped with the proper tools.

Tools required for examining large networks or performing live data capture are substantially more expensive than those used to search individual data sources. Generally, it is not possible to bring down a corporate network while the investigative team captures images of thousands of drives. Costs in time and materials would be prohibitive, as would be the negative impact of downtime on the company. Specialized software is needed to capture, preserve, and document the data. Additional tools are needed for data reduction. Filtering out the general network chatter and unrelated business documents can be a time-consuming process.

Keeping up with newer technology is essential, as is constant refresher training. The organization must continually assess its current capabilities and apply them to what imminent future needs are likely to be. As technology advances, investigative tools and techniques need to advance as well. Cases are won and lost on the ability of investigators to extract evidence. If a forensics team finds itself faced with a technology it doesn't understand, there will be no time for on-the-job training.

CRIMINAL PROCEDURE MANAGEMENT

Defining precisely what constitutes computer crime is very difficult to do. Fortunately, it is not up to the investigator to determine what is and what is not criminal activity. However, some definitions have been presented by various experts. Reyes (2007) states that a computer crime will exhibit one or more of the following characteristics:

- The computer is the object, or the data in the computer are the objects, of the act.
- The computer creates a unique environment or unique form of assets.
- The computer is the instrument or the tool of the act.
- The computer represents a symbol used for intimidation or deception.

Generally speaking, computer crimes are little different from conventional crimes. Somebody stole something, somebody hurt somebody else, somebody committed fraud, or somebody possessed or distributed something that is illegal to own (contraband). While not an exhaustive list of possible computer crimes, the following is a list of the most commonly investigated:

- Auction or online retail fraud
- Child pornography
- Child endangerment
- Counterfeiting
- Cyberstalking
- Forgery

- Gambling
- Identity theft
- Piracy (software, literature, and music)
- Prostitution
- Securities fraud
- Theft of services

Prosecution of criminal cases requires a somewhat different approach than do civil cases. Legal restrictions are stricter, and the investigator is more likely to be impacted by constitutional limitations regarding search and seizure or privacy. Failure to abide by all applicable regulations will almost certainly result in having all collected evidence suppressed because of technicalities. Many civil investigations are not impacted as severely by constitutional law because there is no representative of the government involved in the investigation. To assure that the investigation succeeds, management of a criminal division needs to have someone with a strong legal background. Courts will use the **Federal Rules of Evidence** to decide whether or not to allow evidence to be admitted in an individual case.

For the same reasons, reporting procedures and chain of custody must be rigorously followed by each person involved in an investigation, whether they are involved directly or peripherally. Even a minor departure from best practice is likely to be challenged by opposing counsel. Because of this, selection of personnel becomes a greater challenge. A technical whiz with little or no documentation ability is likely to fail in criminal investigation. Anyone who demonstrates a disregard for authority is a poor candidate for investigating criminal cases.

Tools used in criminal cases are subject to a tighter scrutiny than those used in civil cases. When a person's life or liberty hangs in the balance, judges and juries are less sympathetic to a technician who cannot verify that the tools used to extract the evidence being presented are reliable. Software and hardware tools used by the organization must be recognized by the court for use, and the techniques used by investigators must be diligently documented to show there was no deviation from accepted standard procedures.

Funding is likely to be more limited in criminal work than in civil investigations. Money will be coming from budget-strapped government entities or from law offices watching every dime. In some cases, courts will apply the Zubulake test to determine if costs should be shifted from one party to the other. This test is based on findings from the case *Zubulake v. UBS Warburg* (217 F.R.D. at 320, 2003) where the judge issued a list of seven factors to be considered in ordering discovery (and in reassigning costs). These factors are to be considered in order of importance, the most important being listed first:

1. The extent to which the request is specifically tailored to discover relevant information
2. The availability of such information from other sources
3. The total cost of production compared to the amount in controversy
4. The total cost of production compared to the resources available to each party
5. The relative ability of each party to control costs and its incentive to do so
6. The importance of the issues at stake in the **litigation**
7. The relative benefits to the parties of obtaining the information

IDENTIFYING THE STAKEHOLDERS

In any investigation, there are going to be a large number of people with a vested interest in the outcome. These people are the **stakeholders.** Stakeholders vary in each investigation, depending in part on the scope of the investigation and in part on the raw size of the organization and the data set involved. Sometimes it is easy for the investigator to become overwhelmed by the sheer number of people involved. In all cases, it is safe to assume that there are two primary stakeholders with a greater investment than any other. Those are the accused and the accuser.

The accuser is the easiest to identify. This is the person or the organization that initiated the inquiry to begin with. As simple as that may seem, all too often the actual accuser gets left in the wake of bureaucracy and procedure. This is particularly true in cases that are destined to be presented before a court. Lawyers suddenly take the place of the stakeholders, and the assumption becomes that suddenly they *are* the primary stakeholders. A good investigator never lets this happen. Communications may be with these attorneys as representatives of the stakeholders, but the primary stakeholders remain the accused and the accuser.

Depending on the magnitude and the scope of the case, there might be a wide variety of secondary stakeholders—or none at all. To be a stakeholder of any kind, an individual or organization must have something to gain or lose from the outcome of the investigation. In spite of possible arguments to the contrary, this does not include the news media. Key stakeholders include

- Decision makers: Those who have the authority to initiate or to cancel an investigation or to reassign personnel.

- Mediators: Judges or third-party arbitrators who are responsible for deciding the outcome of the case or issue decisions pertaining to procedure.
- Customers: People or organizations downstream from the accused or accuser who will be directly impacted by the decision. For example, in *i4i Limited Partnership v. Microsoft Corporation*, virtually every reseller of Microsoft Word was impacted (*i4i v. Microsoft Corporation*, 6:07VC113, 2009).
- Process owners: People or organizations whose actions may have contributed to the case or whose operations were or will be impacted by the case.

Extraordinary circumstances can lead to unexpected stakeholders. The Exxon-Valdez incident in 1989 started out as the accidental grounding of an oil tanker that resulted in Exxon's launch of an investigation into the actions of the ship's captain. Before it was over, there were more than 38,000 litigants, including individuals, agencies, and environmental organizations, and three different sets of judges involved in a variety of decisions (Lebedoff 1997). That's a lot of stakeholders.

THE ART OF DOCUMENTATION

Any individual who lacks organizational skills or who finds it difficult to keep accurate notes as he works is not a likely candidate for the position of digital investigator. The vast majority of work the investigator does is documentation. There are five levels of documentation that must be either maintained or created during the course of each case study:

- General case documentation
- Procedural documentation
- Process documentation
- Case timeline
- Evidence chain of custody

Every one of these is important to winning a case should it make its way to court. Faulty, incomplete, or missing documentation can destroy an otherwise meticulously prepared case. In addition to these items, there is also the final report, but that will be covered elsewhere in this book.

THE CRAFT OF PROJECT MANAGEMENT

While this book is not intended to be a treatise on what makes a good project manager, it should be pointed out that good project management practices can facilitate the smooth completion of an investigation from beginning to end. Virtually all of the principles defined in the Project Management Institute's (PMI) *Project Management Book of Knowledge* (PMBOK) apply directly to the investigatory process. Wysocki (2009) defines a project as "a sequence of unique, complex, and connected activities that have one goal or purpose and that must be completed by a specific time, within budget, and according to specification."

Like all other projects, a digital forensics investigation involves multiple stakeholders and a defined scope, and has specific objectives that must be pursued. Multiple people will be involved, requiring the project leader to manage people's time, to assure that tasks are assigned to the person most skilling in performing the work involved, and to keep everything in budget and on time.

GENERAL CASE DOCUMENTATION

Case documentation begins the moment you are asked to consider investigating an incident. Even if an investigator or agency chooses not to accept a case (assuming that possibility exists), it may later become necessary to explain why the case was turned away. Another thing the investigator needs to keep in mind is that anything recorded during the case is **discoverable.** To be discoverable means that opposing counsel has the right to examine and analyze data collected during the process. If an investigator takes written notes or uses a digital voice recorder to make verbal observations, copies of the notes and audio files must be made available to the opposition if requested. Therefore, great care should be taken in the creation of documentation.

A number of factors need to be addressed in the basic case documentation:

- What is the name and contact information for the organization involved in the incident? Record every individual contacted during the investigation, that person's role in the process, and when, where, and how he or she was contacted.
- When was the investigative agency notified, and who initially took the information? Record exact dates and times.
- A description of the incident, both in technical terms and in lay terms.
- When was the incident discovered?
- When did the incident occur? This may be a best-guess scenario.
- Who discovered the incident?
- To whom was the incident reported? This means anyone who learned of it, regardless of rank and file.
- What systems, information, or resources were impacted by the event? This includes hardware, organizational entities, and people.

- Is there any preliminary information that suggests how the offending actions were accomplished?
- What is the impact of the incident on the individual or organization affected? This includes financial impact, impact on the systems involved, and any effect it may have had on the health or mental welfare of individuals involved.
- What actions were taken between discovery of the incident and reporting it to authorities? This means everything that was done, including simple files searches.
- Who are the stakeholders as they are identified?
- As soon as possible, provide a detailed inventory of all hardware (and possibly software) that is involved in the incident. If hardware is seized, provide a separate, itemized list of seized equipment.
- Have all copies of all pertinent documentation, such as warrants, summons, written correspondence, and so forth, been added to the case file?

Any other generic information that does not fit directly into one of the other reporting categories would be included in this section. This would include expense reports, timesheets, and any other general recordkeeping.

PROCEDURAL DOCUMENTATION

During the course of the investigation, a number of tasks will be performed. The history of these tasks should be maintained as painstakingly as possible. The investigator should describe every step taken, the tools used to perform specific tasks, a description of the procedure, and a brief summary of the results. Detailed results can be included in the final report. When describing a technical process, process documentation should be provided whenever possible (as described in the next section).

Anytime the investigator chooses not to follow recommended best practice, it is essential to record the action being taken, what the recommended procedure would normally be, and what actual procedure is being used, and to explain precisely why the deviation is occurring. For the longest time, the best practice when coming upon a running suspect system was to pull the plug. The reasoning was that an orderly shutdown of the system overwrote a lot of data and drastically altered paging files. However, in a live network event that is still transpiring, it may be necessary to collect information from active memory, including current network connections, user connections, and possibly cached passwords. Shutting down the system would kill all that information. The proper course would then be to perform a live analysis and document precisely why the action was taken.

The following is a summary of events and tasks that should be meticulously reported. Some organizations performing investigations on a full-time basis have a template that the investigator follows, filling in the results as tasks are completed.

- Document the condition of the original scene, including a list of hardware found, status (on/off, logged on/logged off, etc.), along with photographs or a video tape.
- Record the names and contact information of all individuals interviewed during the investigations. A summary (or if possible, a transcript) of the interview should be provided as an attachment.
- If equipment is seized, document the make, model, and serial numbers of each device. Provide documentation authorizing the seizure as a separate attachment.
- Record the exact time materials were seized, the location it was taken from, and the name and contact information of the person performing the action.
- If equipment is transported, provide a detailed description of how the devices were packaged if antistatic or Faraday protection was provided. If not, why not?
- Describe the location where seized materials were taken, including the location and type of storage facilities used to house the materials. Record the name and contact information of the person transporting each item.
- Whenever live data acquisition is deemed necessary, record the following:
  - What type of date was acquired (memory dump, system files, paging files, etc.)?
  - What tools and procedures were used to connect to the suspect machine?
  - What tools and procedures were used to acquire the data?
  - What was the time and date the data was imaged, and what was the time and date reported by the device from which the data was acquired? The two are not always the same.
  - What are the type, make, model, and serial number of the target device to which the data was copied?
  - What is the condition of the target device (new, forensically cleaned, data-wiped, or formatted)?
  - What are the MD5 and SHA-2 hash calculations of the image?

- When devices are imaged for later analysis, record the following:
  - The type, make, model, and serial numbers of source devices
  - The type, make, model, and serial numbers of target devices
  - Precautions taken to avoid contamination or loss of data in evidence
  - For disk drives:
    - Drive parameters of disk drives, both target and source
    - Jumper settings
    - Master/slave configuration if IDE
    - Device ID if SCSI or SATA
  - For optical or flash drives:
    - Make, model, and capacity
    - Mounted or not mounted at time of seizure
    - Inventory of blank or used media
  - For seized media:
    - Form of disks (CD, DVD, Zip, etc.)
    - Capacity of disks
    - Number and type of seized disks
    - Possible evidence that there are missing disks (empty jewel boxes, etc.)
  - The date and time of each action taken.
  - The process used for mounting the seized device, including mechanisms in place to assure write-protection
  - The process and tools used to acquire the forensic image
  - MD5 and SHA-2 hash calculations of the image before and after acquisition
- Photograph computer systems before and after disassembling for transport.
- During the examination and analysis of data, record each procedure in detail, identifying any tool used. Record beginning and ending hash calculations of source data, explaining any discrepancies that may occur.
- Above all: Maintain an unbroken chain of custody that includes each piece of evidence handled throughout the course of the investigation.

As is readily apparent, case documentation is not to be taken lightly. While individuals should be treated as innocent until proven guilty, sources of evidence by default get the opposite treatment. The astute investigator always assumes that any case he or she is working will eventually end up in court. Even the seemingly benign cases, such as uncovering evidence of employee misconduct, can end up in court as a civil (or even criminal) court case. Poor documentation can endanger what would otherwise be a sound case.

PROCESS DOCUMENTATION

Unless an investigator or an organization utilizes homegrown tools, most process documentation is likely to come from the vendors providing the hardware or software used. There are some pieces of documentation that must be generated by the agency. Process documentation includes

- User manuals
- Installation manuals
- Readme files stored on installation media
- Updates to manuals posted online by the vendor
- Logs showing updates, upgrades, or patch installations

This is the type of documentation that does not necessarily need to be provided with each investigation report. It must, however, be available if demanded by opposing counsel, a judge, or arbitrator. There are situations that occur where process documentation is used to support or refute claims that proper procedure was followed during specific steps in the investigation.

BUILDING THE TIMELINE

Key to virtually every investigation involving computer or network activity is the creation of an accurate history of events related to the incident under investigation. By creating an easily comprehensible report of the order of events that occurred, the investigator can more easily and more accurately show correlation between those events. For example, it is easier to associate a specific user to the origination of a particular file if the timeline shows that the file was created at a time when it can be shown unequivocally that the user was logged onto the computer or network.

The timeline (Figure 1.2) needs to start from a time just before the incident was known to begin or was initially discovered to the point when the evidentiary materials were acquired for analysis. This is why it is essential that the investigator do nothing that could alter the **metadata** of files stored on the computer. Metadata is information about files that can be either stored within the file itself

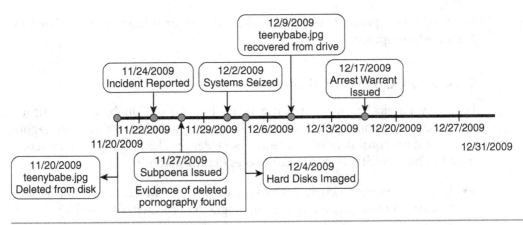

Figure 1.2 A good timeline is essential in communicating the order of events to outside parties of interest.

or extracted from other repositories, such as the Windows master file tables or registry. Three critical pieces of information are the *creation* date, *last accessed* date, and *last modified* date. Together these form the file's **MAC** (modified, accessed, and created) data. Simply viewing a file in a browser or application alters the accessed data. Copying a file from one location to another can modify both the creation and modified dates if forensically acceptable methods are not used. Metadata and ways of protecting and analyzing it will be covered in greater detail in Chapters 9 and 10.

Network and user logon activity are also critical to creating a timeline, as are Internet and e-mail usage. There are various tools that help the investigator validate times that certain events occurred. MACtime is a common forensic tool that can extract a history of user activity on a system. It creates an ASCII timeline of file activity. X-Ways Trace can be used to extract and analyze Internet history. In a network environment, event tracking in utilities such as Microsoft's Event Viewer, the registry, or log files can reveal valuable information that can be used for assembling a credible timeline.

Timelines can be assembled in graphical form that makes it easy for laypeople such as lawyers and judges to understand. Some of the forensic suites (notably Encase) produce automated timelines. Others, such as the Forensic Tool Kit, do not. It is possible, but not necessarily pleasant, to create a timeline using commercial products such as Microsoft Visio, Excel, or OpenOffice. Excel is very cumbersome for this task and is not recommended. Microsoft Visio produces more polished timelines but is limited by the fact that each event must be entered into the timeline separately. A better use of the investigator's time is to invest in a proprietary product such as Timeline Maker for Windows or Bee Docs for Macintosh computers.

CHAIN OF CUSTODY REPORTS

For every physical unit of evidence taken into possession by an investigator or agency, there must be a continuously maintained chain of custody report. Consider it the equivalent of a timeline for evidence. The chain of custody report must be able to verify several critical pieces of information:

- Identify the item precisely, listing type of evidence, make, model, and serial number (if relevant), and make a photograph of the item (if possible).
- Specify when was the item taken into possession.
- Identify where or from whom the item was seized.
- Record who acquired the item along with the time and date acquired.
- Document who transported the item and how was it transported.
- Document how was the item stored during transport.
- Regularly record how the item was stored during possession.
- Provide a continual log, showing the time and date of each time it was checked out for examination, the purpose for checking it out, and the time and date it was checked back in for storage, identifying who had possession of the item during that time.

While an item is in possession of an individual investigator, that person should document what steps were taken to preserve the integrity of the evidence while in possession. Such documentation needs to include a precise identification of the device in possession (as defined above) and what controls were in place to protect the device from electrostatic discharge, electromagnetic interference, and other potential sources of data corruption and other protections. Document what methods were used to prevent data from being inadvertently written to the device (write-blocker devices, software write-protection, etc.). Generate before and after hash values to confirm that the data source did not change while in possession. If it did change, document what process caused the change, along with how and why the change occurred.

Any deviation from standard documentation procedures in preparing the chain of custody can, and most likely *will*, lead to challenges from opposing counsel and can possibly cause the evidence to be thrown out. No breaks can exist in the timeline, because this indicates an opportunity for the data to be replaced, corrupted, or modified.

CASE LAW: CHAIN OF CUSTODY

It is inevitably a good idea to present a flawless chain of custody in order to avoid having evidence declared inadmissible. The courts have vacillated in how they treat evidence in regards to "missing links" in the chain. In *Jeter v. Commonwealth*, Justice Roberts of the Twelfth Virginia Appellate Court wrote, "When a 'vital link' in the possession and treatment of the evidence is left to conjecture, the chain of custody is incomplete, and the evidence is inadmissible" (*Jeter v. Commonwealth* 2005).

Conversely, in *Hargrove v. Commonwealth*, the defendant argued that since the chain of custody did not include any signed statements or testimony from the officer who delivered the evidence to the laboratory, nor was there any evidence that an authorized agent accepted delivery of the evidence at the lab, the integrity of the evidence was in doubt. In denying this appeal, Justice Felton wrote, "It concluded that because the evidence container was received at the lab 'sealed and intact,' there was no evidence that it was subject to tampering between the time it left the police evidence room and the time that it was removed from the lab storage locker. We conclude that the trial court did not err in admitting the evidence container and the certificate of its analysis" (*Hargrove v. Commonwealth* 2009).

CHAPTER REVIEW

1. In what ways does Casey's six-step model differ from the earlier four-step models of digital investigation? What is new, and what has changed?
2. Where in the Casey model would one begin to ascertain precisely what legal documentation would be required for a particular investigation?
3. Is *Zubulake v. UBS Warburg* more relevant to a criminal case or a civil matter? Explain your answer.
4. Discuss the difference between procedural documentation and process documentation. In which document would you explain what steps you took during the examination of a file system?
5. During the process of examination, you have reason to suspect that files that were deleted may still exist. What is the process for locating intact files in unallocated disk space?

CHAPTER EXERCISES

1. Look up at least one criminal case that involved data carving. Was the technique useful for the prosecution or for the defense?

2. Think of as many ways as possible in which a civil case involving electronic discovery of specific e-mails would differ from a criminal cases in which a search of a suspect's e-mail archives must be conducted. Don't try to get too specific here, as this is simply an overview chapter.

3. Throughout the investigation, a myriad of actions are performed. At what point does the chain of custody begin, and how is it relevant at each subsequent stage?

REFERENCES

Anson, S., and S. Bunting. 2007. *Mastering Windows network forensics and investigation.* Boca Raton: Sybex.

Casey, E. 2004. *Digital evidence and computer crime.* New York: Elsevier Academic Press.

Hargrove v. Commonwealth. 2009. Record No. 2410-07-2. Court of Appeals of Virginia Published Opinions. www.courts.state.va.us/wpcap.htm (accessed April 8, 2010).

Hargrove v. Commonwealth, 44 Va. App. 733, 607 S.E.2d 734 (2009). www.lexisone.com/lx1/caselaw/freecaselaw?action=OCLGetCaseDetail&format=FULL&sourceID=bdjcca&searchTerm=eGjb.diCa.aadj.eeWH&searchFlag=y&l1loc=FCLOW (accessed April 8, 2010).

Jeter v. Commonwealth, 44 Va. App. 733, 737, 607 S.E.2d 734 (2005).

Kruse, W., and J. Heiser. 2001. *Computer forensics: Incident response essentials.* Boston: Addison-Wesley.

Lebedoff, D. 1997. *Cleaning up: The Exxon Valdez case—The story behind the biggest legal bonanza of our time.* New York: Free Press.

Marcella, A., Jr., and D. Menendez. 2008. *Cyber forensics: A field manual for collecting, examining, and preserving evidence of computer crimes, 2nd ed.* Florida: Auerbach Publications.

Reyes, A. 2007. *Cyber crime investigations.* Rockland: Syngress Publishing

Wysocki, R. 2009. *Effective project management: Traditional, agile, extreme.* 5th ed. Indianapolis: John Wiley & Sons.

Zubulake v. UBS Warburg , 217 F.R.D. at 320 (2003).

LAWS AFFECTING FORENSIC INVESTIGATIONS

One of the challenges facing a digital forensics investigator (DFI) in any case ever tackled is making sure that everything that is done is done within the parameters of the law. Even the internal corporate survey of a company-owned computer can be impacted by a variety of rules and regulations. Some are legislated regulations, and some fall under the category of constitutional law. The DFI does not need to be a lawyer to succeed. Legal counsel should be involved in every case an agency or organization undertakes. The investigator does, however, need to know enough law to keep out of trouble—and to prevent his or her case from being scrapped due to legal breaches. There are three areas this chapter will cover concerning the legal aspects of investigation:

- Constitutional rights and restrictions
- Legislated privacy regulations
- Working beneath the corporate shield

This chapter provides an overview of these topics, while the following chapters will go into more detail. The reader should keep in mind that the author is not a lawyer and this cannot be taken as legal counsel, but rather a survey of law. Always consult with legal counsel if there is any question about how to proceed with a specific case or situation.

CONSTITUTIONAL IMPLICATIONS OF FORENSIC INVESTIGATION

When the United States was initially founded, the men who led the way to freedom realized that a formal statement of purpose was necessary to keep a fledgling nation from falling apart within a few generations. To this extent, they crafted what we now know as the Constitution of the United States. Knowing that nothing ever stays the same, they built into this document the mechanisms by which it could be modified. These modifications are known as *amendments*. To date, there are 27 amendments to the Constitution. Should the American people decide that they wanted to add a twenty-eighth, they would have to do two things (U.S. Constitution, Article V):

- A two-thirds majority of both houses of Congress would have to pass a proposal for the amendment.
- Three-fourths of the states would have to ratify the amendment in their state legislatures.

The first ten amendments are lumped together in what is popularly known as the Bill of Rights. Amendments One through Eight guarantee individual liberties, while Nine and Ten work together to assure that powers not specifically delegated under constitutional law remain with the states. The amendment that affects the DFI more than any other is the *Fourth Amendment*.

THE FOURTH AMENDMENT

One of the abuses that enraged colonial citizens more than any other was the *Writ of Assistance*. While this sounds benign enough, a writ of assistance was a general warrant that allowed any government agent to enter a home or business without permission and rip it apart looking for any evidence that the residents were involved in undesirable behavior. Under British rule, the government agent didn't need to specify what crime was being investigated or what evidence was the target of the search. The writ of assistance allowed general "fishing expeditions" and was frequently used by local officials indiscriminately—often simply as a means of demonstrating who was in charge.

The first paragraph of the Fourth Amendment clearly states the purpose of the document. The remaining pages clarify the intent and meaning of the amendment in very granular detail. The first paragraph says:

> The right of the people to be secure in their persons, houses, papers, and effects, against unreasonable searches and seizures, shall not be violated; and no Warrants

shall issue but upon probable cause, supported by Oath or affirmation, and particularly describing the place to be searched, and the persons or things to be seized. (U.S. Constitution, Fourth Amendment)

There are two key phrases in this paragraph that surface repeatedly in the process of any criminal investigation. The phrases "unreasonable search and seizure" and "probable cause" have generated reams of legal documents defining what they mean and how they apply to specific cases. There are some notable exceptions to the Fourth Amendment, which will be discussed in the next chapter. However, for the most part, the amendment provides very specific guidelines to how investigations may be conducted.

Unreasonable Search and Seizure

Any time that there is a question about the legality of a search or the seizure of evidence, a judge will consider the answers to two questions:

- Was there actually a search, and was it by government agents?
- Was said search reasonable in all aspects?

The first question seems to be easy to answer, at least superficially. It is actually more difficult than it may appear. However, the mere fact that someone had their house, or their computer, rifled by an investigator does not necessarily fulfill the legal definition of a search. Under constitutional law only legal representatives of the government are implicated. So the judge will ask, "Was the search conducted by an agent of the government?" If not, the Fourth Amendment does not apply. Once again, the glass that covers this question can become cloudy. Who is an **agent of the government?** Obviously, a law enforcement official qualifies. But does a private investigator? That can depend on who hired the investigator and the circumstances by which that person came to conduct the search. If the federal government, or a state or local government, requested the services of the investigator, that person becomes an agent of the government and is subject to constitutional law.

In *The United States v. Howard et al.* (1985), both of these conditions were addressed. In Paragraph 24, the Judiciary states, "We agree with defendants that a consent clause in an insurance contract does not insulate from the Fourth Amendment a search by a private investigator who acts as an agent of the government to gather incriminating evidence for use in a criminal proceeding." The point of this statement is that while a private investigator (PI) acting alone is not subject to Fourth Amendment restraints under normal circumstances, one working at the request of the government is. In this particular case, the court determined that the information collected by the PI was obtained prior to the government contacting the investigator. Therefore, at the time the information was gathered, the PI was not acting as a government agent, and therefore the information was admissible. The ruling states in Paragraph 25, "Nevertheless, where, as here, the intent of the private party conducting the search is entirely independent of the government's intent to collect evidence for use in a criminal prosecution, we hold that the private party is not an agent of the government" (752 F.2d 220, 17 Fed. R. Evid. Serv. 383).

Once the existence of a search is confirmed, the judge must determine if the search was reasonable. He or she asks, "Did the subject of the search have a **reasonable expectation of privacy** regarding the object of the search?" This question also has two underlying concepts. Can the person who thinks his rights were violated demonstrate a reasonable expectation of privacy, either actual or subjective, regarding the object of the search? An actual expectation of privacy would be exemplified by a person's wallet or purse or home. A subjective expectation is defined as one that society in general would recognize. That can be more difficult to determine, as evidenced by the plethora of cases going through the courts. As of this writing, there are cases regarding the transmission of text over an Internet connection, the right of employers to search their own computers, the use of video surveillance in schools, and so on and so forth. There are even cases involving convicted criminals serving time in jail.

Probable Cause

In order for a law enforcement official to obtain a warrant, there must first be a strong indication of probable cause. The USLegal dictionary defines probable cause as "the level of evidence held by a rational and objective observer necessary to justify logically accusing a specific suspect of a particular crime based upon reliable objective facts" (USLegal 2009).

Probable cause must exist before a judge will issue a warrant, but it can also be sufficient justification for performing a search without a warrant. In theory, probable cause is a reason for action known *ex ante* (meaning "before the fact"). An investigator cannot break into an apartment, discover a cache of drugs, and then claim probable cause for the search. Performing a warrantless search based on probable cause runs the risk of having all evidence obtained during the search disallowed and opens the door for civil litigation by the person whose rights were violated.

THE SEQUENCE OF SEARCH AND SEIZURE

Typically, the routine execution of a search warrant goes something like this. The investigator requests a search warrant based on specific parameters (which will be discussed in the next chapter). A judge agrees the request is legitimate and reasonable and issues the warrant. It is a two-stage process. You search (and find), and then you seize. The investigators search the scene and confiscate any evidentiary material they may find. It doesn't always work that way with digital evidence.

To the extent that you are authorized to search for certain items that are likely to contain evidence—such as computers, cell phones, digital media, and so on—this is the order in which a computer investigation is handled as well. However, most computer searches occur in four stages. An initial search locates computer equipment or media as defined in the subpoena. That material is seized and transported to another location. The actual search does not occur until the contents of the device are imaged, which is a process that generally occurs at the new location distant from the suspected scene of the crime. A logical search of the computer or media contents occurs, and any evidentiary digital information is located, copied, and archived. This extended process leaves open many legal challenges and arguments. Some of these will be addressed in the next chapter, and some have yet to be addressed by the courts.

THE FIFTH AMENDMENT

When drafting the Fifth Amendment, the goal of the authors was to prevent the government from ever forcing a citizen to provide self-incriminating testimony. Too many years of having confessions beaten out of them by agents of the British crown left a bad taste in the mouths of our founding fathers. According to the amendment, no person should ever "be compelled in any criminal case to be a witness against himself." (US Constitution, Amendment V).

So how does this impact the digital investigation? Virtually every resource on the network, all cloud resources, and any encrypted drive will be protected by a password. While courts have been somewhat divided on the issue of whether divulging a password is a form of testimony, the general consensus has been that it is. Therefore, in any criminal investigation, while it certainly won't hurt to ask the suspect for a password, if the person refuses, they are likely to claim their rights under the Fifth Amendment.

Even if you have a warrant to search the computer, or even if the person has given his consent, extracted password-protected materials fall under the closed container rule. As such, if a password is not voluntarily provided, you will have to resort to other methods to gain access.

FIRST AMENDMENT PROTECTIONS

Another level of **privileged information** is any material that might be protected under the First Amendment to the Constitution. The First Amendment is very short and to the point. It says the following:

> Congress shall make no law respecting an establishment of religion, or prohibiting the free exercise thereof; or abridging the freedom of speech, or of the press; or the right of the people peaceably to assemble, and to petition the Government for a redress of grievances.

The amendment itself isn't very descriptive about what part of free press is actually covered. Several Supreme Court cases have further defined the rights provided by the amendment. A pivotal case was decided in 1938 in *Lovell v. City of Griffin* [303 U.S. 444 (1938)]. The opinion written by Chief Justice Hughes offered the first official definition of what constituted "the press." He defined the press as "every sort of publication which affords a vehicle of information and opinion." That is a fairly wide description, and it did not define specifically what rights the press had.

Branzburg v. Hayes addressed that issue in 1972 when the court ruled that the First Amendment did not allow a journalist to refuse a subpoena issued by a grand jury. The fact that the case was a 5–4 split decision suggests just how divisive the issue was. At issue was whether or not a journalist had the right to refuse to testify before a grand jury based on First Amendment protections. The court said no.

The key lessons to be learned are twofold. One cannot get a search warrant to search a newspaper office or other publication. It just won't happen. However, one *can* request and be granted a subpoena demanding that the publication hand over specifically defined information.

YOUR ISP AND THE FIRST AMENDMENT

Freedom of the press has been a given in American culture for so long that the phrase is part of the average citizen's everyday vocabulary. First Amendment debates typically center around libel, threatening speech, and obscenity. Additionally, they focus on the government's limited power to censor what the press offers to the public.

In today's cyberworld, it is becoming more difficult to determine what is actually "press" and what is some everyday Joe spewing out libelous rants or issuing potentially criminal threats. Is a blog a valid part of "the press"? Assuming we agree that it is, when a blog does publish something libelous, who is responsible? The blogger, who could be considered the reporter and insulated from indemnification? Or the ISP, who could be considered the publisher and therefore responsible for all contents it manages?

Since there has been relative silence on the part of the courts in this regard, many service providers take it upon themselves to filter content in an effort to avoid potential prosecution. Others are far more lenient. Examples of this are YouTube and LiveJournal.

YouTube provides a platform for people to showcase videos they make. YouTube is relatively careful about monitoring videos for pornographic content, hate messages, and so forth. Any video deemed unsuitable may be deleted without the owner's notification or consent. Conversely, LiveJournal had to face the threat of an advertising boycott before it purged its system of suspected pedophiles (Tushnet 2008). Then, when it did so, it deleted the accounts of many people who were members of a book club discussing Nabakov's *Lolita*.

Another issue faced by ISPs is what to do when a subscriber is involved in the distribution of pirated intellectual property. The Digital Millennium Copyright Act (DMCA) basically provides the ISP a "safe harbor" from liability as long as it adopts and enforces specific policies regarding copyright infringement.

When faced with copyright infringement issues, the courts have frequently used the "dance hall proprietor versus landlord" argument. In the dance hall scenario, a dance hall owner hires a band to play. The band plays an entire mix of copyrighted songs without obtaining permission from the copyright holders of those songs. In this situation, both the band and the proprietor are considered to be in violation. This is because the band is committing the act, and the proprietor is vicariously involved because the proprietor has the control to stop the violation if he or she chooses. Additionally, the proprietor profits directly from the violation.

A landlord, on the other hand, is *not* held liable for such activities that occur inside of the premise where the violation occurs. The landlord does not have as much control over what occurs once the renter takes possession of the property. Landlords lack sufficient control over tenants to be able to enforce rules.

THE RIGHT TO PRIVACY

Many people are surprised when they learn that the right to privacy is not guaranteed under the Constitution. Our legislature has filled this void by passing a number of laws protecting individuals from having their private lives exposed to anyone who cares to look. This is a sufficiently detailed subject that an entire chapter is devoted to it later in this book. For now it is only necessary to provide a general overview of the principles and list some of the key laws that affect the DFI.

The first legal precedence for privacy laws can be traced to an article written in 1890 by Warren and Brandeis entitled *The Right to Privacy* (Warren and Brandeis 1890). In this article, the authors note that "new inventions" and technology threaten the personal lives of individuals. The new inventions of which they wrote were film cameras and the ability to publish actual photographs of people instead of mere line drawings.

For many years, cases involving privacy rights bounced around the courts. The principle finally benefited from a formal definition when *The California Law Review* published the article entitled "Privacy" by William Prosser. In this article, Prosser defined four specific areas of law pertaining to individual privacy. To quote from his article , these areas are

- Intrusion upon a plaintiff's seclusion or solitude, or into his private affairs
- Public disclosure of embarrassing private facts about the plaintiff
- Publicity which places the plaintiff in a false light in the public eye
- Appropriation, for the defendant's advantage, of the plaintiff's name or likeness (Prosser 1960, 389)

The discerning eye notes that there is no mention of "intrusion into the plaintiff's hard disk or file system." This, along with most other activities of the investigator, falls under the seclusion and solitude tort. Subsequent laws passed over the years have more precisely defined a person's right to privacy. Among the prominent laws that contain privacy restrictions are

- The Fair Credit Reporting Act of 1970
- The Privacy Act of 1974
- The Equal Credit Opportunity Act of 1974
- The Electronic Communications Privacy Act of 1986
- Health Insurance Portability and Accountability Act of 1996
- The Gramm-Leach-Bliley Act of 1999
- Privacy of Consumer Financial Information; Final Rule (2000)
- The Fair Debt Collection Practices Act of 2006
- The Family Educational Rights and Privacy Act of 2008

This is just a small sampling of the myriad of laws governing the subject. In addition, many states have their own statutes that may be more restrictive than federal legislation. Another thing to be cautious of is that laws are revised constantly and new ones are passed.

THE EXPERT WITNESS

An expert witness is "a person who is a specialist in a subject, often technical, who may present his/her expert opinion without having been a witness to any occurrence relating to the lawsuit or criminal case" (The People's Law Dictionary 2010). Generally speaking, any **testimony** that relates material not actually witnessed by the speaker is covered under a tenet called the **hearsay rule.** Except under very specific mitigating circumstances, hearsay is not allowable as evidence. The expert witness is one of those notable exceptions.

There is no regulatory agency that monitors "expert status" or any such thing as an expert certification. Courts do, however, specify the types of witnesses who can give testimony and the types of evidence that are admissible. These rules are covered in the Federal Rules of Evidence in criminal cases and the Federal Rules of Civil Procedure in civil cases. The two types of witnesses defined are **eyewitnesses** and **expert witnesses.** Eyewitnesses are those who had firsthand experience with at least one aspect of the crime. Expert witnesses were never there, and cannot offer any firsthand information at all, but have been accepted by the court as being qualified to testify about a specific technical aspect of the case.

Rules 702 and 703 of the Federal Rules of Evidence provide the guidelines for expert testimony. Rule 702 dictates when it will be allowed, and Rule 703 explains the bases for providing such testimony. Rule 702 states that expert testimony is allowable when "scientific, technical, or other specialized knowledge will assist the trier of fact to understand the evidence or to determine a fact in issue" (FRE 2009). Three conditions apply to allowing expert testimony:

- The testimony is based on sufficient facts and data.
- The testimony is derived from reliable principles and methodology.
- The witness can demonstrate that the principles and methodology have been properly applied to the interpretation of facts.

There are two ways to become recognized as an expert witness. Either all parties involved in the case can agree in principle that the person being presented is an expert in the related field, or the judge can make a ruling determining that he or she recognizes the person as an expert. A key tool in determining a person's qualifications as an expert is the **curriculum vitae** (CV). This Latin term means literally "course of life" and is a functional equivalent of a résumé.

In the final act, it is not the length of the alphabet behind a person's name or the list of degrees boasted, and it is not even the CV that determines whether a person can sit an expert witness or not. It is the decision of the judge presiding over the case.

Then there is the question of expert witness neutrality. Jensen (1993) quoted an unidentified lawyer as saying, "I would go into court with an uncommitted, objective independent expert about as willingly as I would occupy a foxhole with a couple of noncombatant soldiers." This statement infers that at least this particular attorney is unwilling to accept neutrality in an expert witness. Judges take a slightly different view. Bender (2002) quoted the Fifth Court of Appeals as having stated, "Experts whose opinions are available to the highest bidder have no place testifying in a court of law before a jury and with the imprimatur of the trial judge's decision that he is an expert." Perhaps the person hiring an expert witness should pay heed to another old quote, "Caveat emptor" (let the buyer beware).

CHAPTER REVIEW

1. Three different amendments to the Constitution affect how the forensic analyst performs an investigation. List the three amendments and describe what individual rights each one impacts.

2. A man was brought to trial after employees at a computer repair shop discovered child pornography on his computer. He tried to get the evidence disqualified as the result of an illegal search, but the judge denied his motion. What was the reasoning behind the denial?

3. Why is it that the owner of a nightclub can be found liable for copyright infringement violations committed by the band playing on a Saturday night, but that the owner of the building from which the hall space is rented is not found liable?

4. Describe the hearsay rule in your own terms, and explain how it relates to the concept of an expert witness.

5. Which constitutional amendment guarantees an individual's right to privacy, and how can those rights be enforced?

CHAPTER EXERCISES

1. Download and review Gramm-Leach-Bliley, HIPAA, and Sarbanes-Oxley. Each of these pieces of legislation have some commonalities and some major differences. What are the main commonly shared features, and how do they significantly differ?

2. Search Google Scholar for a legal case that involves a warrantless search that was accepted by the court. Briefly describe the case, and explain how the search may have been considered allowable under constitutional law.

REFERENCES

Bender, R. 2002. Liability for the psychiatrist expert witness. *American Journal of Psychiatry* 159:1819–25.

Branzburg v. Hayes, 408 U.S. 665 (1972).

Federal Evidence Review (FRE). 2009. Federal rules of evidence. www.FederalEvidence.com (accessed December 16, 2009).

Jensen, E. G. 1993. When "hired guns" backfire: The witness immunity doctrine and the negligent expert witness. *University of Missouri at Kansas City Law Rev.* 62:185–210.

Prosser, W. 1960. Privacy. *California Law Review* 48(3):389.

The People's Law Dictionary. 2010. Expert witness. http://dictionary.law.com/Default.aspx?selected=700 (accessed January 22, 2010).

The United States v. Howard et al., 752 F.2d 220 (6th Cir. 1985).

Tushnet, R. August 2008. *Power without responsibility: Intermediaries and the First Amendment.* George Law Faculty Working Papers.

U.S. Constitution, Amendment Four.

U.S. Constitution, Article V.

USLegal. 2009. Probable cause and legal definition. http://definitions.uslegal.com/p/probable-cause/ (accessed January 14, 2009).

Warren, S., and L. Brandeis. 1890. The right to privacy. *The Harvard Law Review* (4)3.

SEARCH WARRANTS AND SUBPOENAS

One of the motivating factors of the Revolutionary War was the general warrant. England maintained the philosophy that a man's house was his castle and that a government official could not search without a warrant. Unfortunately, it was far too easy for representatives of the English Crown in Colonial America to get a warrant, and then the warrant was a writ of assistance, more commonly known as a general warrant. With such a warrant in hand, the official could ransack a person's home looking for anything and everything that may have been of interest to the official. After America successfully seceded from British control, one of the first things our founding fathers did was establish in the Bill of Rights language specifically prohibiting unreasonable search and seizure. These rights were defined in the Fourth Amendment to the Constitution.

Unless otherwise stated in the warrant, the document must be exercised in "normal business hours," and the executor of the warrant must announce his or her presence. Exceptions to these rules are the no-knock warrant and the after-hours warrant. These will be discussed in further detail later in this chapter.

Laws governing the acquisition and execution of search warrants have evolved and expanded over the years. It seems each year a new challenge to Fourth Amendment interpretation reaches the courts. In the wake of 9/11, it became even more difficult for average investigators to understand their own rights and responsibilities as the Patriot Act expanded some of the government's right to act. Add to this the fact that different courts have interpreted the Fourth Amendment in different ways, and it is understandable that it gets so confusing.

DISTINGUISHING BETWEEN WARRANTS AND SUBPOENAS

What is the difference between a search warrant and a subpoena? While both perform similar functions, they are quite different in scope and in execution. A **search warrant** is an order issued by a judge that gives government officials express permission to enter a specifically defined property with the intent of searching the premises for evidence of a specific crime. To convince a judge that a warrant is in order, an investigator must show two things. First there must be probable cause. Probable cause consists of a statement (an **affidavit**) filed by the government first stating that it believes with reasonable certainty that a crime has been committed, is being committed, or is about to be committed, and second, explaining in as much detail as possible what evidence already exists that such a crime exists.

Along with probable cause, the request for a warrant must fulfill **particularity requirements.** This fascinating phrase simply means that the request must identify with reasonable accuracy precisely what location is to be searched, what materials or evidence are being sought, and what may and may not be seized. Traditional search restrictions require that officers search only in places defined by the warrant, looking for items that fall within the descriptive parameters of the warrant, and they can look only in spaces that could conceivably hold the object being sought. In other words, if an investigator is looking for a stolen car, he may not look in the driver's jewelry box.

When a warrant is issued, it is done so by a judge, at the request of a government official or agency. It is not necessary for the target of the search to be present or to even be aware that the warrant is being requested. More often than not, the person or persons subject to the search first learn of the warrant when it is handed to them. The warrant will occur whether the victim likes it or not. There is no challenge for a warrant presented at the door. It gives the government permission to enter.

A **subpoena** is an order to appear before the court or an order to produce documents or other evidence as defined in the subpoena. A subpoena can be issued that demands both the presence of the person and that the person bring materials with him or her. This type of subpoena is known as a **subpoena duces tecum.** The Latin phrase means "to bring with you under penalty of punishment." Unlike a warrant, the target of a subpoena can respond with a motion to quash the subpoena. If the motion is successful, the order is rescinded. Valid reasons for quashing a subpoena include (Portman and Jacobs 1998)

- Insufficient time to respond to the demands listed.
- Subpoena calls for the disclosure of protected information.

- Compliance places an undue burden on the recipient.
- Compliance requires that the recipient travel excessive distance.
- Subpoena requests information not relevant to the matter of litigation.
- Information requested is readily available from other sources.

Subpoenas can be issued by either federal or state courts. A state subpoena cannot be enforced upon an individual who resides in another state and is *not* a party of the litigation. A federal subpoena is valid regardless of where it is issued or where it is enforced within the legal jurisdiction of United States government.

What Is a Search and When Is It Legal?

Throughout the remainder of this chapter and elsewhere in the book, the words **search** and **seizure** will be used repeatedly. The definition of what constitutes a search is a fairly broad interpretation. Most case law interprets any entrance into a home or office as a search, whether the investigator actively "looks" for something or not. USLegal defines a search as an examination of a person's body, his or her property, or any area that another reasonable person would consider private (USLegal 2010). Therefore, examining a person's telephone constitutes a search. Simply looking through the window of a private home or office is "searching" the place.

The *U.S. v. Carey* (1999) police officers executed a warrant to search a computer for evidence of drug trafficking. While performing the search, the officers came across a large number of images they considered to be child pornography. Using a doctrine known as "plain view," they extended their search to include child pornography and charged Carey with possession of such materials. The plain view doctrine states that items seen in the course of an investigation that exist in plain view can be examined without need for a search warrant. On appeal, the court disagreed with this interpretation, saying that the files were only evident as pornographic in nature if opened. The images were excluded as evidence, and the pornography charges didn't stick.

Seizure is the physical acquisition and confiscation of items found during the search. It can also refer to the detention of a person. Typically, warrants issued by the court grant both the right to search a person or property and the right to seize any evidentiary materials found. The permission to search granted within the warrant may be somewhat generic, identifying no more than an address and whether to search the entire premises or just specific areas of the property. The instructions as to what may be seized by the search team are generally more specific.

The question of when it is legal is more difficult to answer. Clearly, any time a duly appointed justice of a state or federal court issues a warrant to perform the search, the search *as defined in the warrant* is legal. If the search exceeds the scope of the warrant, then it becomes an illegal search. Also, if the search is performed by a private citizen who is not acting as an agent of the government, there is no Fourth Amendment protection against the results of the search. There may be other legal remedies that the victim of the search may pursue. That is a matter for that person to discuss with a competent attorney. However, the court is unlikely to disallow the evidence found under constitutional grounds.

Just because a warrant isn't issued, that does not necessarily mean that a search conducted without one is illegal. There are several circumstances where warrant-less searches are allowed by law. To be illegal under any circumstances, a search must violate "a person's reasonable expectation of privacy" (DOJ 2008). Reasonable expectation of privacy is determined by two factors:

- Does the subject's behavior indicate an expectation of privacy?
- Is that expectation one that society is prepared to accept as reasonable?

How does a person's behavior indicate his or her expectation? A person running naked down the street certainly has no cause to complain if people point and laugh. That same person in the privacy of his shower most certainly does. This is an exaggerated example, but it makes the point. That is where society's acceptance comes into play. The man running down the street is something that the average citizen considers a bit strange. Society does not expect him to assume his public display is an invasion of his privacy, even if in his own mind he thinks he's on a private beach. Unfortunately, most situations are not so easily determined. As DOJ points out, there is no bright line that defines privacy. A few examples of situations where a person *can* expect privacy are defined in the following decisions:

- *Payton v. New York*, 445 U.S. 573 (1980): Privacy inside a person's home is guaranteed, even in the process of making an arrest. A warrantless arrest is specifically unconstitutional.
- *Katz v. United States*, 389 U.S. 347 (1967): Privacy inside a closed telephone booth is assumed because the closed door of the booth gives the person a reasonable expectation of privacy.
- *United States v. Ross*, 456 U.S. 798 (1982): Privacy of the contents of opaque containers is different from the privacy (or lack thereof) in an automobile. A closed container within the automobile is not subject to search without a warrant even if reasonable cause opens the door to an automobile search. This **closed container** clause has been interpreted to include computers,

computer media, and other items that must be mounted on a system before they can be viewed (see below).

- *United States v. Barth*, 26 F. Supp. 2d 929 (1998): Privacy of the contents on a computer's hard drive is essentially the same as that of a closed container.
- *United States v. Reyes*, 922 F. Supp. 818 (1996): Privacy of the contents of a paging device is essentially the same as that of a closed container.

Conversely, courts have also made some notable decisions about where a reasonable expectation of privacy does not exist:

- *Oliver v. United States*, 466 U.S. 170 (1984): Activities conducted in an open field dispel any reasonable expectation of privacy, as anyone—not just legal authorities—can view their activities.
- *California v. Greenwood*, 466 U.S. 35 (1988): Garbage deposited outside of a person's property has been left exposed to the view of anyone who looks.
- *Rakas v. Illinois*, 439 U.S. 128 (1978): Privacy does not exist inside of a stranger's house entered with intent to commit robbery. Constitutional protection enjoyed by the owner does not vicariously pass on to an intruder.
- *United States v. David*, 756 F. Supp. 1385 (1991): A password openly displayed on a computer monitor falls under the plain view exception.
- *United States v. Lyons*, 992 F.2d 1029 (1993): Privacy of the contents of a computer the individual has stolen does not pass from the owner to the thief.

As mentioned in Chapter 1, "The Anatomy of a Digital Investigation," the digital forensic investigator has a more complex formula for searches. The warrant that allows the search of the premises may specify that all computing devices, communication devices, and so forth may be seized. However, after transporting these devices back to the lab for examination, it is equally necessary to have a warrant that identifies what information stores may be searched. A key example is when a warrant is issued to search for information regarding financial fraud of some sort. If, during the course of the search, evidence is uncovered that suggests another crime—such as the distribution of child pornography—a new and separate warrant must be issued.

Any rights to privacy regarding stored electronic information can be relinquished when control of the device or of the data is relinquished to a third party. An individual who brings a computer in for service runs the risk that the repair technician might stumble across evidence of criminal behavior. If that person reports the evidence to authorities, who subsequently obtain a search warrant, there is no recourse against the repairman. Data that is copied to a CD and shipped across the country remains private as long as it is in transit. Once the recipient takes control, the rights of the original sender can vary, depending on circumstances. If circumstances dictate that the "sender" retains control of the "package," then expectation of privacy is retained. *United States v. Most* (1989) allowed that when a person leaves a closed plastic bag with a third party, intending to retrieve it in the near future, then the expectation of privacy is retained. Conversely, in *United States v. Horowitz* (1986), an e-mail message that had arrived at its destination did not afford privacy protection to the original sender of the message.

Aside from the "expectation of privacy" issue, there are other exceptions that allow a warrantless search. These will be discussed later in this chapter.

BASIC ELEMENTS OF OBTAINING A WARRANT

First and foremost—only a judge can issue a search warrant. It can be a federal, state, or territorial judge, or it can be a U.S. magistrate judge. The warrant can be issued only to a legally authorized law enforcement official. To obtain a warrant, a law enforcement official will file a written statement called an **affidavit** that must show

- Probable cause
- Particularity of place
- Particularity of items to be searched

When considering the warrant, a judge can refuse to issue on the basis of any one or more of these requirements. Probable cause was covered in detail in Chapter 2, "Laws Affecting Forensic Investigations." To recap, it basically says that the requestor has a reason to suspect that a crime has been committed, is being committed, or is about to be committed and that evidence of such crime exists at the place to be searched. Federal warrant requirements are spelled out in Title 18, Part II, Chapter 205 – Searches and Seizures.

Special circumstances may prevent an official from being able to provide an affidavit in a timely manner. Rule 41b of the Federal Rules of Evidence (DOJ 2008) also allows a judge, at his or her discretion, to issue a warrant based on sworn testimony or by recorded testimony. When an applicant is requesting a warrant based on sworn testimony, the judge must place the applicant under oath and make a verbatim recording of the testimony given.

Once issued, a warrant is good for only a limited period of time. Unless otherwise specified, Federal Rules of Evidence specifies a default expiration of ten days from the date of issuance. In addition to the particularity issues mentioned previously, the warrant will also specify a magistrate judge to whom the warrant must be returned once it has been executed.

The officer executing the warrant must record the exact time and date the warrant was carried out. If any items are seized during the search, the target of the warrant must be provided a copy of an inventory of everything taken. Another copy of this inventory must accompany the warrant when it is returned to the court. Whoever carries out the warrant must issue a receipt for all items seized along with the inventory.

A defendant who is subject to a search and seizure action initiated by a legally executed warrant has no recourse against the search. However, the defendant may have counsel present during the search. If there is any reason to suspect that the warrant was issued improperly, the defendant can issue a motion to suppress any evidence uncovered by the search.

NO-KNOCK WARRANTS

Unless otherwise stated, an officer executing a search or arrest warrant must abide by the *knock and announce rule.* According to this general rule, when executing a warrant, the officer should knock, announce the intention of the search team, and allow residents of the location being searched time to respond to the knock. The Supreme Court identified key advantages of knock and announce in *Hudson v. Michigan* (2006) as protecting the safety of the officers against defensive reaction by the defendants and protecting property from damage. Justice Scalia noted in his opinion, "Until a valid warrant has issued, citizens are entitled to shield their persons, houses, papers, and effects" (Hudson v. Michigan 2006). His opinion recognizes the fact that, lacking knowledge of a pending warrant being legally served, residents of the building may proactively defend their position.

The courts recognize that sometimes circumstances require that suspects not be notified of a pending search. If there is reason to believe that suspects may aggressively repel a search, that the subjects of the search are likely to escape, or that evidence is likely to be destroyed in the time it takes for officers to wait for a response, the courts may issue a **no-knock warrant.** This gives officers serving a warrant specific permission in writing to break down the door and enter unannounced. Generally speaking, in order to obtain a no-knock warrant, officers requesting the document must show reasonable suspicion that one of the aforementioned conditions exists.

In cases where digital information is a primary target of the search, there may be reason to believe that the suspect may employ a "kill switch." This colorful term refers to any mechanism, hardware or software, that can quickly and effectively destroy data stored on a system. No-knock warrants are frequently requested under such circumstances.

AFTER-HOURS WARRANTS

Rule 41 of the FRCP states that warrants are to be executed during "normal day-time hours" unless otherwise specified; 41a(2) specifies daytime hours as being between 6:00 a.m. and 10:00 p.m. local time. The same exceptions that allow a no-knock warrant can be applied to after-hours warrants. If any one of the three exigent circumstances exists, a judge may issue a warrant that can be executed at any time of the day or night.

SNEAK AND PEEK WARRANTS

FRCP specifies that those with an interest in a property that is the subject of a search should be notified of the government's intent to perform said search. The Patriot Act of 2001 provided law enforcement with a new tool called the *delayed notice*. Under Title 18, Part 1, Chapter 121, § 2705, the court can order notification of a search delayed by up to 90 days. It lists the following circumstances as reasonable cause to issue such a delay:

- Endangering the life or physical safety of an individual
- Flight from prosecution
- Destruction of or tampering with evidence
- Intimidation of potential witnesses
- Otherwise seriously jeopardizing an investigation or unduly delaying a trial

What the rule basically says is that, under such a warrant, a government agent may surreptitiously enter the premises to be searched and conduct the search without the knowledge of the individuals under scrutiny.

Under the conditions of a **sneak and peek warrant,** officers may not seize any material evidence. However, if the judge issuing the warrant determines that there is reasonable necessity for seizure, he or she may issue an order allowing an exception. If such an exception is issued, the officers executing the search may be permitted to surreptitiously copy documents or computer files.

Section 206 of the Patriot Act modified earlier interpretations of sneak and peak by authorizing government officials to solicit third-party assistance in tracking down information about a suspect. Specifically, it empowers a warrant to authorize the search of third-party records for information even when there is no specifically identified person named as the target of the search. This allows the investigator to attempt to track communications by unknown parties who are regularly changing their telephone numbers or taking other evasive action to avoid detection by government authorities. The growing popularity of and ease of access to cheap, prepaid throwaway telephones mounts a strong case for this statute.

THE PLAIN VIEW DOCTRINE

Earlier in the chapter, I mentioned that one long-standing exception to the requirement for a warrant is the **plain view doctrine.** In general searches, the doctrine provides that evidence may be seized without a warrant whenever evidence of an incriminating nature is clearly evident and the officers invoking plain view are in the process of executing a legally issued warrant for a search or arrest when the evidence is found. In other words, if a police officer has a warrant to search a house for controlled substances and there is a video involving child pornography playing when they enter, the pornography can be seized. Additionally, the "plain view" evidence can be used as a probable cause for issuing a new warrant to search for child pornography.

When used in reference to computer searches, plain view can get a bit more confusing. File names, techniques for hiding files, and other technological issues mean that a thorough search mandates opening—or at least examining—any file that is even remotely suspicious. Therefore, it is not unusual that a search legally authorized by one warrant opens, for plain view, evidence of another crime *not* authorized by the warrant. In theory, when this happens, the investigator should immediately stop the search and wait to see if a new warrant will be issued based on evidence found.

Opponents of plain view computer searches complain that lack of specific guidance regarding plain view doctrine with respect to computer searches has led to too many investigators abusing the privilege. Long after sufficient evidence has been found to support the crime under investigation, they continue to probe, "fishing" for evidence of other crimes.

It is not uncommon for a judge to require investigators to submit a *search protocol* in potentially tricky situations. A search protocol is a statement that identifies the processes and procedures that the investigator will use and what precautions will be taken to limit the search to incriminating or exculpatory evidence related to the suspected crime. Any deviations from the approved protocol would have to be submitted and approved before allowed.

The problem with that approach is that the investigator has no way of knowing in advance what steps will be required. If the suspect is using encryption, that will change the situation. What methods has the suspected used to hide or disguise files? What outside influences will come into play?

In 2009, the U.S. Court of Appeals for the Ninth Circuit filed an *en banc* opinion in the case of *U.S. v. Comprehensive Drug Testing* (2009) in which it issued instructions for all judges presiding in the circuit to stop issuing warrants involving computer searches unless the government gives up its right to the plain view doctrine. If the investigator requesting the warrant refused to waive the doctrine, the judge was to do one of two things. He or she could refuse to issue the warrant—regardless of the circumstances justifying said warrant. Or the warrant could be issued with the provision that a third party separate "seizable from nonseizable data under the supervision of the court."

Needless to say, reaction to that ruling was mixed. In an article posted on the Alameda County's District Attorney's Office, the author (unidentified) stated,

> Moreover, it demonstrates an almost paranoidal obsession with computer privacy. And it is hard to avoid the conclusion that it was driven largely by the recent embarrassing revelations concerning the contents of the home computer of the judge who wrote the opinion. In fact, while the judge was adjudicating this appeal, a panel of federal judges was investigating his use of the computer at the request of the Supreme Court. As a result, the judge was publicly rebuked for "exhibiting poor judgment." (Office of the District Attorney, Alameda County 2009)

Within three months, the Ninth Circuit decision was challenged. As of this writing the dust has not yet settled.

THE WARRANTLESS SEARCH

The concept of the warrantless search has been an issue of contention since the Bill of Rights first made its way into our Constitution. For well over a century, it was basically a nonissue. No warrant—no search. In 1914, the Supreme Court instituted the *exclusionary rule* (*Weeks v. U.S.* 1914), which states that any evidence collected by federal agents as a result of an illegal search cannot be used against the defendant in court. Prior to this decision, evidence collected illegally could be used as evidence, but the defendant could pursue charges against those who carried out the search.

Since the 1914 decision specifically named federal agents in its decision, for many years, officers involved in a federal investigation would enlist the assistance of local law enforcement officers to "collect" evidence, which they would turn over to federal agents for use. This changed in 1961 when the court decided in *Mapp v. Ohio*

(1961) that the exclusionary rule applied to all government agents, regardless of their level of jurisdiction.

However, the courts in other decisions have maintained the government's rights to perform searches and seizures without first obtaining a warrant under certain circumstances. Among these mitigating circumstances are

- Searches incident to arrest
- Searches with consent
- Special needs searches involving public employees

All of these exceptions can be applied to physical searches as well as digital investigations. However, some circumstances arise in cases involving digital data that do not arise in more conventional searches.

SEARCHES INCIDENT TO ARREST

Arresting officers have the right to search a suspect at the scene of the arrest without first obtaining a warrant. This is allowed in order to protect the arresting officers, and any bystanders in the area, from being harmed by a weapon the arrestee might have concealed, and in order to prevent the destruction of evidence. This search is limited to the person being arrested and the immediate area over which the suspect might have reasonable and immediate control. The limitations to this exception were decided in *Chimel v. California* (1969).

Prior to *Chimel*, the case that most frequently dictated warrantless search incident to arrest was *Weeks*. While in the 1914 case, the court did overturn a decision on the basis of evidence obtained with no warrant at all, it basically condoned the search of a suspect being legally arrested. In the landmark decision, the court wrote, "While an incidental seizure of incriminating papers, made in the execution of a legal warrant, and their use as evidence, may be justified, and a collateral issue will not be raised to ascertain the source of competent evidence" (*Weeks* 1914).

Terry v. Ohio (1968) further defined the concept of warrantless searches, extending the option to situations where the suspect might not necessarily be the subject of an arrest. In this decision, the court questioned the meaning of the word "reasonable" in the Fourth Amendment restriction against unreasonable searches and seizures. The case came about when Cleveland detective Martin McFadden observed two "suspicious characters" passing the same location several times, and then pausing to engage in brief conversations. Suspecting that the two were about to commit a robbery, McFadden approached the men to question them. During the engagement, he patted one of the men down and discovered a concealed firearm.

The defense for the suspects claimed that their Fourth Amendment rights were violated by an unreasonable search without a warrant.

The Supreme Court, under Chief Justice Earl Warren, determined that there are certain circumstances where probable cause allows for a search to be conducted without a warrant. Four reasons were listed:

- A law enforcement officer's personal observations
- Reliable hearsay
- Behavior fitting a criminal profile
- Unprovoked flight

Unprovoked flight seems as though it would need little explanation. It did require a Supreme Court decision to clarify the intent of the law. *Illinois v. Wardlow* (2000) was one case that determined what constituted unprovoked flight. In this case, the suspect, Wardlow, fled when he witnessed multiple police cars approaching him. Officers pursued him, and when they caught up, searched him and found a concealed weapon. In this case, the Supreme Court determined that flight in a high crime area did not necessarily provide the reasonable cause for police to search. The decision did confirm that Wardlow's Fourth Amendment rights had not been violated but that his mere flight from the sight of a police officer did not constitute suspicious behavior.

It is also against the law for law enforcement to use racial profiling in lieu of criminal profiling. Performing random searches on individuals with Arabic features is not legal, even if there has been "reliable hearsay" of a terrorist threat involving Arab nationals.

SEARCHES WITH CONSENT

In the event that someone with the authority to do so gives consent for government officials to search a specific area, evidence located during the search can be deemed admissible even in the absence of a warrant. Issues that might arise under these circumstances include

- Person giving consent might not have authority.
- Prosecution must be able to prove that the consent was voluntary.
- Officials performing the search must comply with any restrictions placed on the scope of the search by the person granting permission.
- The person granting consent may revoke that consent at any time, without notice.

A common question that arises any time a consent-to-search issue is contested is "Who has the authority to give consent?" The answer to this question varies greatly with the circumstances, and any time there is doubt, an investigator should do one of two things. The safest option is to obtain a search warrant. This completely sidesteps the consent issue since, with the warrant, no consent is required. The second option is to let your legal counsel make the decision. There have been some court decisions that lend general guidelines in three categories of consent:

- Personal property
- Private sector organizations
- Public sector organizations

Each of these issues has specific questions that will be asked and conditions that must be met to constitute a legal consent to search.

Personal Property

When searching a private residence, there are two conditions the court may consider when deciding whether there was legal consent to search the premises or computer systems. **Actual authority** to consent occurs when the target of the search is directly owned and controlled by the person giving the consent, or when an individual has expressly been authorized by the owner to give consent. As an example, Joe Citizen is the only resident at 2 Mockingbird Lane, and when the police knock on the door, he says he has nothing to hide and lets them in, giving the officers permission to look around. Additionally, someone with power of attorney to settle an estate would have actual authority to grant permission for a search.

The second set of circumstances is more complicated. That is **apparent authority** to consent. Apparent authority occurs when the person giving the consent has the genuine appearance of having the authority. This can happen when the person actually believes he or she has the right to give permission, and when the officers conducting the search have no reason to suspect this is not the case. Examples of this concept would be the owner of a house who has an adult offspring still living at home or two adults sharing a residence with common control. Both situations have examples in case law.

Schneckloth v. Bustamonte (1973) was a Supreme Court case that formalized the principle that a search without warrant was valid in the presence of voluntary consent. *United States v. Matlock* (1974) prompted a more granular definition of the principle. Matlock concerned a case of cohabitation by two adults. The defendant was arrested on the front lawn of the house he shared with Gayle Graff (and others). Arresting officers did not ask the suspect which room he occupied, nor did they request his permission to search the premises. The search was accomplished on the permission of Ms. Graff. In this decision the court determined that since statements made by Graff to the police indicated that she and Matlock were married, they had reasonable cause to assume she had the authority to grant permission to search the quarters they jointly shared. It has even been decided that a guest in a house has apparent authority to consent to search an area where visitors would normally be received, provided that guest can demonstrate that he or she has been given access to the house in the owner's absence (*People v. Ledesma* 2006).

In the event that two cohabitants of a residence have equal authority to grant or refuse permission, the situation gets complicated as well. In the absence of one or more of the cohabitants, those present may grant permission to search. Another offshoot of Matlock was that the court decided that the absent cohabitant did *not* have the right to revoke permission, stating that "mutual use of the property carries with it the risk that one of the occupants might permit a search of the common areas" (*U.S. v. Matlock* 1974).

However, in the presence of all cohabitants of equal authority, if even one of those residents objects to the search, apparent authority is not likely to be recognized by the courts. *Georgia v. Randolph* (2006) addressed this issue. In doing so, the court itemized several circumstances where permission may be assumed:

- A recognized hierarchy (e.g., an adult caretaker with a noncompetent ward)
- Objection of an absent cohabitant
- Reasonable fear for the safety of someone inside the premises
- The victim of domestic violence while the victim collects his or her belongings
- Reasonable fear that evidence may be destroyed

In general, parents have actual authority to give permission to search rooms occupied by their children. They cannot, however, grant permission to search an area that is under exclusive control of the child. An example of exclusive control would be a girl's jewelry box that has been locked by the child. Even in the case of adult-aged children, the parents have actual authority in situations where the child does not pay rent for the room. In the event that the child *does* pay rent, the relationship shifts from parent/child to landlord/tenant, and as long as the rent is not in arrears, the tenant relationship assumes priority (*People v. Oodham* 2000).

Private Sector Organizations

Two apparently conflicting principles come into play when considering who has consent to search a computer owned by a corporation or nongovernment nonprofit entity. The first of these is the fact that even though they do not own the space they occupy or the computers they work on, and even though they share this space with other people, workers still can express a reasonable expectation of privacy. This issue was addressed as early as 1968 in *Mancusi v. DeForte*. In this decision Justice Harlan wrote, "It seems clear that if DeForte had occupied a 'private' office in the union headquarters, and union records had been seized from a desk or a filing cabinet in that office, he would have had standing" (*Mancusi v. DeForte* 1968).

However, in most circumstances, the employer has a broader authority to consent to the search of any area or computer owned or controlled by the organization. This right becomes virtually indisputable in the presence of a published employee guideline or log-on banner that expressly states that the company reserves the right to monitor activity on their premises. *United States v. Ziegler* affirmed the company's right to search its own computers in 2006. Judge Diarmuid F. O'Scannlain wrote in his opinion for the Ninth Circuit, "Employer monitoring is largely an assumed practice, and thus we think a disseminated computer-use policy is entirely sufficient to defeat any expectation that an employee might nonetheless harbor" (*United States v. Ziegler* 2001).

For an outsider obtaining permission to search the computers or premises of a private organization, it is essential that the permission be obtained from someone who actually has the right to grant such permission. In some cases, it is clear. Other situations require careful thought. Officers of the organization, such as the president or CEO, a branch manager, or someone with assigned authority over the premises, can be perceived as having **ostensible authority.** This phrase defines the effect that someone in charge has on others, particularly those unfamiliar with the organization. An officer informed by such a person that he or she was in charge and could present reasonable evidence thereof would have no reason to believe otherwise. A receptionist would not have ostensible authority—nor would a man in coveralls cleaning the ashtrays. However, a self-assured woman with a nametag sporting the title "Manager" would convey such authority.

Public Sector Organizations

Public employees enjoy even less protection against warrantless searches than do private sector employees. There does not need to be any evidence of misdeeds on the part of the person being investigated. The government has the right to enforce a *special needs* search on any employee's computer at any time. This means that the reason for the search is to fulfill some specific need by the government. All that needs to be demonstrated is that

- The search is work related, and not intended to collect evidence for a crime, and
- The search is justifiable in its inception and permissible in its scope.

The guidelines for such a search are laid out in *U.S. v. Simons*, 206 F3d 392 (2000). In this case, a government employee was already suspected of storing pornographic images on a work computer. In the ensuing search, investigators found evidence of child pornography. Since the original search was work related and justifiable, the evidence of criminal activity was admissible in court.

SUBPOENAS

A subpoena does not give the bearer any right to search a person or location (except as an inspection). Nor does it allow the bearer to seize any material evidence. It can do one of two things:

- Command a person to appear (either with or without requested physical evidence)
- Command a person or organization to surrender or allow to be examined tangible evidence as defined by the order

The Federal Rules of Civil Procedure outline how subpoenas are issued, served, and executed. In order to be legal, a subpoena must identify the court that issued it. Somewhere on the document it must clearly identify the title of the action requiring the evidence, the court in which the action is being heard, and the action number assigned. The document must clearly state where the person is to appear (if relevant), what evidence must be presented (if relevant), and the time and date that the action is taking place.

To be legal, a subpoena must be served. That means it must be delivered by hand. The person serving the subpoena cannot be a party to the action and must be over the age of 18 years. In the event that the subpoena requires the production of documents or other tangible evidence, then notice must be served allowing time to produce that evidence.

When requesting that a subpoena be served on another party, the requestor must take reasonable steps to assure that there is no undue financial or other burden placed on the person asked to appear or produce. If a subpoena is requesting the production of documents, then if the presence of an individual is also required, that must be stated separately. Once presented with a subpoena, the recipient has the right to file an objection and request that the order be quashed.

Only the issuing court may quash a subpoena. There are some situations where the court is required to quash a subpoena and other times when it may be permitted to, should it so desire. It must quash a subpoena if the recipient can demonstrate any of the following:

- Does not allow a reasonable time to comply
- Requires someone who is not a party to the action to travel more than 100 miles
- Requires the disclosure of privileged information
- Subjects the person to undue burden (a judgment of the court)

The court is permitted (but not required) to quash a subpoena if it

- Requires the person affected to provide trade secrets, confidential information, or other potentially sensitive information
- Requires the person affected to disclose an unretained expert's opinion or information that does not describe specific occurrences in dispute and results from the expert's study that was not requested by a party
- Requires someone who is not a party to the action to incur substantial expense to travel to the location

As an alternative to quashing a subpoena, a judge may also propose alternative conditions, based on the respondent's objections. The judge may take this action if the issuing party does two things:

- Shows that that the testimony or material evidence is critical to the proceedings and cannot otherwise be obtained with undue hardship
- Provides reasonable compensation for the subpoenaed party

Assuming all requirements for a subpoena have been met, and all objections addressed, if the subpoena is continued by the court, failure to comply can result in the subpoenaed party being held in contempt of court.

CHAPTER REVIEW

1. You have just been served with a writ ordering you to appear before the court, bearing a particular set of documents. What type of document did you receive?
2. The order you received gives you only three days to locate and prepare more than a hundred files. Your document imaging specialist is on vacation, and

you have not been able to contact her. What option do you have in order to keep from violating the court order?

3. Discuss how a computer system compares to a sealed container in the eyes of the court when executing a warrant. Under what conditions can you search and/or seize such a container?

4. Describe in your own words the concept of particularity, and identify the two forms that it takes.

5. A warrant has been issued to search the premises of a suspected narcotics trafficker. Those tasked with executing the warrant have been authorized to delay notifying the subject of the warrant for seven days. What type of warrant is this?

CHAPTER EXERCISES

1. Locate online a sample affidavit requesting a search warrant to be issued. As of this writing, such a sample exists at www.quatloos.com/jan0303 nealsearchaffidavit.pdf. Fill out your own affadavit requesting a warrant to search the computer systems and premises of Billy Bob Drayton of 12 Redneck Lane in Brokaw, Alaska. You suspect him of possessing several terabytes of illegal music downloads.

2. Research at least one court case in which evidence was challenged as fruits of an illegal search, where the investigators claimed protection under the plain view doctrine. Was the evidence allowed or not? Explain the reasoning behind the decision.

3. Describe in your own words the difference between actual authority and apparent authority. Locate a case in which apparent authority was exercised.

REFERENCES

California v. Greenwood, 466 U.S. 35 (1988).

Chimel v. California, 395 U.S. 752 (1969).

Georgia v. Randolph, 547 U.S. 103 (2006).

Hudson v. Michigan, 547 U.S. 586 (2006).

Illinois v. Wardlow, 528 U.S. 119 (2000).

Katz v. United States, 389 U.S. 347 (1967).

Mancusi v. DeForte, 392 U.S. 364 (1968).

Mapp v. Ohio, 367 U.S. 643 (1961).

Office of the District Attorney, Alameda County. 2009. Recent case report: U.S. v. Comprehensive Drug Testing, Inc. *Point of View Online.* http://le.alcoda.org/publications/point_of_view/files/CompHealth.pdf (accessed February 10, 2009).

Oliver v. United States, 466 U.S. 170 (1984).

Payton v. New York, 445 U.S. 573 (1980).

People v. Ledesma, 39 Cal. 4th 657 (2006).

People v. Oodham, 81 Cal. App. 4th 1 (2000).

Portman, R., and J. Jacobs. 1998. Responding to third-party subpoenas. www.thefreelibrary.com/Responding+to+third-party+subpoenas-a020519358 (accessed February 1, 2010).

Rakas v. Illinois, 439 U.S. 128 (1978).

Schneckloth v. Bustamonte, 412 U.S. 218 (1973).

Terry v. Ohio, 392 U.S. 1 (1968).

U.S. Department of Justice. 2008. *Federal rules of evidence.* Washington, DC.

U.S. v. Carey, 172 F.3d 1268 (10th Cir. 1999).

U.S. v. Comprehensive Drug Testing, Inc., 579 F3d 989 (2009).

U.S. v. Simons, 206 F3d 392 (2000).

U.S. v. Ziegler, 497 F3d 890 (2001).

United States v. Barth, 26 F. Supp. 2d 929 (1998).

United States v. David, 756 F. Supp. 1385 (1991).

United States v. Horowitz, 806 F.2d 1222 (1986).

United States v. Lyons, 992 F.2d 1029 (1993).

United States v. Matlock, 415 U.S. 164 (1974).

United States v. Most, 876 F.2d 191 (1989).

United States v. Reyes, 922 F. Supp. 818 (1996).

United States v. Ross, 456 U.S. 798 (1982).

USC Title 18, Part 1, Chapter 121, § 2705.

USC Title 18, Part II, Chapter 205.

USLegal (2010). Search law and legal definition. http://definitions.uslegal.com/s/search/ (accessed February 4, 2010).

Weeks v. United States, 232 U.S. 383 (1914).

LEGISLATED PRIVACY CONCERNS

In Chapter 2, "Laws Affecting Forensic Investigations," emphasis was placed on the difference between constitutional rights and legislated privileges. It is a common misconception that a person's right to privacy is guaranteed under the Constitution. That is, in fact, not the case. Nowhere in the Constitution is there any mention of privacy. Attempts have been made to generously interpret the Fourth Amendment to infer such rights. However, the language in that amendment is very specific. It guards American citizens against unreasonable search and seizure—not invasions of privacy.

Considering the omission of privacy rights to be an oversight by our founding fathers, Congress has passed a litany of legislation guaranteeing that certain activities and information will remain private under the law. Those same laws, in most cases, dictate what exceptions exist and what methods can be used to acquire private information and remain in compliance with the law. This chapter covers a small collection of the laws that most typically impact a digital forensic examination.

Chapter 2 touched briefly on this subject, and in that chapter a short list of legislation was presented. This is the list that will be covered in this chapter. To recap, those laws include

- The Fair Credit Reporting Act of 1970
- The Privacy Act of 1974
- The Equal Credit Opportunity Act of 1974
- The Electronic Communications Privacy Act of 1986
- Health Insurance Portability and Accountability Act of 1996

- The Gramm-Leach-Bliley Act of 1999
- The Fair Debt Collection Practices Act of 2006
- The Family Educational Rights and Privacy Act of 2008

It should be noted that the laws are listed in the chronological order in which they were passed. In this chapter, they will be discussed by the category of protection that they provide. These categories include

- General privacy
- Financial legislation
- Health care and education legislation

Also, note that since these are pieces of legislation and not constitutional law, any one of them is subject to change at the whim of the current administration in control of our political system.

GENERAL PRIVACY

There have not been the large numbers of laws passed in this regard simply because the general public has accepted that the laws passed seem to cover the bases sufficiently. As one would expect, the arguments surrounding how they are enforced continue with each year, which is why we have lawyers and courts. Two laws that will be covered in this chapter are

- The Privacy Act of 1974
- The Electronic Communications Privacy Act of 1986

THE PRIVACY ACT OF 1974

5 U.S.C. § 552a, otherwise known as The Privacy Act, was passed in 1974 in response to concerns about how information collected and stored in computerized databases could impact the private lives of average citizens. The law followed a report by the Department of Health, Education, and Welfare (HEW) entitled *Records, Computers, and the Rights of Citizens*. HEW recommended that Congress pass legislation that codified what information could be retained, how it could be used, and who had the right to see it. The report listed the following requirements for such legislation (HEW 1973):

- No recordkeeping system should exist whose very existence is kept secret from the public.

- Individuals must have some mechanism for learning what information is retained in a database and how that information is used.

- Individuals must be able to prevent information that was obtained for a specific purpose from being used or made available for other purposes without permission.

- If information retained in a database is incorrect, there must some mechanism by which an individual can have corrections made.

- Any organization creating, maintaining, using, or disseminating records of identifiable personal data must assure the reliability of the data for their intended use and must take precaution to prevent misuse of the data.

In 1974, the Privacy Act was passed, addressing each of these concerns. Some restrictions to the bill do apply. For one, the legislation applies only to U.S. citizens and permanent residents of the United States. Therefore, an exchange student or a person living in the country on a temporary work visa cannot sue for damages under this statute. Also, the law was written to apply only to federal agencies. This restriction is what led to the passage of several seemingly similar laws in later years that applied to specific industries.

As passed, the law allows individuals to request access to their records. It provides guidance for how an individual can submit a request for corrections to be made—but it also allows the agency receiving the request to deny it. The law places limitations on the government's right to disclose information—but it also provides a dozen different exceptions that allow the government to do what it pleases with confidential information. **Audit** trails must be maintained that identify when and to whom any given record was shared.

Law enforcement is granted numerous exceptions in virtually every aspect of the law. Any law enforcement official or agency is exempt from the law if the records contain

- Information about offenders, either alleged or convicted
- Information compiled for the purposes of criminal investigation
- Any information collected about an individual throughout the course of enforcing law, from arrest to release

If a citizen can demonstrate that any rights accorded by this law have been violated, that person can file civil action against the agency and the official committing the alleged violation. The court will privately examine the records in question and make a determination as to whether the defendant properly invoked a legitimate exception to the law. If the court finds the violation to be willful and intentional, it can grant a settlement of actual damages plus legal expenses. Additionally, if the court finds the violation to be willful and intentional, it can find the official guilty of a misdemeanor and fine the individual up to $5000.

THE ELECTRONIC COMMUNICATIONS PRIVACY ACT OF 1986

The Electronic Communications Privacy Act (ECPA) was actually an offshoot of another law passed many years earlier. ECPA was passed as an amendment to the Omnibus Control and Safe Streets Act of 1968—more frequently referred to as the Wiretap Act. Wiretap had been passed in order to limit government access to private communications over electronic media. This particular bill prohibited government agents from employing any means to intercept a transmission of any sort over wire or airwaves without using due process—which generally requires a warrant (see Chapter 3, "Search Warrants and Subpoenas") unless the action falls under one of the exemptions defined under the act.

A key modification included in ECPA was the Stored Communications Act (SCA). SCA was a subset of ECPA that separately defined electronic communications services (ECS) and remote computing services (RCS). The roles of each of these services received different levels of protection under the law. DOJ has defined ECS as a service available to the general public that temporarily stores data that was sent by a subscriber *to or from a third party*. RCS is a service that processes customer files and/or stores them on behalf of the customer *for that customer's use*. A significant difference between the two services is the presence of the third party. Information stored for the customer by a service provider falls under one of three categories:

- Basic subscriber information includes the name and address of the customer, what types of services the customer receives from the provider, length of service, certain identifiers (including telephone numbers, account numbers, subscriber numbers, etc.), assigned IP addresses, and payment information (which can include any credit card numbers left on file by the customer). Telephone connection records, along with session times and durations fall under this category.

- Records or other information regarding the customer fall into a second category. This would include any information collected about a customer by the provider that does not fall under the basic subscriber information, and does not include any content of stored files or communications. This category includes "transactional" records, such as account logs, history logs, cell site history, and so forth.

- Content is the most protected of the information types defined under SCA. This includes any stored files, messages, or other data generated by the customer, and not by some automated process. Stored voice mails, other audio recordings, video, and other images all fall under the definition of content. It would also include certain automatically generated information, such as message headers and metadata.

According to 18 U.S.C. 2703 c (1)(C), a service provider can voluntarily provide certain types of information requested by an investigator. In all but the most extreme circumstances, information should be obtained through a warrant, a court order, or a subpoena. This eliminates any possibility that opposing counsel could suggest that the provider was "compelled to consent."

Under SCA, an investigator can ask a judge to issue a **preservation order.** This is a legal decree to the provider to take any and all steps necessary to assure the preservation of records, log files, or other evidence defined in the order until a warrant or subpoena can be legally issued. A preservation order can be issued in writing, by fax, or by e-mail. They are good for up to 90 days, with an option for the investigator or agency to request an additional 90-day renewal.

FINANCIAL LEGISLATION

This category of legislation covers what information can and cannot be shared by banks, mortgage companies, and other companies that collect information in order to make decisions about money, to collect information about money, or to collect debts. Financial institutions are notoriously strict about protecting customer data as a result of these laws. When conducting any sort of investigation that requires accessing financial records, it will be essential to collect the necessary legal documentation before proceeding. Additionally, these laws are frequently cited during electronic discovery in the course of a civil proceeding:

- The Fair Credit Reporting Act Of 1970
- Right to Financial Privacy Act
- The Gramm-Leach-Bliley Act Of 1999
- Fair Debt Collection Practices Act of 2006

There is a lot of overlap to these laws. Still, each one covers a different aspect of legislation. Passing familiarity with each of them is a good idea.

THE FAIR CREDIT REPORTING ACT OF 1970

The Fair Credit Reporting Act (FCRA) is an act of legislation that lays down some guidelines that consumer reporting agencies (CRA) must follow in reporting on the activities and history of individual consumers. CRAs are the agencies that collect consumers' payment histories into a large database and then provide that information, at a charge, to other companies that subscribe to their services. The three primary CRAs are Equifax, Experian, and TransUnion. However, under the law, any organization that collects information about consumer activity, credit, and payment history falls under the definition.

FCRA states that a consumer has the right to know what information is contained within his or her file. Every consumer is allowed to request a credit report at no charge one time every year. CRAs can (and will) charge for any additional reports requested. There are some circumstances that require the CRA to provide a report at no charge regardless of how many times a consumer has received a report in the previous year:

- Adverse action is taken against a consumer because of information contained in a report.
- A consumer is the victim of identity theft.
- The file contains inaccurate information as a result of fraud.
- The requesting consumer is on public assistance.
- The requesting consumer is unemployed but anticipates applying for employment within the next 60 days.

Information contained within the reports can be provided only to certain entities under specific circumstances. These are identified in § 604. Permissible Purposes of Consumer Reports of the act. Clearly, the consumer described in the report can authorize its release at any time. Law enforcement can obtain a report only through consent of the consumer or by way of a court-issued subpoena.

THE RIGHT TO FINANCIAL PRIVACY ACT OF 1978

The Right to Financial Privacy Act was passed in 1978 to limit the circumstances under which a government agency can obtain records about an individual from a financial institution. The law states that no government official or agency can obtain financial records of a person or organization without due process. The entity requesting the records must obtain an administrative subpoena or a court-issued summons before it can access records. In order to obtain such a court order or summons, the entity must demonstrate that there is a legitimate reason to believe that the records are relevant to an ongoing investigation and that a copy of the summons or subpoena was either delivered to or mailed to the last known address of the owner of the records requested.

One paragraph in the law gives the financial institution a substantial amount of leeway in notifying the government of suspected crimes being committed by an account-holder. Section 1103, Paragraph C, says, "Nothing in this title shall preclude any financial institution, or any officer, employee, or agent of a financial institution, from notifying a Government authority that such institution, or officer, employee, or agent has information which may be relevant to a possible violation of any statute or regulation." It goes on, later in the paragraph, to say that no state law, constitutional requirement, or regulation can prevent an institution or officer of an institution from reporting criminal behavior. All the institution can report is the identifying information of the account-holder, be it a corporation or individual, along with a description of the suspected criminal behavior. From there, the government must use that information to pursue a subpoena to collect any other information it needs in order to pursue an investigation.

In 2001, the law was amended in order for law enforcement and intelligence agencies to obtain information without the consumer's knowledge as long as all other legal requirements were met. If it can be demonstrated that there is a danger to national security, of physical injury to another person, serious property damage, or flight to avoid prosecution, the government may serve a warrant on the institution with an order of delayed notification to the entity under investigation. This means that the government can get a subpoena, do a thorough search of the customer's records, and *then* notify the customer of its intent. This prevents a suspect from destroying evidence, manipulating records, or otherwise throwing a wrench into the investigation.

THE GRAHAM-LEACH-BLILEY ACT OF 1999

The Graham-Leach-Bliley Act of 1999 has more of an impact on financial institutions than it does on civil or criminal investigations. Its impact on the forensic examination is almost exclusively related to electronic discovery. Therefore, the investigator dealing with financial institutions needs to be aware of what the act encompasses, should an investigation include such an organization. Its basic purpose was to formalize the Financial Privacy Act, defining what government agencies had the right to enforce the regulations, and granting certain states' agencies regulatory rights. It also introduced the Safeguards Act, which requires that financial institutions have a documented security infrastructure in place to protect a customer's private and financial information.

The key provision of Graham-Leach-Bliley affecting a legal investigation is the *pretexting provision*. This provision prohibits anyone or any organization from obtaining information from a financial organization by providing false information about why the information is needed. Not that any investigator would ever do such a thing. Another issue discussed by the act is that of document retention and availability of documents in e-discovery motions.

THE FAIR DEBT COLLECTION PRACTICES ACT OF 2006

The Fair Debt Collection Practices Act (FDPA) is another law that has but minimal impact on investigators but may have a peripheral impact. This law was passed in 2006 in response to predatory actions used by debt collection agencies and their employees in their efforts to recovered monies owed. It specified a set of ethical guidelines for debt collectors to follow, which will not be covered here. Additionally, the act specifies how and when information can be shared by financial organizations with such agencies, or between agencies.

Law enforcement may become involved when investigating identity theft, fraudulent check-passing, or forgery. It allows information to be shared with law enforcement without a warrant, *with the authorization of the person whose name is on the check or whose identity is being used.* People operating under a misappropriated identity are not protected by the law in any way.

PRIVACY IN HEALTH CARE AND EDUCATION

While there are numerous laws passed in the arena of health care and legislation, the two that are of concern here are the Health Insurance Portability and Accountability Act of 1996 and the Family Educational Rights and Privacy Act of 2008. It is likely that civil investigations will be impacted more by these acts than will criminal investigations, but familiarity is required under either circumstance.

THE HEALTH INSURANCE PORTABILITY AND ACCOUNTABILITY ACT OF 1996

The Health Insurance Portability and Accountability Act (HIPAA) of 1996 applies to the insurance and health industries. It also impacts banks and other financial organizations in how they interact with the organizations impacted by the law. HIPAA dictates standards for conducting health care transactions and maintenance of health plans, and defines end users' rights when it comes to general health care issues. The law defines specific rules concerning a person's rights to privacy and the confidentiality of both financial and health-related data.

The main thrust of the regulation is to mandate how and when medical facilities or practitioners can exchange a patient's information. It also specifies that the entities covered by the regulation may provide information to law enforcement under specific circumstances. Obviously, a recipient of a legally issued subpoena or search warrant must comply with the order. It may also comply with written administrative requests of law enforcement, providing that the request is accompanied by a written request that specifies the information sought and an affidavit stating that the materials requested are relevant and material to an ongoing legal matter.

Information regarding identifying characteristics pertaining to missing persons, fugitives, suspects in ongoing criminal investigations, or material witnesses may be provided without requiring a warrant. This information can include the person's name and address, social security number, blood type, and Rh factor. If the person is known to have been injured or to be dead, the institution can also provide dates and times of treatments or the date and time of death if appropriate. Descriptions of any distinguishing characteristics, such as birthmarks or scars, is also permitted. The institution may not share DNA or tissue samples, blood samples, dental records, or the results of analyses without a legally issued subpoena or warrant.

Medical facilities may approach law enforcement with voluntary information in cases of child abuse, domestic violence, or neglect and provide the information allowable under an administrative request. In some circumstances, the facility may be required to contact law enforcement. Gunshot wounds and stab wounds must be reported. If a death is suspected to be the result of criminal activity, it must be reported.

THE FAMILY EDUCATIONAL RIGHTS AND PRIVACY ACT OF 2008

The Family Educational Rights and Privacy Act of 2008 (FERPA) controls the distribution of private information about students. It dictates that parents and eligible students must have a right to examine any of the student's records maintained by an educational institution. Only the parent or eligible student may review the records except under specific circumstances. These include (as written in the act)

- School officials with legitimate educational interest
- Other schools to which a student is transferring

- Specified officials for audit or evaluation purposes
- Appropriate parties in connection with financial aid to a student
- Organizations conducting certain studies for or on behalf of the school
- Accrediting organizations
- To comply with a judicial order or lawfully issued subpoena
- Appropriate officials in cases of health and safety emergencies
- State and local authorities, within a juvenile justice system, pursuant to specific state law

There is certain information that the school is allowed to provide in a published directory. This includes names and addresses, dates and places of birth, any awards received by the students, and the dates that the student attended the institution. If such a directory exists, parents and students must be notified of its existence and must have the right to request that the information not be disclosed.

It is important that investigators be familiar with state laws in this regard. Different states have different regulations regarding how law enforcement may access student records.

PRIVILEGED INFORMATION

Assume for a moment that an investigator is presented with a case with a proper warrant intact and legal counsel has mitigated the privacy issues. Does that mean that the investigation can now dig out anything related to the case as defined by the warrant? Not necessarily. There are certain forms of information deemed privileged by law. Four areas of privileged information to be careful about are

- Attorney/client privilege
- Doctor/patient privilege
- Work/product doctrine
- Protected intellectual property

ATTORNEY/CLIENT PRIVILEGE

The only privileged information defined in the Federal Rules of Evidence is that of attorney/client privilege. The U.S. Department of Justice (DOJ) publishes a manual entitled *Searching and Seizing Computers and Obtaining Electronic Evidence in Criminal Investigations* (DOJ 2009) that further defines federal concerns regarding privileged information that are handled by DOJ attorneys. If a case expands to the point where disinterested third parties become involved, then 42 U.S.C. § 2000aa-11(a); 28 C.F.R. comes into play. This regulation prohibits federal law enforcement officers from obtaining privileged documents from attorneys, physicians, or clergy. The investigator also needs to be aware that certain state and local laws also protect physician/patient information and in some cases proprietary intellectual property.

The Government Enforcement Bulletin defines attorney/client privilege in the following way: "Communications shared in the course of an internal investigation, including documents which contain or constitute communications between employees and in-house or outside counsel, are subject to the attorney-client privilege if they are made with a reasonable expectation of, and in confidence between, privileged persons, and for the purpose of seeking, obtaining, or providing legal assistance or advice" (Jonas and Keefe 1996). Rule 502 of the Federal Rules of Evidence sets specific conditions for maintaining confidentiality between an attorney and client.

The right of client/attorney privilege was established in a landmark Supreme Court case, *Upjohn v. United States.* The U.S. Court of Appeals for the Sixth Circuit ruled on appeal that existing client/attorney privilege laws did not apply to information exchanged by middle management employees of the corporation and the organization's legal counsel. In an opinion presented by Justice William Rehnquist, the court issued a ruling that even employees of the rank and file were protected.

PHYSICIAN/PATIENT PRIVILEGE

Federal Rules of Evidence make no mention of physician/patient privilege. However, most state jurisdictions have rules pertaining to this professional relationship. This is an area that will require careful consultation with a lawyer familiar with the jurisdiction that has power over a case. There is legal precedent for not invoking this privilege. In *Tarasoff v. Regents of the University of California* (17 Cal. 3d 425, 551 P.2d 334, 131 Cal. Rptr. 14), California's Supreme Court contended that medical professionals have a legal obligation to notify authorities when they know that actions by a patient are potentially harmful to another person. Since each state writes its own statutes regarding this privilege, it is essential to follow the advice of an attorney when this privilege is invoked.

WORK-PRODUCT DOCTRINE

The *work-product doctrine* is a legal principle that applies to documents or other evidentiary material that an individual or organization prepares in anticipation of litigation. The person or organization under investigation can seek a **protective order** rendering those documents undiscoverable. Unlike client/attorney privilege, materials protected under the work-product doctrine can be overcome under two sets of circumstances. First, if it can be demonstrated that facts critical to the investigation can only be found in the "protected" documents, a judge can issue an order to produce the requested materials. Second, if the entity seeking the information can prove undue hardship caused by discovering the information from any source other than the protected documents, the judge can order discovery.

PROTECTED INTELLECTUAL PROPERTY

By law, proprietary information, such as corporate trade secrets, is not protected by law. However, it is possible for the party subject to the search to negotiate limited review of such files. An article published in *Corporate Counsel's Quarterly* recommends that companies or individuals with such information stored on a device subject to search notify the agents executing the warrant that such records exist and insist that those records be sealed until legal review (Vizy 2005).

While a search warrant may preclude an investigator from obtaining certain information, it is possible that a judge may issue a subpoena, ordering the surrender of the requested information

CASE LAW: WHEN PRIVILEGED DOCUMENTS AREN'T

As stated in the previous sections, work product and privileged documents are generally protected information and not available as evidence. The court can change that situation with the strike of a gavel if it so chooses. In *United States ex rel. Baker v. Cmty. Health Sys., Inc.,* a judge determined that the government had unfairly issued litigation holds (in its own systems) in a way that **prejudiced** the defense. Its response was described as lackadaisical. As a result, critical information was destroyed prior to the hold order being put into place. The judge sanctioned the government by ordering it to turn over all government documents, including privileged information and work product, to the defense for review. Culpability and prejudice were listed in the court order as the motivation for issuing sanctions in the case.

TAINT TEAMS

The courts have recognized that it may not be possible to extract legitimate evidence from electronic sources without coming in contact with privileged information.

In order to protect both sides of the investigation, the courts have acknowledged the necessity for independent teams of professionals to examine and identify those documents that qualify as privileged. Such a team is called the **taint team.** The taint team is generally composed of lawyers and law enforcement officials who have no vested interest in the case.

The validity of taint teams is supported in the DOJ manual entitled *Searching and Seizing Computers and Obtaining Electronic Evidence in Criminal Investigations* cited earlier. The manual refers to the taint team as an ethical wall between the evidence and the prosecution that prevents privileged information from being viewed by the wrong people.

Taint teams have repeatedly fallen under attack. In 2006, the U.S. Court of Appeals for the Sixth Circuit rejected the use of taint teams on grand jury subpoenas. In this decision, the court declared that a third party's interest in protecting its privileged information outweighed the government's need to form a taint team. For such investigations, the courts were directed to appoint a special master who would supervise the examination of documents and determine what was privileged and what was not (U.S. Court of Appeals for the Sixth Circuit 2006).

In 2006, the offices of Representative William Jefferson (D-Louisiana) were raided by the FBI. Jefferson's attorneys attempted to have all documents seized during the raid declared inadmissible. Their argument was that the search violated the defendant's right under the Constitution's Speech and Debate Clause. The premise of this clause is that the legislative branch should be protected from intimidation or threat by the executive branch. Such a search, they insisted, represented such a threat (Dettelbach and Conley 2008). Initially, the concept of the taint team won out, with the lower court ruling that the filtering of information provided by the taint team was sufficient to protect Jefferson from executive intrusion. However, on appeal, the District of Columbia Court of Appeals overturned that decision and allowed the congressman to review all documents before releasing them to the government.

CHAPTER REVIEW

1. The Privacy Act of 1974 allows that no recordkeeping system should be in place whose very existence is kept secret from the public. Discuss some of the requirements set forth by the act that opens government records to the public. Would this act have a significant impact on the digital investigator? If so, how?

2. The Electronic Communications Privacy Act was one of the first pieces of legislation to address a preservation order. What is a preservation order? When is it likely to become relevant to an investigation?

3. How is the digital investigation affected by the Fair Credit Reporting Act?

4. What are four different types of information that can be claimed as "privileged"?

5. What is a taint team, and how does it come into play in the course of an investigation?

CHAPTER EXERCISES

1. EPIC.ORG is an organization that touts itself as being focused on "public attention on emerging civil liberties issues and to protect privacy." Browse to its Web site at http://epic.org/privacy/litigation, and scroll through some of its cases. Discuss whether or not the cases filed by the organization are based on the Constitution, on legal precedent, or on political position.

2. The recording industry has made headlines in recent years with a series of high-profile cases in which the Recording Industry Association of America has targeted college students who host musical downloads on their computers in college dorms. Verizon sued the organization to prevent the execution of a subpoena. It lost. Read the case *Verizon v. RIAA* (available at the time of this writing at http://epic.org/privacy/copyright/verizon/) and have an open discussion about the merits (or lack thereof) in this case.

REFERENCES

CardReport. Equal Credit Opportunity Act. www.cardreport.com/laws/ecoa. html (accessed February 22, 2010).

Department of Education. 2008. *The Family Educational Rights and Privacy Act of 2008.* www2.ed.gov/policy/gen/guid/fpco/ferpa/index.html (accessed March 2, 2010).

Department of Health, Education, and Welfare. 1973. *Records, computers, and the rights of citizens.* http://epic.org/privacy/hew1973report/ (accessed February 19, 2010).

Department of Justice. 2009. *Searching and seizing computers and obtaining electronic evidence in criminal investigations.* Washington, DC: Executive Office for United States Attorneys.

Dettelbach, S., and J. Conley J. 2008. Knock, knock! The Rep. William Jefferson search case and its implications in the attorney-client context. *Andrews Litigation Reporter,* 22(9)

Federal Deposit Insurance Corporation. 1978. *Right to Financial Privacy Act.* www.fdic.gov/regulations/compliance/manual/pdf/VIII-3.1.pdf (accessed February 22, 2010).

Federal Trade Commission. 2009. *Fair Credit Reporting Act.* www.ftc.gov/os/statutes/fcradoc.pdf (accessed February 21, 2010).

Federal Trade Commission. 2006. *Fair Debt Collection Act.* www.ftc.gov/bcp/edu/pubs/consumer/credit/cre27.pdf (accessed March 1, 2010).

Jonas, S., and R. Keefe. 1996. *Government enforcement bulletin.* www.wilmerhale.com/publications/ whpubsdetail.Aspx?Publication=2075 (accessed January 20, 2010)

Senate Banking Committee.1999. *Graham-Leach-Bliley Act.* http://banking.senate.gov/conf/confrpt.htm (accessed March 1, 2010).

The Electronic Communications Privacy Act of 1986, Public Law 99-508. http://cpsr.org/issues/privacy/ecpa86/ (accessed February 19, 2010).

U.S. Court of Appeals for the Sixth Circuit. 2006. In re Grand Jury Subpoenas 04-124-03.

U.S. Department of Health and Human Services. 1996. HIPAA frequent questions. www.hhs.gov/hipaafaq/permitted/law/505.html (accessed March 2, 2010).

United States ex rel. Baker v. Cmty. Health Sys., Inc., No. 05-279 WJ/ACT, 2012 WL 5387069.

Vizy, N. 2005. Handling a search warrant. *Corporate Counsel's Quarterly,* 21(2).

THE ADMISSIBILITY OF EVIDENCE

When an archaeologist makes a new discovery, the burden of proof falls on the researcher to show beyond a shadow of a doubt that the discovery is authentic and genuine. The same holds true of the gems the digital investigator uncovers during an investigation. It isn't sufficient that we find the smoking gun. We have to find it in a manner that the courts find acceptable, or it will be dismissed. Another difference is that the investigator has to prove that the evidence is not only genuine, but relevant. Relevance is a function of admissibility. Whether or not evidence is admissible in court depends on a surprising number of factors. Throughout this book, the mantra has been *document, document, and then document how you documented.* Perhaps it hasn't been said quite so succinctly, but still, documentation is the key to everything. This chapter will discuss what makes evidence admissible and how the investigator can assure that the work accomplished makes its way into court.

WHAT MAKES EVIDENCE ADMISSIBLE?

Any information or exhibits that are to be presented in a court case, whether it be civil or criminal, will be subjected to scrutiny by both sides as well as by the judge in order to determine whether or not that evidence meets the general guidelines for **admissibility.** If the court will allow the evidence to be presented, it is admissible. A number of factors go into making this decision. Some of the questions that will be asked are

- Is the evidence relevant?
- Is the evidence authentic and credible?
- Is the evidence competent?

All three of these conditions must be met before the material will be allowed in court. So to clarify matters as much as possible, a detailed discussion of each one is in order. In considering any of these questions, a concept of American law known as the *exclusionary rule* must be kept in mind at all times. This basic tenet of American law states that if evidence is collected in violation of the law, or in violation of a person's constitutional rights, that evidence must be excluded from all court proceedings.

Environmental Law Publishing (2010) has posted a rather complex flowchart that helps determine the admissibility of evidence. The diagram takes into consideration various factors involved when a court would or would not allow evidence. A simplified version of this flowchart, limited to those conditions likely to be encountered in a digital examination, is seen in Figure 5.1.

Is the Evidence Relevant?

"The fundamental rule governing the admissibility of evidence is that it must be relevant" (*Wilson v. R* 1970). If relevance cannot be established, the discussion can stop right here. None of the other factors covered in this chapter will be . . . well, relevant. The evidence will immediately be disallowed.

To be considered **relevant**, the evidence in question must satisfy two conditions. First and foremost, it must be **material**. Material means that it directly relates to the case being presented. If the prosecution is trying to prove that a man is guilty of bank fraud and presents files from his computer showing that he visited pornography sites with regularity, this is going to raise an instant objection from the defense.

The second condition of relevance is that the material is **probative**. That means it proves something that will help get at the truth of the situation. This works hand in hand with the material aspect of relevance. If the suspect possesses several account numbers for accounts that do not belong to him, it proves that he was showing an interest in other people's business matters. The history of pornography sites proves something, but nothing that is material to the case.

Is the Evidence Authentic?

There are several things to examine in order to establish the authenticity of evidence as well. We must consider the credibility of the information presented.

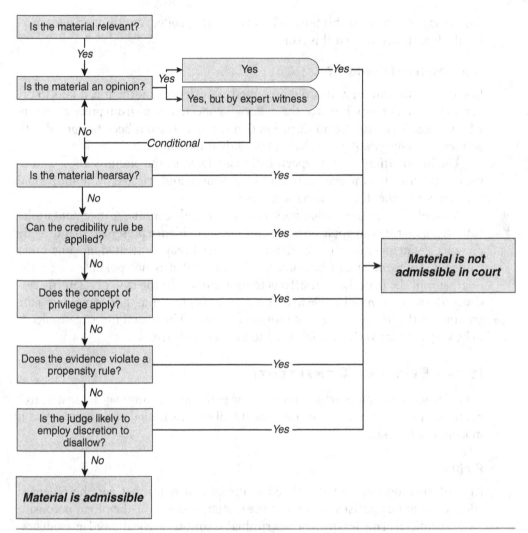

Figure 5.1 A flowchart of the admissibility of evidence

It must be factual information and not a person's opinion, with the exception that an expert witness may be called upon to express an opinion based on professional experience or specialized training.

Is the Material an Opinion?

Strictly speaking, digital evidence will not fall under the category of an opinion. The material either exists or it doesn't. However, the interpretation of material found may be subject to this test. As an investigator, collect anything of relevance. Let the legal team sort out this issue.

Is the Material Credible?

In order to ascertain that material presented as evidence is authentic, it falls to the investigator to demonstrate that the materials collected came from precisely where it is claimed. There can be no suspicion that the evidence has been tampered with or altered in any way. A good chain of custody is mandatory.

The information must be specifically associated to the circumstances and to the person linked to the events. It must be produced and attested by an individual who can verify that these associations exist.

Most of all, the information must be truthful and accurate. A statement under oath that a carrot is an apple does not make it so. Evidence presented that directly presents a statement or other evidentiary material may be treated like any other witness's statement. It can be considered hearsay if it is not possible to get the originator of the material to testify as to its accuracy. In the case of scientific evidence, the witness must be able to defray any doubts that might arise regarding the accuracy of the process used to obtain the evidence. The digital investigator needs to be very familiar with the tools used to extract evidence.

IS THE EVIDENCE COMPETENT?

For evidence to be **competent,** it must not be prejudicial in any way. It must be free of any statutory constraints. It must satisfy all constitutional constraints. And it must not be hearsay.

Prejudice

Any information not directly related to the case at hand that has the potential effect of swaying a jurist's opinion in the matter, one way or the other, is considered prejudicial. This is why a prior criminal record is rarely allowed as evidence. A person who is being tried for robbing a liquor store is unduly prejudiced if the prosecution shows that she was convicted three times for shoplifting. If considered unfairly prejudicial, even evidence germane to the case may be excluded. Federal Rule 403 says that the probative value of the evidence must not be outweighed by the danger of unfair prejudice (FRE, Rule 403, 2011).

Statutory Restraints

Some information cannot be presented as evidence because of the protected nature of the information. Privileged information is generated in a variety of ways.

Chapter 16, "Litigation and Electronic Discovery," will cover this subject in more detail. For now suffice it to say that if information collected constitutes communication between a person and a priest, a doctor, or a lawyer, it is going to get kicked out of court.

Constitutional Constraints

The rights of the people are guaranteed under the Constitution. It is one of the fundamental tenets of our society. If evidence is obtained as a result of a blatant violation of those rights, it cannot be admitted as evidence, no matter how solidly it proves the case. Anybody who has seen Dirty Harry in action knows all about that. The First and Fourth Amendments to the Constitution are the amendments most frequently cited in evidence hearings, but circumstances can easily bring others into play.

Some court decisions have stated that forcing a suspect to reveal a password violates the Fifth Amendment as it applies to self-incrimination. In March 2012, a federal judge ordered Ramona Fricosu to provide an unencrypted copy of encrypted information from her hard drive (*United States v. Fricosu* 2012). The judge, Robert Blackburn, ruled that requiring the suspect to unencrypt the hard drive was not a violation of Fifth Amendment rights (Hunt and Varner 2012).

This ruling seemingly contradicts the decision handed down in *U.S. v. John Doe* (2012) where evidence was disallowed because the defendant had been forced to reveal the password to an encrypted drive. Which interpretation is correct is likely to be determined by the Supreme Court. As of this writing, *Fricosu* is still under appeal. The moral of these two stories is that it isn't up to the investigator to decide what is right and what is wrong. Let the legal minds fight it out, and until a decision is handed down, do nothing that could compromise the evidence.

Hearsay

Hearsay is any statement that is made outside of the proceedings by any person (or thing, as we will see later on) who is not under oath at the time the statement is made. Courts take a dim view of "he said–she said" arguments on the witness stand. The Law Commission in 1995 had this to say about hearsay: "Where a representation of any fact is made otherwise than by a person, but depends for its accuracy on information supplied by a person, it should not be admissible as evidence of the fact unless it is proved that the information was accurate" (Sommer 1998).

For every rule, there are exceptions, and the hearsay rule is no exception. Several of the hearsay exceptions related to oral testimony are not relevant to this discussion and will be ignored. Exception No. 6, Records of a Regularly Conducted

Activity, specifically relates to digital investigation. This includes records created by the business in the course of regular business activity as well as automatically generated records, such as log files (FRU 2012).

The Exclusionary Rule

Protection under the Fourth Amendment includes searches of a person's possessions as well as his home. This includes his automobile, briefcase, cell phone, and any other object that could be classified as a "container." The Fifth Amendment prevents people from being forced to testify against themselves. The alleged witches of Salem had their constitutional rights violated when they were forced to confess under duress. It is a pity for them that the Constitution had not yet been written. Lastly, the Sixth Amendment guarantees a person the right to counsel. The latter does not affect the digital investigator as often but should be kept on the back burner as a possible problem to deal with.

When a search or seizure of property is done in violation of a suspect's constitutional rights, the *exclusionary rule* dictates that any evidence from such a search or seizure must be excluded as evidence. A key factor to consider here is that only a search and seizure performed by an agent of the government can be considered a violation of a suspect's constitutional rights. There will be more on that when we talk about digital vigilantes later in this chapter.

Some version of the exclusionary rule has existed in U.S. legal doctrine since even before America was an independent country. Chief Justice Mansfield wrote in 1769 that the courts should disregard any evidence that was provided under duress, regardless of how convincing that evidence might be (Davies 2003).

Disregarding evidence obtained during an illegal search was affirmed by the Supreme Court in 1914 (*Weeks v. U.S.* 1914). This trial centered on an alleged scam to sell lottery tickets by mail. During this era, state-run lotteries did not exist, and any form of such activity was illegal. Law enforcement officials searched Weeks's home and found the evidence they needed to prosecute.

Justice Day, writing for the majority, stated that "there was involved in the order refusing the application a denial of the constitutional rights of the accused." The Supreme Court ruling reversed the decisions of the lower courts affirming Weeks's conviction.

KEEPING EVIDENCE AUTHENTIC

For the most part, relevance and competence are matters for the legal minds to argue out. Verifying that the data is authentic, and keeping it that way throughout the entire cycle of the investigation, from instigation to conclusion, is the job of the investigative team. The process of documentation (to be discussed in greater detail in Chapter 17, "Case Management and Report Writing") is a key component to having your evidence accepted in court.

There are three areas of discussion that need to be addressed. First of all, it is necessary to keep the search of all information systems legal and within the scope of authorization. Searching a computer system is no different than searching a home. Unless the owner has given explicit permission for the search to be conducted, some form of legal authorization, such as a court order, a warrant, or a subpoena, will be required. Chapter 3, "Search Warrants and Subpoenas," covered this subject in greater detail.

While doing the search, there are additional concerns to keep in mind. What is the plain view doctrine, and how does it impact your work? Are there multiple users who regularly make use of the computer system being searched? Does your authorization define a specific scope for the search to be conducted?

PLAIN VIEW DOCTRINE

Generally speaking, the plain view doctrine is a rule that specifies that a search and seizure of evidence can be done without a warrant any time that the official making the search finds evidence of a crime that is clearly visible without the need for an entry or a search. Court decisions have specified that there can be no reasonable expectation of privacy regarding an item that is located in a way anyone can see (*Horton v. California* 1990). The classic example of this situation is when a police officer pulls a driver over for a speeding violation and sees a baggie full of white powder on the front seat.

This premise easily comes into play during any digital investigation, and the investigator needs to tread carefully when it does. What would the correct approach be if, while searching for evidence of mail fraud, the investigator finds child pornography "in plain sight"? Mantei (2011) identifies three categories under which the plain view doctrine might impact the digital investigator:

- The inadvertence approach
- The prophylactic test approach
- The computers as containers approach

These different approaches were defined based on different court rulings that have occurred over the years. While the following discussion focuses primarily on how the government handled specific criminal cases, the principles will apply to any forensic evidence.

The Inadvertence Approach

Did the investigator come across the evidence "in plain view" accidentally or as the result of a systematic search? Defining plain view under this standard is based on a decision handed down by the U.S. Federal Circuit Court in *U.S. v. Carey*. In this historic case, the investigators were given permission by the owner of the computer to perform a search. Despite having consent, the officers obtained a search warrant for evidence regarding the sale and distribution of controlled substances. During the search, police officers found a number of files with sexually suggestive file names. After viewing several of these files, they found files containing child pornography. Additional charges of transporting and possessing goods containing or including child pornography were filed against the defendant.

Initially, the courts allowed the files as evidence, citing that the evidence had been obtained while executing a legally obtained search warrant. On appeal, the Tenth Circuit overturned this decision. Using the officers' own testimony as a guide, the court pointed out that the files used to indict Carey were not found "in plain view" inadvertently, but rather after a systematic search consuming a substantial amount of time. The first files seen, which prompted the search, while pornographic in nature, did not contain child pornography and therefore were not evidence that a crime had been committed. In any case, the files were not regarding the sale and distribution of controlled substances.

This approach was further fortified in *U.S. v. Mann* (2010), where child pornography was discovered during an investigation into criminal voyeurism. While a large number of files were admitted as evidence, files flagged with *known file filter* (KFF) alerts were disallowed as evidence because the court decided that a KFF comparison identified the file as child pornography and therefore the investigators should have known they were outside of the scope of their investigation. A new warrant would have been required to search for child pornography.

The Prophylactic Test

In a nationally publicized case, *U.S. v. Comprehensive Drug Testing, Inc.*, the Ninth Circuit outlined a series of rules that evidence must pass in order to be considered "in plain view." In searching for records specific to certain professional athletes named in a warrant, a directory containing targeted files was seized and transported offsite for analysis. During this time, the names of other nationally recognizable athletes were discovered in the directory listings. The defense filed a FRCP 41(g) motion to have the evidence returned to the defendant and removed as evidence due to an unlawful search and seizure. The Ninth Circuit granted this motion and defined the following rules for applying plain view.

The government had to "forswear reliance on the plain view doctrine or similar doctrine," and if the government refused to accept a waiver of that nature, the judge "should order that the seizable and non-seizable data be separated by an independent third party under the supervision of the court, or deny the warrant altogether." The decision stated that the government also had to state the "actual degree of such risks" that failure to immediately execute a warrant will result in the destruction data (*U.S. v. Comprehensive Drug Testing, Inc.* 2008).

This completely contradicts the Fourth Circuit's decision that a computer search must "by implication, authorize at least a cursory review of each file on the computer" (*U.S. v. Williams* 2010a). The backlash to *U.S. v. Comprehensive* was such that in a later document, the Ninth Circuit clarified that these were to be considered guidelines and not rules to be followed. However, at least for the time being, courts have different precedents from which to act. Each must be considered.

Computers as Containers

In 2010, police officers obtained a search warrant that allowed them to search and seize computers belonging to Karol and Curtis Williams. The warrant specified "computer systems and digital storage media, videotapes, videotape recorders, documents, [and] photographs" (*U.S. v. Williams* 2010b). The purpose of the warrant was to investigate a complaint from a local church that they had received e-mails threatening young boys attending their Sunday school classes.

During the subsequent search, investigators discovered thousands of images of young boys. Thirty-nine of these images were classified as pornographic, and as a result of the search, Williams was indicted on child pornography charges. In Williams's defense, he claimed that the search of his computers represented a violation of his Fourth Amendment rights because the search of his computers exceeded the scope of the warrant as issued.

In rejecting Williams's appeal, the Fourth Circuit pointed out that the warrant authorized the search of each of the data storage devices or media specified in the warrant. Because the warrant instructed investigators to search for any evidence supporting the church's complaint, the court decided that in order to ascertain the evidentiary value of any given file, that file had to be opened and viewed. In the decision, the Fourth Circuit correctly pointed out that file names and extensions were invalid search constants because either one could be changed to conceal the actual contents of the file. The computer system was compared to "filing cabinets or other closed containers" (*U.S. v. Williams,* 2010b). Once a warrant was issued for the container, each item in the container could be examined.

DEALING WITH MULTIPLE USERS

For many years, operating systems (OSs) have been designed from the ground up to support multiple users. Each OS maintains separate user profiles to manage preferences and separate containers for storing user files (Figure 5.2). Legal issues face any investigator searching a computer system used by more than one person.

It is not at all uncommon for computers owned by corporate entities or other organizations to be used by more than one person. Even privately owned computers are likely to be configured with multiple user accounts. My Macintosh at home has accounts for my wife, both of my children, me, and even my sister-in-law.

Any time multiple users are involved, the issue of privacy becomes somewhat convoluted. How to deal with search warrants and subpoenas is also impacted when there exists the possibility that any given file on the system could have been created by any one of several people. Whether legal or civil in nature, each case revolves around the concept of an individual's "reasonable expectation of privacy." If your warrant specifies User A, how does a general search of the hard disk preclude the possibility that files from User B will be discovered and viewed?

A password-encoded account that is managed on the local computer is a strong suggestion that users have a reasonable expectation of privacy. However, on most networks, passwords are managed by the network operating system and not on local security accounts. When this happens, while each computer onto which a

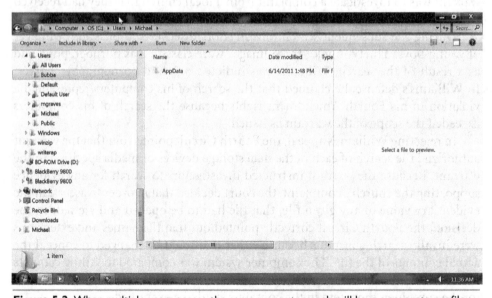

Figure 5.2 When multiple users access the same computer, each will have a separate profile.

user logs on will have a profile for that account, it is not necessarily true that files created, modified, or downloaded by that user will be stored in a profile-specific location. Such inconsistent behavior exacerbates the problems faced by the digital investigator.

These difficulties can be a little different, depending on whether the search is being conducted on the basis of the *consent search doctrine* or in response to a warrant or subpoena. Since warrants and subpoenas are covered in Chapter 3, "Search Warrants and Subpoenas," only the consent search doctrine will be discussed in this section.

THE CONSENT SEARCH DOCTRINE

As has already been discussed at great length, the whole reason behind the necessity for search warrants is the Fourth Amendment. This particular document guarantees that citizens do not need to fear unreasonable searches or seizure of their property. Only by way of a legally executed warrant could a government official search a citizen's property.

The Supreme Court has spent the last couple of centuries fine-tuning the definition of "unreasonable." The courts defined a two-component test of any situation to ascertain the level of reasonability. First of all, does the individual have a "subjective expectation of privacy"? And secondly, would society in general be "prepared to recognize [it] as reasonable" (*Katz v. U.S.* 1967)?

One exception to the Fourth Amendment, carved out early in the game, was that any time the owner voluntarily consented to having his or her property searched, any evidence discovered as a result of that search was considered to be legally obtained. Subsequent court cases even determined that it did not necessarily have to be the actual owner of the property that granted consent for the search.

U.S. v. Matlock (1974) determined that anyone who possessed "common authority" over a property could grant consent to its search. In this decision, the court was quite clear that vested interest in the property extended beyond the concept of ownership. If the owner shared common access with a roommate or a family member, then that person also had the authority to grant permission to search those areas to which the person was granted access.

Such common authority is not without limitations. *U.S. v. Block* specified that while a person might have the authority to enter a room, this did not automatically render the authority to search everything within the room. The case in point involved a mother who granted permission for police to search the footlocker of her 23-year-old son. While she did have the authority to grant access to the room, because as owner of the house she automatically had that privilege, she could not grant permission to search a locked footlocker owned by her son. The line of demarcation was that she did not own the footlocker, did not have permission to open it, and subsequently did not have "access."

CASE LAW: *U.S.* v. *FRANK GARY BUCKNER*

In 2003, police entered the home of Frank Gary Buckner with the verbal consent of Buckner's wife, Michelle. At this time, Ms. Buckner said for the officers "to take whatever [they] needed" and that she "want[ed] to be as cooperative as she could be" (*U.S. v. Frank Gary Buckner* 2007). The officers seized the computer belonging to Mr. Buckner and transported it offsite for forensic analysis. Evidence found on the computer led to 20 counts of wire fraud and 12 counts of mail fraud. The defense tried to have evidence derived from the computer search suppressed, contending that since the computer was password-protected and nobody could sign on to the computer or view the files without knowing the password, then only he could give permission for a search of the computer. The motion to suppress was denied and Buckner filed a conditional plea of guilty.

The condition of his plea reserved the right for him to appeal based on the denial of his motion to suppress. On appeal, Buckner did not challenge the right of police to seize the computer. He did, however, contend that the search of the computer without a warrant was unconstitutional and therefore the evidence was obtained illegally. In its decision, the U.S. Court of Appeals determined not only that Ms. Buckner had common authority over the computer but also that apparent authority existed for her to grant permission to the officers to search the computer. The motion to suppress was affirmed and Buckner lost the appeal.

The natural question that arose from these decisions was: Who has "apparent authority" to grant permission for a search? While the concept of common authority is clearly defined, to what extent must the investigator go to determine that a person granting permission actually has the authority to do so?

Illinois v. Rodriguez set the precedent for that decision in 1990. In this landmark decision, police responded to a call at the residence of Dorothy Jackson, who complained that Rodriguez was assaulting her daughter. According to police records, Ms. Jackson gave the officers every reason to believe that she had the authority to allow police to search the property. In the ensuing search, illegal contraband was discovered, which led to the arrest of Rodriguez. No warrant was issued because the police assumed none was needed in the presence of consent.

Rodriguez argued at his trial that Jackson did not have the authority to consent to such a search, since she no longer lived in the apartment and had not done so for several weeks. The argument was initially successful, and the lower court ruled on behalf of Rodriquez. The case wound its way all the way to the Supreme Court, where Justice Scalia, writing for the majority option, cited that Fourth Amendment rights are not violated when law enforcement "reasonably (though erroneously) believe that the person who has consented to their entry is a resident of the premises" (*Illinois v. Rodriquez* 1990).

So after this lengthy and possibly meandering discussion of what constitutes permission, how does this affect the digital investigation? The question of multiple accounts on a computer was asked in 2001. In a situation where one individual granted permission to search a computer, it was made clear to the investigating officers that there was another user on the computer, that both users had a password-protected account, and that both maintained their own file folders. The court decided that permission by one user on a shared system did not give police the right to search the files of the other user (*Trulock v. Freeh* 2001). The court analogized this to the locked footlocker in *U.S. v. Block*. Reference this to the earlier section, "Computers as Containers."

A distinct problem is manifested when investigators use generic forensic tools to search for files on the hard disk. As discussed in Chapter 8, "Finding Lost Files," many of the search tools are run against a forensic image of an entire drive. These tools do not necessarily know what files are owned by which users. Unlike encryption, which renders a file unreadable to general text searches, files that are only managed by password security are readily found by tools such as Encase, FTK, and such. While some of the more advanced versions of these tools are able to identify which user owns any particular file, the majority do not. Open-source or generic utilities such as strings or GREP and file carving utilities like Scalpel are unable to distinguish between users.

In *U.S. v. Andrus* (2007), McKay, the justice presiding, defines two legal issues key to any search of a system involving multiple users. The first questions whether or not users exhibit a determined attempt to keep their data private. Use of encryption and password-protected files is strongly indicative that they do. The second issue at stake is whether the investigating entity is employing any form of technology that allows the search to go beyond its authorized scope.

Using Encase as an example, McKay notes that software is capable of ignoring password protection in the process of finding and opening files. He concludes that investigators are then under the obligation to inquire into the level of access and what authority the person granting permission has over the system (*U.S. v. Andrus* 2007). A person with full administrative privileges on the system can obviously change any password on the system in order to gain access. But does the ability by necessity grant the right?

DEFINING THE SCOPE OF THE SEARCH

Regardless of whether the search for evidence is inspired by civil or criminal action or whether it is being conducted with consent or the result of a court order, it remains true that there will be a specific limit to the extent of the search. A search warrant will outline specific parameters that define the scope. Law enforcement officials are learning that a search scope that is too loosely defined will almost certainly lead to an appeal. Judges are more cognizant of this as well. In a civil investigation or an internal operation, it is up to the legal team to define the scope of the desired search.

Search warrants must be specific. Specificity is defined by two factors. The first is **particularity**. Particularity means that the warrant must clearly state what is being sought in the context of the search. A warrant that authorizes the search and seizure of "computers and storage media under the control of the defendant" would be considered overly broad if the "defendant" was a corporate entity. In this case, it would be necessary to identify which computer or computers were being sought and the specific media. That same description might be sufficient in a search of a private individual's residence. It is always the decision of the legal counsel as to what items to search and not that of the investigator.

The second factor is **breadth.** Under the breadth factor, the scope of the warrant is limited to the probable cause upon which the original warrant is based. In other words, if the probable cause is in regard to income tax evasion, the searchers cannot confiscate pornographic material. If such evidence is found in plain sight, in order to seize the materials, a new warrant should be requested defining the new scope.

In a civil or internal investigation, the scope will be defined by the person or committee making the assignment. Civil litigation is generally preceded by a discovery meeting in which each side states what documentation it expects the other side to produce. E-discovery and its related processes are covered in more detail in Chapter 16, "Litigation and Electronic Discovery." Internal investigations are usually subject to less regulatory oversight. As such, instructions may be very well defined or they may be very loose. It is important to make sure everybody is on the same page before the investigation starts. Regardless of the situation, any time the search looks like it is taking the investigator outside of the defined scope, the time has come to take a step back and find out if additional guidance is in order.

WHEN THE CONSTITUTION DOESN'T APPLY

Much of the discussion in this chapter has been based on criminal investigations. Since these are cases that are prosecuted by government entities, the watchful eye of the Constitution rules every step. There are situations, however, when the courts cannot enforce constitutional law. In civil cases involving private individuals, the FRCP applies, which has a different set of rules for introducing evidence (See Chapter 16). Another situation that clouds the issue of constitutionality is evidence provided by the digital vigilante.

CIVIL LITIGATION AND INTERNAL INVESTIGATION

Internal corporate investigations are generally not impacted by constitutional limitations. However, a word of caution is in order. In the event that such an inquiry leads to the discovery of criminal activity and subsequent charges, any deficiencies in the investigation will be called into question. Legal counsel should be consulted in any situation where future prosecution is a possibility. Since this subject is covered in Chapter 16, there is little need to duplicate the material here.

DIGITAL VIGILANTES

People have long had a perverse admiration for the vigilante. Most of the super-heroes charging through the theaters are vigilantes. The law can't act because its hands are tied by legal issues, or by their own incompetence or lack of concern. So a dedicated private citizen with special powers takes the law into his own hands. Vigilantes go far back into history. Where would merry old England have been without Robin Hood?

The realm of digital investigation is not without its share of these types of people. Well-trained hackers make the news when they break into a bank system and make off with thousands of credit card numbers. Not so much is heard when a hacker breaks into a system and produces evidence of a major crime in progress. Police have informants everywhere—even on the Net. But is the evidence uncovered by a vigilante admissible as evidence in court?

While law enforcement has made great strides in combating cybercrime in the past few years, it still has a way to go. According to Brenner (2007), the reason for this is our current model of law enforcement, because the assumptions it makes about crime do not hold true to digital criminology. The whole concept of "jurisdiction" makes no sense when there are no border guards to find contraband in the electronic luggage. When credit card information is stolen from an online store in Boston, but the perpetrator pressed the Enter key that initiated the crime in Pakistan, who goes after the bad guy, and which courts handle the civil case? Brenner suggests that the actions of vigilantes should be encouraged, although she argues that they should be controlled—deputized as it were. But how would that impact the constitutionality of the actions?

When Is the Private Search Constitutional?

Consider this case as an introduction to the discussion. In *U.S. v. Bradley Joseph Steiger* (2003), the defendant was arrested and charged with multiple counts of possessing child pornography and receiving it by way of interstate and foreign commerce. The evidence that led to law enforcement obtaining a police warrant came from an anonymous tip provided in an e-mail from a person who identified himself only as Unknownuser. Steiger attempted to have the evidence uncovered as a result of that warrant suppressed because Unknownuser was working as an agent for the government and as such had searched his computer illegally in violation of the Wiretap Act. Additionally, law enforcement failed to include the fact that the evidence provided by Unknownuser was obtained illegally when they applied for their search warrant.

In denying these motions to suppress, Justice Goodwin of the Eleventh Circuit made two observations regarding a search by private individuals. The first was that a search conducted by a private individual, whether legally conducted or not, did not implicate the Fourth Amendment. The second observation was that the court had to decide whether or not a private citizen was acting as an agent for the government when conducting the search. The latter decision is based on the answers to two questions.

Did the government know of, and authorize, the search? In Steiger, the answer was that it clearly did not. The search was conducted long before the government was made aware that a violation had occurred. Had an authorized agent of either a state or federal government agency suggested that Unknownuser conduct the search, then the hacker would have clearly been working as a government agent, whether paid or unpaid. The additional inference is that, had such an agency been aware that Unknownuser was going to perform such a search before the fact, their acquiescence to the search would render the hacker as a government agent.

Was the private individual's primary purpose to assist the government or to further its own ends? It is very difficult to ascertain the motives of a person. In light of the fact that this particular search was done prior to law enforcement being aware of a violation, there was no evidence to support a claim that the hacker's motive was to help the U.S. government.

A third question addressed by the decision that was related to the issuance of a warrant rather than the legality of the search focused on whether a warrant is legal if the affidavit uses illegally obtained information in submitting the request. Responding to this challenge, Goodwin wrote, "Because information obtained by a private person is not subject to the Fourth Amendment's exclusionary rule, a statement that the anonymous source had hacked into Steiger's computer to obtain that information would not have affected the magistrate's finding of probable cause" (*U.S. v. Bradley Joseph Steiger* 2003).

When Is the Private Search Unconstitutional?

The same vigilante from Steiger became the focus of another court decision later that same year. When Unknownuser sent information about another alleged child pornography site, an FBI agent named Faulkner contacted him with a response sometimes known as "the wink and the nod." Faulkner wrote that he could not authorize Unknownuser to conduct any searches because that would make him an agent of the government and none of the information discovered would be admissible in court. On the other hand, Faulkner added, if Unknownuser happened to stumble across such material, he would be delighted to hear about it.

In *U.S. v. Jarrett,* the District Court found that such an arrangement clearly indicated that Faulkner was aware that a search would take place and tacitly condoned such a search. That made Unknownuser an agent of the government. The evidence was suppressed.

The government appealed the decision and successfully had the evidence reinstated. However, its success was based on another factor rather than knowledge of the hacker's activities. The decision of the Appeals Court stated that the agency relationship was dependent on the degree to which the government participated in the actions. The government neither participated nor instructed the hacker in any manner, and the case was ordered to be retried with the evidence included. According to the decision, the informant would become an agent of the government if the government did "affirmatively encourage, initiate or instigate the private action" (*U.S. v. William Anderson Jarret 2003*).

When Is the Warrant Legal?

The concept was revisited in 2007 with a new twist. An anonymous caller told police of a Sprint PCS Web site that displayed images similar to those in Steiger. The caller gave the agent the user ID and password for the site in the course of the conversation. The agent who received the call had no trouble accessing the Web site and downloaded the images as evidence to present in his request for a warrant. The warrant led to a search of the defendant's apartment, which uncovered sufficient evidence for an arrest. The defendant voluntarily confessed when confronted with the evidence.

At trial, the defendant moved to have the evidence suppressed, based on the fact that while the tipster was not covered by Fourth Amendment restrictions, the agent who viewed the site clearly was. The site was password protected; therefore, downloading the images in the process of requesting a warrant was a violation of the defendant's rights. The evidence found while searching the apartment, as well as the defendant's confession, defense claimed, should be suppressed as being the "fruit of a poisonous tree."

The motion was denied. While the court conceded that the password protection employed on the site demonstrated the defendant's expectation of privacy, the fact that the defendant freely shared the user name eroded that expectation. In the decision, the court wrote, "For example, there can be no reasonable expectation of privacy in matters voluntarily disclosed or entrusted to third parties, even those disclosed to a person with whom one has a confidential business relationship" (*U.S. v. Kendra D'Andrea* 2007).

Vigilantes Today

Law enforcement continues to use digital vigilantes in the same manner as they have used street informants for years. Additionally, not all such informants are actively looking for criminal activity. In *U.S. v. Barth*, the District Court decided that while a person has a reasonable expectation of privacy regarding their computer files, that privacy is lost when the computer is dropped off to a computer repair facility for service. The rationale is that in order to service the computer, the technicians have to be able to access the contents. If they reveal what they've found to law enforcement officials, no violation of the Fourth Amendment has occurred.

In the corporate environment, a situation arises in which all employees sign employee policy forms acknowledging that they are aware that the organization may, at its discretion, monitor their activities and even search their computers. Management or IT personnel who subsequently turn over material they find to law enforcement officials do not violate any laws.

A civilian group called Perverted Justice exposed hundreds of alleged pedophiles on a Web site after their members posed as underage girls and agreed to meet for a secret tryst. They avoid the implications of being considered agents of the government by enforcing a simple rule. They never contact the police. If the police contact them about a specific individual posted on their Web site, they happily provide any information they can.

Another group, Artists Against 419, go after scam artists. They go after phishing sites and other fraudulent sites, and have used questionable tactics in their war against cybercrime. The list of individuals and organizations that fight crime in digital costumes instead of masks and capes grows every year. The legal battle as to whether their results are legally admissible as evidence continues.

CHAPTER REVIEW

1. What are the three primary factors that determine whether evidence collected during an investigation will be admissible in court? Briefly discuss each of these factors.

2. Explain in your own words the exclusionary rule. How is it related to the three factors of admissibility?

3. What is the plain view doctrine, and why does it have such a significant impact on digital forensics? What are three approaches to ascertaining whether the doctrine applies to a specific case?

4. Explain particularity, and discuss how evidence might be suppressed if the court determines that it is absent in a particular warrant.

5. Under what circumstances is a digital search not covered under the Constitution?

CHAPTER EXERCISES

1. Look up *U.S. v. Cioffi*, 2009. How did the defense successfully argue to have evidence collected during the search of the defendant's e-mail archives suppressed? What are two principles discussed in this chapter that were invoked?

2. Review the case *U.S. v. Paul V. Burdulis*. In this motion to suppress, the defense attempted to have evidence suppressed on the grounds that the warrant lacked particularity and that it did not establish probable cause that the evidence described in the warrant could be found in the locations defined in the warrant. What was the outcome of that motion, and what principle discussed in this chapter was cited by the judge in making his decision?

REFERENCES

Department of Justice. 2004. *Forensic examination of digital evidence: A guide for law enforcement.* www.ojp.usdoj.gov/nij/pubs-sum/199408.htm (accessed February 12, 2012).

Brenner, S. 2007. Private-public sector cooperation in combating cybercrime: In search of a model. *Journal of International Commercial Law and Technology* 2(2):58.

Davies, T. 2003. Farther and farther from the original Fifth Amendment: The recharacterization of the right against self-incrimination as a "trial right" in Chavez v. Martinez. *Tennessee Law Review* 70:987–1045.

Environmental Law Publishing. 2010. Flowchart of the rules for the admissibility of evidence. www.envlaw.com.au/handout6.pdf (accessed May 22, 2013).

Horton v. California, 496 U.S. 128, 133 (1990).

Hunt, H., and C. Varner. 2012. United States: 5th Amendment self-incrimination and computer encryption passwords. www.mondaq.com/unitedstates/x/167962/Software/5th+Amendment+SelfIncrimination+Computer+Encryption+Passwords (accessed March 12, 2012).

Illinois v. Rodriguez 497 U.S. 177 (1990).

Katz v. United States 389 U.S. 347 (1967).

National Institute of Justice. 2004. The computer forensic tool testing program. www.nij.gov/topics/ forensics/evidence/digital/ standards/cftt.htm (accessed March 9, 2010).

Sommer, P. 1998. Digital footprints: Assessing computer evidence. *Criminal Law Review* (December):61.

Trulock v. Freeh, 275 F.3d 391 (4th Cir. 2001).

U.S. v. Andrus, 483 F.3d 711 (10th Cir. 2007).

U.S. v. Bradley Joseph Steiger, 318 F.3d 1039 (11th Cir. 2003).

U.S. v. Carey, 172 F.3d 1268 (10th Cir. 1999).

U.S. v. Comprehensive Drug Testing, Inc., D.C. No. CV-04-00707-2008.

U.S. v. Frank Gary Buckner, 473 F.3d 551 (2007).

U.S. v. Kendra D'Andrea, 497 F. Supp.2d 117 (2007).

U.S. v. Mann, 592 F.3d at 780 (2010).

U.S. v. Matlock, 415 U.S. 164 (1974).

U.S. v. William Anderson Jarret, 338 F.3d 339 (2003).

U.S. v. Williams, 592 F.3d 511, 521, 523 (4th Cir. 2010a).

U.S. v. Williams, 592 F.3d 511, 521, 523 (4th Cir. 2010b) p. 1003.

United States Of America, v. John Doe, Appellant, WL 579433, Nos. 11–12268 & 11–15421 (2012).

United States v. Fricosu, No. 10-cr-00509-REB-02 (2012).

Weeks v. United States, 232 U.S. 383 (1914).

Wilson v. R, 44 ALJR 221 (per Barwick CJ); ss55-56 EA (1970).

FIRST RESPONSE AND THE DIGITAL INVESTIGATOR

The actions that are taken—or are not taken—in the first hours of any investigation are often the ones that will later help or hinder the search for evidence. Far too often, the first people on the scene know too little about collecting and archiving digital evidence, and they do more harm than good. In recent years, law enforcement agencies around the world have spent a great deal of time and money training personnel to deal with digital information at the scene of a crime in a more effective manner. In 2001, the U.S. Department of Justice (DOJ) published a paper entitled *Electronic Crime Scene Investigation: A Guide for First Responders* as a preliminary set of guidelines for law enforcement to follow when first on the scene. While some of the recommendations contained in the paper have subsequently been superseded by updated recommendations, for the most part it is still recommended reading for all law enforcement personnel.

FORENSICS AND COMPUTER SCIENCE

Due to the popularity of several television shows featuring the forensic end of law enforcement, the public has developed an almost jaundiced eye toward the subject. In fact, the term *CSI effect* was coined to describe the public perception that all hard drives could be analyzed, all passwords cracked, and all DNA evidence analyzed in 60 minutes or less. Another misconception is that every investigator involved in digital forensics is a computer scientist. This is not always the case, nor is it necessary for it to be.

DEFINING DIGITAL FORENSICS

The word *forensic* is derived from the Latin word *forensis*, meaning "public." This Latin term is the same root as of the word "forum." *The Merriam-Webster Online Dictionary* (2009) defines the word **forensic** as "belonging to, used in, or suitable to courts of judicature or public discussion and debate." The astute reader immediately notices that there is nothing about science or computers in the definition. Further reading will show that in addition to digital forensics and forensic science, there are also fields such as entomological forensics, forensic psychiatry, etymological forensics, and a plethora of other terms related to presenting information regarding specific areas of study to the courts. For the purposes of this book, the definition of *digital forensics* will be the one used by Marcella and Menendez in their book *Cyber Forensics: A Field Manual for Collecting, Examining, and Preserving Evidence of Computer Crimes*. They define computer forensics as a discipline that combines elements of law and computer science in order to collect and analyze computer data from a variety of computer systems, networks, storage devices, and other devices using digital communications as the source and flow of information in a way that is admissible as evidence in a court of law (Marcella and Menendez 2008, 5).

While this book will deal with internal investigations as well as civil and criminal enquiries, the philosophy will always remain the same. If the job is important enough for the client to engage the services of a forensics professional, it is important enough that the case should hold up in court if it should come to that. Prepare every case as if it will appear before a judge.

COMPUTER SCIENCE AND DIGITAL FORENSICS

Analyzing stores of digital information does require a substantial knowledge about how computer systems work, how file systems work, and how operating systems (OSs) access and store data. It does not, however, presuppose that every digital forensic investigator (DFI) is qualified as a computer scientist. The knowledge required to extract deleted files and trace e-mails across the planet is completely different from the knowledge required to design a microchip, write the code for an OS, or design and build a file server.

The digital investigator will do well to have a strong understanding of file systems. Good hardware skills are in order so that hard disks can be removed without damage and information extracted from firmware stored on devices in the computer. Without a solid foundation in basic networking skills, it will not be possible for the DFI to track the actions of an individual breaking into a corporate network over a TCP/IP connection.

The best way to understand the difference between a computer scientist and the digital investigator is that the scientist knows a great deal about a specifically defined body of knowledge, while the DFI must have a familiarity with a wide range of subject matter. So while the argument goes on about whether or not digital forensics is a science, suffice it to say that to be a good DFI, a person must be a scientist, an artist, a craftsman, as well as a very good detective.

LOCARD'S EXCHANGE PRINCIPLE

Edmond Locard was a scientist living in Lyon, France, who first postulated in the early part of the twentieth century that everything that enters a crime scene does two things. It leaves part of itself behind, and it takes part of the scene with it. Paul L. Kirk further refined that principle in his book *Crime Investigation: Physical Evidence and the Police Laboratory*, when he said:

> Wherever he steps, whatever he touches, whatever he leaves, even unconsciously, will serve as a silent witness against him. Not only his fingerprints or his footprints, but his hair, the fibers from his clothes, the glass he breaks, the tool mark he leaves, the paint he scratches, the blood or semen he deposits or collects. All of these and more bear mute witness against him. This is evidence that does not forget. It is not confused by the excitement of the moment. It is not absent because human witnesses are. It is factual evidence. Physical evidence cannot be wrong, it cannot perjure itself, it cannot be wholly absent. Only human failure to find it, study and understand it, can diminish its value. (Kirk 1953)

While the French scientist and the famed professor of criminology from the University of California, Berkeley, were both referring to physical evidence, the principles they espouse hold just as true to the digital world as they do the physical. Every file copied to a hard disk changes the electrical charges on the disk's platter, makes changes to the file system, alters and creates files, and even makes changes in the registry. When a knowledgeable criminal goes to great efforts to disguise these changes, all that happens is that more changes occur.

The indisputable fact that investigators must constantly keep in the backs of their minds is that actions they perform can have the same effect if they are not careful. One primary law reigns supreme in the world of digital investigation. Do Not Change the Evidence. This concept will be repeated again and again throughout this book.

COMPARING DIGITAL EVIDENCE TO PHYSICAL EVIDENCE

Casey (2001) states that there are two types of evidence: that which possesses class characteristics and that which possesses individual characteristics. Class characteristics define an aspect shared by a large group of similar objects or people. Individual characteristics are traits unique to a particular sample. For example, if there are two white 2007 Saturn Sky convertibles parked side by side in a lot, the drivers might have trouble distinguishing which vehicle is theirs. However, one of them has a New York license plate, and the other is from Massachusetts. As a group, both vehicles qualify as "cars." Two class characteristics that they share are that they are both Saturn Skys and they are both white. The license plate gives each one an individual characteristic.

Why does the white color not qualify as an individual characteristic? If it was the only white Saturn Sky in the world, it most certainly would. Even if the investigator could point out that there were only ten white Saturn Skys in the whole world, and only four are in the United States, the color would still qualify. But with nearly 20% of this specific make and model on the road being white, the color only gives us a more narrowly defined class characteristic.

Additionally, evidence can be patent, or it can be latent. These terms are most commonly used when describing transient evidence, such as fingerprints; but they can apply to virtually any evidence. Patent evidence is something easily seen, picked up, handled, and photographed. Using fingerprints as an example, a patent fingerprint is the big, gooey thumbprint in blood that every investigator dreams of finding but never does. The more common latent fingerprint is the one that is only picked up by the observant eye and must be dusted, lifted, and processed before it can be identified.

The vast majority of digital evidence is latent. Even the documents that might appear to be patent on the outset are latent. Just because a Microsoft Word document opens easily in a wide variety of word processing applications for anybody in the world to read does not make it patent evidence. There are two reasons for that. First, the document does not open by itself. It requires a rather complex computer application to be launched by the user or the computer, then the application has to load the document, and second, it can be read on the screen. Or someone can print it out. Once it is printed on paper, the paper document can be considered evidence—*but it cannot be considered the same piece of evidence as the electronic version.* That is a key difference. Why?

- The paper document contains none of the metadata of the electronic file.
  - It does not prove who created the document.
  - There is no indication on when the document was created.

- Judges and juries cannot see if the printed document was modified since its creation.
- The electronic file could contain additional information concealed in either the metadata, in steganographically concealed form, or tucked into the structure of the file.
- The paper document does not indicate what computer housed it when it was discovered or how many times it has been copied from computer to computer.

Physical and digital evidence differ in several other substantial aspects as well. A key difference is in longevity and stability. Over the past few years, several people have been released from prison based on comparisons of DNA samples that were several years old. Earl Washington was released in 2000 after serving 16 years in prison. The DNA samples from 1984 proved that he did not commit the crime for which he was convicted (ACLU 2003). More recently, viable samples of DNA were taken from skeletons of Vikings over 1,000 years old (Melchior et al. 2008). While the Vikings from which the samples were extracted were not suspected of any crime (not recently, anyway), the incident demonstrates how long a sample can be retained and successfully used as evidence. Similarly, digital investigators need to be able to demonstrate how long the evidence they collect can remain viable in its environment. As we will see, memory does not retain evidence as satisfactorily as magnetic media.

A floppy disk from just a few years ago might be unreadable without special help. The information stored on a live computer system changes every second that the system is running. Computer data is extremely volatile and easily deleted, and can be destroyed, either intentionally or accidentally, with a few mouse clicks. It will be an amazing feat if archaeologists a thousand years from now are able to read a DVD unearthed from a radioactive ruin.

The DFI can generally retrieve a deleted file, either partially or fully, and that floppy disk can probably be read by the professional investigator. The hard part comes in proving that the evidence is reliable. As discussed in the previous chapter, evidence must be authentic and it must be relevant. The Federal Rules of Evidence (U.S. DOJ 2008) is a 41-page document that clearly defines what evidence is, how it must be handled and presented, and a myriad of other regulations. It is imperative that the investigator understands the rules—especially as they pertain to authenticity and relevance.

Relating these two characteristics to digital evidence, remember the following: For the evidence to be authentic, the DFI must be able to prove that the information presented came from where he or she claims and was not altered in any way during examination, and that there was no opportunity for it to have been replaced or altered in the interim. To be relevant, the information must have a bearing on the event being investigated, either directly or indirectly. If a DFI is tasked to locate pornography and in the process unearths evidence of illegal gambling, then great pains must be taken to preserve the newly found evidence while at the same time pretending it doesn't exist. Until authorization is issued that allows the extraction of that data, it is not relevant to the case at hand.

This brings up the final issue to be discussed pertaining to evidence. In addition to its authenticity and relevance, it must be legally obtained. In Chapter 1, "The Anatomy of a Digital Investigation," there was a brief discussion on three types of investigation—internal, civil, and criminal—and it was pointed out that different regulations and laws govern how the types of investigation may be conducted. The criminal investigation is the most restrictive in terms of legal requirements. As mentioned before, the DFI should always treat every project as if it were a criminal investigation unless circumstances or orders dictate otherwise.

CONTROLLING THE SCENE OF THE CRIME

The first thing a DFI has to do is determine precisely what the scene of the crime actually is. At a genuine crime scene where a dozen emergency vehicles, a SWAT team, and the mayor are competing for attention, it might be pretty obvious. When conducting an internal investigation to determine whether or not a recently axed employee took confidential information with her when she left, there is no evidence of a real crime. All anyone really has is a suspicion. In either situation, there will be a specifically defined "area" that the DFI will be allowed to enter. There are protocols to follow.

DETERMINING WHO IS IN CHARGE

Who is in charge can frequently be the most difficult question to answer—especially in internal investigations or civil litigation. As a DFI, one thing will always remain constant. Whoever is in charge, it isn't you. Always remember that when the general walks into a room of colonels and asks, "Who's in charge here?" the answer is always, "You, sir." Except in this line of work, rank is not always prominently displayed, nor is it always indicative of who is in charge.

Find out as soon as possible what the chain of command is, and respect that chain. As soon as possible, the DFI should create a document that defines who has what authority, as it is defined to him or her, and include that with the case documentation.

In internal investigations, the organization contracting the services will almost certainly assign a person to conduct the investigation. This person will act as the DFI's primary contact and work through him or her to access whatever resources are required to complete the task at hand.

Civil cases will generally be initiated by either the counsel for the plaintiff or the counsel for the defendant. In these situations, the DFI will be reporting directly to one (or more) of the attorneys representing in the case. By default, the focus of the investigation will be to prove one side's claim over the other. Depending on which side the DFI represents, access to the data might be easy, or it might be dependent on what is released as a result of an e-discovery order.

Criminal cases can get very confusing. There must be a determination of what level of government (state or federal) or what agency has jurisdiction. Once jurisdiction is assigned, a lead investigator will be appointed. This is the person to whom the DFI will most likely report. Warrants will specify precisely what and where the DFI can search and what type of information is being sought.

SECURING THE SCENE

The first rule of any newly developing case is Safety First. In a case involving computer crime, it is unlikely that the safety of any people is at risk; but it is not out of the question either. Consider the situation where a pedophile is actively luring a young child into a predatory situation. Securing the child would take precedence over securing the data.

Following the safety of people, the DFI must consider the safety and integrity of the computer, the data, or the network. If a network intrusion is in process, then it essential to secure critical data on the network before worrying about who is after it. Preferably, a way can be found to lock down proprietary information without alerting intruders that they have been detected.

Now is the time to secure the evidence. A rule espoused by DOJ in its first responders' guide is this: If it is off, leave it off. If it is on, leave it on. Consider the volatile data, such as active memory, paging files, and so forth. Do not assume that only the computer systems present can hold data. The following items are very likely to have information valuable to the investigation:

- PDAs
- Digital music players
- External storage devices (hard disks, flash drives, etc.)
- Cell phones
- Caller ID boxes

- Answering machines
- Digital cameras
- Digital audio recorders

This is merely a list of the obvious devices. The astute DFI will survey the scene with a critical eye to determine if other possible sources of digital evidence exist. If one or more computers are running, it is a good idea to get a digital photograph of the screen. Be particularly cognizant of USB drives. The BitLocker encryption used by Windows Vista (and later) adds an extra layer of security by allowing the user to configure the encryption keys to be read from a thumb drive. Such a device that doesn't appear to have any other useable data stored on it is likely a candidate for hardware encryption keys.

If a device such as a cell phone is present and on, secure the device immediately in a Faraday bag to prevent outside intervention. A Faraday bag is an enclosure engineered of a variety of materials that work together to block all electromagnetic radiation. Do not turn the device off. Document it properly, and transport it as soon as possible to a secure place for analysis if the field investigator is not equipped to handle it on the scene.

DOCUMENTING THE SCENE

As part of the case documentation, it is important to have an accurate description of the scene as it was initially found. A high-quality digital video camera should be part of every DFI's arsenal of tools. Video documentation is valuable for identifying what was at the scene when it was first uncovered. Position of user interface devices (is the mouse on the right or left side of the keyboard?) can be used as evidence later on down the road. Examine all suspect systems and make notes of the following:

- Record the brand, make, model, and serial number of every device present.
- Note whether the computers present are on, off, or in sleep mode.
- Determine if the computers are part of a network.
- Look for a modem. If present, determine whether it is connected to another system somewhere.
- Record the status of all lights on the system. Flashing network lights can indicate a live TCP/IP connection.
- Listen to the system for excessive hard disk activity. This could indicate an active connection or data transfer.

- Identify any peripherals that are installed or connected. Document them whether they are to be collected or not.
- Look for documentation specific to devices not currently present. This could suggest other devices exist somewhere that might be relevant to the investigation.
- Photograph the back of the computer, and identify what devices are plugged into what ports.

Before the investigator leaves the scene, each person present should be added to a contact list with names, titles, phone numbers, and e-mail addresses for future contact. Provide a brief description of their role in the drama.

IDENTIFYING THE DATA SOURCES

The investigator began identifying data sources during the documentation of the scene. The inventory of hardware taken will identify the obvious sources of potential evidence. Now it is time to look for the less obvious. Here is where the investigator finally becomes an investigator. Look for documentation for devices that do not exist. The reason for this is to help find sources of data not present at the scene of the initial investigation. For example, there might be no sign of a digital camera, nor any memory cards for such a device present at the scene. But the presence of the owner's manual for a professional digital camera suggests that it exists somewhere. It also suggests approaches to take while searching hard disks, DVDs, and such.

Many of the popular "all-in-one" copy/scanner/printer machines have a function known as scan once/print many. In order to perform this technological trickery, the page (or pages) being printed are stored in memory. This should be checked and recorded.

A proprietary cable hanging out of a FireWire port tells the investigator to find whatever device gets connected to that cable. In some cases, the cable can help identify the device in question.

Look around for evidence that the suspect makes use of Internet storage or operates a Web site, even if Internet data transfer is not the issue. It has become more common for people to use offsite storage for information they don't want prying eyes to see. Web site hosting ranges from inexpensive to free and provides several megabytes or even multiple gigabytes of storage space on the Internet service provider's (ISP) server farm. What better way to provide global access to contraband information than to set up a secure Web site and distribute the material via unpublished Universal Resource Locators (URL)?

Interview anyone who may have useful information. The person or persons under investigation may or may not prove to be cooperative in providing passwords or locations of other data sources. However, other people can prove to be a wealth of information, especially in environments where there are multiple users and multiple systems. I was involved in one situation where the receptionist knew the user names and passwords of each person in her office. Security is a wonderful thing. Other bits of information that may be of use would be whether or not the suspect system or systems were used by multiple individuals. What was the primary use for the system?

Carefully search the area for concealed passwords that will allow investigators to gain access to data sources. Encrypted hard disks, Web sites, Internet services, and so forth will all require password authentication for access. In another situation I worked, a sticky note with the sentence "Pick up alphabits" gained the investigators access to an encrypted drive. The actual password turned out to be *@lphab1ts* .

Don't overlook a laser printer. It won't by necessity store any useful digital information, but the transfer roller can possibly retain an image of the last document printed. This may change in the very near future. Researchers at Purdue University have proposed a process by which characteristics of specific printers can be embedded in every page created on the machine (Chiang et al. 2008).

HANDLING EVIDENCE

On the scene there are a variety of evidence sources, and not all of them are digital. Prior to handling any physical evidence, confirm with the lead investigator that all preliminary processing has been completed. Depending on the level of effort going into the case, this may include photographing the scene, identifying and collecting fingerprints, and possibly collecting DNA samples. Once the DFI has the authority to begin collecting devices, there are procedures to follow to insure that the integrity of the data is not impacted.

EVIDENCE HANDLING WORKFLOW

From beginning to end, a repeatable and logical process contributes to consistent success. The acquisition of evidentiary materials is a significant step that can impact the entire case and therefore should be accomplished systematically and efficiently. The basic steps in collecting equipment are

1. Identify the evidence.
2. Photograph the evidence in situ (if possible).

3. Document the evidence (where found, by whom, make, model, serial number, etc.).

4. Package the evidence for transport.

5. Transport the evidence.

6. Store the evidence while in possession.

All of these steps are noted in the chain of custody with time, date, location, personnel involved, and case number documented. Figure 6.1 is an illustration of the workflow used in processing evidence.

CHAIN OF CUSTODY

A critical function of any investigation is the continuous process of logging each and every action that is taken on or against a piece of evidence and recording every movement that evidence makes. This log of actions and movement is called the **chain of custody.** From the instant an object is identified as having evidentiary value, these records become a living document that is updated with every touch. Even if an object is simply removed from a cabinet to be viewed by a supervisor, that action must be recorded. During the actual examination of the evidence, the chain of custody must match up to the procedural log (which will be discussed in more detail later in the book). If an action is recorded in the procedural log and there is no entry in the chain of custody to show that the material changed hands from evidence storage to the investigator, the entire chain is broken. The chain of custody can be challenged, and the evidence can potentially be declared inadmissible.

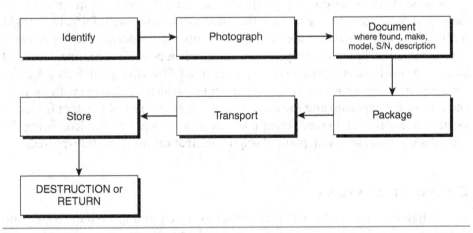

Figure 6.1 Evidence-handling workflow

In *United States v. McKeever,* the court defined a seven-part test for determining the usability of evidence in court. In this particular situation, the list referenced video tapes used as evidence; however, this list (now known as the McKeever test) has been used as the precedent of other forms of evidence. The seven parts of the McKeever test are (words in parenthesis added by author) as follows:

1. The recording device (or computer) was capable of making the recording.
2. The operator of the device (or computer) was competent to make the recording.
3. The recording (or data file or artifact) is authentic and correct.
4. No changes, additions, or deletions have been made to the recording (or forensic image).
5. The recording (or digital evidence) has been preserved in the manner as seen by the court.
6. The speakers (heard or seen in the recording or identified in the digital files) are identified.
7. The conversation recorded (or material stored on the computer) was made voluntarily and not induced in any way.

Digital cases do not always involve tape recordings. However, the McKeever test can be applied to any form of evidence. While chain of custody is not specifically listed, it is addressed in points 3, 4, and 5. If there is any moment in which a critical piece of evidence cannot be accounted for, a case can be made that it is not the same device or file, that alterations may have been made, or that the evidence has been tampered with or corrupted.

A good chain of custody log specifically identifies the evidence in a way that is clear to all who read the log or view the evidence. Identifying information might include data such as make, model, and serial number of the device. The log is generally accompanied by a photograph of the device when possible. The time, date, and location at which the evidence was seized is recorded. From that point forward, every person who has any exposure to the evidence must be identified, along with the time and date of the exposure and the reason for it. Every transfer of the item from one location to another and every action taken against it must be recorded, listing the time, date, persons involved, point of origin, destination, and how transported.

COMPUTER SYSTEMS

It is unlikely that the DFI will ever collect every computer system from a site unless the investigation centers on an individual or a very small organization.

Therefore, it is likely that individual computers will be selectively seized. There may be laptop computers, standalone computers, and perhaps networked computers. Standalone computers are desktop machines or workstations that are not connected to a corporate or organizational network. This could include laptops. Network workstations can be more complex and should be treated differently.

Standalone Computers

Whether a desktop PC or a laptop, the standalone computer is identified by the fact that it is not joined to a larger network. Note that even private residences can have relatively complex networks configured these days. Therefore, it is not safe to assume that just because a computer is being seized from an individual's house it should not be checked for network connectivity. It could be part of a home network or linked to a corporate network via a *virtual private network* (VPN). A VPN is a way of configuring a network connection over the Internet, allowing people to work at home. This is a very common situation in today's business environment.

Earlier in the chapter, it was heavily emphasized that everything about the system should be documented, including status, condition, make, model, and serial number. The DFI should make sure this process is completed before anything is touched. If the computer is on, but the monitor is off, turn the monitor on and give it time to fire up. If the monitor is on, move on to the next step. If the desktop is visible, make a photograph of the screen as it is displayed. If the monitor is on but there is no apparent display, move the mouse slightly in an attempt to wake the system. If the system wakes, photograph the display. If not, do *not* push any buttons or press any keys.

Now is the time to determine if there should be any attempt to capture live information from the system. That is a very complex issue that will be discussed in more detail later on. For now, suffice it to say that if live capture is decided to be the best choice, move to that step. If the system is to be packed up and carried away for analysis, remove the power cable from the back of the computer. Do not unplug it from the wall, and do not shut the system down gracefully. If the system is a laptop or other portable system, remove the battery (if possible). Note that many models of laptop computer offer the option of installing a second battery in a multipurpose bay. Verify if this is the situation, and if so, remove that battery as well.

Check floppy disk drives, if present, for the presence of diskettes. If found, remove the diskette from the drive, being cautious not to pollute any potential evidence such as latent fingerprints. Store the media in antistatic sleeves. Do not remove CDs or DVDs from their respective drives.

Prior to transport, place a layer of tape over the power plug connector and over all drive bays or slots. Label cables and connectors so that they can be reconnected precisely as they were when disconnected. While transporting the evidence, label it as fragile and confidential. Make sure that a chain of custody is maintained from the moment of seizure to the moment of return.

Networked Computers

In a complex environment such as a corporate network or a governmental organization, it may not be possible to seize individual computers or components. At this point, live capture becomes the norm. It won't be simply local data that serves as possible evidence. Specialized procedures and utilities are used in processing this type of environment. See Chapter 12, "Searching the Network," for a detailed description of processes used. However, there is a good deal of information to be collected by first responders:

- Contact information for network administrators
- A list of affected hardware, including servers, switches, routers, and workstations
- Copies of relevant log files, as described in Chapter 12, "Searching the Network"
- Live analysis of current network connections, open sessions, and open files on suspect systems
- A topographic map of the network, if available

PHOTOGRAPHING EVIDENCE

Items collected during first response should be photographed in exactly the place and position where they are initially found. Digital cameras should be configured to place a time-date stamp into the actual image as well as embedded in the image metadata. Demonstrating that the creation date of the image matches that of the time-date stamp displayed on the image lends credibility to the fact that investigators indeed found the materials at the time and place where they claim. The photographs may also be used to demonstrate that the device under investigation is the same one found at the scene.

DOCUMENTING EVIDENCE

At the time evidentiary materials are collected, several things should be recorded. Here is where the chain of custody starts. The chain of custody will record every movement it makes, every person who has had possession, and every place it has been stored. It starts with documenting

- Where the evidence was found
- Time and date the evidence was collected
- Who found the evidence
- Description of the evidence
- Make, model, and S/N of device (if applicable)

PACKAGING EVIDENCE

When preparing evidence to be moved from the scene of the incident to the location where it will be stored until the conclusion of the investigation, it is essential that proper care is taken. It is not sufficient to simply throw a computer onto the back seat of a car and drive it to the lab. Materials collected should be packaged in appropriate containers that are well padded against temperature and physical impact. Devices such as cell phones should be protected from exposure to electromagnetic waves as well. The Faraday bags mentioned earlier in the chapter are used for this purpose. Each package should be labeled, indicating to what case it relates, time and date collected, and a brief description of contents.

TRANSPORTING EVIDENCE

How evidence is transported from the scene to its destination can be critical to the success of the case. The investigator needs to be able to demonstrate that there were no opportunities for evidence to be altered, tampered with, or otherwise compromised. When arriving on the scene, the team should be prepared with proper packaging materials for packing and transporting evidence. Critical items include

- Packing boxes
- Antistatic bags
- Antistatic bubble wrap
- Cable ties
- Packing tape
- Evidence tape
- Faraday containers
- A hand truck

Before packaging components, be sure to label each one with the following concepts in mind. You must be able to match components to systems in order to examine them precisely as they existed in situ. If multiple users are involved, devices must be identified as to primary user. When devices are seized from multiple rooms or locations, the originating location must be listed.

While transporting evidence, follow these rules:

- Electronic devices and media must be protected from electronic and magnetic interference.
- Devices (especially computers) must be protected from impact or excessive vibration.
- Evidence must be protected from heat and humidity.
- Precautions must be taken to prevent loss or theft of evidence materials.
- The chain of custody report must be rigorously maintained.

Always remember that in a contested situation, the opposition will be looking for any opportunity to discredit the procedures or practices at every step of the way.

STORING EVIDENCE

Many of the rules of transporting evidence apply equally to the storage of evidence. As soon as any piece of evidence arrives at a storage facility, it must be inventoried, identified, and stored safely according to the type of material it represents. Be aware of how long any particular piece of evidence might reside in storage. Devices that depend on batteries require special attention. If the batteries are allowed to die, there is a strong potential for losing valuable data. If a power adapter or alternate power supply cannot be provided, the device should be processed immediately. A high-capacity uninterrupted power supply is a good addition to the field kit.

Some devices, such as cell phones or other networked devices, might require that they be stored in a manner that prevents unauthorized access. Faraday boxes are useful for this. Some larger facilities are equipped with Faraday rooms. These allow the devices to be stored and examined without danger of outside interaction.

In all cases, evidence materials need to be protected from heat, humidity, electromagnetic exposure, and other damaging environmental conditions. This would include contaminating or oxidizing gases or particulate matter such as dust and sand. All storage lockers or rooms should be constructed from fire-retardant materials with an automated fire extinguishing system.

Wiles and Reyes (2007) list four factors that a secure evidence storage facility must meet:

- Access to storage is limited to the evidence custodian.
- All access to the evidence locker is rigorously documented.
- Chain of custody for all items in possession of the facility must be rigorously maintained.
- Some form of independently auditing the aforementioned rules exists.

Physical access to the storage area should be highly restricted. Documented rules and regulations for storage and access must be prepared and followed to the letter. Twenty-four-hour video surveillance and intrusion detection systems should be installed that meet these requirements:

- Video capture and recording equipment is not accessible to anyone but authorized personnel.
- Images taken by the system must be of sufficient quality to be usable.
- Surveillance views should include all entrance and exit points for the storage area as well as the public access area.
- Intrusion detection should be able to detect entry through doors and windows as well as catastrophic entry that would include the destruction of walls, floors, and ceilings.
- Walls, floors, and ceilings should be hardened to deflect forced entry.
- Air ducts and other conduits should be sized to prevent human entry.
- Air filtration and other systems should be designed to prevent the infiltration of harmful substances.

Security systems for accessing the evidence storage areas should include some form of twin-check system. These checks can include password access, biometric recognitions (such as retinal scans or fingerprint identification), security cards, tokens, and so forth.

DESTRUCTION OR RETURN OF EVIDENCE

The phrase "destruction of evidence" usually sends chills down the spine of a good investigator. Inadvertent destruction or spoilage of evidence is the one event that nearly all practices are designed to avoid. However, once a case is concluded, one of two things will happen to evidence materials. Either it will be returned to the original owner or it will be destroyed. Generally speaking, courts will order the destruction of certain types of evidence, including pornography, evidence of illegal gambling, and contraband such as pirated software or other stolen intellectual property. Also, if seized hardware is ordered by the courts to be donated to another organization, all data contained by the target devices must be destroyed. Laws can vary from state to state. It is not the responsibility of the investigator to decide whether or not to destroy evidentiary materials. Such orders would come from officers of the court in criminal cases or possibly from officers of the corporation in the case of internal investigations.

Should the request to destroy materials be made, make sure that the request comes in writing and that it is made by someone with authority to make such a request. Once the decision to destroy is finalized, it is time to select the method of destruction. Many state and federal organizations require the physical destruction of the media storing the sensitive data. Where possible, this would include incineration. Devices such as hard drives or optical disks that either cannot be incinerated or would pose health or environmental hazards if incinerated can be destroyed in some very creative and stress-relieving methods. While working for a federal agency, I was once asked to destroy a number of hard disk drives using a large sledge hammer. Other methods include driving a spike through the disk and physically dismantling the drive.

If the device is to be reused, but the data destroyed, there are a number of data wiping utilities that can do the job effectively enough that the average user could never extract it—and that most professionals would find difficult, if not impossible, to recover. One method that is free and quite effective is the use of the dd utility. The command dd if5/dev/urandom of5/dev/hda will overwrite the entire contents of the hard disk identified as hda by the system with random data. Repeating this operation several times, followed by a format of the drive, will sanitize the device for future use. dd if5/dev/zero of5/dev/hda is a command that will overwrite the device with zeros.

WIPE.EXE is a Windows utility for cleansing disk drives. This interesting little applet has an additional talent for deleting files selectively, and it can remove residual entries in the MFT. Also available for Windows is a freeware program called Active@KillDisk (AKD). AKD is recognized by the Department of Defense as conforming to all government standards for data destruction. This free download is currently available at http://killdisk.com/.

Linux users have several options as well. The dd utility previously mentioned works on all file systems and can be run from either a Windows or a Linux machine. Most, if not all, Linux distributions ship with a utility called Shred that deletes the inode for the file and overwrites the allocated space with zeros. A more powerful option is the Disk Scrub Utility that destroys the inode and overwrites the allocated space with one or more passes over the space.

CHAPTER REVIEW

1. Explain Locard's principle, and describe how it is relevant to a digital investigation.

2. List three or four things that can be described as class characteristics and three or four others that qualify as individual characteristics. Use a house as an example.

3. You have a printed version of a document along with the digital file that was used to create that document. List two things that the digital document has that the paper document doesn't. What are two pieces of evidence that might be obtained from the paper document that you wouldn't get from the digital file?

4. What makes the transportation of evidence such a critical factor in an investigation. Explain how the opposition might latch onto an error in the transportation cycle to disqualify evidence.

5. Describe the function of a Faraday box, and explain what purpose it serves in the evidence collection process.

CHAPTER EXERCISES

1. Using the information provided in this chapter, put together a shopping list of items that a first responder should always have at immediate disposal in a field kit. Using current pricing, provide your manager (or instructor) with a purchase requisition that includes items, prices, and a total.

2. You have been assigned to investigate whether or not an employee at a local hospital has been accessing patient records and selling information to online pharmacies. It is your first day of the investigation. Put together a list of data sources that must be examined during the investigation.

3. Using a standard word processing application, such as Microsoft Word or OpenOffice, create a standard template that you will use as a chain of custody for the remainder of this text.

REFERENCES

American Civil Liberties Union. 2003. *A question of innocence.* www.aclu.org/capital-punishment/question-innocence (accessed December 22, 2009).

Casey, E. 2001. *Digital evidence and computer crime.* New York: Elsevier Academic Press.

Chiang, P., N. Khanna, et al. 2009. Printer and scanner forensics. *IEEE Signal Processing Magazine* 26(2):72–83.

Kirk, P. 1953. *Crime investigation: Physical evidence and the police laboratory,* p.4. New York: Laboratory Interscience Publishers.

Marcella, A., and R. S. Menendez. 2008. *Cyber forensics: A field manual for collecting, examining, and preserving evidence of computer crimes* . New York: Auerbach Publications.

Melchior, L., T. Kivisild, N. Lynnerup, and J. Dissing. 2008. Evidence of authentic DNA from Danish Viking Age skeletons untouched by humans for 1,000 years. *PLoS ONE.* www.plosone.org/article/info 3Adoi 2F10.13712Fjournal.pone.0002214 (accessed December 24, 2009).

Merriam-Webster Online Dictionary. s.v. "forensic." http://www.merriam-webster.com/dictionary/forensic (accessed May 23, 2013).

U.S. Department of Justice. 2001. *Electronic crime scene investigation: A guide for first responders.* Washington, DC: National Institute of Justice.

U.S. Department of Justice. 2008. *Federal rules of evidence.* Washington, DC.

Wiles, J., and A. Reyes. 2007. *The best damn cybercrime and digital forensics book: Period.* Burlington: Syngress Publishing.

DATA ACQUISITION

A key rule of digital forensic investigation is that one never works with the original data. In some cases, as with live memory, that isn't feasible in any case. The primary reason, however, is that working on a copy offers several advantages:

- The hash codes of the original can be compared to the copy to assure authenticity.
- If one makes a mistake, it is easy enough to start over on a fresh copy.
- The approach used for one type of data may not work well with another type, and a fresh copy, complete with matching hash values, assures integrity of the data.
- Loss, theft, or corruption of the copy image does not end the investigation.
- The courts insist that investigators work that way unless demonstrably impossible.

This chapter deals with acquiring forensic images of various types of data. The most commonly imaged device is currently still the hard drive, but that is rapidly changing as more cases rely on evidence derived from cell phones. However, the first line of data often seen by the investigator is a live and running system. Therefore, a live memory capture is where this chapter will begin.

ORDER OF VOLATILITY

If there is one constant in the world of computers, it is that data is volatile. Even information "safely" stored on a hard disk can be wiped. To the investigator, it is critical that information be collected based on its degree of volatility. The *Guidelines for Evidence Collection and Archiving* (Brezinski and Killalea 2002) lists the following priority list for data acquisition:

- Registers, cache
- Routing tables, ARP cache, process tables, kernel statistics, memory
- Temporary file systems
- Disk
- Remote logging and monitoring data that is relevant to the system in question
- Physical configuration, network topology
- Archival media

The first two items can only be collected effectively by doing a live memory capture, as described in the next section. On a laptop computer, it is possible to collect historical artifacts of previous live sessions by copying the hibernation file from the hard disk. Processes, routing tables, and other volatile information from the session immediately prior to the system going into hibernation will be part of this file.

Additionally, any system that has ever "blue-screened" will have a .DMP file stored some place on the hard drive. Depending on the OS of the system involved and how the system was configured, this may be a truncated "snapshot" of memory, or it may be a complete memory dump. While this data archive may not have anything directly related to the current system status, it is possible that evidence of previous events may be derived. It may even contribute toward building an effective time line.

MEMORY AND RUNNING PROCESSES

In the old days when a computer was suspected to contain data that would be of value to a legal investigation, the first-response team would immediately pull the plug on the machine, pack it up, and haul it back to the lab for analysis. The philosophy behind this thinking was that performing a graceful shutdown on a running machine would overwrite files and delete temporary files that might be of use later on down the road.

Recent years have seen the increasing importance of live response to incidents. Live response is the collection of data from a running machine that will be forever lost if it is shut down for removal. The advantages of live response are numerous. Information that will not be available from static archives can be used to establish remote connections. It may be possible to retrieve passwords from computer memory. And while the system is still logged in by the original users, an encrypted disk is available to the investigator without requiring a password.

One of the primary reasons for live response is to be able to acquire a live memory capture that as closely as possible represents the running state of the computer at the time of the incident. The sooner the capture is made, the more accurate the results will be. In any case, an exact replica of the state of the machine at the moment of the incident will never be possible.

For one thing, the investigator will always be the victim of Locard's exchange principle. This fundamental truth states that the mere act of taking a snapshot of the memory image is intrinsically altering it in some way. Merely moving the mouse changes the contents of RAM to a certain extent. Attaching an external drive makes additional changes to memory, as well as changes to the Windows Registry (if using a Windows operating system). Every step of the acquisition process should be documented, if possible. This makes it easier to factually justify any minor differences in data sets that may emerge.

In addition to the changes made by the investigator, the simple passage of time affects what is captured. Every minute that passes results in some changes to system memory. The amount of change that occurs over time is directly related to the amount of installed memory on the system. A study by Walters and Petroni (2007) showed that after ten minutes standing idle, a system with 256MB of RAM (low by today's standards) was approximately 93% identical to the initial measured state. An identical system configured with 512MB retained a similarity of 98%.

While 93% seems significant, it also means that 7% changed. At 120 minutes, these numbers dropped to 79.8% and 96%, respectively. Any activity on the machine at all would dramatically decrease the similarity. This includes simple network connectivity with no overt action by the user.

As a live-response function, it is necessary for the investigator to understand that the process is going to alter the computer as it is executed. Nobody will be able to come along later in the investigation and repeat the process. Much of what the technician does is wholly dependent on the (possibly false) assumption that the OS running on the machine is reliable and not infected with a rootkit. It is possible that mistakes made at this point are unredeemable.

The downside to that approach was that live data, such as routing tables, running processes, and user data stored in memory (including passwords), but not yet written to the drive, is permanently lost. It is also possible to detect the presence of a *rootkit* before it can do any damage. Rootkits are small applications installed on a computer by an intruder that can successfully conceal themselves from standard system utilities. They can allow the intruder to take control of the machine or to intercept and send pseudo-responses back to the OS. Therefore, it often becomes desirable to grab a copy of live memory while the machine is still running and *then* pull the plug. There are several forensically valuable pieces of information that can be collected from a running computer that would be irretrievably lost if the computer were powered down before it was captured:

- Passwords in plain text
- Running processes
- Unencrypted data that is stored in encrypted form on the hard drive
- Instant messages
- Currently logged-in user information
- Open ports
- Evidence of attached devices

Much of the information found in memory can be particularly valuable whenever the situation involves breaches across the network or the Internet—especially if there is any possibility that there may still be open ports to the perpetrator. If it is deemed necessary to perform a live query of the system, it is also possible to connect to the target system with a tool such as *Netcat* and execute commands remotely on the system with minimal impact on static information stored on the computer.

One thing the investigator needs to keep in mind is that making a hash of the memory image for later comparison is not a viable option. The contents of memory are dynamically changing all the time. The connection made to the computer to collect and analyze data made some changes. This is unavoidable. But the impact can be kept to a minimum if the proper tools and technique are used.

A final point to be made is that system memory—as defined by the installed memory chips in the computer—and addressable memory are not the same thing. A system with 4GB of installed memory does not have 4GB of addressable memory. Different approaches to estimating memory can deliver different values. Look at Figure 7.1, for example. Typing the mem command in a command prompt yields these results.

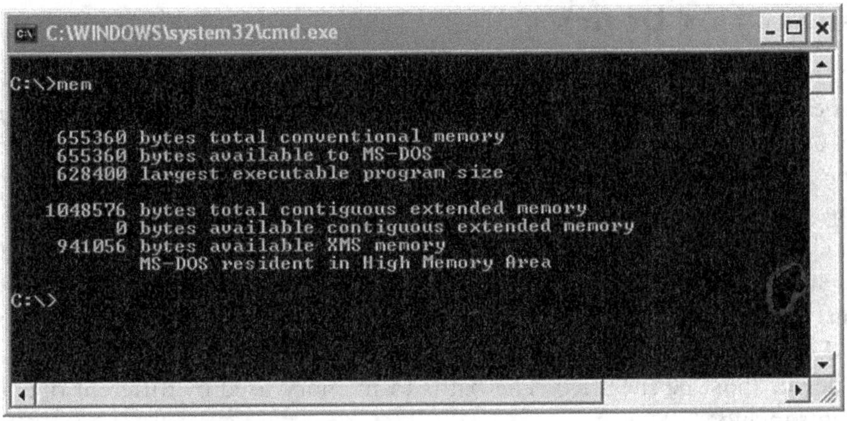

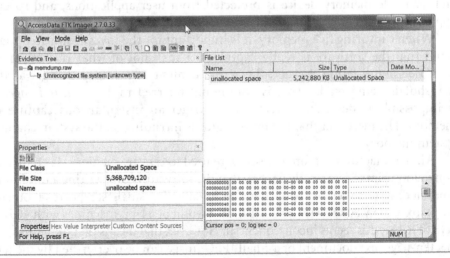

```
C:\WINDOWS\system32\cmd.exe

C:\>mem

     655360 bytes total conventional memory
     655360 bytes available to MS-DOS
     628400 largest executable program size

    1048576 bytes total contiguous extended memory
          0 bytes available contiguous extended memory
     941056 bytes available XMS memory
            MS-DOS resident in High Memory Area

C:\>
```

Figure 7.1 MEM reports 4GB of RAM

According to WIN64DD (Figure 7.2), the total addressable space is 5,368,709,120 bytes. In binary, this works out to precisely 5GB. Why is this? Other devices attached to the system bus are also equipped with memory. For example, the hard disk on the system currently in use by the author contains 32MB of cache memory. A video card can have several megabytes to more than a gigabyte of addressable memory. A typical SCSI adapter has anywhere from 512MB to as much as 4GB of addressable memory as well. Therefore, a system with 4GB of installed RAM will generate an address space to support these extra devices.

Figure 7.2 A forensic memory capture utility recognizes 5GB of addressable memory.

MEMORY AS A DEVICE

The thing to remember about memory is that it is just another device. Devices can be accessed in either **user mode** or **kernel mode.** User mode is a low-privilege level of access. Certain commands or processes just aren't allowed. Kernel mode is the level of access granted to the core operating system and to the CPU. Anything goes. Memory is a highly protected device, so accessing it indirectly can be a challenge. All operating systems need a path to any data, and that includes data stored on devices. User-mode access to memory is denied by the OS; only kernel-mode calls are accepted. Therefore, devices utilities that directly access RAM or device cache memory must do so in kernel mode. To do so, the path to the device must be specified. The paths to memory used by different operating systems include

- Linux, Unix, and OSX: `/dev/mem and/dev/kmem`
- Windows 2000, XP, and so on: `//physicalmemory`

The Windows path can look a bit confusing to the beginner, but is actually quite simple. The dot between the two sets of backslashes is replaced by an IP address or computer name. For example, if the investigator is connected to a suspect computer over a Netcat connection that has an IP address of 192.168.2.1, the string would be `\\192.168.2.1\PhysicalMemory`.

It is possible to directly copy RAM from the machine on computers running Windows XP or earlier using readily available utilities. With Windows XP, SP2, and later, the memory device is protected from user applications, and special applications are required to obtain a memory capture.

When capturing live memory, it is important for the investigator to understand that the software is really capturing a snapshot of what is in memory for a fleeting duration. In fact, the actual content of memory changes as the snapshot is being made. This is commonly referred to as a *smear image*. It is impossible under current technology to get an instantaneous capture of memory. The mere fact that the investigator is intruding on the system changes system memory.

All manufacturers of forensic software used to capture memory claim to have "small footprints." By this, they mean that the software is overwriting a minimum amount of system memory while it makes its copy. The smallest reported footprint is approximately 80KB (HBGary 2010). In a world of 64-bit machines with 4GB to 8GB of RAM, this seems inconsequential. However, that means that the equivalent of a ten-page text document or a small JPEG image can be overwritten by the tool designed to capture it.

SOFTWARE MEMORY CAPTURE

Most forensic software suites offer some form of memory capture and analysis utility as part of the package. Encase offers the HBGary solution. Access Data's FTK offers RAM dump analysis as part of its basic package. There are also a number of open-source utilities on the market that accomplish this task. The following sections describe some interesting utilities, along with how they work and what tricks they can do.

Memoryze

Mandiant Systems is a developer of forensic software that offers the community a free utility for capturing images of live memory. This utility, called Memoryze, not only captures an image of memory from a target system but also provides tools for analyzing the data obtained. It boasts the ability to interface with the 64-bit systems managed by Vista and Windows 7.

An interesting aspect of Memoryze is that the investigator can first acquire a copy of the memory as an image and then perform certain live analysis tasks on the running system. Some of the things Memoryze can do include

- Identify running processes
- Identify open ports
- Identify memory handles
- Find and identify loaded DLLs
- Identify running device drivers
- Identify all loaded modules, including executables and DLLs

It can also detect the presence of rootkits and hooks to operating system components. (A hook is a string of code inserted into a program to perform a specific function. Many programs, including operating systems, include interfaces for accepting user input or for directing the application based on user input. Hackers might use these interfaces for inserting malevolent code.)

WinDD

The *DD* (short for disk dump) utility has been a favorite among Linux users for many years. It can capture bit-level images of drives or partitions, and even live memory, without affecting the contents of the source data. WinDD is a Windows-based version of this utility. It is a freely available utility distributed by SourceNet and described as "Safe, effort-free backup for FAT, FAT32, NTFS, ext2, ext3 partitions."

Current versions of WinDD include Win32dd and Win64dd, which are supplied in the MoonSols toolkit. These tools allow for a raw memory dump from the target device to a specified file. The executables represent 32-bit and 64-bit versions of the utility for specific Windows operating systems.

WinDD is best run from over a network connection, although it can be run from a write-protected USB device as well. Applications can be run remotely over a network on target machines using a utility called Netcat. Netcat establishes a TCP/IP connection between the local machine and a target device, and then allows the user to "plant" an executable on the target machine.

Either the USB or the Netcat method will leave footprints on the machine under investigation. A footprint is the amount of live memory that is overwritten by the executable core of the device loaded in order to capture the memory image. The smaller the footprint, the better. Any data you overwrite might be data you wish you had later. Be aware that inserting a USB device also makes other changes to the system. These changes include loading device drivers (which overwrites memory) and making changes to the registry. The executable of WinDD has a footprint of slightly less than 1MB.

FTK Imager

While primarily known for its abilities to image physical disks, FTK Imager from Access Data can also be used to capture a memory image. Imager is a Windows tool that can run from an external device, such as a USB drive or CD-ROM. It is included with the Helix CD and can be obtained as a free download from http://accessdata.com/support/adownloads#FTKImager. One caveat to Imager is that Access Data does not guarantee that the utility will not make write attempts to the target drive. Personal tests by the author indicate that it in fact *does* write to the target disk. Therefore, it is highly recommended that a write-protect device such as the Wiebetech Forensic Ultra Dock be used (as described later in the chapter) between the source and the target disks.

The *verify image* option calculates either an **MD5** or SHA1 hash of the acquired image. This option should be routinely selected. The format of the image file can be Access Data's proprietary *Smart* format, EO1 as used by Encase Data, or the raw DD image format. More details on image format are presented later in this chapter. In addition to the actual image created by the utility, a **log file** is generated that includes the following investigator-defined information:

- Case data
- Case number
- Evidence identification number

- Description
- Examiner name
- Notes
- Disk information (drive geometry, make and model, interface, volume size, and number of sectors)
- Time and date the acquisition started
- Time and date the acquisition completed
- A list of segments that failed to copy successfully
- Image verification results, include hash values calculated

The image and log files will be stored in the target location configured by the investigator.

HARDWARE MEMORY CAPTURE

Memory can be captured by hardware devices or forensic utilities designed for the task. One proposed hardware device patented by Brian Carrier and Joe Grand is the Tribble. Named after the Star Trek creature, the Tribble is a device that, if installed in a host computer, can capture memory with no need for intrusive software elements. As of this writing, the Tribble exists only as a proof of concept device, so it could not be tested. One shortcoming pointed out by Carrier (2004) in his paper *A Hardware-Based Memory Acquisition Procedure for Digital Investigations* is that the device must be installed in the machine prior to the incident under investigation. Postmortem installation will not accomplish anything. Therefore, it might be a useful preemptive tool for larger organizations, but it is not likely to be of much use to the field investigator.

The research done by Carrier has led to some interesting products that are currently available. Two devices are of particular interest. Forensic Dossier by Logicube is a hardware/software combination that can capture up to 8TB of stored data as well as capture live memory. Its NetConnect Live Acquisition permits the capture of running memory as well as up to 8GB of static storage from the same target machine.

Memory Grabber Forensic Tool by System Research and Application Corporation is a PCMCIA card that grabs memory from laptops or other devices equipped with a compatible slot. Memory Grabber is OS agnostic, meaning it ignores the operating system in use on the system and only makes a copy of data that exists in physical memory. When plugged into the suspect computer, the card provides an interface to a controlled system running forensics software that can be used to analyze the image.

PROCEDURES IN COLLECTING LIVE DATA

Because the information collected during live capture cannot be repeated, it is essential that the investigator document every step taken in the process. It won't be possible for anyone else to re-create the same image to verify results. There is only one shot at a good image.

- Document preliminary information, including
  - Date and time
  - Complete log of the command history
  - A photograph of the scene as found
  - Operating system running on machine
- Document the exact time of each step in the capture process to establish an audit trail of each forensic tool or command used.
- Collect all types of volatile system and network information:
  - Memory dump
  - Paging files
  - Hibernation files
- Document time that the process is completed.

Regardless of the investigator's choice of utility for conducting the capture, it is essential that it be run from a collection of binaries known to be good. There always exists the possibility that a perpetrator may have planted rootkits or other malware into the host operating system of the target device. Run the executables from a read-only device, such as a CD-ROM or a USB device configured to run in read-only mode. While it is true that there will be a measurable impact on memory by the insertion of the device (remember Locard's principle?), the choice is relative clear. By capturing live memory, the investigator runs the risk of losing some evidence. Not capturing it at all guarantees that none of the potential evidence that exists in RAM will be collected.

Collecting a memory dump with free utilities is possible. The DD utility allows a raw dump of memory. It will work with any version of UNIX or Linux and any version of OSX prior to 10.4. It is a command-line utility. To be successful, the command must be configured with the *input file* (if), which is the target you are trying to acquire, and an *output file* (of), where the target image is to be stored. Some optional triggers include specifying a block size and some conversion options. For a forensic copy, the conversion option *noerror* is generally necessary. The noerror option forces the utility to continue working even if it encounters an error. Without this trigger, the utility will stop on the first error it encounters. An example of a memory capture in Windows is as follows:

From a command prompt, type

```
dd if= \.\\PhysicalMemory of=F:\Evidence\memory.dd conv=noerror
```

This will put the image of the memory onto a flash drive, in the Evidence directory. The problem with a DD image is that typical memory diagnostic utilities won't open them. String searches for possible passwords are possible, but getting a process map out of the file can be problematic.

Dedicated forensic utilities, such as Access Data Corporation's FTK Imager, will create an image that can be analyzed in FTK. In this utility, a live process tree can be extracted.

Once the dump file has been collected, run a hashing utility against the file. Then, make two copies. Hash both copies, and confirm that the values match. One copy will become the archive copy and will only be used for making additional working copies. The other becomes the initial working copy used for analysis.

Under no circumstances should an application that modifies MAC data on stored files be utilized. This includes system utilities such as COPY, XCOPY, MOVE, TAR, and several others. Before using a utility in the field, test it to verify that MAC data is left untouched.

ACQUIRING MEDIA

The process of capturing forensic copies of hard disks is more straightforward than that of memory capture. The information the investigator is targeting exists as a static record. As long as the media being copied is not changed, the process is verifiable and repeatable. Several types of media may be targeted in any given investigation:

- Hard disks
- Floppy disks
- Zip disks
- Optical disks (CD-ROM, DVD, etc.)
- USB flash media (thumb drives, memory cards, etc.)
- Removable and portable hard disks
- Personal electronic devices (digital recorders, music players, PDAs, telephones, etc.)

There are several key points to remember. Encrypted devices can be a problem. Unless you have or can acquire the password, once the device has been shut off, the encrypted data is a collection of meaningless bits and bytes. Several options exist for recovering passwords (to be discussed later in the book), so the copy should be made. However, if encryption is known to exist, as much information as possible should be collected during live response. As with every other aspect of the investigation, every step of the process should be documented, including the steps that were taken, who performed each task, and what tools were used. All target media where copies of suspect data are to be stored should be brand new, or at the very least forensically wiped using DoD-approved tools. The target media should be hashed prior to copying and the hash of the copy compared. Matching values indicated a forensically sound copy.

The tools used for acquiring media copies must provide write protection to the source. Most operating system utilities used to copy data make numerous changes. This must not be allowed. Forensic tools, such as the Wiebetech device shown in Figure 7.3, intercept any calls made by the operating system and return the anticipated response, without actually writing any data to the media.

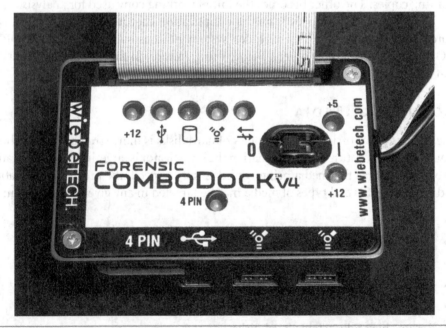

Figure 7.3 The Forensic Combodock is a forensically sound write-protected port replicator for acquiring copies of digital media.

CASE LAW: A LEGAL ARGUMENT FOR A GOOD IMAGING PROCESS

In *The State of Ohio v. Cook*, defense counsel attempted to discredit the forensic image used to convict Brian Cook for the possession of potentially pornographic images of children. On appeal, defense contended that the process used to capture the image was invalid.

The initial search was visual and consisted of finding and subsequently copying files from a hard disk to floppy disks by an interested party not associated with the government. A warrant was issued and the computer subsequently seized in April of 1999. While a mirror image was made of the hard disk at the time, an image made with a forensically sound tool was not made until two years later, as the case was coming to trial.

Defense argued that the first image was not forensically sound and that the second was taken too long after the events occurred, and therefore the evidence was unreliable. The entire process of acquiring the disk, from the removal of the device to its subsequent imaging, was called into question. On appeal, the court found that since there was ample documentation that the processes used were reliable and that there was little or no possibility of tampering with the evidence, all evidence was admissible. The conviction was upheld.

FILE FORMATS FOR DISK IMAGES

Another thing to consider is the format in which to save the image file. There are several basic file formats generally used by the forensic community for storing images:

- DD Images (bit-for-bit)
- Expert Witness Format (EWF)
- Advanced Forensic Format (AFF)
- Safeback (by NTI)
- ILook Imager
- ProDiscover File Format

Each of these formats has its own advantages and disadvantages. Many investigators (including this author) prefer to store an image in both DD and one of the other compressed formats whenever possible. The last four items on the list are all proprietary and will not be discussed in this chapter. I did, however, feel a need to make sure that readers were aware of their existence.

DD Images

A time-tested and easily **authenticated** format is the bit copy generated by the DD utility discussed earlier in the chapter. Several different analysis tools can mount this image as a virtual drive, allowing it to be searched with file system utilities. Since DD does not incorporate any form of file compression, the resultant image can be quite large. This can be overcome in the Linux/UNIX version of DD by using the command in conjunction with the SPLIT command. This is made possible by the fact that DD (as with most *nix command-line utilities) can be piped to another command. Piping is an action that sends the output of one command over to another command for processing. Multiple pipes are possible. An example of the DD utility used in place with the SPLIT utility is

```
dd if=/dev/hda | split -b 2000m - /mnt/hdb/
```

In the above command, the source of the data being copied is identified as /dev/hda, which is the *nix way of identifying the primary hard disk on the first controller. In Windows, this would be the C:\ drive. The pipe character informs the command to output the results of DD to SPLIT. The –b trigger defines the block size into which the target file will be split, with the number immediately following identifying the block size. The default value, with no letter following the number, tells SPLIT that the block size is measured in bytes. The 2000m qualifier specifies a block size of 2000MB (or 2GB). Had the number been followed by a k, the block size would have been 2000KB, or 2MB. The dash following the block size is rather important. It tells the SPLIT command to read from standard input. Lastly, /mnt/hdd/ identifies the target medium for the files as the mounted hard disk identified by the kernel as HDB. This means that it is the second IDE device located on the machine. Linux recognizes USB drives as SCSI devices, so in the above example, the first USB thumb drive installed on the system would be seen as SDA instead of HDA.

Expert Witness Format (EWF)

Some of the proprietary forensic suites incorporate proprietary file formats. Encase by Guidance Software can save image files into a format called the Expert Witness Format (EWF). Several other suites, including FTK and PyFlag, have embedded EWF support even if they do not utilize the format by default. Linux users can obtain EWF images using utilities such as EWFACQUIRE.

The EWF format copies the target image, breaks it into 32Kb chunks, compresses the chunks, and then stores them together in a single file. As the chunks are generated, the EWF algorithm creates relative indexes that can be used by the applications that support the format for random access of the data in the image. Certain predefined metadata, including jump tables and file pointers, can be stored in the header to speed up random searches. (Jump tables tell the file system what clusters on a hard disk to skip over to when a file is fragmented on the drive.)

Some limitations to EWF should be noted. With Encase version 5 and earlier, EWF was limited to 2GB file sizes. This was due to a 31-bit offset value embedded in the code. Target disks larger than 2GB had to be split and then recombined for processing. Version 6 gets around that limitation by replacing the 31-bit offset with a base offset (see sidebar on offsets for an explanation).

WHAT IS AN OFFSET?

Computers store and then subsequently find data by assigning address ranges. A base address is typically a memory area equivalent to a single piece of data as wide as the OS can read in a single operation. This is the *base address.* A 32-bit OS has a base address 32 bits wide, while a 64-bit OS has a 64-bit address. Simple, isn't it? However, often, an application needs to assign much larger areas. An offset value is a method of addressing that the OS uses to locate information in memory beyond the absolute address.

The early versions of Encase used an addressing mechanism known as *absolute direct.* This provided an effective address of the absolute address plus a specified *jump* to the next address. In the case of EWF, the jump was 31 bits wide. Two to the 31st power results in a value of 2,147,483,648—or effectively, 2GB (see Figure 7.4).

| Load | Register | 31-bit Address | Load | Register | 31-bit Address |

Figure 7.4 Indexed absolute addressing

The base + offset addressing scheme allows the programmer (or program) to assign any size of address to a function. A 32-bit processor will allow a 32-bit address to be assigned. By 32-bit address, this does not mean that the address is only 32-bits wide, but rather a 32-bit value. Two to the 32nd power is 4,294,967,296, so a 32-bit processor allows a 4GB address to be defined. A 64-bit processor could handle 18 *petabytes.* This ought to be more than any investigator will ever need—to paraphrase a famous quotation.

Advanced Forensic Format (AFF)

The Advanced Forensic Format is the choice preferred by many investigators. A key advantage of AFF is that it allows arbitrary metadata to be stored with the target image. To use an example of what this means, an open-source tool called AImage allows the operator to define several custom fields for metadata storage. In addition to the disk image, it also stores the version of the library tools used to create the image (AFFLIB), identifies the computer from which the image was acquired, prompts the investigator to enter her name, and identifies the sector size used by the device acquired. An advantage of AFF was that it introduced the capability of compressing the image, allowing larger targets to be acquired. Data was acquired from the target in 16MB "pages."

AFF was not without its shortcomings. The original incarnation of AFF (version 1) was unable to acquire live memory images. The names generated for the segments created during capture were not encrypted. And the 16MB page size led to issues in capturing the NTFS MFT metafiles. AFF Version 4 (AFF4) overcomes most of the faults of AFF1. Data can be captured in segments or streams. This means that fragmented information (such as the NTFS MFT) can be easily captured. Segment capture can be used for acquiring smaller blocks of data. The actual target image is created as an image stream in order to retain an accurate hash value of the image. The actual image will be stored in multiple segments, with each segment identified with a Uniform Resource Name (URN).

PROPRIETARY FORMATS

Several forensic software manufacturers support file formats specific to their products. There are Safeback (by NTI), ILook Image, Paraben's Forensic Image Format, and the ProDiscover File Format. Since this text attempts to be as vendor-neutral as possible, there is no detailed discussion of these formats. However, a general familiarity of each one is important.

Safeback

The developers of Safeback do not publish any specific details concerning their product line. Therefore, the technical details surrounding it are not available for study. They describe the file structure as self-authenticating. By this, they mean that SHA256 hash values are calculated before and after capture.

Safeback can be launched from a boot disk or operated remotely over a network. Disk images can consist of bit-by-bit copies of entire devices, or individual partitions. As with any other forensically sound utility, Safeback copies slack space and unallocated space. While it works, it maintains a time-date stamped audit trail of each activity performed by the software on the target device.

iLook

As with Safeback, the technical details of iLook Investigator are not published. It is provided by the Internal Revenue Service only to qualified law enforcement officers and agencies. The software is available in 32-bit and 64-bit versions. The imaging utility that is provided, IXimager, will output the source file into any one of three formats.

The iLook Default Image Format (IDIF) stores the image in compressed form. An interesting feature of this format is its proclaimed ability to detect changes to the source image that occur after the beginning of the capture event. The application reportedly logs any user activity that occurs during this time. (Insomuch as the author works in private industry and education, the software was not available for review and testing.) The iLook Raw Bitstream Format (IRBF) is identical to IDIF in all aspects, except that it stores the final image as a raw binary file. No compression is performed. The iLook Encrypted Image Format (IEIF) stores the final image in encrypted form, as its name implies. A user key is required to access the image.

IXimager runs from either a bootable CD or a bootable floppy diskette. It can acquire images of RAID systems as well as individual volumes. Images can also be acquired over FireWire, SCSI, or USB connections. The files produced by IXimager can be read and analyzed only by iLook Investigator. In order for the image file to be accessed outside of Investigator, it must first be converted into raw bitstream format, similar to the output of the DD utility described earlier.

Prodiscover Format

Prodiscover is a product by Technology Pathways that provides a relatively complete suite of tools to the forensic investigator. It provides bit-for-bit copies of a hard disk or other device, and captures hidden areas, including slack space, HPA partitions, and unallocated space. Links to alternate data streams are maintained, and can subsequently be analyzed and the data recovered.

A Prodiscover file consists of five parts. A 16-bit file header includes a hash signature to validate the file along with a version number for that file. Following the file header is a 681-byte image header that contains user inputted metadata, including investigator name and case information. This is followed by the data block. If an uncompressed file was selected at the beginning of the capture, this will be a single binary file. If file compression was selected, there will be a series of blocks of compressed data. The fourth section exists only when file compression is selected. It is a data array that identifies the compressed blocks in the previous section along with their respective sizes. The last section is an error log of any I/O errors that occurred during capture.

CHAPTER REVIEW

1. Why is it important what order you follow in collecting evidentiary material? Discuss the order of volatility and why this is critical.

2. What are some important pieces of evidence that can be collected from a live memory capture? What are some tools you can use to capture live memory?

3. You are acquiring memory from a Dell laptop equipped with 4GB of RAM. Your memory image is 5GB. Explain the discrepancy. Your colleague used a different tool and did get a 4GB image. Why is that?

4. What is a "footprint" in memory, and what significance does it have to your work?

5. A lot of emphasis was placed on the necessity of using a write-protection device when capturing images of media. What does a write-protection device do, and why is its function so important?

CHAPTER EXERCISES

1. Go online and research some tools that would be valuable in collecting both live memory images and images of various forms of media. Put together a shopping list for your manager that includes one list that adheres to a tight budget and another in which cost is no object.

2. See if you can find a court case in which a live memory image of a computer played a significant role in the outcome.

3. You have three tools that you want to test for their ability to do memory capture. Put together a test script that you will use in testing. What are the various things you will be examining?

REFERENCES

Brezinski, D., and T. Killalea. 2002. *Guidelines for evidence collection and archiving.* www.faqs.org/rfcs/rfc3227.html (accessed July 5, 2011).

Carrier, B. 2004. A hardware-based memory acquisition procedure for digital investigations. *Digital Investigation Journal* 1(1):59.

HBGary. 2010. Fastdump—A memory acquisition tool. www.hbgary.com/solutions/memory-forensics/ (accessed August 17, 2010).

State v. Cook, 149 Ohio App. 3d 422 - Ohio: Court of Appeals, 2nd Appellate Dist. (2002).

Walters, A., and N. Petroni. 2007. *Volatools: Integrating volatile memory forensics into the digital investigation process. A white paper by Black Box, Inc.* www.orkspace.net/secdocs/Conferences/ BlackHat/Federal/2007/Volatools_-Integrating_Volatile_Memory_Forensics_ into_the_Digital_Investigation_Process-paper.pdf (accessed July 12, 2011).

FINDING LOST FILES

Here is where the actual archaeology of the digital forensics expert comes into play. Digging out the "lost data" is one of the more challenging aspects of the trade. For anyone who has been on the technical side of computers for any length of time, it is old news that a deleted file hasn't gone anywhere. Until overwritten, the data from that file stays where it's at. Depending on the operating system in use, it can either be very easy to restore a file or very difficult.

From a forensics point of view, however, it isn't just deleted files that are of concern. The investigator needs to be able to recognize the presence of hidden files, disguised files, and invisible files as well. Again, how easy that is to do depends entirely upon the OS in play. This chapter describes standard file recovery techniques as well as some tricks used by more technically astute individuals for keeping files away from unwelcome eyes. Note that standard OS file recovery utilities are routine material in conventional computer books and will not be covered in detail in this chapter.

FILE RECOVERY

Once a file has been deleted and subsequently removed from the Recycle Bin or trash can or whatever adorable analogy the operating system uses, it falls to third-party utilities to regenerate the file if necessary. The vast majority of commercial file recovery applications can perform a successful recovery only if none of the sectors originally assigned by the file system to that file have been overwritten. Some of the more advanced utilities can extract partial data from unallocated space. The digital investigator is interested in those types of utilities.

Most of the forensic suites offer file-recovery options. This is one area that is blessed with several open-source applications as well. To understand how file and data recovery work, it is essential to have at least a rudimentary understanding of how the file system manages data in memory and in storage systems. While this is more thoroughly covered in a book dedicated to operating systems, a brief overview of the two main file system types are in order. The following pages will discuss file management in Windows file systems and in the various flavors of UNIX, including Linux and Macintosh OS-X.

THE MICROSOFT FILE SYSTEM

Over the years, Windows systems have seen several file systems evolve. The venerable old File Allocation Table (FAT) system originated with MS-DOS, and each Windows version shipped with improvements to the file system. Over the years, Microsoft has shipped OS versions using the following file systems:

- FAT12 (FAT with 12-bit file table entries)
- FAT16 (FAT with 16-bit file table entries)
- FAT32 (FAT with 32-bit file table entries)
- NTFS 1.0 (released with NT 3.1)
- NTFS 1.1 (released with NT 3.5)
- NTFS 1.2 (released with NT 3.51 and 4.0, frequently called NTFS 4.0 because of the NT version)
- NTFS 3.0 (released with Windows 2000)
- NTFS 3.1 (released with Windows XP and later)

Storage devices store data in storage units called **sectors.** The average magnetic device is divided in millions of sectors containing 512 bytes each. (Note that the newer *Advanced Disk Format* released in 2010 features a 4KB sector.) When a hard disk is formatted, it is divided into partitions and clusters. A **partition** is nothing more than a section of a disk. When a contractor builds a house, the main structure consists of four walls and a roof most of the time. However, it is pretty rare that those four walls contain only one room. Usually interior walls divide the house into several rooms. Hard disks can be treated the same way. A 1TB hard disk can be divided into any number of different partitions of different sizes, and each partition will be recognized by the OS as a separate drive, even though it is not.

Partitions come in one of two forms: a primary partition or an extended partition. A *primary partition* is one that is defined in the master boot record of the hard drive and can be turned into a bootable partition. There can only be four primary partitions on any given physical disk. Primary partitions can be further divided into *extended partitions*. How many extended partitions a computer can have is entirely dependent on the file system in use. With most early file systems, a system was limited by the number of letters in the alphabet. Modern file systems overcome even that limitation.

As mentioned, a hard disk is divided sectors. However, most file systems can't read a single sector if the partition is larger than 520MB. Anywhere from 4 to as many as 64 sectors are collected together into file allocation units (FAU). A more common term used interchangeably with FAU is **cluster**. (This book will use the term cluster.) Table 8.1 lists some commonly seen partition sizes along with the default cluster size. No cluster can hold data from more than one file. Depending on the file system in use and the size of the formatted partition, a cluster could potentially be as large as 32KB. If a file is only 800 bytes, it occupies a full cluster, and the remaining 31KB+ become disk slack. It holds no data, yet at the same time, it is prevented from holding data. Hang onto that thought for a few pages.

File Allocation Tables

The *File Allocation Table* file system was one of the earliest of Microsoft file systems. Originally introduced with MS-DOS, it remained the default file system for the company's operating systems up to and including Windows NT. There were several versions of the file system, described briefly as follows (Microsoft 2011).

FAT12 FAT12 was the original file system used by the first version of MS-DOS in 1980. It is still the file system of choice for all floppy disks and hard disks

Table 8.1 Common File Systems and Partition Sizing

FS	Min./Max Partition Size	Cluster Size Min/Max
FAT16	<16MB/2G	2KB/32KB
FAT32	<260MB/2,048GB	2KB/32KB
NTFS 1.1	<500MB/8GB	512B/8KB
NTFS 3.0	<500MB/16EB	512B/64KB

(or partitions) under 16MB. Running across a hard disk in FAT12 will be a true accomplishment for any digital archaeologist. However, it is still relatively common to encounter floppy disks.

The number 12 is derived from the fact that the OS only supported 12-bit file table entries. The 12-bit limitation meant that a FAT12 volume could only address 4,086 clusters. The astute mind notices and points out that 2 to the 12th power equals 4,096. The difference is due to reserved clusters used by the file system, and therefore not available to the OS. Clusters ranged from a single sector (512 bytes) to four sectors (2KB).

File names in FAT12 consisted of something called the 8.3 format. Up to eight characters could be used for the file name, with three characters reserved for the file extension. The "dot" character was reserved as a separator between the file name and the extension.

FAT16 With the introduction of 16-bit CPUs in the late 1980s, larger disk systems and file names became more important. FAT16 extended the file entry to 16 bits. Theoretically, the file system could address hard disks as large as 2GB. However, in that era, BIOS limitation came into play. A FAT16 volume can hold as many as 65,524 clusters, and each cluster will consist of between 4 and 64 sectors, depending on how the disk is formatted. As with FAT12, the reason the file system cannot access the full 65,536 clusters that can be theoretically addressed is because of reserved sectors.

FAT16 used exactly the same file name convention as FAT12. The 2GB limitation means that hard disks larger than 2GB had to be divided into multiple partitions. A 40GB hard disk would require 20 partitions as the very least. This rendered FAT16 of limited use as disks became larger.

FAT32 FAT32 first appeared in Windows 95, Service Pack 3. Having read the previous two sections, it is almost automatic to jump to the conclusion that FAT32 used 32-bit file table entries. To do so would be wrong. FAT32 reserves four bits of the structure for internal use, leaving a 28-bit entry. In theory, FAT32 allowed up to 2TB volumes. However, because of performance limitations introduced by system BIOS, such large file table entries are not supported by most computers of that era. The computer holds certain pieces of information in RAM at all times. The FAT structure for a 2GB partition is over two megabytes. Most computers built in the late 1990s were not suitably equipped to store this large of a file in memory and were forced to store the file tables to virtual memory. A volume with a terabyte of files would require more virtual memory than Windows could easily access.

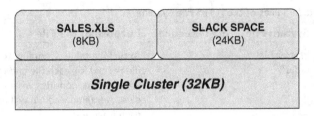

Figure 8.1 Only a single file can occupy any given cluster. Data from another file cannot coexist.

An issue specific to FAT32 that is of significant relevance to the digital investigator is the amount of slack space caused by large partitions: 32KB clusters meant that if a file was only 2KB, there was a total of 30KB that went unused. A 2KB file that overwrote a 32KB cluster leaves behind a lot of potential evidence for the investigator to find (see Figure 8.1).

NTFS

The NTFS file system is managed by several *metadata files* that collectively make up a sophisticated relational database. Simply put, a metadata file is a file that contains descriptive information about other data. The Master File Table (MFT) is the file that does the most work and gets all the press, but there are several other metadata files that are essential to OS stability and that can be useful to the digital forensics investigator. Table 8.2 defines the various metadata files as defined by Microsoft. It should be noted that to the forensic investigator, the two metafiles most commonly examined are $Mft and $BadClus. The other files are included for completeness.

Every file or directory ever created in NTFS has at least one record. If a file is fragmented, it will have at least as many entries as there are fragments. Additionally, as attributes are piled onto the resource, it is possible that new entries will be required to accommodate the additional metadata generated.

The metadata files do not reside within the confines of the traditional file system. Even if an advanced user selects options in Windows Explorer to view hidden files, system files, and so forth, the metadata files will not be visible in Explorer. However, a cluster-level search tool, such as Briggs Software's Directory Snoop, will allow you to view and even edit them (a highly dangerous operation and definitely not recommended). Figure 8.2 shows Directory Snoop revealing the metadata files. As is easy to see, some of these are not small files. On this particular machine, the $MFT file is in excess of 135MB.

Table 8.2 Metadata Files of the NTFS File System

File Name	System File	MFT Record	Purpose of the File
$Mft	Master file table	0	Actual file table. Contains at least one base file record for each file and folder on the volume that identifies what clusters host file data. A fragmented file will have a record for each fragment.
$MftMirr	Master file table 2	1	Duplicate image of first four records of MFT. Fault tolerance against single-sector failure.
$LogFile	Log file	2	Provides information for file system journaling. It retains records of changes to the file system.
$Volume	Volume	3	Identifies volume label (as configured by the user) and volume version (assigned by the OS).
$AttrDef	Attribute definitions	4	Defines attributes of files and folders on volume. These include *hidden*, *read-only*, and other file system attributes.
$	Root file name index	5	Index of files in system root. Too many files in the root directory can impact system performance
$Bitmap	Cluster bitmap	6	A representation of the volume showing which clusters are in use.
$Boot	Boot sector	7	Code used to mount the volume that defines the file system along with bootstrap loader code and a pointer to the OS boot files used if the volume is bootable.
$BadClus	Bad cluster file	8	Maps bad clusters for the volume.
$Secure	Security file	9	Contains security descriptors for files contained within the volume. Services running in the OS that maintain file-level security are dependent on this metafile.
$Upcase	Upcase table	10	Conversion table for translating lowercase characters into matching Unicode uppercase characters.
$Extend	NTFS extensions	11	Defines optional extensions including quota definitions, reparse point data, and others.
		12-15	Not currently used.

Source: Microsoft 2010.

Name	Del	Size	Modified	Accessed	Created	Record	Parent	Flags	Na	Attr
$AttrDef		2560	2006-12-04 13:00:25.96	2006-12-04 13:00:25.96	2006-12-04 13:00:25.96	4	5	0006	3	
$BadClus		0	2006-12-04 13:00:25.96	2006-12-04 13:00:25.96	2006-12-04 13:00:25.96	8	5	0006	3	
$Bitmap		7629120	2006-12-04 13:00:25.96	2006-12-04 13:00:25.96	2006-12-04 13:00:25.96	6	5	0006	3	
$Boot		8192	2006-12-04 13:00:25.96	2006-12-04 13:00:25.96	2006-12-04 13:00:25.96	7	5	0006	3	
$LogFile		67108864	2006-12-04 13:00:25.96	2006-12-04 13:00:25.96	2006-12-04 13:00:25.96	2	5	0006	3	
$MFT		135118848	2006-12-04 13:00:25.96	2006-12-04 13:00:25.96	2006-12-04 13:00:25.96	0	5	0006	3	
$MFTMir		4096	2006-12-04 13:00:25.96	2006-12-04 13:00:25.96	2006-12-04 13:00:25.96	1	5	0006	3	
$Secure		0	2006-12-04 13:00:25.96	2006-12-04 13:00:25.96	2006-12-04 13:00:25.96	9	5	0006	3	
$UpCase		131072	2006-12-04 13:00:25.96	2006-12-04 13:00:25.96	2006-12-04 13:00:25.96	10	5	0006	3	
$Volume		0	2006-12-04 13:00:25.96	2006-12-04 13:00:25.96	2006-12-04 13:00:25.96	3	5	0006	3	
acl.ini		213	2007-02-12 11:10:12.36	2009-11-23 10:18:15.36	2009-05-05 15:02:04.47	74761	5	0020	3	

Figure 8.2 A third-party utility, such as Directory Snoop, allows the investigator to access cluster-level information, including the NTFS metadata files.

UNIX/Linux File System Metadata

Linux operating systems can use Ext2, Ext3, Ext4, or Reiser file systems. UNIX uses the UNIX File System (UFS). Each file system approaches the issue of data storage and mapping in slightly different ways. However, the overall process and theory are similar between the Linux and UNIX systems. The following is only a brief discussion from a balloonist's view.

Most Linux systems employ one of the Ext file systems. Ext2 is a legacy system and rarely used in new installations. Ext3 and Ext4 have different levels of complexity but can coexist on the same system. Their basic structure is the same, and therefore the following discussion pertains to those two versions.

Linux treats all file systems as though they are a common set of objects. In Ext*, these objects are

- Superblock
- Inode
- Dentry
- File

At the root of each file system is the superblock. The superblock is the "master node." It contains information about the file system itself. Size, status, and definitions of other objects within the file system, such as the inodes and dentries, are contained in the superblock. The objects that a user recognizes as "the file system," such as files or directories, are represented in Linux as an inode. The inode (short for index node) contains all the metadata used by the file system to manage objects. This information includes

- File owner
- File type
- File permissions

- Modify/Access/Create (MAC) information
- File size
- Pointers to the blocks hosting the file
- Number of links to the file

The dentries act like a telephone book, identifying what inode numbers are assigned to specific file names. The file is the container that is viewable by the user. Ext3 maintains a directory cache of the most recently used items to speed up performance.

UNDERSTANDING SLACK SPACE

A digital investigator will spend a great deal of time digging information out of slack space. Therefore, it is essential to know precisely what slack space is, and how to read it. Slack space is disk space allocated to a file but not actually used by the file. To understand this requires a brief discussion of disk geometry.

Disks store information in clusters, which are built out of sectors. Operating systems format disks into clusters, which, depending on the file system chosen and the partition size created, could range from 1 to 64 sectors. Table 8.3 lists various

Table 8.3 Cluster Sizes in Different File Systems

Volume Size	FAT16	FAT32	NTFS
7MB to 16MB	2KB	Not supported	512 bytes
17MB to 32MB	512 bytes	Not supported	512 bytes
33MB to 64MB	1KB	512 bytes	512 bytes
65MB to 128MB	2KB	1KB	512 bytes
129MB to 256MB	4KB	2KB	512 bytes
257MB to 512MB	8KB	4KB	512 bytes
513MB to 1,024MB	16KB	4KB	1KB
1,025MB to 2GB	32KB	4KB	2KB
2GB to 4GB	64KB	4KB	4KB
4GB to 8GB	Not supported	4KB	4KB
8GB to 16GB	Not supported	8KB	4KB
16GB to 32GB	Not supported	16KB	4KB
32GB to 2TB	Not supported	Not supported	4KB

Source: Technet 2011.

combinations of file system, partition size, and cluster size an investigator is likely to encounter. For the purposes of this explanation, the 64-sector cluster will be used. That represents a data unit of 32KB.

Any individual cluster can be assigned to only a single file. Think of each cluster as being a kitchen canister with rigorously enforced standards. The one labeled "Salt" can only contain salt. Your 32-ounce container can contain up to 32 ounces of salt. But if you have only 2 ounces, you cannot fill the remaining space with flour. If you try to put flour in, all of the contents would be unusable. Your kitchen containers might let you make that mistake, but the file system won't.

Now, here is where the analogy breaks down. If you relabel the salt canister with the name "Flour," you can now fill the container with 32 ounces of flour. The average person washes the canister thoroughly before changing contents. The file system does not. It simply replaces the salt in the canister with flour—and worse yet, it starts from the bottom and works upward. So if you have a 32-ounce container of salt, change the name to Flour, and start filling it, a whole bunch of salt remains. In other words, the data in a reallocated cluster is not overwritten.

Figure 8.3 illustrates this concept. In this illustration, the nursery rhyme *Twinkle, Twinkle, Little Star* was hosted by cluster 154926645. The file was erased and replace by *Mary Had a Little Lamb*, which did not require as much space. So the file system overwrote the bytes it required, but left certain characters from the previous file behind. The astute investigator can retrieve the remaining characters from the erased file to determine if they have any relevance to the investigation at hand. While such information may not be the proverbial smoking gun, it may provide powerful evidence of where the smoke came from.

Up until recently, a disk sector was 512 bytes. Of that 512 bytes, about 40 bytes were used for sector mapping and 40 bytes for error correction. The *International Disk Drive Equipment and Materials Association* (IDEMA) developed the *Long Block Data* (LBD) standard that defined 4KB sectors. Disk drive manufacturers have incorporated this new standard in the Advanced Format. Since file systems

Figure 8.3 An example of slack space. The faded text represents data left behind by a previous file.

such as NTFS, ext3, and HFS all use 4KB as a default cluster, once usage of LBD becomes universal, the concept of the cluster will be reexamined.

UNDERSTANDING UNALLOCATED SPACE

Occasionally, a beginning practitioner has difficulty understanding the difference between slack space and unallocated space. In a way, they are similar, but realistically, they are quite different. Unallocated space can be considered as slack space for the entire volume. It is any hard disk space that is not currently identified within the file system as hosting live file data. Those clusters have not been assigned, or "allocated" as it were, to any given file. It is available for use, should the operating system need to store a new file or to extend an existing file into additional clusters.

Just because a cluster is unallocated does not necessarily mean it is empty. When a user deletes a file, the clusters assigned by the file system to that file are marked as free, and the space is now unallocated. The data is not affected unless one of two things happen. The first is if the file system identifies the cluster as free and uses it for another file. In that case, if the cluster is not completely overwritten, it may be possible to extract data from the part of the cluster not completely overwritten. This is the "slack space" that was discussed in the previous section.

The second thing that can destroy the data in unallocated clusters is to use a wipe utility. Such a utility overwrites the data repeatedly with 0s and 1s, deleting the data between each pass. Some utilities perform as many as 32 passes. The average digital forensic lab will be unable to retrieve any data from clusters subjected to such a wipe. However, some highly specialized facilities have equipment that can extract information from drives on a molecular level. This, however, is far beyond the scope of this book.

Assuming that a wipe utility has not been used, most forensic suites have the capability of searching slack space as though it were a file. They can search for text using string searches. Data-carving utilities (discussed later in the chapter) can find entire files as long as they exist intact.

Sometimes it is a matter of finding specific data, and not recovering an entire file. To find text strings in slack space, a couple of utilities are quite useful—GREP and strings. Both utilities are available in either *nix or Windows variations.

GREP

GREP is an acronym for *Global/Regular Express/Print*. Originally developed for UNIX, all flavors of Linux support it as well. It is a command-line utility and requires at least a rudimentary understanding of using a *terminal emulator*.

Terminal emulators are programs that operate within the graphical environment of the OS, but provide pure command-line services. This is frequently called simply the *shell*. Such shells include Terminal, XTerm, BASH, Konsole, and about a thousand others.

GREP has over 40 different command-line tags that modify its behavior. Therefore, a complete discussion would require a small book on its own. To get the condensed version of the GREP manual, type MAN GREP at the Linux command prompt, and it will display a detailed description of each trigger.

The tricks that GREP can perform that are of interest to the investigator are somewhat simpler. It can extract strings of text from binary files. This is useful if data has been embedded in another file. For example, a music file might have strings of text embedded between the file header and the sample blocks. GREP can look for specific patterns. This is useful if you are looking for files that contain certain words.

If the investigator is looking for passwords in a live memory capture, GREP can be used to find all text strings that fall within a size range. For example, if one knows that the password policy requires passwords between 8 and 15 characters, then the memory image file can be search for all text strings in that range and ignore all others.

Strings

Strings is available in both the *nix and the Windows platforms and is equally useful. By default, the utility will display any text string longer than four characters. However, as with the GREP utility, command-line triggers allow the user to modify this behavior. The -n trigger allows the user to specify a minimum string length. Strings can search individual files, or it can search folders. If the folders option is used, it can be told to search folders recursively. This means that all nested folders within folders within folders can be searched using the parameters specified.

THE DELETED FILE

The best way to understand how files can be recovered is to understand what happens when they are deleted. Different operating systems deal with the deleted file in different ways.

FAT16 deleted the file simply by replacing the first character of the file name with an illegal character. The file name was then rendered "invisible" to the operating system and did not show up in directory listings, nor are the file names visible to applications. The data remained intact on all clusters until the file system needed that cluster for another file. Recovering a deleted file required only that the user have disk-level access in order to replace the illegal character at the beginning of the file name with a legal character. It did not matter if the correct character was used or not. However, the OS has no way of dealing with partially overwritten clusters. So if a cluster had been reallocated, one of two things would happen. Either the file would be reported as corrupt and the application would fail to load it, or it would load the file, and where foreign data had replaced original data, the information would appear as gibberish.

Later versions of Windows introduced the Recycle Bin. In those versions, when a user deletes a file it is reallocated to the Recycle Bin. It is not "placed" or "moved" there. The actual data that comprises the file stays precisely where it was before the user elected to delete it. The FAT entries are simply rewritten to place the file in a hidden folder called Recycled. (Note that if you have more than one drive in your computer, you'll have a Recycled folder for each drive.) The file is then renamed. The original name and location of the file are stored in a hidden index file, called INFO2 (or INFO, if you're using Windows 95), located in the Recycled folder. When you open the Recycle Bin, click a file, and choose Restore, the original path is read from the INFO file, the file is renamed, and its directory entry restored.

A file is in no danger of being lost until it is removed from the Recycle Bin. Even then, the file data is not deleted. What happens is that Windows changes the name of the file by changing the first character of the file name to an illegal character (as previously discussed in the previous section). The file system alters the file's directory entry to indicate the space occupied by this file is no longer needed and is available for use. Until that space is needed, it still remains intact. However, if the operating system needs space for another file, those clusters may be overwritten. Until it is overwritten, the raw data still exists on the hard disk and may be recoverable by third-party applications.

The implications of this are twofold. If the deleted file contains information that must never again see the light of day, then steps must be taken to permanently erase the data. There are a number of utilities available that will accomplish this task. Note that many file deletion products claim to meet Department of Defense specifications for a clean file wipe, citing a need for data to be overwritten seven times. In fact the *Clearing and Sanitizing Matrix* (U.S. DoD 2006) generally referenced does not make such a statement. In fact, it states that in order to sanitize a disk containing classified information, the disk must be degaussed with a Type I or Type II degausser or destroyed.

For acceptable destruction methods, incineration, melting, disintegrating, pulverizing, or shredding are all listed as acceptable methods. These latter methods are not very conducive to data recovery. Only for nonclassified information is any method involving overwriting considered to be acceptable. The method of deleting nonclassified information from a disk is to "overwrite all addressable locations with a character, its complement, then a random character and verify" (U.S. DOD 2006). The implication here is that even data that has been overwritten is potentially recoverable.

Implication number two is that if there is need to recover that file, one can dramatically increase the chances of being able to recover a deleted file by halting any subsequent disk activity. If the OS decides it wants to recycle one or more of the sectors used by the file, the difficulty of recovering it increases by several magnitudes. That is why many published guidelines suggest turning off a suspect computer by pulling the power plug from the back of the system. A graceful shutdown writes a myriad of files to the hard disk in the process of shutting down. These new files, or newly relocated files, can potentially overwrite sectors that the investigator might want to later recover.

THE FILE RECOVERY PROCESS

The author assumes that readers of this book are already familiar with the process of recovering a file from standard Recycle and Trash bins. This text will concentrate on locating and extracting files that have been removed from those locations.

There are numerous third-party utilities that can successfully restore files from the NTFS file system. An inexpensive option that the reader can use to follow along is Directory Snoop from Briggs Software. A free download allows 25 uses before a license is required. As of this writing the licensed version, as used here, is around $40.

In this example, a file named Test_Document.doc was saved to the DA_Temp folder. The file was subsequently deleted. For the purposes of this demonstration, the Recycle Bin was emptied prior to deletion, making Test_Document.doc the only file present. Windows Explorer still reports this file as present in the Recycle folder (Figure 8.4). Next, the file was removed from the Recycle Bin. As one might expect, there are no longer any entries in Explorer. However, the data remain intact on the clusters it occupied until overwritten by another file. Additionally, the MFT entries may still exist.

So how does one go about finding this ephemeral data? Numerous file recovery utilities exist that, with varying degrees of success, can restore a file that has not been overwritten. A few more sophisticated utilities can restore the data from partially overwritten files. All of the major forensic suites provide functionality for recovering deleted data.

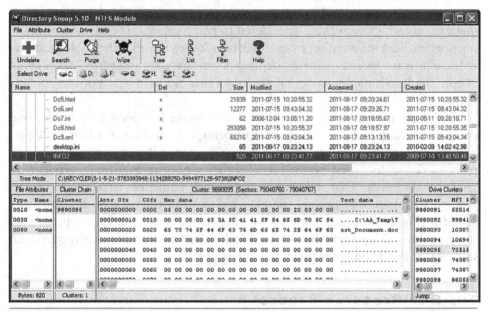

Figure 8.4 The INFO2 directory holds recycled files.

MFT entries are not immediately deleted after a file is erased. The entries are simply marked as free, becoming available if needed. Disk editors enable the investigator to read and copy into a file the information contained by MFT entries remaining from deleted files. This can include information such as file name, file extension, and possibly a pointer to the next MFT entry. This suggests the size of the file was larger than the cluster size in use by the file system.

In this example, Directory Snoop finds two entries that correspond to the deleted file. The file names do not correspond. The author knew to look in the Recycle Bin for the deleted file rather than in the original directory. Why? As mentioned earlier, the initial erasure of the file simply moved the file from its original director to the Recycle directory. The Windows 7 file system maintains a hidden, read-only file called $Recycle Bin where deleted files are maintained. (Windows XP and earlier utilized INFO2 files.) They are renamed by the file system to prevent naming conflicts in the inevitable case where the user recreates the file under the same name. When the Recycle Bin is emptied, the files are simply deleted from *that* directory, and the space is allocated by the file system as available.

Notice in Figure 8.5 that there are multiple subdirectories of Recycle Bin. Each of those folders is the recycle bin for a specific user account on the machine. This explains why each user sees only her deleted files and not those of other users who share the machine. The deleted files continue to appear, and using the utility are easily restored as long as the file has not been overwritten. With this utility and

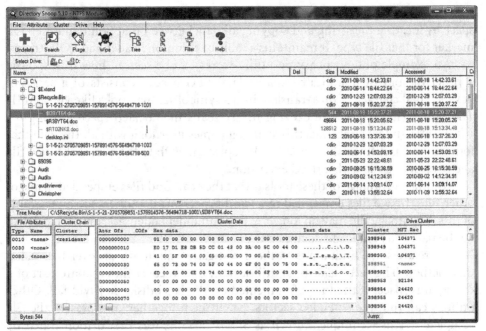

Figure 8.5 Every user on the system has a separate folder in the Recycle Bin.

several others like it, it is possible to restore the remaining data from slack space even after a cluster has been allocated to a new file.

DATA CARVING

It has been mentioned numerous times in this book that until overwritten, files continue to exist on most media. However, without the support of a file system in place, a file must be returned to an approximation of its original structure before it can be opened. The process of **data carving** extracts the string of binary code that makes up a file and copies it into a contiguous file that is readable by the file system. By nature, each type of file has a specific file structure. The file header is unique to each type of file. Additionally, different file types support different classes of metadata. The payload contains the actual data.

HOW DATA CARVING WORKS

Forensic investigators make use of special utilities to extract complete files from slack space or unallocated space. They utilize an understanding of basic file structure in order to perform their magic. Every file has a header, and every file has an end of file (EOF) marker. Headers for any given file are a specific string that tells the OS what type of data is contained within. The utility finds files in slack space by locating the string and copying all data between that point and the EOF marker for that file type. It maintains a table of common header and EOF strings.

An example of how a carving utility works can be seen in how it would dig a JPEG file out of unallocated space. The JPEG header consists of a series of hexadecimal characters that translate into a symbol set that looks like ÿØÿà..JFIF. The EOF string is ÿÛ. The carving utility scans unallocated space looking for ÿØÿà..JFIF, and when it finds this string, it copies it—along with all the data that follows—until it finds the string ÿÛ. It copies the EOF to the end of the new file and saves it as a file with a JPEG extension.

Another advantage of these tools is that they can find files embedded inside of other files. Image files embedded in a word processing document are an example of this. The image file may no longer exist as an independent file on the hard disk but be part of a composite document.

There are some limitations to the investigator's ability to uncover files using this method. The vast majority of utilities can only recover files that are part of a contiguous space. If the file is fragmented on the hard disk, they will fail. Other utilities can find the extended sectors, patch them together, and present the file completely. This technique, known as SmartCarving, was first demonstrated by Pal, Sencar, and Memon (2008) in response to the 2007 Digital Forensics Research Workshop (DFRWS) challenge. A company called Digital Assembly now distributes a suite of utilities called Adroit Photo Forensics that incorporates this technology.

Conventional data carving utilities rely on certain conditions to be successful. Those parameters in part depend on the technique used by the file carving utility. The most common utilities use either block-based or header/footer analysis. However, in general the following applies to all except SmartCarving utilities. The file signature (that part of the header that identifies the type of file) must be present and intact. The file is not fragmented. The utility must be able to account for file block size variables. A condition that does not preclude success, but can make life difficult for the investigator is when the file signature is so common that it is likely to appear repeatedly as a character string in numerous files. This causes a great number of false positives to be reported.

A block-based file carver starts out by finding a known header string. Then, it examines each block of data in turn, using data modeling to determine if the next block scanned meets the expected data for that type of file. Each data block that fits the model is added to the file.

Header/footer utilities start out by using a search string engine to scan the unallocated space, looking for known file headers. Next, the utility performs a mapping function. It bounces down the input file, one block at a time, looking for the first occurrence of the file footer identified with that file. By default, most applications use the 512-byte block to match the sector size of most hard drives. All of the data between the header and footer is assumed to be associated with that file and is "cut and pasted" into a new file and given an arbitrary name, followed by the default extension for that file type. Any data remaining in a 512-byte block that follows the EOF marker is dropped. The file is copied to the target evidence drive into a folder selected by the investigator. As mentioned earlier, common header strings result in false positives.

Each invalid header results in a new file being started. When the footer is reached, the new file is copied to the target drive. If a single contiguous stream of data yields a dozen "headers" before finding a valid footer, then 12 files will be generated. Only one will be the actual file, but all of the others will still be copied to the target evidence drive. On a large project this can have a major impact on resources.

Another source of failure for data carving utilities is the fragmented file. The header and footer of the file may be separated by one or more clusters owned by a different file.

DATA CARVING TOOLS

As previously mentioned, all commercial forensic suites offer powerful file recovery tools. This includes data carving. For those not blessed with the budget for such fancy toys, there are two open-source utilities that are worth examining: Foremost and Scalpel. The following is a brief overview of these tools.

Foremost

Foremost (downloaded from http://foremost.sourceforge.net/) is a Linux data carving utility that can extract files from their entirety from unallocated space (assuming, of course that the file still exists in its entirety.) Originally developed by the U.S. Air Force Office of Special Investigations, it has been released to the public domain for general use. It is primarily header/footer based but does examine block content to verify file type. The utility can work on a live system or a forensic image file.

Foremost is a command-line utility that must be run with root privileges for maximum success. Several triggers allow the investigator to customize the output of the results. While not a conclusive list of triggers, the more useful to the investigator include

- -i Input file. Allows the user to specify a specific file for Foremost to analyze.
- -o Output directory. Allows user to specify the directory in which the output file will be stored.

- -v Verbose. Runs in verbose mode, providing more information about running state and file statistics.

- -q Quick mode. Only searches each block for header information. Speeds up the search but misses embedded files.

- -Q Quiet mode. Suppresses error messages.

- -w Write audit mode. Creates a list of files found without extracting any files.

- -k Allows the user to specify the size of the data chunk scanned by Foremost. (Note that there must be sufficient free RAM for whatever size is specified.)

- -b Block size. Specifies the block size to be used. Allows known cluster sizes to be configured, speeding up the process. Default is 512 bytes.

- -t File type. Specifies the type of file for the search (DOC, JPEG, TIF, etc.).

- -s Skip blocks. Specifies how many data blocks to scan past before beginning the search for header information. Useful for scanning images of large drives where boot sectors, file system metadata, and root directories can be skipped.

An example of Foremost at work follows (note that the command is typed all one line):

```
FOREMOST -t jpeg, tif, bmp - /usr/documents/
evidence/diskimage.dd -o/usr/documents/evidence/results
```

In the above example, the utility has been asked to search for all JPEG, TIF, and BMP images located in a disk image created by the DD utility. The image file named diskimage.dd, located in the /usr/documents/evidence directory of the mounted drive, is the file being examined. If diskimage.dd is located in a different directory or on a different partition, Foremost will generate a "file not found" error.

The output of the search will be stored in directory named /usr/documents/evidence/results. Files will be stored with randomly generated names followed by the appropriate extension. For example, the output directory might contain files such as 65544361.jpg, 35719997.jpg, 44002899.jpg, and so forth.

If the audit trigger is specified, an additional file named audit.txt will be generated by Foremost and stored in the target directory. A cautionary note here is that Foremost is not intelligent enough to create a directory that does not exist. Therefore, the investigator must first create the desired target direct prior to running the utility.

Carver-Recovery

Carver-recovery is another open-source utility (download from https://carver-recovery.googlecode.com/files/Portable_Executable.zip) that looks for file headers and footers in order to perform its function. Scalpel scans the target drive twice. In the first pass, it is reading data in large chunks. While the chunk size is user definable, the default setting is 10MB. As the application performs this scan, it keeps a log of the location of each header it finds for which it was configured to search. It also looks for footers, creating a log of each hit. On the second pass, the indexes created during the first pass are used to determine what chunks hold potential files and is able to skip over all chunks that do not offer potential evidence. This process makes for a somewhat faster operation in theory. In practice, the results varied widely.

The author used three sample image files and used Foremost and Scalpel to look for images. The images consisted of

- 2GB USB drive: 6 undeleted and 2 deleted images
- 40MB partition from a FAT32 hard disk: 20 undeleted and 10 deleted images
- 40GB hard disk: 20 undeleted and 10 deleted images (source of partition above)

The test results were rather interesting. On the 2GB USB drive, Foremost finished the job about 27 minutes and 45 seconds (27m45s), whereas Scalpel took 26m17s. Both utilities extracted the undeleted files with ease, while neither was able to identify or extract the deleted files. While Scalpel was somewhat faster, it was not a significant difference. The reason that the flash drive did not allow for the recovery of deleted drives was that flash memory is not magnetic media and stores data in a completely different manner. It uses microtransistors to store data, and when a file is deleted, all transistors are set to "off."

The 40MB file took 38m47s for Scalpel to process. Foremost beat it out with a 22m17s time. The time savings came at a cost, however. Foremost found but nine of the ten deleted files, whereas Scalpel identified all of them. The 40GB test was particularly revealing. Scalpel finished the job, finding all files in 4h32m38s. Processing the image file in Foremost was unsuccessful.

CHAPTER REVIEW

1. Explain in your own words how the file system in use on a computer system can be significant to the investigator when looking for evidence. What makes

the search approach different between file systems? What makes a search more or less difficult with any given file system?

2. You have to find any files on a computer that are related to a specific case. You know that the suspect's name is Priscilla, that she was dealing in the international pornography trade, and that one of the suspected suppliers is in the state of Georgia. What utilities can help you find files, and how is it that they can help?

3. Why is it that a file that has been deleted by the user can be recovered intact? Shouldn't the data be permanently erased when a file is deleted?

4. How does slack space differ from unallocated space? How are they similar?

5. What process is used to recover files intact out of unallocated space?

CHAPTER EXERCISES

1. Using either online resources or the library, research at least two criminal or civil cases in which recovered files played a significant role in how the case played out.

2. On your own hard disk, try to find some files that were deleted in the past and recover them. Are you able to use them?

REFERENCES

Microsoft. 2010. The NTFS file system. *Technet.* http://technet.microsoft.com/en-us/library/cc976808.aspx (accessed July 22, 2011).

Microsoft. 2011. File systems. *Technet.* http://technet.microsoft.com/en-us/library/cc938437.aspx (accessed July 18, 2011).

Pal, A., T. Sencar, and N. Memon. 2008. Detecting file fragmentation point using sequential hypothesis testing. *Digital Investigations* (Fall). http://digital-assembly.com/technology/research/pubs/dfrws2008.pdf (accessed August 24, 2011).

U.S. Department of Defense. 2006. *Clearing and sanitizing matrix.* DoD 5220.22-M.

DOCUMENT 9 ANALYSIS

One of the great challenges for a digital investigator comes when the evidence is in plain sight but can't be found—or isn't recognized for what it is. Perhaps a file isn't what it says it is. On the simplest level, a JPEG image file might be renamed with an AVI extension, making it appear to be a video file. More complex techniques employed by the bad guys include embedding files within files (alternate data streams) or even burying small files in the Windows Registry. This chapter covers some of these techniques and how to uncover the evidence.

FILE IDENTIFICATION

In theory, the easiest aspect of a file search is the process of identifying what kind of file it is. The Windows file systems (and less universally, other file systems as well) use the file extension as a file identifier. A file with the name of IMAGE. JPG is an image file using the Joint Photographic Expert Group file compression algorithm. Usually. However, file systems do not enforce extension rules. If a user changes the extension of a file in Windows, the only action the operating system takes is to present the warning shown in Figure 9.1.

Once the extension is changed, the Windows default actions for the newly assigned extension will apply to the file. An example of a default action is the double-click of the mouse. In Windows, a double-click opens the file in the application associated with that file type. A file with a .doc extension opens in Microsoft Word. When the extension is changed, double-clicking on the file in Windows Explorer

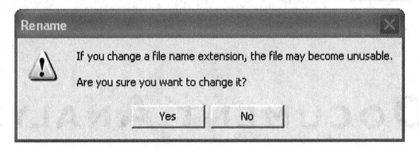

Figure 9.1 Changing a file extension in Windows only prompts a warning.

will not elicit the expected behavior. In the example shown in Figure 9.2, the file CyberControls Forensic Approach.pdf has been renamed to CyberControls Forensic Approach.tif. Double-clicking on the file in Explorer brought up the Office Picture Manager application, which could not open a PDF file. So Windows displayed a small square with a red X instead of the PDF. Right-clicking on the file and selecting Open With, and then selecting Adobe Reader opens the file correctly.

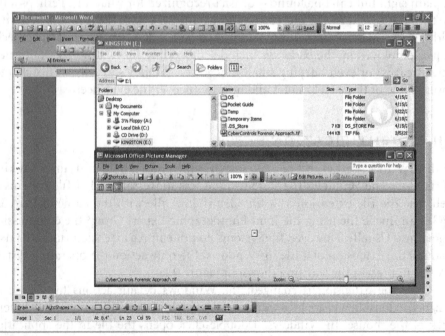

Figure 9.2 Windows default actions do not behave as expected when a file extension has been changed.

What does this little exercise imply? For one thing, it becomes clear that changing the extension does nothing to alter the structure of the file. It is doubtful anyone thought it would. Additionally, changing the extension did not affect the ability of the correct host application to open the file. Therefore, there is something else in the file structure that determines whether or not an application can open a file.

FILE STRUCTURE

Any file stored by any file system used by a computer must have similar structure or there can be no cross-platform compatibility. However, anyone who has experience using more than one OS knows that a Microsoft Word document can be opened with either Word for Macintosh or Word for Windows. Additionally, third-party applications such as OpenOffice have no trouble opening the files of either version of Word.

The extension, discussed briefly in the previous section, acts as a superficial identifier of file type. If unaltered, most applications have no difficulty identifying files by extension. If asked to open a file with an unfamiliar extension, the application will dig a little deeper into the file. There are several internal identifiers that files use to introduce themselves. These include file metadata and file structure.

FILE METADATA

Files can contain two types of metadata that applications use to recognize and open the file. Internal metadata is contained within the file and can consist of a binary string or a text string. Three commonly used metadata containers are the *MFT attributes*, the *file header*, and the *magic number*.

MFT Attributes

The NTFS file system used by current Windows OSs places certain information concerning the file into the metadata files. Chapter 8, "Finding Lost Files," contains a table of the metadata files used by NTFS, along with a description of each file. The metadata files are created when the disk is first formatted to NTFS. After that, every file copied to the drive owns at least one MFT record. MFT records contain certain attributes that define the entry to the OS. Table 9.1 lists the MFT attributes used by NTFS, along with the hexadecimal value assigned to each attribute.

The reason for understanding the various attributes is that some of the utilities used key on those attributes when they search for file data. An important

Table 9.1   NTFS Attributes

Attribute Name	Hexadecimal Value
Unused	0x00
Standard Information	0x10
File Name	0x30
Object ID	0x40
Security Descriptor	0x50
Volume Name	0x60
Volume Information	0x70
Data	0x80
Index Root	0x90
Index Allocation	0xA0
Bitmap	0xB0
Reparse Point	0xC0
EA Information	0xD0
EA	0xE0
Property Set	0xF0
Logged Utility Stream	0x100
First User-Defined Attribute	0x1000
End of Attributes (records)	0xffffffff

aspect to remember is that file content is considered an attribute of the file. It is the *data* attribute and carries the hex value of 0x80. This value is useful to utilities such as Directory Snoop in that it allows the application to identify the part of the file that is specifically user data. Figure 9.3 illustrates how Directory Snoop reads the file attribute types.

Additionally, MFT records can be examined to see if a file that no longer exists perhaps once did. While the Windows metafiles are not directly viewable by most applications, a disk editor such as Directory Snoop allows this task to be accomplished. In Figure 9.4, we see the entry for a file called redstateicon.png. The file no longer exists on my hard disk, but a string search of the $MFT metafile in Directory Snoop found this record. While most of the information is gibberish to the average person, directory Snoop does tell us the file name and what application is the default program to open the file. Additionally, it tells us what the legacy MS-DOS file name is as well.

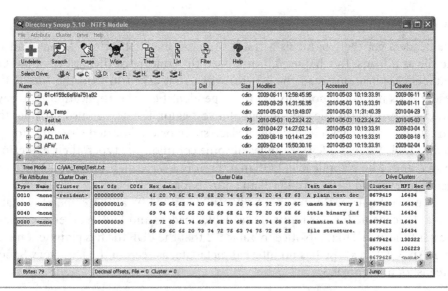

Figure 9.3 Not all files contain internal metadata.

```
FILEO  ˪ ˊΛ%              ˪ 8  Àˡ  ˩            |    8↵  ˪ o      ┼                    H
↑    ¶ü'½ᴶᴶÊ «ó½‼êÉ  ‾QO-''Î  ¶ü'½ᴶᴶÊ            | m Æ-''Î m Æ-''Î m Æ-''Î
€      ᴶ b  ↑    nâ     m    Æ-''Î m Æ-''Î m Æ-''Î  ¿
        ┼ r e d S t a t e I c o n . p n g  €  0  x      ˪ Z  ↑   í         m
Æ-''Î m Æ-''Î m Æ-''Î m Æ-''Î                ⚭ R E D S T A ~ 1 . P N G
. p n 0  €      ᴶ b   ↑   í       m Æ-''Î m Æ-''Î m Æ-''Î
          ┼ r e d S t a t e I cˡ n . p n g        €        ↑    ·   ↑
%PNG
→  IHDR      ▯-   2Ĭ½   ┼tEXtSoftware Adobe ImageReadyqEe<
  1IDATxÚdOK₁Q¶ÀÎèM´ã"ˆ2úo◀Ùù"\´ú-F˚ᴶADª(▯"▯scP´3,°}ÐªVòªváʌ³ Š‹gÞü»½;E     ]
8œsîûq/<%'Þ(ˡÈK%Ð¿θªYY6T†Š+™ ÙçҐ(˟     çÅ÷|%◀#œß?óˈ▯À»eã$;EQ⊦-«4ù=àIm▯ù«┬|
xÀêâ.fÝï0âX8Ñ0O%yÀMà┼cPW◀šfOC22ᴢÎ¶ₐh‼*ˡ ᴶ íá&. 'Z´ñ-ó%n·‡Vy›sé4₁C₂<|Sz¼tÀ·³◀òòÙ&Çv0
-,ØÇ%ĥfÐá>#cÑi«gû®▯ÀáQh>ÆÀ¾½ÄH•üRŽ¶0-,'┼,üf=‡°õí²-¹-"ú•¬qJµ¦üqîñ%A á…•ÎGµm
  ÍD®B , ÿÿÿÿ,yG◀
|   .EO  ˪ äã%                ˪ 8   àˡ  ˩            |    9↵  ˪ t      ┼                    H
↑    ᴬΛ*½ᴶÊ «ó½‼êÉ  ‾QO-''Î  ᴶΛ*½ᴶÊ            | m Æ-''Î m Æ-''Î m Æ-''Î
↑    t   ↑   nâ     m    Æ-''Î m Æ-''Î m Æ-''Î  ¿
        ┼ n o t C o n n e c t e d S t a t e I c o n . p n g ↑   0   x        ˪ Z
  ↑   í     m Æ-''Î m Æ-''Î m Æ-''Î                  ⚭ N O T C
O N ~ 1 . P N G S t a 0         ᴶ t  ↑   í      m  Æ-''Î m Æ-''Î m Æ-''Î m
Æ-''Î           ·  ·       ↑   ┼ n oˡ C o n n e c t e d S t a t e I c o n . p n
g      €    ·  ·          ↑   %PNG
→  IHDR      ▯-   2Ĭ½   ┼tEXtSoftware Adobe ImageReadyqEe<
  1IDATxÚdOK₁Q¶ÀÎèM´ã"ˆ2úo◀Ùù"\´ú-F˚ᴶADª(▯"▯scP´3,°}ÐªVòªváʌ³Š‹gÞü»½;E     ]
8œsîûq/<%'Þ(ˡÈK%Ð¿θªYY6T†Š+™ ÙçҐ(˟     çÅ÷|%◀#œß?óˈ▯À»eã$;EQ⊦-«4ù=àIm▯ù«┬|
xÀêâ.fÝï0âX8Ñ0O%yÀMà┼cPW◀šfOC22ᴢÎ¶ₐh‼*ˡ ᴶ íá&. 'Z´ñ-ó%n·‡Vy›sé4₁C₂<|Sz¼tÀ·³◀òòÙ&Çv0
-,ØÇ%ĥfÐá>#cÑi«gû®▯ÀáQh>ÆÀ¾½ÄH•üRŽ¶0-,'┼,üf=‡°õí²-¹-"ú•¬qJµ¦üqîñ%A á…•ÎGµm
IEND®B , ÿÿÿÿ,yG◀                         ˪ FILEO ˪ µy%                  ˪ 8   Àˡ ◀
```

Figure 9.4 This Notepad file is cut and pasted from a copy of the MFT record found in the NTFS $MFT metafile.

File Header

File headers get their name as a result of being the first string of data read by the file as it loads. In Chapter 8, I discussed the concept of file headers and EOF markers. Applications read these bytes when first asked to load the file. If the header does not correspond to the file type identified, the application may have difficulty loading the file. To the digital investigator, the header also provides the starting point for carving files out of slack space or unallocated space on storage media. Table 9.2 lists a few examples of some common file types, their extension, header, and, where applicable, EOF marker. It is a *very* small sample—to attempt including every file type would fill an entire book.

A general rule of thumb (not universally applied by all developers) is that a humanly readable file has humanly readable headers and EOF markers. A binary file has binary metadata. Notice in Table 9.2 that the PDF file has plain text metadata. An ASCII text file has no internal metadata, as seen in the Directory Snoop screenshot in Figure 9.3.

Table 9.2 Sample File Structure and Metadata

File Type	Ext.	Start (hex)	Start	End
Word Doc	.doc	DOCF	ÐÏà	ô9²q
PDF	.pdf	255 0 4446	%PDF	%%EOF
Windows Media	.wma	30 26 B2 75 8E 66 CF 11 or A6 D9 00 AA 00 62 CE 6C	0&²u.fï. or ¡Ù.ª.bÎl	Ñvll/llyúØllœ ÔÂ–Êl
JPEG	.jpg	FFD8 FFEO	ÿØÿà	ÿÙ
Excel Worksheet	.xls	DOCF	ÐÏà	0x000a
TIF file	.tif	49 49 2A	II*	......
Bitmap	.bmp	42 4D	BM	......
Ping File	.png	8950 4E47	‰PNG	IEND®B`,...
GIF	.gif	47 49 46 38 37 61 or 47 49 46 38 39 61	GIF87a or GIF87b	.;
RTF	.rtf	7B 5C 72 74 66 31	{\rtfl	\par }}
ID3	.mp3	49 44 33 03	ID3...	LAME3.98.UUU
MPEG3	.mp3	00 00 01 Bx	00 00 01 B7	...*
MPEG2	.mpg	00 00 01 B4	00 00 01 B9	...¦
AOL Art File	.art	4A 47 03 0E or 4A 47 04 0E	JG..	ÐË.. or ÏÇË

Magic Numbers

Magic numbers are really nothing more than another method of structuring a header. Files incorporating magic numbers embed a file signature consisting of hexadecimal code into the first few bytes of the file to identify the file type. The term is derived from the Linux and UNIX (*nix) file system. The Linux Information Project (LIP 2006) defines the magic number as occupying the first six bytes of the file. Many programs use the magic number as the first step in identifying a file type. However, as with the file header, there are certain files, such as ASCII text files, HTML, and source code cabinets, that do not incorporate magic numbers.

Identifying a file by the magic number method does incorporate a small degree of latency (additional processing overhead required by an application to perform a specific set of tasks). Most Linux builds have defined lists of magic numbers in various directories. Among these are (Darwin 1999)

- `/usr/share/file/magic.mgc`—Compiled list of magic numbers
- `/usr/share/file/magic`—Default list of magic numbers
- `/usr/share/file/magic.mime.mgc`—Default compiled list that will display mime types when the -i trigger is used
- `/usr/share/file/magic.mime`—Default list that will display mime types when the -i trigger is used

In Linux, the `file(1)` command can be used to identify a file by its type. One of the command's first tests is to attempt to read a magic number and compare the number it finds to one or more of the magic number lists above. The digital forensic examiner can use a disk editor to view a file and examine the magic number directly in an effort to identify the file type.

UNDERSTANDING METADATA

The word *metadata* gets thrown around a lot and is used in more than one context. Earlier in this book, a loose definition of metadata was presented that simply defined it as data that describes data. However, metadata can exist in multiple forms. The operating system maintains information about files in various repositories. As discussed in the previous chapter, the NTFS file system makes use of a series of metadata files. Individual files can also contain information stored within the file that defines the file. Additionally, many applications, such as document management systems, maintain separate files containing metadata. All of these sources can be a gold mine of information for an investigator. *Aguilar v.*

Immigration and Customs Enforcement (2008) determined that the three types of metadata relevant to digital evidence include

- System metadata—Information generated by the file system or document management system
- Substantive metadata—Information that defines modifications to a document
- Embedded metadata—Information embedded by the application that creates or edits the file

Substantive metadata can fall within either of the other categories. Another form of metadata that exists that is important to the investigator is external metadata. Many document and image management software solutions maintain large amounts of information in the form of a database. Indexing, file modification, tracking, and auditing information is stored in separate files maintained by the application. Each of these types of metadata will be discussed over the next few pages.

SYSTEM METADATA

Chapter 8 introduced the concept of metadata usage by the OS. All file systems maintain vast amounts of information about the files and directories stored on the volumes they control. The fact is—the file system *is* the metadata that the operating system uses to manage files on the various media it controls. To be certain, there are physical aspects of the file system, such as the mapping of file allocation units on the drive itself, but that mapping is meaningless without the directions that tell the OS or the applications how to get there from here.

It isn't just hard disks that have volumes of metadata. CD-ROMs, DVDs, and even thumb drives need some form of file table that informs the system how and where files are store. Every computer running needs to be able to mount multiple file systems. The hard disk uses its system. As mentioned in the previous chapter, Linux systems might be formatted with the Ext2, Ext3, or Ext4 or perhaps the Reiser file system. Windows typically uses NTFS, although some legacy systems may use one of the several versions of FAT. Even an NTFS-based computer needs to be able to read FAT if that is how a USB flash drive was formatted. And in order to read CD-ROMs or DVDs, the ISO-9660 or the ECMA-167 file system must be mounted. Understanding how these files systems work is far beyond the scope of this book. However, a brief overview of how and where the system metadata is stored is essential for the digital investigator.

Value of OS Metadata

The useful aspect of OS metadata in the process of digital investigation is the ability to prove the existence of a deleted document and to research the timeline of a document. OS metadata does not help identify contents of files, aside from file type. A critical piece of information found here is the *modify/access/create* (MAC) data. Disks formatted with NTFS offer the additional attribute of entry modified (EM). EM notes the last time the MFT entry in the NTFS metafiles was modified. MAC information is valuable for creating a time line of events, as long as care is taken in analyzing and interpreting the data. It is important that the tools used by a forensic investigator are tested and verified to *not* alter MAC data.

All files stored on any file system are stamped with the time and date they were created, the last time they were accessed, and the last time they were modified. MAC data is easily viewed using a wide variety of commercial and shareware utilities. Figure 9.5 shows an example. Used in conjunction with other information found on the computer, it might be possible to identify what user was the last to access or modify a file and perhaps even who created it. A short discussion about each of the MAC attributes is in order here.

Create The create attribute on a file is generated the first time that the file is saved to the file system. Note that it is *not* necessarily the date that the file was originally saved. How can this be? Two things commonly affect the create date. If a user copies a file from one location to another, even though the two files are identical, each will have a different create date. The source file will show the date it was initially saved to that disk, while the new copy will have a create attribute that shows the time and date that it was first saved to the target drive.

Forensics		<dir>	2010-01-06 17:56:40	2010-05-06	2010-01-06 17:56:41.00	8	2 d	8 F
Directory Snoop		<dir>	2010-04-16 14:30:12	2010-04-19	2010-04-16 14:30:10.40	41	3 d	204950 C
Downloads		<dir>	2009-05-13 06:41:56	2010-04-16	2009-05-13 06:41:57.56	6	2 d	6301 C
Encase		<dir>	2009-09-17 13:02:52	2010-01-05	2009-09-17 13:02:51.14	19	2 d	327690 E
Forms		<dir>	2010-01-09 09:17:26	2010-01-21	2010-01-09 09:16:58.00	34	2 d	739656 F
Linux		<dir>	2009-11-05 09:01:12	2010-01-05	2009-11-05 09:01:11.21	21	2 d	884310 L
New Folder	x	<dir>	2010-04-16 14:30:12	2010-04-16	2010-04-16 14:30:10.40	39	2 d	(204950) ?
Practice		<dir>	2010-02-05 09:37:22	2010-02-05	2010-02-05 09:37:21.14	36	2 d	1574790 F
Research		<dir>	2010-01-06 17:56:40	2010-05-06	2010-01-06 17:56:41.00	11	2 d	24441 F
Screenshots		<dir>	2009-05-13 06:44:04	2009-05-13	2009-05-13 06:44:05.03	13	2 d	28365 S
Wiebetech		<dir>	2009-12-31 09:17:24	2010-01-05	2009-12-31 09:17:23.67	23	2 d	721456 W
Working		<dir>	2010-01-25 10:57:20	2010-05-10	2009-05-13 06:44:05.76	17	2 d	28657 W
_FRDI_CH2.doc		82	2010-04-10 09:31:08	2010-05-07	2010-04-10 09:31:08.81	25	3 ah	33662 _
_Word Work File D_190095863	x	82	2010-04-10 09:31:08	2010-04-10	2010-04-10 09:31:08.81	28	4 ah	(33662) ?
.DS_Store		6148	2010-04-10 09:27:20	2010-04-11	2010-04-10 09:27:21.63	9	2 ah	4542 C
?U_TE~3.PDF	x	640293	2009-12-31 09:23:36	2010-01-06	2009-12-31 09:23:33.46	33	1 a	(739933) ?
01_01.TIF		135460	2009-04-17 09:56:28	2010-04-10	2009-09-25 11:26:47.83	38	1 a	853218 C
2005_CDIA_Revisied.pdf		40839	2009-04-01 10:16:58	2010-02-24	2009-05-13 06:41:57.52	3	3 a	6296 ?
FCIV.EXE		84784	2004-05-13 14:26:48	2010-01-22	2009-05-13 06:43:58.38	8	1 a	24429 F
FRDI CH2.DOC		70144	2010-04-10 09:31:08	2010-04-10	2010-04-10 09:31:08.64	32	1 a	33663 F

Figure 9.5 Several readily available utilities allow the user to view the currently active MAC data for a file.

The other way that create-attribute time stamps are modified is through a file system utility that allows a user to intentionally modify the attribute. There are several commercial and shareware applications that allow this. Therefore, by itself the create attribute doesn't prove much of anything. It serves only as supplemental evidence to support other findings. Most applications that are used to generate files also embed creation metadata within the file. If a comparison of the two values shows a difference, there is sufficient cause for the investigator to look more deeply.

Access The access attribute is the most volatile attribute of a file. Any time any user views, opens, copies, or backs up a file, this attribute is modified by the file system. Each time an executable is run, its access time is modified. Even the activity of antivirus scanning software has been known to alter the access time stamp. In fact, merely right-clicking on a file in Explorer and selecting Properties alters the access time stamp. There is no way for the investigator to accurately ascertain what action was invoked upon the file—only that one of them was. Many applications provide far more detail in their metadata concerning access information. For example, using the proper utilities, it is possible to identify the previous ten times that a document was accessed.

Modify The modify time stamp is arguably the most valuable of the time/date attributes contained within a file. This information tells when the contents of the file were last altered. Any change to the file content sufficient to alter its hash value (which is virtually any change at all) is sufficient to reset this value. Actions that change the access and create attributes do not impact modify times. The act of moving or copying a file has no impact. These actions, however, will likely impact the attributes of the folder containing the files. For example, if a user copies NOVEL.DOC from C:\Documents to C:\User\Documents, the attributes of NOVEL.DOC will change as follows:

- SOURCE FILE ENTITY — C:\Documents\NOVEL.DOC—Create time remains the same, access time is reset, modify time remains the same.
- SOURCE FILE CONTAINER — C:\Documents—Create time remains the same, access time is reset, modify time remains the same.
- DESTINATION FILE ENTITY—C:\User\Documents\NOVEL.DOC—Create time is reset, access time is reset, modify time remains the same.
- DESTINATION FILE CONTAINER — C:\User\Documents—Create time remains the same, access time is reset, modify time is reset.

Entry Modified The *entry modified* attribute (unique to NTFS) is modified each time any of the other three attributes is changed for any reason. It basically says that something in the metadata that comprises the MFT entry for the file has changes. There is no indication of which attribute changed. By itself, this tells the investigator little, if anything. However, it does suggest that further examination is in order.

The MAC time stamps can all be easily viewed in Windows Explorer or in one of the Linux File browsers. Figure 9.6 shows these attributes displayed in the file properties of a file stored on a Windows machine. (The problem with this

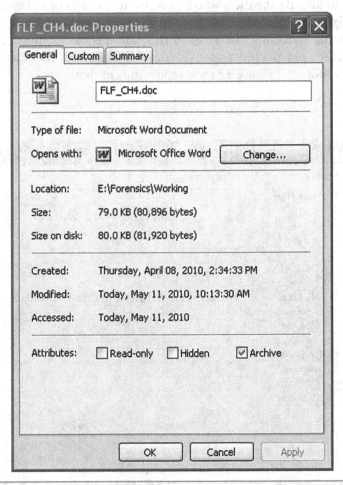

Figure 9.6 Windows Explorer is capable of displaying the Created, Accessed, and Modified file attributes.

approach is that merely viewing the file alters the accessed time stamp and is not acceptable procedure in the investigative process.) The entry modified attribute is not so easily viewed.

Using MAC

One of the first things an investigator does when approaching a new inquiry is to ask "Who did what, and when did they do it?" The who part is usually the more difficult question to answer, although the when can usually be narrowed down to a relatively narrow time frame. Once a specific time has been identified, it might be possible to identify the users who had access to the data or to begin the search for who might have gained access from beyond the network. Many applications feature filtering functions that assist in this task. Figure 9.7 illustrates a simple filter (a function of Directory Snoop) to locate all document files that were modified on a specific date. Figure 9.8 shows the results of that filter.

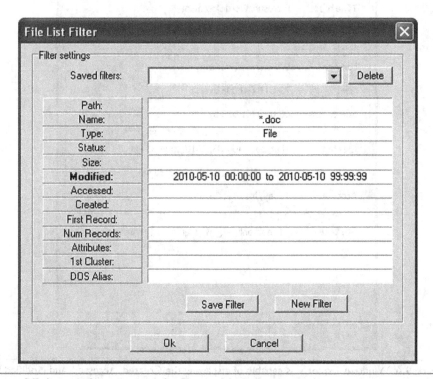

Figure 9.7 A simple filter to search for files modified on a certain date

Path	Name	Del	Size	Modified	Accessed	Created
E:\Documents\Michael\Passed Lives\	Passed Lives.doc		817152	2010-05-10 10:37:32	2010-05-10	2009-05-13 06:41:53.65
E:\Documents\Michael\Passed Lives\	Passed_Lives_2007.doc		653312	2010-05-10 15:48:18	2010-05-10	2009-05-13 06:41:54.03
E:\Forensics\Research\	Microsoft Office 2007 Document Metadata XML Parts S...		36864	2010-05-10 15:26:28	2010-05-10	2010-05-10 15:26:24.95
E:\Forensics\Working\	DA_CH5(2).doc	x	83968	2010-05-10 11:15:04	2010-05-10	2010-05-10 11:15:02.18
E:\Forensics\Working\	FIL_CH11.DOC		50688	2010-05-10 10:33:48	2010-05-10	2010-04-10 09:23:24.23
E:\Forensics\Working\	PROPOSAL.DOC		254464	2010-05-10 10:35:02	2010-05-10	2010-01-26 08:22:37.72
E:\manuscripts\	Pandora Notes.doc		43008	2010-05-10 10:36:44	2010-05-10	2009-05-13 06:44:09.22

Figure 9.8 The results of the filter illustrated in Figure 9.7

Obviously, a typical investigation will involve many different file types and events. Commercial forensic software often features a timeline functionality that allows multiple queries to be processed simultaneously. Once a time frame has been identified, the investigator may want to identify all files created or modified during that window. Perhaps it is important to know that a specific application ran during that time period.

The Sleuth Kit, an open-source application running on the Linux platform, can generate timelines on virtually any file system. With The Sleuth Kit, the process consists of two parts. The fls utility collects the temporal data associated with each file on the system and collects it into a single file, called the *body file*. This is basically just a pipe-delimited ASCII text file that contains one line for each file, listing MAC data. (Pipe-delimited simply means that the file is a text file holding records, and each record is separated by the pipe character—the one that shares the backslash key over the right Enter key.) Once the body file has been built, the MACtime program can be used to build a timeline based on parameters selected by the investigator. The Sleuth Kit includes the ability to build the timelines as do all commercial forensic suites.

Keep in mind that the full timeline of a case is produced from more than simply file access or creation times. A full timeline includes data extracted from

- MAC data
- System logs
- Event logs
- E-mails
- Internet history
- File metadata

Analysis of these items is covered in other parts of this book. Too much reliance on file system metadata can be dangerous, since antiforensic utilities allow knowledgeable users to alter that data to read whatever they want it to.

Document Management Systems

Departmental or enterprise document management (DM) systems generate large amounts of metadata that gets stored in separate files maintained by the application. While the overall process of document management is beyond the scope of this book, it is important to understand that when such a system is in place, information that can be critical to an investigation or inquiry can be found in places other than the file system or from within the file.

Different developers approach document management in a variety of ways. Therefore, it is not possible to review every possible configuration or option; there are some generalities that are common between most products. Virtually all of them offer version control, check-in/check-out functionality, auditing, and history tracking. The actual documents are stored as files in an archive. The document archive may be called an archive, or it may be a cabinet, a repository, or a directory. It is not uncommon for an archive containing hundreds or even thousands of documents to exist as a single file managed by a database, such as Oracle or SQL Server.

The typical document management solution is client/server based. A common configuration is to have a database server handle the functions of security and indexing, and a dedicated storage device such as a Storage Area Network (SAN) or Network Attached Storage (NAS) head to warehouse the data. The files are not necessarily of the same type. A DM solution might host PDF files, TIFF files, document files, spreadsheets, and multimedia files—all in the same cabinet. The application can be programmed to automatically perform automatic document retention/destruction policies. For example, if a loan application is intended to be kept for seven years after the loan is rejected, the DM solution might automatically delete the file at seven years and one day. Any time there is potential for litigation, there should be a preservation order requested to immediately suspend such automatic destruction of documents and logs and to preserve all files that may be relevant to an investigation.

EMBEDDED AND SUBSTANTIVE METADATA

The majority of applications that create or edit user files also generate important metadata that is contained within the file structure. Some of this information is viewable within some functionality of the program, while some of it can only be examined with specialized applications. Some of the embedded metadata is generated by the application, while some of it can be added by the user. Figure 9.9 shows some of the viewable metadata of Microsoft Word at the time of writing.

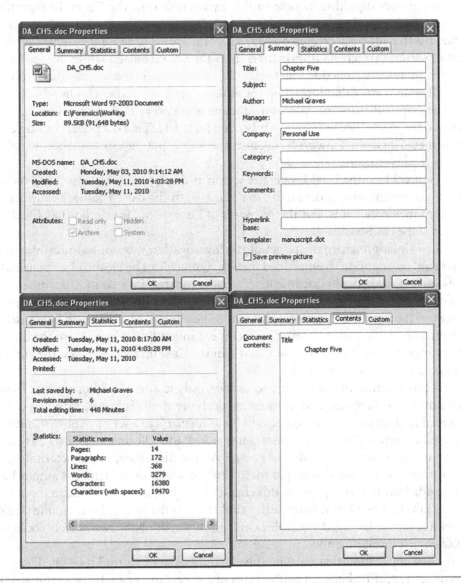

Figure 9.9 A compilation of four of the five Properties screens from a Microsoft Word document reveals the viewable metadata of this application. The fifth screen is of little or no relevance to the investigator.

Much of the metadata defined as substantive falls under the category of embedded metadata. Substantive metadata includes information such as embedded fonts, line and paragraph spacing, indents, and so forth.

An interesting thing to note in this image is that in the General Properties screen, the create date is reported as May 3, 2010, yet in the Statistics screen, it is shown as having been created on May 11, 2010. This is because the General Properties screen extracts its information from the OS metadata, while the Statistics screen represents embedded metadata. The difference is most likely the result of a fatal system error that locked up the author's system on May 11. On reboot, the file was opened from the Microsoft document recovery option. Apparently, this altered the create date within the embedded metadata. This is a perfect example of how metadata cannot always be taken at face value, but requires intelligent analysis by the investigator.

Figure 9.10 is the final Properties screen as displayed by Microsoft. Virtually all of this information is data that can be entered by the user. These are considered custom metadata fields. For the purposes of illustration, the author has filled in some of the fields available.

In a situation where the target of the investigation was not technically astute and paid no attention to embedded metadata, much can be gleaned from an analysis of this data. If the document is being compared to a control document, a difference in revision numbers might suggest that the document was altered between the times that the two documents were altered. Also, the field in Statistics identifying the last user to save the document might be different from the document owner, if such information is saved in the Custom field, or from the author as saved in the Summary field.

A more technically astute suspect is very likely to alter this information. There are numerous shareware and freeware applications on the Internet, as well as commercial applications, whose sole reason for existence is to alter or remove metadata from documents. Therefore, if a user wants to hide this information, it isn't difficult.

Another thing to consider as a result of this discussion is the nefarious use that the metadata files can be put to. In this particular document, the author has embedded the first two pages of this chapter into the Comments field in the summary tab (Figure 9.11). A drug dealer could store a list of suppliers, a pimp could have a complete listing of available talent, or hundreds of phone numbers could be hidden in a similar manner.

Each application that creates embedded metadata can read its own. There is some compatibility between applications of a suite, but not a lot. For example, the embedded metadata of a PowerPoint file can indicate how many slides are in a presentation. Of what use is that to Word? Music files can host a large amount of

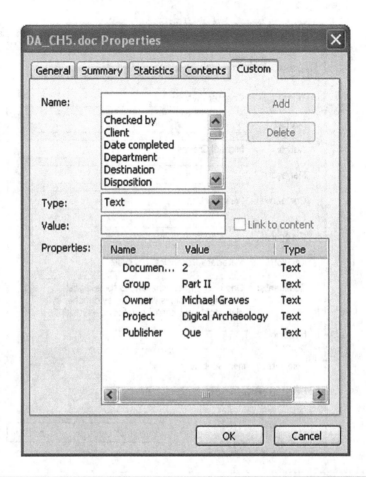

Figure 9.10 Some applications allow the user to add personalized information in custom metadata fields.

data viewable in applications such as iTunes or Windows Media that identifies the song title, composer, artist, and dozens of other bits of information. Figure 9.12 shows just a fraction of the data available from the metadata of typical music files.

The majority of document metadata is easily viewable from within the application that created the file. Viewing the document properties exposes most of the metadata in Word, and there is a wide variety of metadata editors out there for image and music files.

Some critical metadata is hidden. A rather embarrassing incident happened to the British government in 2003, when a spokesperson released a dossier supposedly

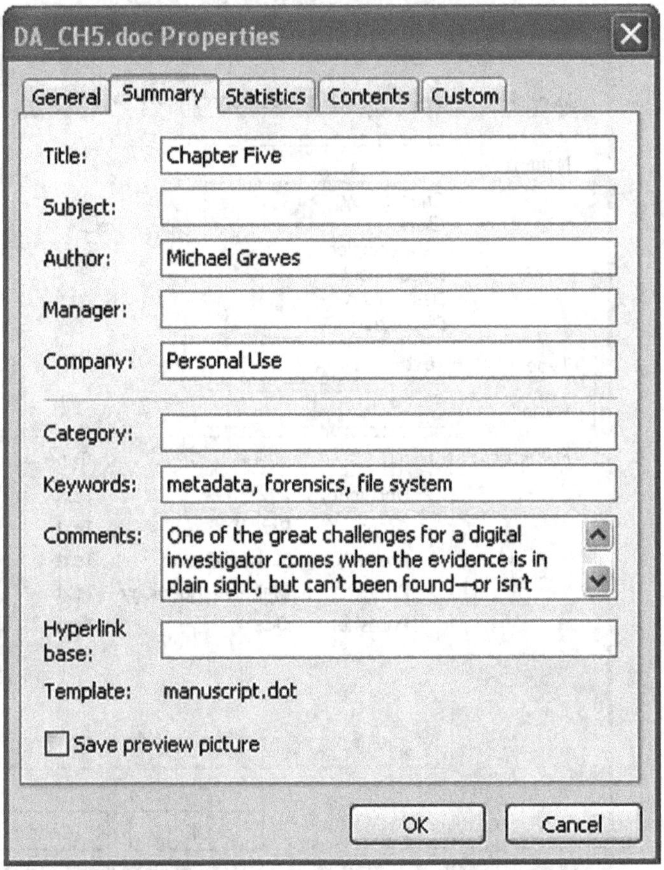

Figure 9.11 A relatively large amount of user data can be stored in the hidden metadata fields of a typical document.

produced by their intelligence services. Dr. Glen Rangwala of Cambridge University was able to prove that the document was actually produced by a U.S. researcher by extracting the revision logs from the document (Thompson 2003). These logs are not visible through any conventional method but can be viewed by way of several third-party utilities. One utility called DocScrubber is a free utility from Java-Cool Software that can do this. Figure 9.13 shows the metadata uncovered from a document by this utility that reveals eight different revisions by three authors (only two of which appear in the screenshot).

Figure 9.12 Most files created by user applications embed large amounts of custom metadata into the file package.

A sample of useful data that can be extracted from a documents metadata includes

- User name
- User initials
- Organization name (if configured on the system)
- Computer name
- Document storage location
- Names of previous authors
- Revision log (Word, Excel)
- Version log (Word)
- Template file name (Word, PowerPoint)
- Hidden text (Word, Excel)
- Globally Unique Identifiers (GUIDs)

```
 1   DOC SCRUBBER v1.1
 2   Analysis Performed at 8:09:36 AM on 5/26/2010
 3   File Analyzed: E:\Documents\Systems\GX270.doc
 4
 5   Title:
 6   Author: Michael Graves
 7   Company: Personal Use
 8   Keywords:
 9   Subject:
10   Comments:
11   Template Used: Normal.dot
12   Application: Microsoft Word 9.0
13   Created: 7/28/2005 1:28:00 PM
14   Last Saved: 11/22/2005 5:57:00 PM
15   Last Edited By: Wm. Rollins
16   Last Printed: 11/22/2005 5:56:00 PM
17   Page Count: 1
18   Word Count: 202
19   Character Count: 1157
20   Revision Count: 10
21   Total Editing Time (minutes): 24
22
23   Unique Identifier (GUID): Not Found.
24   Recent Hyperlinks List: Not Found.
25
26   Revision Log: Found 7 hidden revision(s)
27   "Michael Graves" edited file: "D:\Documents and Settings\Michael Graves\Desktop\Doc1.doc"
28   "Michael Graves" edited file: "C:\Shared\Internet For XP signon.doc"
29   "Michael Graves" edited file: "C:\Documents and Settings\52750\Application
     Data\Microsoft\Word\AutoRecovery save of Internet For XP signon.asd"
30   "Wm. Rollins" edited file: "C:\Shared\GX270.doc"
31   "Wm. Rollins" edited file: "C:\Shared\GX270.doc"
32   "Wm. Rollins" edited file: "C:\Shared\GX270.doc"
33   "Wm. Rollins" edited file: "E:\Documents\Systems\GX270.doc"
```

Figure 9.13 Revision logs can reveal much about a document that is not visible from the application.

Most applications can be configured to not save certain information, and there are also third-party utilities that can "cleanse" a document of this information. Therefore, it should not be expected that every document will expose each and all of these bits of data. For an example of examining a specific document, see the sidebar entitled *Digging Deeper into the Document History*.

DIGGING DEEPER INTO THE DOCUMENT HISTORY

For the forensic investigator, finding a file is only the beginning of the search. After that, the real fun begins. Who really created it, and was it altered in the meantime? Are there other versions out there somewhere? In this exercise, the reader should refer to Figure 9.12 and look at some of the information that DocScrubber provided in its analysis of the sample document.

The metadata shows that the original author was the same person as the one who wrote this book. However, it was last edited by Wm. Rollins, and in fact, the last several edits were done by Mr. or Ms. Rollins. This may be meaningless, unless of course, Mr. Graves insists that he did all of the work on the document and that there was no opportunity for anyone to make any changes . . . or unless M. Rollins is claiming to be the original author.

One piece of information that requires a bit of interpretation is found in lines 20 and 21. DocScrubber reports 10 versions of this file, but an editing time of 24 minutes. Even if the revision logs are not available, this suggests that the file has been renamed at some time. Why is that? Unless one is a very fast editor and typist, 2.4 minutes per edit seems to suggest very fast work on somebody's part. On the other hand, if a file is renamed and then reopened, it is seen as a new file the first time it is opened and the editing clock starts over. Perhaps the investigator might find another copy of this file elsewhere under a different name. Do a strings search for some text extracted from the file.

The file was also printed on 11/22. That suggests that the possibility that hard copy of the file has been distributed. Only the investigator will know if this is a significant factor or not, but it certainly brings suspicion to the claim "Nobody else has seen this file."

The metadata log also tells us the file changed names twice along the way. The first change, from Doc1.doc to Internet for XP Signon.doc, won't come as any surprise. That shows the creation of the document and the first file name it was saved under. Then after M. Rollins takes control of the file, it suddenly becomes GX270.doc. So this is where the reported editing time began. Now, if this was a large file with only 22 minutes of editing time, we would have additional reason to be suspicious of any claim that Rollins was the author.

We also see an autorecovery file (Internet for XP Signon.asd) listed. Can we find a temporary file on the system that contains a different version of this file? Does the file still exist under its original name, and what differences can we find?

Additional embedded metadata that can be found in documents includes a substantial amount of user data that "hides" in the file. The formulae used in a spreadsheet are contained within the file. Unless it is hidden, a user can view the syntax of a formula by clicking on a cell that contains a formula. A document with the Track Changes feature enabled might contain large amounts of information embedded in the file. Some of the embedded metadata contained in a file includes

- Formulae
- Hyperlinks
- Hidden columns
- Tracked edits

- Fields
- Database links
- Embedded object information
- Hidden text or numbers
- Alternate streams

MINING THE TEMPORARY FILES

Modern operating systems rely very heavily on the services of temporary files that are created in the process of running an application, editing files, or performing searches. The general idea is that once a temporary file is no longer needed, the OS automatically deletes that file. However, not all temporary files are successfully deleted by the OS. An improper shutdown of the system results in a large number of temporary files that are permanently stored on the hard disk. So in essence, they are no longer temporary. By knowing the extension and default locations of temporary files created by specific applications, the investigator can go looking for specific types of files. According to a Microsoft article (Technet 2005), there are three sets of circumstances that result in temporary files:

- Files created by desktop applications to facilitate editing (undo files, scratch files, and so forth)
- Backwardly compatible applications that require swap files in order to run on the current system (such as MS-DOS files running on a Windows system)
- Spooler files created when a print job is sent to the printer

Internet Explorer, as well as virtually all other Internet browsers, also keeps a cache of files from recently visited Web sites so that the page will load more quickly if the user returns to that site. Additionally, many applications create "autosave" files so that if the system crashes while the user is working on a document, all unsaved work will not necessarily be lost. Some temporary files can be identified by characters added to the file name. Table 9.3 is a list of some of the commonly produced temporary files that can be found on a typical system. Note that the default locations listed can be changed by the user with most, if not all, of the applications listed. A little searching might be required on the part of the investigator.

Table 9.3 Some Common Temporary Files

Identifier	Application(s)	Description	Location
*.abk	Corel Draw	Automatic backup	%user%\Application Data\Local\Temp
*.asd	Microsoft Word	Autorecover file	%user%\Application Data\Microsoft\ Word\Startup
*.asv or .arf	DataCad	Autosave file	DataCad Program Directory
*.bak	Firefox	Bookmark backup	%APPDATA%\Mozilla\Firefox\Profiles\xxxxxxxx.default\ (where xxxxxxxx is a random set of numbers)
*.bak	MS Word	V6.x backup file	Same folder as original file
*.bdb	MS Works	Works database backup	Same folder as original file
*.bk!, *.bll	WordPerfect for Windows	Document backup	Documents and Settings\%user%\Application Data\Corel\WordPerfect\(ver)\Backup
*.bkl (-9)	WordPerfect for Windows	Document backup	Documents and Settings\\%user%\Application Data\Corel\WordPerfect\(ver)\Backup
*.bks	MS Works	Works spreadsheet backup	Same folder as original file
*.blk	WordPerfect	Temporary file	Documents and Settings\\%user%\Application Data\Corel\WordPerfect\(ver)\Backup
*.bps	MS Works	Works document backup	Same folder as original file
*.chk	Check Disk/WordPerfect	Fragments of files saved by ScanDisk and CheckDisk process, WordPerfect temporary file	CheckDisk files are stored in the root directory. WordPerfect CHK files are in a user-configurable directory.
*.cnv	WordPerfect for Windows	Temporary file	Documents and Settings\\%user%\Application Data\Corel\WordPerfect\(ver)\Backup
*.da0 (-9)	Windows	Registry backup	%windir%\Sysbckup (WIN98 and earlier) System Volume Information folder on WIN2K and up)

Continues

Table 9.3   Some Common Temporary Files—cont'd

Identifier	Application(s)	Description	Location
*.db$	Dbase	Temporary file	DBase Home Directory
*.fnd	Microsoft Explorer	Saved search	Documents and Settings\% user%\Favorites
*.idx	America Online	Temporary Internet Mail file	/program files/america online/ idb
*.in0	General	Backup of an initialization file	Same folder as original file
*.llc	Laplink	Saved connection record	Documents and Settings\% user%\Documents
*.moz	Netscape	Temporary cache file	\Program Files\Netscape\Users\ User\Cache
*.mp3_	OSX	Temporary MP3 music file	Documents and Settings\\% user%\Application Data\ Microsoft\Windows\Temporary Internet Files\Low\Content.IE(v)
*.old	General	Backup file	Same folder as original file
*.pca	PCAnywhere	Registry backup file	Varies with the version of PCAnywhere
*.qbb	QuickBooks	Data backup file	Configured by user
*.qdb	Quicken	Backup file	Configured by user
*.qmd	Quicken	Data backup file	Configured by user
*.set	Microsoft OS	File set for Microsoft backup	Configured by user
*.sik	Microsoft Word	Word backup file (German)	Same folder as original file
*.spc	WordPerfect	WordPerfect temporary file	Documents and Settings\\% user%\Application Data\Corel\ WordPerfect\(ver)\Backup
*.sqb	SyQuest	SyQuest data backup	Configured by user
*.svd	Microsoft Word	Autosave file (early versions)	Same folder as original file
*.t44	dBase IV	Temporary sort file	%DBaseHome%\Temp
*.tmp	General	Temporary file	Various location on drive
*.w40	Windows 95 OS	Backup file	\%windir%\Temp
*.w44	dBase IV	Temporary index file	%DBaseHome%\Temp

Table 9.3 Some Common Temporary Files—cont'd

Identifier	Application(s)	Description	Location
*.wbk	Microsoft Word	Document backup	Same folder as original file AND Documents and Settings\%user%\Application Data\Microsoft\Word
*.xar	Microsoft Excel	Autorecover file	C:\Documents and Settings\ 40032\Application Data\ Microsoft\Excel
*.xlk	Microsoft Excel	Excel backup file	C:\Documents and Settings\ 40032\Application Data\ Microsoft\Excel
~WRD*.doc	Microsoft Word	Autosave file	C:\Documents and Settings\ 40032\Application Data\ Microsoft\Word

This is only a brief list of the most commonly found files and is not intended to be all inclusive. The investigator should be aware of the applications running on the target system and research the types of files created by the application.

Temporary files are automatically deleted by the application or the OS when the system or application is gracefully shut down. However, these files are treated as any other deleted file and, if not overwritten by later files, can still be recovered by most forensic software. Figure 9.14 is a partial listing of automatically deleted files found by Directory Snoop that could potentially be recovered if there was a need.

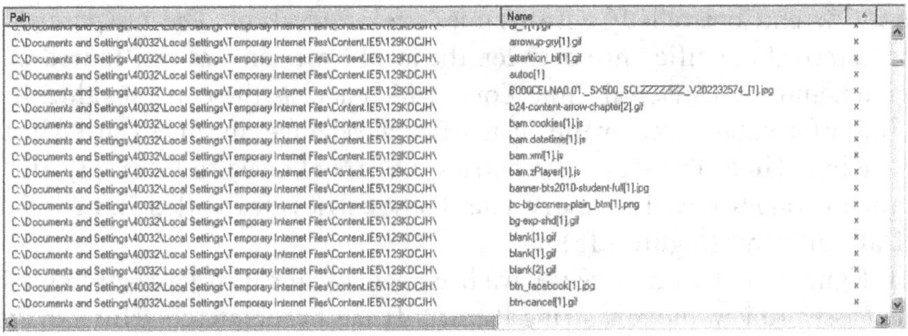

Figure 9.14 Temporary files that are automatically deleted can often still be recovered.

IDENTIFYING ALTERNATE HIDING PLACES OF DATA

So far the discussion of document analysis has centered on examining or finding entire files. For the average user, this is as far as a search needs to go. However, more technically astute individuals will know of other ways to keep information stored on a computer that will completely elude the casual observer, and might possibly escape the notice of a professional if not specifically sought. There are four common repositories for hiding data that an investigator should routinely check (if possible):

- Registry entries
- Document metadata fields
- Bad clusters
- Alternate data streams

There are tools for searching all of these areas. The following pages will discuss some methods for uncovering the intentionally hidden files. The use of bad clusters and alternate data streams for concealing data is not a function of document analysis and will be covered in Chapter 15, "Fighting Antiforensics."

FINDING DATA IN THE REGISTRY

The designated use of the Windows registry is to control how Windows functions. It typically deals with configuration issues, compatibility, functionality, and behavior of the OS and installed applications. It also contains a lot of user-specific data. The nature of registry entries and a Windows applet called *regedit* allows users to embed data in certain types of registry entry.

Some preexisting entries exist that are open for storing user data. An example of this is the time zone information key, located at HKEY_LOCAL_MACHINE\System\CurrentControlSet\Control\TimeZoneInformation. The purpose of this key is to record the difference between the local time zone, as configured on the computer, and the Universal Time Zone, which acts as the control value. It also contains information used by the OS to calculate changes in times caused by Daylight Savings Time. There are two entries that are allowed to be empty and can contain text values as well as binary data. These entries are entitled StandardName and DaylightName (Figure 9.15).

In Figure 9.16, two new keys have been generated called Password and Text. In the Password key, the text string Passw0rd1 has been entered. This can just as easily be an actual password to an encrypted volume or a server. An entire line of text is stored in the Text key. Why couldn't a drug dealer put the name and phone number of his Columbian supplier in a place like this?

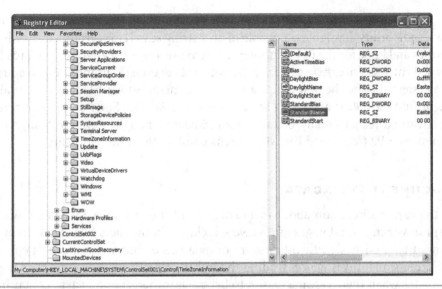

Figure 9.15 Many existing registry entries can be used to conceal user data.

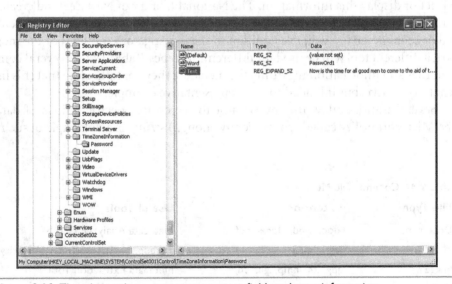

Figure 9.16 The advanced user can create custom fields to house information.

How does the investigator find such information? There is no easy way. Using the regedit utility, it might be possible to do a string search for certain key words or phrases and hope for the best. Another way is to use a registry analyzer to search for unused entries. Since there can easily be hundreds or even thousands of such entries in a system that has been used for a while, this might get a bit tedious, but it also might find the data that a string search leaves out. Paraben Software manufactures an advanced registry analyzer called (conveniently enough) Registry Analyzer as part of their P2 Command Kit. Most forensic suites offer a similar utility.

DOCUMENT METADATA

In the earlier discussion about metadata, one of the examples included a document in which several pages of text were included in the metadata. That example shows that a fairly significant amount of data can be hidden in a document. To the professional investigator, finding the information in a single document is no challenge when there is some reason to believe it is there. On a system containing thousands of documents, finding a single document containing hidden data is more of a challenge.

Different files have different types of metadata and require different tools to extract or display this information. The National Library of New Zealand created a universal Metadata Extraction Tool that works on a wide variety of documents and once mastered is a valuable addition to the investigator's toolkit. For the most part, a different tool will be used for different file types. Table 9.4 lists several common files and information regarding the metadata they contain. Note that this list is not exhaustive, but intended to be a representative example.

Several utilities allow the investigator to search for specific strings of data. The Microsoft utility called (conveniently enough) *strings* is an example of such a

Table 9.4 Common File Metadata

File Type	Extension	Useful Tools
Document	.doc, .wpd, .docx, .pdf	Metadata Analyzer, iScrub
Music	.wav, .mp3	Tuneup, BeaTunes, iTunes, Audacity
Image	.jpg, .tif, .bmp, .gif, .png	Metadata Extraction Tool
Web	.html, .htm	REG, REGGIE
GPS	.xml, .gis	TKME, XKME, Metascribe, Metavist, EPA Metadata Editor

utility. While preparing this chapter, the author embedded the sentence "Hidden data in the metadata fields can be a problem to find in large collections of documents." into the document's description metadata. Now that the sentence has also been placed into the general text, a general content search in Windows Explorer using any phrase contained in the sentence would find this document. Figure 9.17 shows a search based on the phrase "large collections." As it found several documents, the search string may have been too generic.

For the moment, pretend that the sentence is not in the actual document, but resides only in the metadata. The investigator suspects that a document exists with a word, phrase, or name embedded somewhere, but it isn't showing up in a general content search. The strings utility might help if you have a unique string to search by. For the purpose of this example, the author has now embedded the word "dirigible" into the metadata. The reason for such an interesting selection was to simplify the results for this example. The results are shown in Figure 9.18.

The command is used in this manner:

```
strings [-trigger] [file or directory name]
```

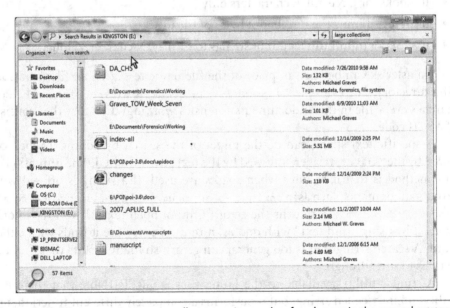

Figure 9.17 Most operating systems allow generic searches for phrases in the general content of files.

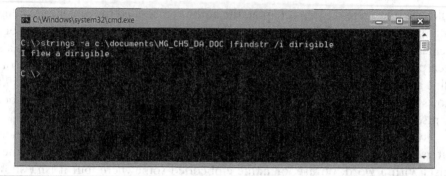

Figure 9.18 The strings command will find a desired text string even if concealed in the metadata.

Available triggers include

- **-s** Searches subdirectories
- **-o** Displays the **offset** within the file where the string is located
- **-a** Looks for ASCII characters only
- **-u** Looks for UNICODE characters only
- **-b [bytes]** Limits the number of bytes of file to scan
- **-n X** Sets a minimum length of strings to display, X characters long.

An asterisk can be used in place of the file name to search all files in a specific directory. For example, `strings -a e:\documents\forensics\working\*` searches every file in the e:\documents\forensics\working\ directory that consists of ASCII code.

A specific text string can be the target of the search by adding a pipe, followed by the `findstr` trigger, followed by the text string desired. The limitation of this method is that it hiccups when spaces are used. If a string is offered with no quotations marks, such as in `strings -a e:\documents\forensics\working\* | findstr find text`, it returns the error, "Cannot open text." If you try to outsmart it by using "find text" with quotes, it returns every file it finds with either word. A search string that is too general can return so many results that they are tedious to sort through.

A similar utility available to the Linux user is GREP. (Note that there is a utility in Linux called string, but it performs a completely different function, not related to text strings.) Grep turns the same tricks as strings in Windows. It does, however, offer a few more options and is considered by many to be a more power-ful tool. The following triggers are available to GREP:

- **-A num** Displays specified number of lines after the matched pattern
- **-B num** Displays specified number of lines before the matched pattern
- **-c** Displays number of matches found for specified text
- **-C** Displays two lines before and after each match
- **-e pattern** Searches for pattern (e.g., eixeixeix)
- **-f file** Uses a pattern from a file
- **-i** Ignores case
- **-l** Lists names of files that contain matches
- **-L** Lists files that have no matches
- **-w** Lists whole words that are matched
- **-x** Lists only whole lines that are matched

If the investigator is simply trying to find documents with suspicious embed-ded metadata, regardless of content, a better solution is one of the various meta-data analysis tools on the market. Virtually all of the professional digital forensic suites sold commercially have some version of a metadata analyzer. Investigators with these at their disposal are well equipped to perform a thorough analysis.

If one finds oneself in the field without such a tool, there are some utilities that will help. Metadata Analyzer can examine an entire folder of Microsoft Word or Excel documents and extract all the conventional fields from the file header, such as author, last editor, file creation date, and so forth. It will also report if there are custom fields containing user-added information. While it does not display that information, at least the investigator knows which files contain user-generated metadata. Figure 9.19 shows a selected document displayed by a report generated by the author. In this example, 33 documents from a folder were analyzed. The one displayed contents four custom fields and is worth further examination. This tool is offered as a free utility by Smart PC Solutions (located at www.smartpctools. com/metadata/).

FINDING DATA IN THE BAD CLUSTERS

Using bad clusters as a way to hide data is more of a theoretical trick than one that is generally seen in the field. The NTFS file system maintains a list and a bitmap of bad clusters it finds during disk checks in the file system's $Badclus metadata file.

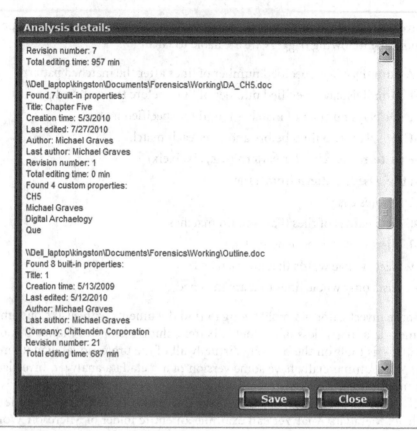

Analysis details

Revision number: 7
Total editing time: 957 min

\\Dell_laptop\kingston\Documents\Forensics\Working\DA_CH5.doc
Found 7 built-in properties:
Title: Chapter Five
Creation time: 5/3/2010
Last edited: 7/27/2010
Author: Michael Graves
Last author: Michael Graves
Revision number: 1
Total editing time: 0 min
Found 4 custom properties:
CH5
Michael Graves
Digital Archaelogy
Que

\\Dell_laptop\kingston\Documents\Forensics\Working\Outline.doc
Found 8 built-in properties:
Title: 1
Creation time: 5/13/2009
Last edited: 5/12/2010
Author: Michael Graves
Last author: Michael Graves
Company: Chittenden Corporation
Revision number: 21
Total editing time: 687 min

Save   Close

Figure 9.19 Metadata Analyzer is but one of several tools that can extract document metadata and display it.

Since the release of IDE drives back in the late 1990s, hard disks have managed bad clusters through the firmware. By editing the $Badclus file to include a block of sectors, these sectors will be excluded from those available to the file system and will not be seen by any traditional tools.

The Metasploit suite has the ability to do this. However, the difficulty of the process, combined with the subsequent difficulty of retrieving the data at will, has all but rendered the technique obsolete. It is very easy to detect that bad clusters are being used. All the investigator has to do is view the contents of the $Badclus file. In a typical Windows system, it is a zero-byte file with no entries. If there are entries, virtually any disk editing tool can easily locate those clusters, and the investigator simply cuts and pastes the data into a new file, saved to any media.

CHAPTER REVIEW

1. What are three forms of metadata that can be useful to an investigator, and how are they of use?

2. Discuss the differences and similarities between Windows file headers and the Linux magic numbers.

3. What is it about MAC data that makes it critically important that an investigator be very careful about how it is used and applied?

4. What types of metadata does Microsoft Word store in documents? Of what value is this information to an investigation?

5. List several types of temporary files that are of use in an investigation, and explain how they can be used.

CHAPTER EXERCISES

1. Download a copy of DocScrubber from www.brightfort.com/docscrubber. html, and install it on a computer. Create a document in Microsoft Word, and have each person in the class copy the file to his or her computer and pass it on to the next person. After the last edit has been made, use Doc-Scrubber to analyze the document. What do you learn from this exercise?

2. Open the file created in the above exercise on each person's computer. After a few minutes, the file will autosave. Try to find the file it creates. (Hint: It carries an extension of .asd.)

REFERENCES

Aguilar v. Immigration and Customs Enforcement Div. of U.S. Dept. of Homeland Sec., 255 F.R.D. 350 (S.D.N.Y. 2008) (No. 07 Civ. 8224 (JGK)(FM)).

Darwin, I. 1999. File(1). www.fileformat.info/info/man-pages/man1/file.1 (accessed May 4, 2010).

Linux Information Project. 2006. Magic number definition. www.linfo.org/magic_number.html (accessed May 4, 2010).

Technet. 2005. Windows temporary files. http://support.microsoft.com/kb/92635 (accessed June 8, 2010).

Thompson, C. 2003. Microsoft word accidentally reveals Iraq-dossier writers. *Collision Detection.* www.collisiondetection.net/mt/archives/2003/07/microsoft_word.php (accessed May 26, 2010).

E-MAIL 10 FORENSICS

Throughout history, people have used various methods of exchanging messages over long distances. In the days of the Roman Empire, long-distance runners acted as couriers, carrying messages back and forth. Trained pigeons have transported notes attached to their legs, and more recently, the U.S. Postal Service has served as an agent for transporting letters back and forth. In the Electronic Age, it is the wonderful world of electronic mail—or, more simply, e-mail—that serves as the transport mechanism for the vast majority of today's written communications.

The relationship of e-mail to crime is convoluted and appears in many forms. Direct criminal activities involving e-mail include phishing attempts, e-mail fraud, and extortion. E-mail can also provide evidence of other crime. Later in the chapter there will be an account of a murder that was solved in Vermont using e-mail correspondence to tie the co-conspirators together with the victim. This same example shows how e-mail evidence can be used to prove a conspiracy. This chapter focuses on finding e-mail, back tracing a message to its source, and analyzing e-mail contents.

E-mail Technology

An investigator who doesn't understand the basic technology behind e-mail communications is going to be at a distinct disadvantage when it comes to using e-mail as evidence of malfeasance. Understanding the technology assists in locating e-mail messages thought to be destroyed and helps prove the source of a message.

An e-mail message at its heart is a simple text message that starts at one computer and traverses a network or the Internet, finally arriving at the destination computer (Figure 10.1). Modern e-mail protocols allow users to send messages more complex than text in the message. Graphics and advanced formatting becomes possible with HTML. Files can be sent by e-mail as an attachment.

HOW E-MAIL TRAVELS

E-mail transport happens at three different levels. The **mail user agent** (MUA) is the application with which the user interfaces. Most computer professionals simply refer to this as the client. The **mail transport agent** (MTA) is responsible for getting the message from the sender to the recipient. The **mail delivery agent** (MDA) sorts out all the e-mail that arrives at a specific location and gets each message to the correct recipient. Dedicated mail server applications, such as Microsoft Exchange Server or the Linux-based SendMail application, provide MTA and MDA services without the average administrator needing to know what part of the application is performing what function. Some of the open-source solutions have separate applications for MTA and MDA.

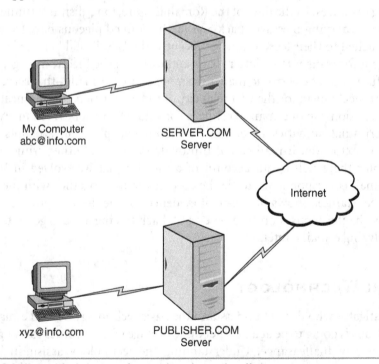

Figure 10.1 A simplified version of conventional e-mail traffic

To get from Point A to Point B, the e-mail starts at the sending computer's *client application,* or more simply, the client. A client is a program running either as a local application on the user's computer or as a Web application from the e-mail provider that supports the transfer back and forth of electronic messages. Once the e-mail's composer clicks on the SEND button, the message begins its path across several *e-mail servers* until the recipient's client sends a request to the server that provides e-mail services for that person to download all new messages. At that point the server sends all the messages that have accumulated. Depending on the client configuration and the policies of the user's ISP, the messages may or may not be deleted from the queue at that point. Every step of this process is a function of the e-mail protocols in use by the various clients and servers in the path.

E-MAIL ADDRESSES

E-mail addresses typically consist of three elements. The first of these is the user name. This is assigned to the individual by the e-mail service provider used by that person. The "at sign" (@) acts as a pointer that indicates of what domain this user is a member. Following the @ is the domain name that hosts the user account. Therefore, if William Robert acquires an e-mail address provided by an organization called *ringbox.com,* his e-mail address might be displayed as billybob@ ringbox.com—or generaluser@somewhere.com, as seen in Figure 10.2. This combination of elements separates him from users billybob@rodeo.com or billybob@ whitehouse.org, which are likely to represent different users, although William *may* have set up accounts with both of those other organizations.

The user name in an e-mail address is not necessarily indicative of the name. Most services allow the user to request a user ID and, if it is available, will provide that ID. For example, the author could request michaelgraves@yahoo.com. However, if that user ID is already taken (which it is), then he must select another ID that is available. Therefore, in the example presented here, if a person is trying to send an e-mail to the author of this book, and assumes that michaelgraves@ yahoo.com is the correct e-mail address, the e-mail is likely to be delivered, but

To...	generaluser@somewhere.com
Cc...	
Subject:	

Figure 10.2 The syntax of a simple e-mail address

not to the person intended. Likewise, if an investigator is searching for e-mails sent by the author, any e-mails carrying that user ID are not going to be his—*unless* the author has deliberately *spoofed* the user ID. Spoofing is a method of altering information to make it appear as if it originated from somewhere else. There will be more on that later.

E-MAIL PROTOCOLS

E-mail transfer requires separate protocols for sending and for receiving messages. As of this writing, Simple Mail Transport Protocol (SMTP) is used for all outbound transmissions of e-mail. Two protocols used for receiving messages are Post Office Protocol, Version 3 (POP3) and the Internet Message Access Protocol (IMAP).

SMTP and ESMTP

Sending e-mail requires the support of SMTP. Extended SMTP (ESMTP) is used as both a mail submission protocol and a mail relay protocol. For the purposes of this book, the differences between the two protocols is inconsequential. (A more detailed description of e-mail protocols can be found later in the chapter.)

The client connects to the server application over TCP/IP port 25 by default. However, due to the onslaught of malware targeting port 25, many ISPs are redirecting traffic to port 587. The client starts out by sending a simple handshaking packet, sometimes called the HELO packet. This packet simply informs the server that *user@domain.com* wants to send a message to *user@otherdomain.com*. The server examines both addresses and determines two things. First, the transmitting e-mail address is valid and is authorized to use the services provided by the server. Second, the recipient address is a valid address. Once the transmitted address is validated, and the recipient address is determined to be a valid syntax, the server accepts the message and attempts to transmit it.

The client will probably not send the e-mail message immediately unless the user uses a Send Now option or if the client has been specifically configured to transmit messages immediately. Most e-mail clients default to a queued transmission schedule by which e-mails build up and are all transmitted at specific intervals, such as every ten minutes. Likewise, the client, when attached to the Internet, will check the server's inbox at similar intervals looking for new incoming messages to download.

POP3

POP3 is the third incarnation of the venerable Post Office Protocol. It is the age-old standard for managing incoming e-mail messages. POP3 allows for standard text messages, attachments, and HTML encoded messages. Messages can be configured to remain on the server after download or be deleted. Once a message transfer is completed, the recipient can disconnect from the Internet and read the messages at leisure. POP3 transfers data over TCP/IP port 110.

IMAP

The **IMAP** (Internet Message Access Protocol) is a more modern protocol than POP3. There are two differences worth noting between IMAP and POP3. A key difference to the investigator is that, unless specifically configured otherwise, IMAP leaves all messages on the server after downloading. Another critical difference is that multiple users can administer the same mailbox. Therefore, just because a message is contained within an IMAP mailbox does not explicitly point to the owner of that mailbox as the person responsible for the message. IMAP uses port 143 for data transfer. IMAP is frequently used by people who use offline storage of e-mail messages or when multiple people administer the same mail box.

E-MAIL CLIENTS

Virtually anyone who owns a computer these days has some form of e-mail client installed on the computer, whether that software is used or not. Nearly every operating system that ships or that is available for download provides an e-mail client (Figure 10.3). A wide variety of clients are available either as a free download or as a part of a commercial software suite. Additionally, e-mail clients may reside on a host Web site and open as a Web page for the user. Some Web-based e-mail services allow the user to interface with a host client, while others offer only Web page support. Table 10.1 lists a representative collection of different e-mail clients, although it is far from being a comprehensive list.

Whichever e-mail client a user has selected, there are some main functions that are always present:

- Create and transmit messages
- Receive messages
- Display list of messages in inbox by header
- Open a message (and associated attachments)
- Add attachments to outgoing messages
- Receive attachments with incoming messages

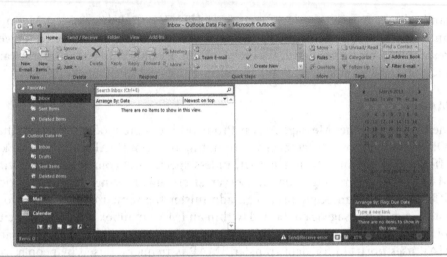

Figure 10.3 Microsoft Outlook is a commonly used e-mail client that is part of the Office suite.

Table 10.1   Common E-mail Clients

Client Software	Distributor	Method of Distribution	Platform
Entourage	Microsoft	Ships with Microsoft Office for MAC	Macintosh
Eudora	Open Source	Free download	Windows/Macintosh
Gmail	Google	Web-based	Web-based
Hotmail	Microsoft	Web-based	Web-based
KMail	Open Source	Ships with several Linux packages	Linux
Mulberry	Open Source	Free download	Cross-platform
OS-X Mail	Apple	Ships with Macintosh OS-X	Macintosh
Outlook	Microsoft	Ships with Microsoft Office	Windows
Outlook Express	Microsoft	Ships with Microsoft Windows	Windows
Pegasus Mail	Open Source	Free download	Cross-platform
Thunderbird	Open Source	Free download	Cross-platform
Yahoo Mail	Yahoo	Web-based	Web-based

The latter two functions are frequently limited or controlled by the e-mail service provider. In order to more efficiently utilize available storage and bandwidth, it is common for e-mail providers to limit the size attachments it will allow.

E-mail clients also control where saved messages are stored and how deleted messages are handled. A typical Windows user with Outlook Express installed and configured as an e-mail client will have one file containing their personal address book and one containing their mail folders. The address book will typically have a *.wab* extension, while the mail folders have a *.mbx* extension. For example, a user whose login ID is robchild will have an address book stored in the robchild.wab file and a set of mail folders in a robchild.mbx file. Users of the dedicated Outlook application will have a single folder with a *.pst* extension.

INFORMATION STORES

The various e-mail clients each have specific mechanisms for storing information. The information typically stored by an e-mail client includes the messages and the folders created by the end user for organizing messages, calendars, address books, and other information (such as notes, reminders, and task lists). Insomuch as there are literally hundreds of e-mail clients, it would be far beyond the scope of this book to cover them all. However, the vast majority of e-mail accounts are accessed by a relative few clients. In the corporate environment, there are even fewer. The different architectures this chapter will cover include

- Microsoft Outlook Express
- Microsoft Live Mail
- Microsoft Outlook
- Microsoft Entourage
- Lotus Notes
- Evolution
- KMail
- OS-X Mail

While there are notable differences in how each of the applications stores data, there are also significant similarities. An effective e-mail client stores messages and schedules in one file and address books in another. The reason for that is that the address book is frequently made available to other applications. For example, the personal address book (PAB) in Outlook can provide addresses, feed mail merges, and do other tasks for Microsoft Word.

There are two major Microsoft e-mail clients—Outlook and Outlook Express (OE). The two applications are somewhat different in how they store information, so a discussion about each one is in order.

OUTLOOK EXPRESS

OE was the default mail client in Windows versions 98 through Vista. Its lengthy reign means that it will appear as the client of choice on a large number of computers still in use. Versions of OE, along with the associated Windows versions, appear in Table 10.2.

OE 4.0 stored data in a file with a .mbx extension. In OE versions using the MBX file format, three files retained user data:

- MBX files: Contain text from all messages stored on system.
- IDX files: Index files for each MBX file. MBX and IDX files occur in pairs.
- NCH files: Retain the folder structure created by the user.

Since OE 4.0 is obsolete and rarely seen in use, there are few (if any) tools available for examining the system.

Subsequent versions all store messaging information in a database file with a .dbx extension. Thus, it is generally referred to as the DBX file. Other files used by other applications also use the same extension; therefore, the .dbx extension is not a positive indicator that the file is a data archive for OE. Two identifiers link a file with the .dbx extension to OE.

When viewing the file in raw format (as one would see it in a disk editor or if capturing the file with a carving utility), the header will begin with 0xCF 0xAD

Table 10.2 Outlook Express Version Evolution

Version	Windows Version	Release Date
OE 4.0	Windows 98	June 1998
OE 5.0	Windows 98SE	June 1999
OE 5.01	Windows 2000	February 2000
OE 5.5	Windows ME	June 2000
OE 6.0	Windows XP	October 2001
OE 6.0, SP2	Windows XP, SP2	August 2004
OE 6.0, SP3	Windows XP, SP2	April 2008

Source: PeoplePC 2011.

0x12 0xFE. Following the header, a **content class identifier** (CLSID) identifies the type of DBX file it is. A CLSID is a string at the beginning of certain types of files that the OS uses to associate the file with a specific application and to define the file as an object within the OS. In this particular case, the CLSID tells Windows that this particular DBX file is associated with Outlook Express and that it is a database object. Versions of OE that use the more common DBX file are more readily examined. Messaging information is stored in .dbx files. These files generally possess user-friendly names, so are easily identified. Typical DBX files include

- INBOX.DBX: The user inbox.
- SENT ITEMS.DBX: Messages sent by the default user.
- DELETED ITEMS.DBX: Contains messages deleted from the inbox.
- DRAFTS.DBX: Messages begun, but not finished, may be stored here, as well as messages waiting for further attention prior to transmission.
- OFFLINE.DBX: Exists on systems where the user has configured Webmail services, such as Hotmail. Does not exist on systems where Webmail accounts have not been configured.
- POP3UIDL.DBX: Tracks messages left on the POP server.
- \<Generic name>.DBX: Database for a user-created mail folder. For example, if the user has a folder called EDUCATION, a file called EDUCATION.DBX will be created.
- \<Newsgroup name>.DBX: If the user subscribes to a news group, a folder will be created for that news group.

The user's address book is stored in a Windows Address Book (WAB) file.

OUTLOOK

The full version of Outlook was designed to be a complete personal organizer, rather than simply an e-mail client. There have been several versions over the years (Table 10.3). Calendar events, contact information, notes, and messages were all stored in databases accessed by a common interface.

Outlook stores data in Personal Folder Files (PST, due to the file extension). By default, PST files are located in the user's Documents and Settings folder created when the user's profile is generated by Windows. However, this is a setting easily changed by the user, and therefore, a general search for PST files should be performed any time Outlook is the preferred application on a computer.

Table 10.3 Microsoft Outlook Versions

Version	Windows Version	Release Date
Outlook 97	Windows 98	January 1997
Outlook 98	Windows 98	June 1998
Outlook 2000	Windows 2000, ME	June 1999
Outlook 2002	XP and 2000	May 2001
Outlook 2003	XP, Vista, Pentium, 128MB+ Ram	November 2003
Outlook 2007	XP SP2+, Vista, Windows 7, 256MB+ Ram	January 2007
Outlook 2010	XP SP3+, Vista, Windows 7, 256MB+ Ram	July 2010
Outlook 2011 for MAC	N/A	October 2010

E-MAIL SERVERS

For two e-mail clients to communicate between one another, there must be at least one e-mail server—but there will most likely be two or more. In a corporate environment, where two employees exchange messages, it is possible for a single server to do all the work, acting as both an SMTP server for outgoing messages and a POP3 or IMAP server for incoming. Two people across the world from each other will each be connecting to their own server, and along the way, the message will bounce across numerous relay servers. Relays don't act as actual e-mail servers but can provide information valuable to an investigation, as will be examined later in this chapter.

SMTP Servers

The SMTP server handles all outgoing messages. In a typical e-mail system, the SMTP server might have an address such as smtp.mwgraves.com. The e-mail client must be configured to connect to the SMTP server whenever it needs to transmit messages. The client connects to the server across port 25 or port 587, depending on how it was configured. The server verifies that the sending account is a valid one and looks at the target address. That address is split into two components—the user ID and the domain name. If the target domain name is the same as the sender's, a subroutine in the e-mail software called a *delivery agent* hands the message off to the POP3 or IMAP server in the domain. If one server is performing both functions, the agent will simply paste a copy of the message into the recipient's inbox folder.

If the message is intended for an external domain, the SMTP server sends a request to a Domain Name Services (DNS) server to resolve the domain name to the IP address of a recipient SMTP server. Once the address is resolved, the server transmits the message to its destination, and then sits back and waits for a response. If the address is good and the message is delivered, an acknowledgment (ACK) packet will be returned to the transmitting server. If the address cannot be resolved, or if the user is not a valid user on the target system, a nonacknowledgment (NACK) packet will be returned. The latter will initiate a delivery failure message by the SMTP server that will go to the sender's POP3 or IMAP server, eventually to be delivered to the user.

The routing protocols used by devices along the way determine the fastest path between source and destination. A message is quite likely to be relayed by numerous intermediate SMTP servers before it reaches the recipient. Each server will append the header with a Received: line.

POP and IMAP Servers

POP3 and IMAP act as the post office for the network. Incoming messages are stored on these servers, waiting for end users to access and download them. With POP3, SMTP retrieves the message from the Internet, copies it to the message queue, and then notifies the SMTP delivery agent that there is a new message. The delivery agent transfers the message to the mail storage folder for distribution by POP3. With IMAP, the "mailbox" resides on the server and not on the user's computer.

This is the root of one key difference between the protocols that is particularly relevant to forensic investigation. While it can be configured to save messages until deleted by the user, the default configuration for a POP server is to delete a message once it is downloaded. IMAP defaults to saving the message on the server until deleted. IMAP also allows a single user to maintain multiple inbox folders, or for several users to share a single inbox.

The ramifications of these differences are significant. If the investigator sees that the suspect uses IMAP, then a strong possibility exists that the ISP still has copies of pertinent messages. However, additional corroboration will be required to verify that the message can be connected to a specific individual. In a shared environment, someone can use the defense that another user is responsible for the message. Conversely, even if a user is the sole owner of an account, there is no reason that the same user can't have other accounts on the system. Deeper digging will be required.

THE ANATOMY OF AN E-MAIL

The fundamental structure of an e-mail is based on a standard called the **Multipurpose Internet Mail Extensions** (MIME). A key functionality of MIME is to define the format of an e-mail. At the very minimum, an e-mail consists of a *header* and the *body*.

The header contains the control information used by servers to identify and direct the journey of the message. It is broken down into numerous fields to be discussed in this section. The body is the text of the message as composed by the author of the message.

Optionally, a message might also contain one or more attachments. An attachment is a separate file that is "paper-clipped" to the message and transmitted alongside of it. Some e-mails contain additional content even when the author did not intentionally add an attachment. Custom signatures added by e-mail clients transfer as embedded images. These images are sent as an attachment and displayed via a hidden link.

STANDARD HEADER INFORMATION

E-mail headers are metadata fields contained in every SMTP message transmitted over the Internet. They consist of multiple fields that contain useful information about the message, from source to destination. There are four header elements common to all e-mail messages. These are all fields that are frequently indexed by popular e-mail clients so that a user can sort messages using any one of these fields. These standard fields are

- TO:
- FROM:
- SUBJECT:
- DATE:

While superficially these seem to be self-explanatory, a little discussion is in order. The *TO:* field contains the name of the addressee(s) as seen in the *current state of the message*. Multiple addressees can be defined for a single e-mail. Each address is separated by either a comma or a semicolon (depending on the e-mail client used). Names in the TO: field should not be considered as definitive. This information can be overwritten and the message retransmitted, or it can be spoofed. When a message arrives in a user's inbox, the mere fact that her name is in the TO: field is no indication that she was the original intended recipient—or the only recipient, for that matter—even if her name is the only one that appears in the TO: field. Mass-mailing software sends the same message to every e-mail address in a database and can even customize the messages to extract information from lists and insert it into the message.

The *FROM:* field is even more likely to contain bogus information. E-mail spoofing changes the information in various MIME fields in order to conceal the origin of the message. Some viruses scour the hard disk of a computer where it just landed and forwards itself to every e-mail address it can locate on the machine. To the recipients of the relayed message, it would appear that this user was the person who originated the message.

The *SUBJECT:* line is optional and may be left empty. It is typically filled in by the original author, and if the e-mail is forwarded or a reply is sent, the e-mail client will automatically append the subject line with the prefix RE: which is an extraction of the Latin word *res,* meaning "pertaining to."

The *DATE:* field specifies on what date the message was sent. This metadata element is generated by the e-mail client that originates the message. Therefore, the time/date stamps on the message will be dependent on the clock set on the client machine. A sender can easily set the clock on her computer to any time and date that she pleases, compose and send a message, and the time stamp on the message will read accordingly. However, the time/date stamps found in other header fields generated by intermediate transport servers will reveal the correct time/date stamp. Time/date stamps on replies will be different from those on original messages, since, to the system, a reply is a new message being sent. As with the other fields, this is easily spoofed.

MIME Header Information

In addition to the obvious fields, there are a number of metadata fields populated by e-mail clients as well as servers along the path of the message. The header information in a typical e-mail message can be extracted easily from the e-mail client (Figure 10.4).

On the Webmail application of my ISP (hosting www.mwgraves.com), the header can be extracted as follows (Figure 10.5):

1. Open the message.
2. Click Mail.
3. Select Show Details.
4. Select All from the Header field.
5. Cut and paste into a word processing application.

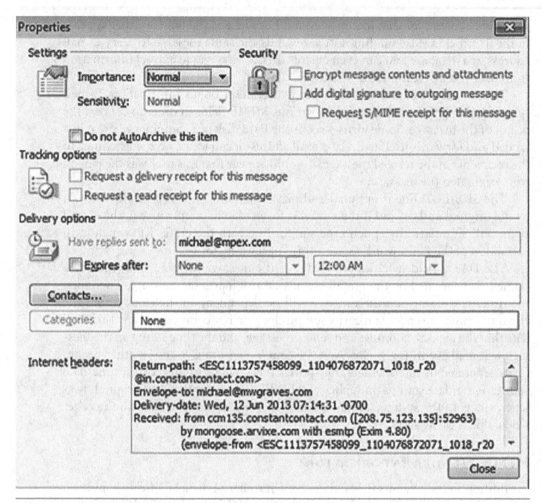

Figure 10.4 Internet headers can be easily extracted from most e-mail clients.

The header information can be extracted from Microsoft Outlook as follows (refer to Figure 10.4):

1. Open the message.
2. Click View.
3. Click Options.
4. Select All from the Internet headers field.
5. Cut and paste into a word processing application.

Figure 10.5 Finding header information in a Webmail application

With Microsoft Entourage (for Macintosh OS-X), the header information can be extracted as follows (Figure 10.6):

1. Open the message.
2. Click View.
3. Click Internet Headers. (A new window will open with the Header Information.)

Header information is read from the bottom line up. The following is an extract from a typical e-mail, along with explanations of the content for specific fields. I have interjected descriptions of key lines in bold that were *not* originally

Figure 10.6 Finding header information in a Microsoft Entourage

part of the header. IP server names and addresses of the network servers have been masked for obvious reasons. In most cases, time and date stamps should always be verified through external sources. Spoofing software can make times and dates to be anything the creator wants them to be.

Received: from exchange.matarin..com (xxx.xxx.xx.xxx) by MYSERVER.matarin. corp.local (xxx.xxx.xx.xxx) with Microsoft SMTP Server id 8.1.358.0; Tue, 6 Oct 2009 02:25:49 -0400	This tells us what server dispensed the message to the client e-mail box.
Received: from Carrier.matarin.Matarin-corp.com ([xxx.xxx.xx.xxx]) by homing. Matarin.Matarin-corp.com with Microsoft SMTPSVC(6.0.3790.3959); Tue, 6 Oct 2009 02:25:49 -0400	This is an intermediate server.

Received: from EMAILSERVER ([xx.xxx.xxx.xxx]) by Carrier.Matarin.Matarin-corp.com over TLS secured channel with Microsoft MTPSVC(6.0.3790.3959); Tue, 6 Oct 2009 02:25:49 -0400

This is another intermediate server.

Received: from mta45.e.bordersstores.com (Not Verified[207.251.97.205]) by Picui with MailMarshal (v6,4,1,5038) id ; Tue, 06 Oct 2009 02:27:06 -0400

This indicates that the recipient e-mail server is running a spam blocker called MailMarshall along with the server name and IP address of the server that transmitted the message.

DomainKey-Signature: a=rsa-sha1; q=dns; c=nofws; s=200505; d=e.borders.com; b=RSIjwxlm VQlkGAP8I/jEaURcC4skYJl-8FI74g0 MhGobvIApV9LADPYq2DI64bpAfxl-IUHmJLR=; h=Date:

Domain Keys are digital signatures for e-mails.

Date: Tue, 6 Oct 2009 06:26:03 +0000

This information is easily spoofed and cannot be trusted without external verifiers.

Message-ID: <bukxz55axsb4lrax-b73qe9jj9pmxjm.3093967756.7575@mta45.e.borders.com>

This is a unique identifier for the message. Only one e-mail in the world will have this. If it is possible get to the ISP or the originating server before the logs are flushed, it might be possible to identify the sender.

List-Unsubscribe: <mailto:rm-0bukxz55 axsb4lraxb73qe9jj9pmxjm@e.borders.com>

Legitimate mass mailers provide an address to query in order to be removed from their mailing list. This field is frequently spoofed by spamming software.

From: Borders Rewards <Borders@e.borders.com>

In this case, the sending user is an anonymous department name.

To: mgraves@mwgraves.com

This is the intended recipient.

BCC: michael@mwgraves.com

Blind Carbon Copy (BCC) indicates that the message that arrived was a copy of an original message sent to the user in the TO: field.

Subject: Your Rewards Coupon Is Here

This is what is contained in the original subject line.

MIME-Version: 1.0

This is the version of Multipurpose Internet Mail Extensions used by server.

Reply-To: "Borders Rewards" <support-bukxz55axsb4lraxb73qe9jj9pmxjm@e.borders.com>

This tells us what e-mail address will receive any REPLY message that I send.

Continues

Content-Type: multipart/alternative; boundary="=bukxz55axsb4lraxb 73qe9jj9pmxjm"	Content type can range from plain text to specific file types. Multipart Alternative refers to a message sent in a mix of plain text and some other file format, such as JPG or HTML.
Return-Path: bo-bukxz55axsb4lraxb73qe9jj-9pmxjm@b.e.borders.com	This is where bounced e-mail messages go when refused by target system.
Envelope-To: michael@mwgraves.com	This told the SMTP servers to send the message to this e-mail address regardless of what was viewable in the TO: field. This is typical of spam messages.
X-OriginalArrivalTime: 06 Oct 2009 06:25:49.0358 (UTC) FILETIME= [D89574E0:01CA464D]	This is the time/date stamp for the message's arrival into the POP mailbox. This is one area where the originator of the e-mail does not have access. A huge disparity between this time stamp and the origination time stamp is cause for further investigation.

TRACING THE SOURCE OF AN E-MAIL

As has been mentioned, one of the key points for the investigator to remember is that much of the information stored in a header can be spoofed. However, the attacker has no control over intermediate servers that exist between the source and target machines. When an e-mail is first generated on the transmitting client computer, the first of the headers is created.

When John sends a message to Sally, John's e-mail client will generate a FROM: header line containing John's e-mail address and a TO: header line with Sally's e-mail address. If John is using a cleverly designed bulk e-mail application, he can configure it to put into the header any FROM: address he chooses to invent. John's client application is configured with the server name and IP address of his SMTP server. He can also tell it to inform the SMTP server that his computer is any name or IP address that he wants it to be.

The SMTP server will take the information provided by John's client and generate the first Received: line, appending his information to the header. The server uses the Domain Name System (DNS) to locate the target mail server identified in Sally's address, which returns the IP address of the target mail server. A mail transfer agent packages the message and transmits it to that IP.

In a perfect world, where there are express routes from every point to every other point, the mail would arrive and the recipient's mail server could append the header with its information and that would be it. However, in the real world there are usually multiple hops along the way. These intermediate mail servers add their signature in the form of a Received: line. They don't identify themselves, but they identify the server from which they received the e-mail. And the next server along the path identifies them. None of the intermediate servers change the all-important message ID.

Each server maintains activity logs. If these activity logs can be obtained from the service provider, they can be used to ascertain certain things. For example, it is quite possible for users to forge message headers to make it appear that messages came from places they didn't or arrived at times of their choice. Comparing the SMTP logs to questionable messages can provide evidence of such tampering.

AN APPROACH TO E-MAIL ANALYSIS

When beginning a forensic examination of a body of e-mail, it is critical for the investigator to remember a few key points.

This is as much a legal matter as it is a technical matter. If working from a warrant, it is likely that the warrant spells out specific subjects or specific identities for which the investigation can target. Exceeding the boundaries of the warrant can result in numerous problems. Evidence can be disqualified, the investigator can lose credibility, or an unintended privacy breach can result in a lawsuit.

In spite of the massive volumes of correspondences a typical e-mail server might yield, only a few of those messages are of any relevance. The case will dictate the legal limitations the investigator faces, while the budget allowed will dictate the scope of the search.

Large volumes of data to sort through will not make the courts, the lawyers, or the clients more forgiving of the investigator who fails to meet deadlines. Time is the constant delimiter.

When the investigator does stumble across the proverbial "smoking gun" that solves the case, he or she will have to explain to anybody that matters just how the evidence was obtained, why it is relevant, and what makes it authentic.

The opposing party is going to do everything in its power to discredit all the work that is done on this side of the investigation. Document everything to make that as difficult as possible.

THE SEARCH

The first step the investigator must take when searching e-mail is to identify all sources of e-mail used on the target system. As seen in the previous sections of this chapter, different e-mail systems store messages (and therefore evidence) in different locations on the computer. In some cases, the evidence will not be on the computer, but somewhere out in the cloud. Web-based systems such as Hotmail, Yahoo Mail, and such typically provide each user with a fixed amount of storage space on which he or she can store messages. Client-based applications such as Outlook and Entourage store them in a database on the local system.

Once the archives have been identified, the search for relevant message threads begins. This of course begs the question, how does one find the few relevant e-mails among hundreds of thousands of messages in perhaps dozens of archives? And once a relevant message is found, how does the investigator keep the thread together? A thread is the complete string of e-mail messages, beginning with the initial message and following through each reply or response, all the way to the final message. Keeping the thread intact is critical if the outcome of the case depends on the reliability of the chain.

Searching the Archives for Strings

Typical command-line text search utilities, such as GREP, fall short in this area. If an investigator is searching for any message that contains the term "infiltrate," after a lengthy search, the utility will return any message that contains the word but will not segregate based on who sent the message. Care must be taken in the selection of search strings as well. Just asking GREP to look for "bright" will return every instance of that string, including words like "brighter," "brightest," "Albright," and "brighten," along with potentially hundreds of alliterations of the string. The investigator must use manual methods to locate and connect the entire e-mail chain from an archive.

Tools such as those by Clearwell, Paraben, and others facilitate this task. Dedicated e-mail analysis software such as these offer far more sophisticated search strategies. The investigator can search multiple keywords simultaneously. Boolean tools allow fine-tuning searches even further. Many offer deduping capabilities, eliminating wasteful duplicate e-mails. Filters that automatically compensate for time zone changes prevent mistakes in time line analysis.

Boolean operators are used in a refined search in order to limit results. A **Boolean** operator is a term that the user adds to a search phrase that is not a term that is searched but rather one that defines the search on a more granular level. Boolean words must be typed in all capital letters. Boolean operations include

- AND: The search must include both words (or both phrases enclosed in quotes).
- OR: The search must include either of the words or quoted phrases, but not necessarily both.

- NEAR: Both words or phrases must be included in the entity, and they must occur in close proximity to one another within the entity.

- \+ or "": Search for the phrase exactly as typed (do not put a space between + and first term of search string).

- \- or NOT: Do not include any entity that contains the following string along with the defined search. For example, typing [car –Ford] (minus the brackets) will bring up every entity within the database that includes the word "Car" but does NOT include "Ford."

Most databases automatically assume the AND operator in any given search. They also do not assume any relationship between words in a phrase. Therefore, the search string [Ford Motor Company] with no quotes will bring up every document that contains "Ford," every document that contains "motor," and every one that contains "company." Enclosing the same three words in quotation marks will return only documents that contain the phrase "Ford Motor Company."

A clear understanding of Boolean search strings facilitates an efficient search. Jason Baron was an investigator involved in many of the massive lawsuits involving the tobacco industry. He reported that the companies involved in the lawsuits generated over 1,700 electronic discovery requests involving e-mail, directed at various government organizations (Baron 2010). One of the search strings he used incorporated ten carefully chosen keywords combined with the names of the litigants and then modified by 35 different combinations of Boolean operators. This one search narrowed a field of over 32 million e-mails down to a "mere" 320,000. The difficult part is that while the search eliminated 99% of the pool, the remaining 1% had to be manually examined for evidentiary value.

A second problem inherent in using only keyword searches as a data mining technique is that such searches also cull out a large number of potentially relevant documents that simply did not contain one of the keyword phrases. Blair and Maron (1985) produced a study that indicated only 20% of relevant documents were located by keyword searches when dealing with large volumes of data. An organization called the Text Retrieval Conference (TReC) wanted to know if this ratio was still relevant after several decades and repeated the study. Their results were nearly identical (TReC 2010).

ANALYZING THE RESULTS

A large search of document archives, whether e-mail or otherwise, will result in four basic categories of result. False positives are those documents that were in no way relevant to the subject of the search, but were nonetheless retrieved during the search process. The evil cousin of the false positive is the false negative. This is the document that is relevant but that the search scheme failed to locate. On the positive side of the discovery ledger are the true positives (relevant documents that were retrieved) and the true negatives (irrelevant documents that were ignored).

There are two phrases with which the investigator should be familiar. *Precision* is the ratio of retrieved documents between true positives and false positives. For example, if an investigator's search of an archive of 32 million files yields 32,000 hits, those hits would be sorted between relevant and irrelevant. The percentage of true positives yielded by the method is the precision ratio. If 80% of those 32,000 files are true positives, then the precision rate is 80%. The other phrase is *recall*. This value is much more difficult to ascertain, and yet it is the source of much of an investigator's pain. Recall is the percentage of relevant documents that were retrieved from the initial mass. If the search technique that yielded 32,000 records actually found only 20% of the files that were relevant, then the recall was only 20%. Precision × Recall = Accuracy. In this example, 20% × 80% = 16%. These are all concepts to remember in Chapter 16, "Litigation and Electronic Discovery," as well, when the discussion about document searches focuses on a discovery request.

ADVANCED SEARCH METHODS

If it is indeed true that a Boolean search has such a low success rate, is there another option? Several attempts have been made at a more targeted approach. For a while, Columbia University worked on a forensics tool called the E-mail Mining Toolkit (EMT). EMT attempted to collect messages into groups that evidenced similar behavioral characteristics. Development of this concept has been discontinued, but the concepts generated a great deal of interest. Among the techniques developed by Columbia were the following (Hershkop 2006):

- Stationary User Profiles: Previous user activity was analyzed using known user accounts. An algorithm developed by the programmers created a histogram of account activity. This histogram was used to compare to other accounts (to ascertain whether a single user made use of multiple accounts) or against unknown message threads to attempt user identification.

- Similar Users: This analysis protocol collected multiple users with similar behavioral characteristics and created composite histograms. Accounts that dramatically deviated from the "norms" identified by these histograms could be considered suspect accounts, worthy of more intense inspection.

- Attachment Statistics: Every e-mail in the target repository is examined for attachments. Proliferation of attachments (retransmission to multiple recipients) provided an indication of certain behavioral traits. The software calculated a number of metrics regarding the cumulative collection of attachments. Among these metrics, incidence rate and spread were usable as a measure of threat.

- Recipient Frequency: The underlying philosophy supporting this approach is that certain types of users receive certain types of e-mails consistently and other types rarely. For example, a medical office or a real estate agency is likely to receive more image files than a library. Some users receive many e-mails from a small number of sources, while others receive large numbers from large numbers of sources. For example, a law office is likely to receive a lot of e-mails, but from a select group of transmitting accounts. A state agency will receive one or two messages each from thousands of individual users. These behavioral characteristics can be used to identify the type of account. An account that transmits millions of messages but receives very few is a strong candidate for investigation as a spam originator.

- Group Communications: Large numbers of messages sent to identifiable groups of users can be used to identify the type of user. Groups of individuals with pronounced similarity in last names are likely family groups. Collections of seemingly unrelated accounts that receive similar types of messages might indicate a club or business organization.

While there has been little progress made in the development of commercial tools that employ these techniques, other researchers have pursued the "concept searching" model, which does not rely on exact keyword matches. Rather, it looks for words related to a particular idea. ContentAnalyst is a company that uses this approach. They provide solutions that can be integrated into other applications that provide advanced search capabilities based on concept searching. Investigators start with a blank data set and feed the application terms that define the search. As the application receives data, it begins to build up the "language" of the project.

An example of this would be searches for messages relating to an automobile accident. Using a Boolean search that included the terms "car," "automobile," "crash," and "accident" would bring up a large number of e-mails at an insurance agency. However, it would miss a message with the header "April Incident" and the message "I trashed my ride yesterday." A well-designed concept search would find these messages as well. It works by creating clusters of phrases that mean the same thing. For wreck, the analyst could tell the application that related terms, such as "accident," "wreck," or any other synonym (either noun or verb) is a valid equivalent. The concept search takes any of the words that have been identified as part of the general cluster and finds messages that include those terms. The well-versed analyst will include related slang terms as well as literate terminology.

ContentAnalyst technology can be found in several document management solutions and is used by several software developers as an advanced search engine for their products. Companies employing this technology include

- Agilex (intelligence applications)
- AnyDoc (document management)
- Datacap (document processing)
- dtSearch (text retrieval)
- eIVia (information management)
- eLumicor (electronic discovery)
- Fastline Technologies (data mining software)
- H&A eDiscovery (litigation support)
- iConect (litigation support)
- kCura (electronic discovery)
- Planet Data (litigation support)
- SAIC (intelligence applications)

This list may not be all inclusive and is likely to expand as more companies recognize the value of the technology.

TRACING THE SOURCE OF AN E-MAIL

Often it is important to locate the source of a message. First, the investigator confirms that the IP address is valid. The **nslookup** command run from a command line will identify the URL of a valid IP address. If the utility cannot not identify the IP address, then that is a very good sign that the IP address in the header is not a valid SMTP server. Figure 10.7 shows the results of an nslookup query.

The first shows a successful query, asking about the identity of an IP address located in the header of a message that arrived from a trusted vendor.

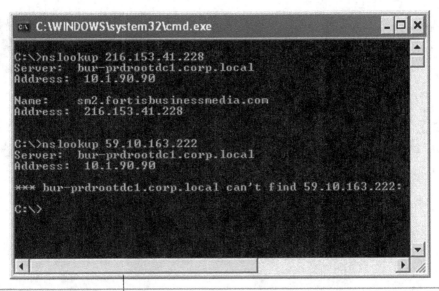

Figure 10.7 Nslookup is a utility that will resolve the host name when provided an IP address.

As expected, the URL reported was a valid address and not unexpected. The second queried address came from an unsolicited offer for a popular drug enhancing male stamina. Unsurprisingly, the query was unsuccessful. The sender spoofed the IP.

The investigator can identify each address using a **WHOIS** lookup if valid. www.whois.com is a database of URLs that provides a significant amount of information. WHOIS can query both by domain name and by IP address. Therefore, an investigator can WHOIS an IP address and find out the name of the domain. A WHOIS query of the author's domain identified the author as the owner of that domain (along with some personal information that was redacted from Figure 10.8) and provided the IP addresses of the servers that hosted the domain. It also provided the contact information for the host provider for the domain, including address and telephone number.

Note that none of these queries identified a specific individual. That is rarely possible without help from the ISP or organization hosting the mail server from which the message originated. In a criminal investigation, it might be possible to subpoena the mail server logs and message archives. During civil litigation, this information can be demanded during the discovery process.

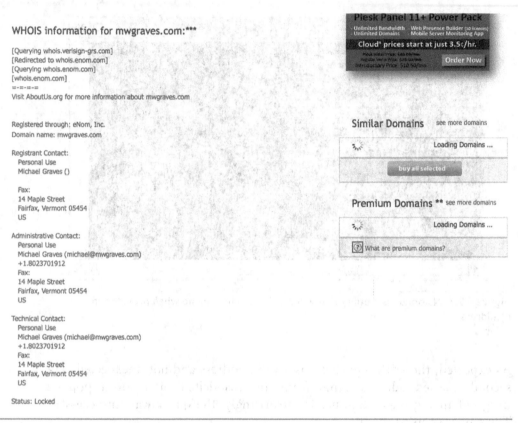

Figure 10.8 The WHOIS database provides a great deal of information about domains and/or IP addresses.

CHAPTER REVIEW

1. Explain the headers that are used in a standard e-mail message and why they are relevant to an investigation. Why is it dangerous to use information you find without some form of collaborative evidence?

2. What information can be extracted from an e-mail header that will allow you to trace a message back to its originating ISP?

3. Explain the concept of information stores. Why is an understanding of how different clients store messaging information critical to the success of an e-mail search?

4. Explain the concepts of *precision* and *recall*. How are they used in e-mail analysis, and what is each one's relevance?

5. What are two network tools of value to the investigator that are freely available on any machine with network access?

CHAPTER EXERCISES

1. Find an example of spam on one of your machines. Extract copies of the headers and analyze the message. See if you can figure out the originating server and, if possible, the ISP that initially forwarded the message.

2. Locate and make a copy of the e-mail store on your personal machine. Use the strings utility to search for several key words or phrases.

REFERENCES

Baron, J. 2010. How do you find anything when you have a billion emails? Author Blog. http://e-discoveryteam.com/2009/03/04/jason-baron-on-search-how (accessed October 22, 2011).

Blair, D., and M. Maron. 1985. An evaluation of retrieval effectiveness for a full-text document retrieval system. *Communications of the ACM* 28(3):293.

Hershkop, S. 2006. Behavior based email analysis with application to spam detection. PhD diss., Columbia University.

PeoplePC. 2011. Common Internet software versions. http://psc.peoplepc.com/articles/email/common-internet-software-versions-noimages.php (accessed December 3, 2011).

TReC. 2010. National Institute of Standards and Technology TREC Legal Track. http://trec-legal.umiacs.umd.edu/ (accessed November 1, 2011).

WEB FORENSICS

11

Often the focus of an investigation eventually finds its way to what a specific individual has been doing on the Internet. Internal investigations might concentrate on whether violations of company policy have occurred. Civil investigations may search for evidence of information tampering, theft of intellectual property (such as illegal downloads of music or other copyrighted material), or the uploading of corporate information to external sites. Many criminal investigations have turned on the evidence that the suspect performed searches specific to the criminal behavior under investigation. This chapter discusses how such information can be extracted from a suspect computer.

INTERNET ADDRESSES

In order to access the Internet, an operating system requires an application-level interface between the user and the OS. From a purely technical standpoint, the World Wide Web is merely a *very* large network. But since it is so large, standard file system managers such as Windows Explorer or the OSX Finder for Macintosh are not up to the task of searching the Web for files. The Web is more complex than a local file system.

Web browsers locate objects on the Web through a **Uniform Resource Locator** (URL). The URL amounts to a user-friendly (sort of, anyway) address to a particular point on the Internet. A typical URL is exemplified in Figure 11.1, which shows

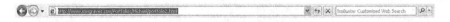

Figure 11.1 A browser's address line points the user to a specific URL.

the address of a Web page maintained by the author. There are several elements to this address.

The letters HTTP identify the **scheme** used by the resource. Generally this refers to the protocol used when accessing the resource. In this example, HTTP indicates the Hypertext Transfer Protocol. This is the standard protocol used by the vast majority of Web pages. Another common denominator is HTTPS, which stands for Hypertext Transfer Protocol Secure. This protocol incorporates encrypting algorithms and allows for the secure transfer of sensitive information such as financial data, personal identification information, and so forth. When making a purchase over the Internet, it is always critical that users verify the page in which they are entering such information employs HTTPS. There is also FTP, which is the File Transfer Protocol. Occasionally, large files are stored on FTP servers, and users are redirected to that site using the FTP protocol. Table 11.1 identifies the most commonly used schemes seen across the Internet.

Following the scheme will be a colon, followed by two forward slashes (://). In the example, the letters WWW indicate that the resource is located on the World Wide Web. This is the prefix of the **fully qualified domain name** (FQDM). Occasionally users may see prefixes such as WWW1, WWW2, or WWW3 in its place.

Table 11.1   URL Schemes in Use

Scheme	Description
http	Hypertext Transfer Protocol
https	Hypertext Transfer Protocol Secure
ftp	File Transfer Protocol
gopher	The Gopher protocol
mailto	Redirects to e-mail address
news	USENET news
nntp	USENET news using NNTP access
telnet	Telnet protocol (interactive interface)
wais	Wide Area Information Servers
file	Host-specific file names
prospero	Prospero Directory Service

This indicates that the browser is retrieving information from an alternative server to the one identified by the URL that serves this location. This is typical of sites that house so much information that it is stored in large server farms and not just a single machine. Many sites are not preceded by the WWW, and it is not required with most modern browsers.

MWGRAVES.COM identifies the specific domain. MWGRAVES is the domain name and COM is the URL suffix that indicates to which *top-level domain* it belongs. The top-level domain indicates which group of name servers will be used when searching for the site. In this example, the URL is of a commercial Web page. As of this writing, there are a total of 312 designated top-level domains (ICANN 2011), including a number of two-character extensions delegated to specific countries. There are several top-level domains (listed in Table 11.2) with which anyone should be familiar.

That completes the minimum requirements for a fully qualified domain name. However, individual files and folders located within the domain are defined in the path segment of the full name. The example in Figure 11.1 is for a Web page located two folder levels (/Portfolios/Michael) deep in the Web site.

WEB BROWSERS

As mentioned earlier, the Web browser is an interface between the user, the OS, and the Internet. A computer may have two or more browsers installed, but only one will be the default browser. This is the application that will open when a

Table 11.2 Primary Top-Level Domains

Extension	Description
.biz	Business
.com	Commercial
.edu	Educational
.gov	Government
.info	Informational
.mil	Military
.net	Network
.org	Organizations (originally nonprofit)
.travel	Sites dedicated to travel
.xxx	Adult content

shortcut to a URL is activated through an application or by a user from the desktop.

When a browser is launched, it first navigates to its *home page.* The home page is configured in the preferences and is whatever Web site the user prefers to see when they first launch the application. This may be a personal Web site or one of the major search engines, such as Yahoo or Google.

How Web Browsers Work

A Web browser, at its most basic, interprets documents created in the Hypertext Markup Language (HTML) and displays them on a computer monitor in formatted form. A browser consists of several major components. They all work together to perform the common function of displaying a Web page.

Externally, the user interface provides the tools that allow the average person to find, download, and read Web pages. Interfaces vary among browsers but commonly include

- An address bar
- Forward and Back buttons
- Bookmarking capabilities
- Intrapage search capabilities
- Configuration utilities

The workhorse of the application is the browser engine. It processes and transmits queries and acts as a controller for the next component, which is the rendering engine. The rendering engine takes the Web page language, such as HTML, and **parses** it, using the information to draw the screens and display content provided by the Web page.

The networking engine talks to other services running on the computer, such as the Domain Name System, to make connections necessary for locating Web resources, connecting to them, and transferring content from source to destination and vice versa.

A key feature of Web browsers that is of relevance to the investigator is that, by default, Internet-based data systems tend to negatively impact on local system performance. In order to minimize this impact, Web browsers cache information. What that means is, when the user visits a page, a copy of the HTML for that page is stored on the local computer. Certain content, such as image files, PDFs, and multimedia content, are copied and stored as well. The reason for doing this is that when the user visits a site repeatedly, the browser does not have to duplicate the efforts of downloading all that material again. It sends out a query to the Web site, asking when was the last time the Web site content changed. If there have been no changes since the last visit, the cached content is loaded.

BROWSING WEB SITES

When a Web site is first opened, a couple of things happen. The URL to that site is logged in the Internet history file. This isn't done simply to keep track of what the user is doing while on the Internet (although it certainly allows for that). This is how the browser keeps track of where to go when a user clicks on the Forward or Back buttons in the browser. Since browsers assume that speed is a critical element for most users and that many users will visit sites more than once, they create a cache of files used by Web pages. These include the HTML files and style sheets that comprise the page, individual images that make up the site, and even script files. These are the temporary Internet files.

The second thing that happens with most, but not all sites, is that a small file called a *cookie* is downloaded to the computer (unless that cookie already exists). A single site might load several cookies to a visitor's computer in a single visit. Cookies are small text files that store certain information about the user and the user's interaction with the site. This is usually information that the user voluntarily provides and not something covertly harvested by some agent launched by the Web site. While cookies can most certainly be used for nefarious purposes, for the most part they are benign tools to enhance the Web experience.

When you navigate to a favorite site and it already knows who you are . . . that is because on a previous visit it stored a cookie. When you go to Amazon.com and suddenly the page is filled with suggestions, it is because Amazon generated a cookie based on your previous searches. None of the Web site's intimate knowledge of a user's behavior comes from information about that person on the company's Web servers. It is all right there on the local hard disk.

A third thing happens in Windows, but it is accomplished by the OS and not the browser. The Web site is recorded in the registry as a "most recently used" (MRU) site. Virtually every application installed in Windows maintains an MRU list in the registry. Even if the files are deleted and then forensically wiped, unless the user takes proactive measures to do so, the entry will remain in the MRU list until it is eventually overwritten.

BROWSER SETTINGS

To do a complete analysis of Internet history on a system, there are several observations the investigator must make at the outset of the investigation. The browser settings must be recorded to start with. One critical setting is how the browser treats browsing history. The Internet Options (Figure 11.2) determine the default settings for how cached files are treated.

In Figure 11.2, the browser has been set to keep history for zero days. That means everything that the user views today will be gone tomorrow. The default setting is ten days. If this setting has not been changed, then the files will automatically delete ten days after it is first cached.

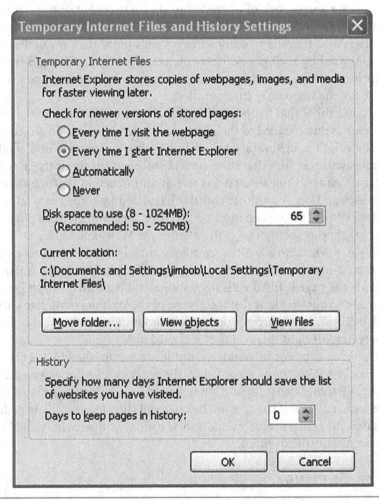

Figure 11.2 The configuration of the browser tells the investigator several things that will be useful in the investigation.

Another thing the configuration window tells the investigator is the directory to which cached files (temporary Internet files) are stored. This will be discussed in more detail in the next section. If a user has chosen to use a different location for any reason, the investigator learns two things. First, somebody knew enough about computer systems to change the default. This is something the prosecutor may use to her advantage later on. Second, we now know exactly where to look for cached files . . . or where to point our file recovery software in an effort to restore deleted cache files.

BROWSER HISTORY

Different browsers store history in different ways. Microsoft's Internet Explorer (IE) stores information useful to the investigator in at least three different places. Users with Windows 2000 and earlier will have a cached version of the history stored in `C:\Documents and Settings\@user:\Local Settings\Temporary Internet Files\Content.IE5\`. This is the default location IE uses for putting pages and images viewed by that particular user. Computers used by multiple users will have a profile for each user. The purpose of this directory is to speed up access to recently or frequently visited Web pages. `C:\Documents and Settings\@user:\Local Settings\History\History.IE5\` stores a noncached history without the actual pages and images. The cookies discussed earlier in the chapter are generally stored in `C:\Documents and Settings\@user:\Cookies\`.

Windows 7 handles cached data a little differently. By default, cached history is in `C:\Users\@user:\AppData\Local\Microsoft\Windows\Temporary Internet Files\Content.IE5`. However, in previous versions of Windows, IE plug-ins failed when attempting to write data to protected folders. In order to mitigate this problem, Windows Vista and Windows 7 create virtual folders in which cached files are stored. These folders are hidden and not accessible to general users.

Cookies will be stored in one of two places, both of which are hidden. `C:\Users\@user:\AppData\Roaming\Microsoft\Windows\Cookies` is the default location. This is where Windows will store cookies whenever possible. In Versions 7 or later, IE offers a "protected mode" operation. If this option is turned on, cookies can only be stored in low-privilege folders. In this case, `C:\Users\@user:\AppData\Roaming\Microsoft\Windows\Cookies\Low` is where the cookies will land.

The above-mentioned locations are all places for the investigator to look if forced to perform a manual examination. Most well-equipped professionals will be using a specialized tool. All of the commercial forensic suites offer Internet history analysis, and all of them are quite good at what they do. On the other hand, for this particular task, it is not necessary to have an expensive tool to do an effective job. Nirsoft

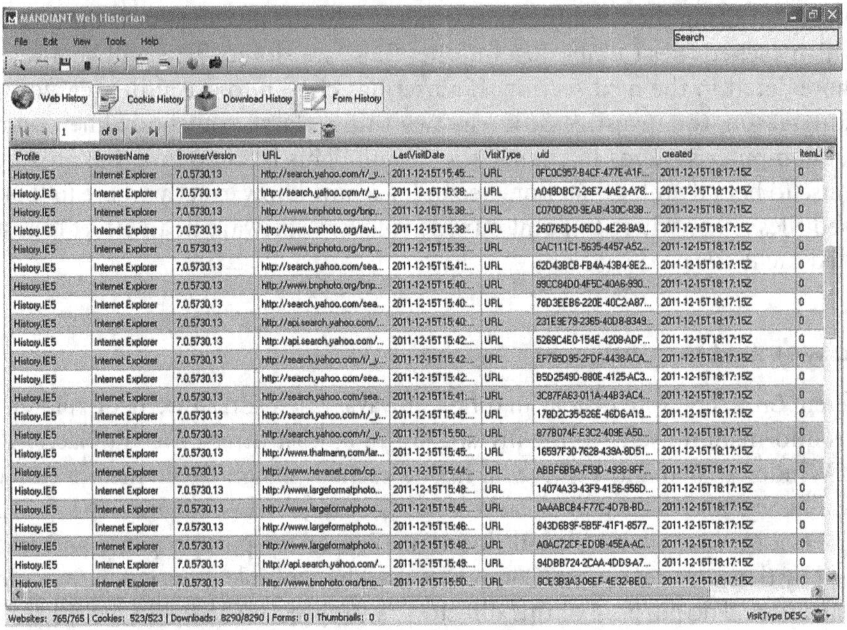

Figure 11.3 Web Historian is just one example of an application that facilitates the analysis of a user's Internet activity.

(www.nirsoft.net) makes available a number of different browser analysis tools as open source freeware. These include specialized history tools for IE, Mozilla, Safari, Chrome, and Opera. The popular Firefox browser is a version of Mozilla and can be analyzed by that utility. Additionally, the Linux forensic application The Sleuth Kit does an excellent job of analyzing Internet history on most browsers.

Another tool called Web Historian is useful whenever the investigator is unsure which browser may have been used. This utility scans the directory structure of the computer and identifies valid history files for IE, Mozilla, Netscape, Safari, and Opera. Web Historian (Figure 11.3) analyzes the files it finds and has the ability to output data into Excel format, HTML, or a comma-delimited text file that can be imported into virtually any database application. When data is output to a spreadsheet or database, an investigator can sort information in a variety of ways. Sorting by **timestamp** and then by URL is a good way to generate a timeline of activity.

ANALYZING USER ACTIVITY

The information located during browser analysis can be used to prove numerous points that a prosecutor needs to address. There are two aspects to conducting an analysis of browser history. The first part consists of finding and identifying specific records. The second aspect of the investigation is analyzing the history.

Identifying Specific Records

As mentioned earlier in this chapter, browser history can be found in more than one place in the file system. In addition to the temporary Internet files stored by the system, a history record exists in the form of .dat files. Also, the cookies stored on the system can be of importance. A user who configures her system to regularly delete history files may not eliminate cookies. Those files identify the Web site from which they originated.

The temporary Internet files will store cached Web pages, images, and PDF files that were downloaded by the browser during every session since the last time the files were cleared. Those files can be extracted and sorted by time stamp, by URL, or by file name by most browser analysis tools. DAT files require specialized software to read, but that does not necessarily mean proprietary or expensive software. Pasco is an open-source utility that will read the DAT files from Internet Explorer, Mozilla, and Netscape. It is programmed to search all of the default file locations for history files and can be told to search an entire volume. Once it finds a history file, it prepares a user-friendly file that displays the information from several different fields located within the file:

- **URL:** The full Web address of the record (including file name)
- **File Name:** The file name as it exists on the local system
- **Record Type:** Whether it was a browsed Web site or one to which the user was redirected
- **Access Time:** At what time the file was last accessed
- **Modified Time:** At what time the file was last changed
- **Directory Name:** The local directory from which the file was retrieved
- **HTTP Headers:** As received by the user when the Web site was first accessed

These records may be sorted in any number of ways. Sorting by URL allows the investigator to identify what files came from which source. Disparate time stamps on files from the same URL indicates that the user repeatedly visited that site—useful in refuting an argument that the user was directed there by malware and did not intend to go there. Sorting by access time allows the investigator to prepare a timeline of the user's activities. If it is necessary to identify specific types of files that were collected, a sort by file name will be useful.

Analyzing Browser History

The goal of the forensic investigator is to support or disprove the hypothesis that someone is either innocent or guilty of the crime for which they have been accused. Simply finding contraband on a computer is not always sufficient evidence to convict someone of a crime. Let us consider a hypothetical case involving illegally downloaded music. In this situation, the prosecutor needs to be able to prove several things:

- The defendant had knowledge of possession of illegal materials (contraband).
- The defendant took specific actions in order to obtain the contraband.
- The defendant had control over the contraband.
- If deleted, the defendant took active measures to destroy the actual materials and/or evidence that such materials once existed.
- There was sufficient quantity of contraband to justify prosecution.

It is not the job of the investigator to prosecute or defend the case. Therefore, this discussion will not explore the legal issues surrounding how each of the above points is defined. The investigator's job is to provide the information the prosecution—or defense, if that is the side being examined—will use in preparing an argument.

Note

For the purposes of this discussion, consider executive management to be the prosecutor in regards to an internal investigation.

Establishing Knowledge of Possession   Simply having a copy of a file on a computer is not proof that the owner of the computer had knowledge of its existence. Two common defenses are these: "It was an unwanted pop-up," and "Somebody else was on my machine." Two approaches can be made to demonstrate knowledge of possession. The *present possession* concept states that since the object is currently in the suspect's possession, that person must know it is there. Therefore, under this precept, simply finding a cached image of the file on the computer's hard disk is not necessarily proof of knowledge.

Many users have no idea that Internet data is stored on their computer. The idea that the user doesn't know about cache can be refuted if that person admits to having cleared the browser cache in the past. If the investigator can find evidence that the user has cleared the cache in the past, this defense is refuted. The presence, or the evidence of past presence in any directory other than the default directories used by the browser, is strong evidence that the file was intentionally saved to that location.

Evidence of deleted files has been accepted as evidence that the user knew of the material's existence. In *The United States v. Tucker* (2001), the defendant claimed that he had no knowledge of possession because the computer automatically stored the images in cache without any intervention on his part. The court finding disagreed with that argument, stating in its decision that possession "is not only evidenced by his showing and manipulation of the images, but also by the telling fact that he took the time to delete the image links from his computer cache file." This demonstrated knowledge of existence and the ability to control the image.

Tools such as Directory Snoop can locate the Master File Table (MFT) entries in the file system metadata long after the file itself has been wiped or overwritten (see Figure 11.4). This concept falls short, however, when the files are deleted by an automatic process such as the IE function that automatically clears cache at predetermined intervals. In this case, intent belongs to the automated process. Corroborating evidence to show that the file was deleted in some other fashion might be needed by the prosecutor. A comparison of the create dates and the delete dates on many of the images in Figure 11.4 shows that the file was deleted on the same day

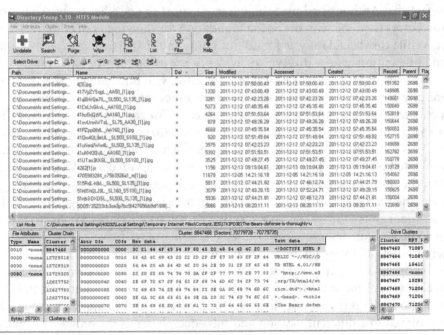

Figure 11.4 Most low-level disk editors, such as Directory Snoop, allow the investigator to view evidence of the previous existence of files long after they are gone.

as it was created. If the browser is only configured to flush the cache every several days, this is evidence of intentional deletion. Unfortunately, it is not much help if the default browser is set to clear the cache upon closing the application.

The idea that another person was on the machine at the time can be a little trickier to disprove. This generally requires the collection of corroborating evidence. Log files showing that the user accessed password-protected information or Web sites are one bit of evidence that can be used. In a Windows system, the Security tab of the Event Viewer might be helpful if it contains data records for that period of time. These logs show log-on and log-off times for every individual who has accessed the computer over time. However, event logs are set to a certain size, and older data moves out as the log fills.

Establishing User Actions The browser history goes a long way in establishing the intent of a user. It is true that many Web sites launch obnoxious pop-up windows that the user did not wish to see and had no intention of launching; however, repeated searches can reveal intent. In *The State of Florida v. Casey Marie Anthony* (2008), the digital investigators were able to demonstrate that Anthony had performed numerous searches for chloroform and its effects. This was in spite of the fact that Anthony had made a concerted effort to erase her browser's history. Prosecutors used the searches as the foundation for showing premeditation in the act. While the defendant was found not guilty in this particular case, it is still a good illustration of how this type of evidence is used in real-life situations.

Web history needs to be examined carefully, with both sides of the argument carefully considered. Occasionally the most innocent of searches brings up the worst sites. And many Web sites generate income for each mouse click they draw for the client Web site (in particular, those specializing in pornographic materials). Less scrupulous Webmasters design pages that instantly generate hundreds of unsolicited pop-ups. This is often referred to as a *pop-up bomb*. While these are often the result of navigating to the type of Web page the prosecutor is hoping to prove, they can also be the result of a Trojan horse received through an e-mail or other innocuous source. The unsuspecting person who has this happen to them is not someone who deserves prosecution. The guilty party may use this as an argument for how an image got on his computer.

A pop-up is an example of a *redirect*. In other words, the user browsed to one URL but either the client or the server responds to the browser application with an HTTP 300 response. This is a message that tells the browser that the requested resource has been moved to a different location and subsequently sends the browser to the new location. Another culprit is the *fast meta refresh*. This is where the Web programmer puts code in the header that automatically sends a refresh command to the browser, and redirects the page to a new URL. One URL is chosen by the user, but the Web page opens one or many alternate pages the person never intended to visit.

A redirected URL of any sort will be identified as such in applications such as Web Historian (see Figure 11.5). The application extracts information from the header to accomplish this. It should be noted, however, that the fact that a page is identified as a redirect is no indication that the resultant artifact is not the result of intent. Redirects can be the result of moved Web pages. If the owners of a Web site move to a different host provider, they certainly don't want to lose traffic because of a new URL. Therefore, they will program redirects for their old URL. Once again, the investigator is looking for corroborating evidence. Pop-up bombs will generate a burst of redirects. A long series of automatic downloads not identified as a redirect, followed by one or two redirects, is not a very strong indication of the user being victimized by a pop-up storm. Conversely, several dozen redirects in a very short period is strong evidence of such an incident.

Another source of potential evidence on a Windows machine is the registry. One can access the Windows registry by clicking Start then Run and typing REGEDIT at the prompt. One registry entry in particular that is of some use is HKEY_CURRENT_USER\Software\Microsoft\Internet Explorer\TYPEDURLs. Another location to examine is HKEY_USERS\.Default\Software\Microsoft\ Internet Explorer\TYPEDURLs. This registry entry stores values that are typed

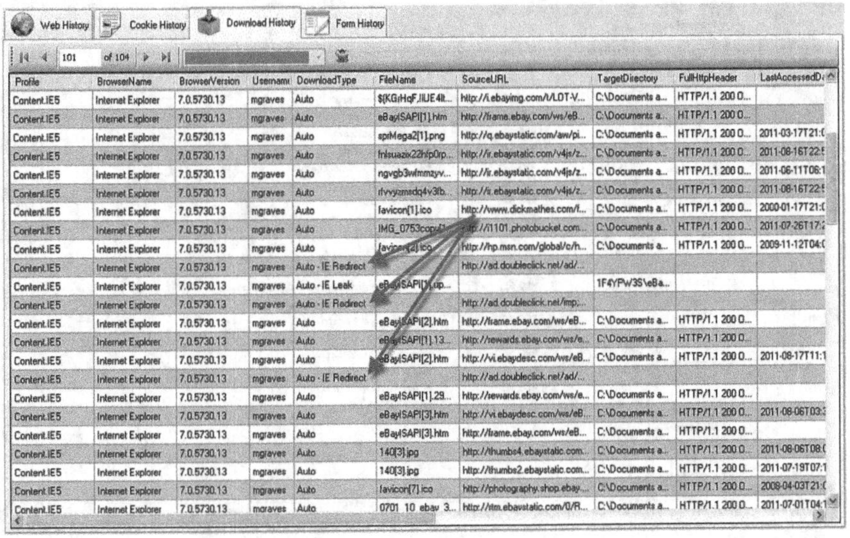

Figure 11.5 An application such as Web Historian can not only display the browser history but can also identify redirects and IE Leaks.

into the browser's address window by an active user. When examining the Typed URL list in the Registry (Figure 11.6), keep two things in mind. Quite a number of these URLs can be stored, and deleting the history or the temporary files in IE does nothing to eliminate them. More importantly, a URL recorded here is a URL that was not very likely "accidentally" accessed. A key point to remember is that typed URLs may not necessarily represent the exact URL typed in by the user. If Auto-Complete is turned on, and the user starts to type a Web address, and then accepts Auto-Complete's "suggestion" of a Web site, that site will now appear in the TYPEDURL registry entry.

Establishing Control of Digital Material   In the Tucker case mentioned earlier, the question arose whether the defendant had any actual control over the files found in the locations managed by the OS and by the browser. His claim was that since the browser saved files against his will, he was not responsible for their presence. The previous sections of this chapter discussed how to ascertain whether sites on a computer were intentionally accessed or were the result of redirects. Another defense frequently mounted is the "Trojan horse" defense: Malware made me do it.

If the investigator is able to demonstrate that the user intentionally navigated to a Web site that downloaded files to the hard drive, they will have a good foundation for

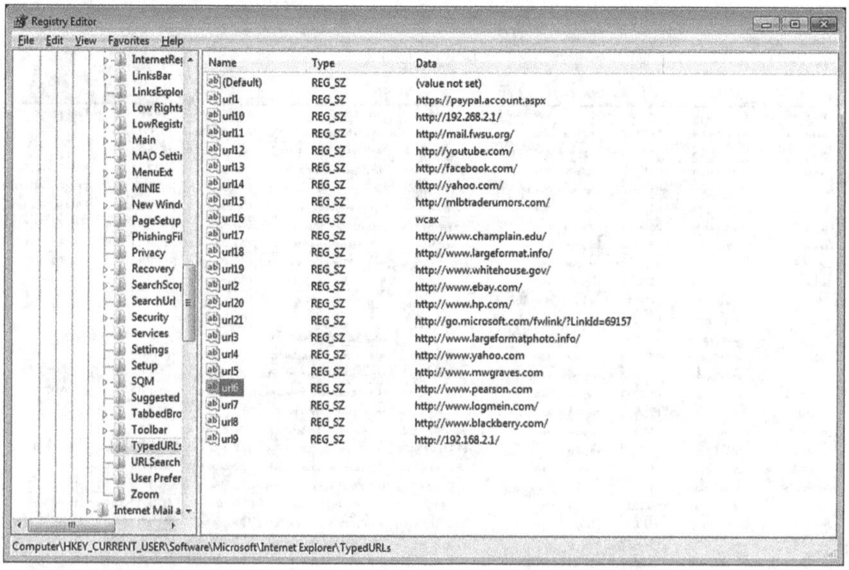

Figure 11.6 The TYPEDURL registry entry shows addresses that were accessed via the address bar of Internet Explorer.

proving both intent and control. If the contraband is stored anywhere else on the computer, such presence indicates the user actively manipulated and controlled the files.

The Trojan horse defense presupposes the existence of malware. Proving the existence of malware is easy enough. Many applications exist that will scan a computer system and report the presence of viruses, worms, and Trojan horses. Such a scan would be the first line of defense for a suspect. However, it should be noted that the presence of malware at the time of the seizure is not sufficient defense. It is essential for the defense to prove that it existed on the computer at the time the contraband materials appeared on the system.

When attempting to establish control over digital information, the investigator needs to establish the exact time the material first appeared on the computer. That would appear in the file properties as the create date. If the last access date is within a few seconds of the create date, there is strong evidence that the file was copied to the file system as part of the browser's automated process. An access date several hours (or days) later is difficult to defend.

Determining Active Measures Were Taken Did the user delete the browser history files, or were they deleted during an automated purge? That can be difficult to prove. Many document management solutions automatically audit file deletions and indicate what user initiated the action, along with an exact time and date. Unless specifically configured in advance, most file systems do not audit file deletion information. Therefore, it is difficult to prove the exact time at which a file disappeared from the system. Once again, the investigator needs to look for corroborative evidence.

Simply deleting a file does not wipe it. A file wipe eliminates the data from the surface of the drive. Look for the presence of file-wiping software on the system. Such software works by overwriting files with 1s, 0s, or random sequences of 1s and 0s. Files that are wiped are generally difficult, if not impossible, to recover. However, the fact that a file was wiped proves intent.

Disk editing software, such as Directory Snoop, helps to establish whether a file was wiped, rather than simply deleted. A few other indicators can show intent. In Figures 11.7 through 11.9, a file has been deleted in one instance and wiped in another. In Windows there are a couple of significant differences between the wiped file and the deleted file. A file deleted by means of Windows file system methods is moved to the Recycle Bin and continues to store data until overwritten by another file. A file wiped by a file-wiping utility remains in its original directory but no longer contains data.

The initial file was the netstats.bat file described elsewhere in this text. The original file was deleted, using Windows Explorer, and then emptied from the Recycle Bin. The file showed up in the Recycler folder as DC5.bat. Finding it was

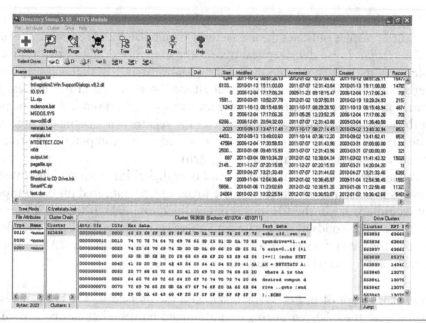

Figure 11.7 A file before deletion

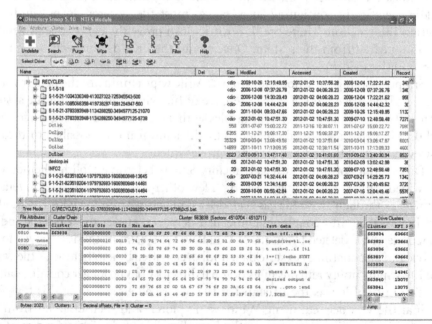

Figure 11.8 A file deleted by means of Windows file system

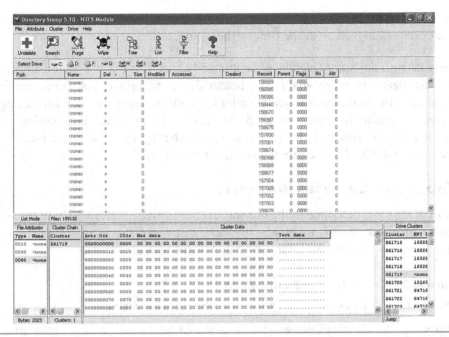

Figure 11.9 A file wiped by a file-wiping utility

simply a matter of knowing to check for deleted files in that folder and then doing a text search for a string known to exist in the file. The deleted file was no longer found in its original directory. An investigator who does not know exactly where to look for a file can either search for a string, for a file name, or for a known hash value (if the file is from one of the national databases of known contraband files). Examining Figure 11.8 shows that the data still exists in the deleted file. A file that is partially overwritten will very likely contain data from the new file that owns the cluster, but may be able to provide evidentiary material from the slack space.

The wiped file shown in Figure 11.9 still exists in the original directory (the root directory in this example). No data remains, as the software completely overwrote the data. Note, however, that the file name remains intact. The software used to delete this file did nothing to alter the MFT metadata. Much of the freely available software used to wipe files works in this manner. More recent products, however, are not so investigator friendly. Some products wipe the metadata as well. The Purge function in Directory Snoop is an example of that. As the name implies, the utility purges the MFT record completely. Recovering the file is out of the question (by any conventional forensic tool, that is), but the fact that it was wiped is a sure sign that user action was taken on the file. Now it is up to the investigator to connect a specific user to that action. As before, that is a matter of identifying what user was logged on at the time of the action.

Determining a Sufficient Quantity of Contraband Exists It is not the responsibility of the investigator to prove what is or is not sufficient material to justify prosecution of the case. In an internal investigation looking into employee misconduct, a single image or music file may be sufficient cause. In criminal prosecution, the investigator will simply indicate how many of what types of files were located in the suspect media. Let the prosecutor take it from there.

TOOLS FOR BROWSER ANALYSIS

Most of the tasks described in the previous sections can be performed by automated tools. Some task-specific tools were mentioned in various sections. Table 11.3 lists several readily available tools for analyzing specific browsers.

Table 11.3 Forensic Tools for Browser Analysis

Product	Browser	Target Information	Source
Pasco	Internet Explorer	INDEX.DAT	Freeware open source
Web Historian	Internet Explorer, Firefox	INDEX.DAT, Cookies, and temporary Internet files	Freeware open source
Index.dat Analyzer 2.5	Internet Explorer	INDEX.DAT	Freeware
Firefox Forensic	Firefox	Cookies, history, and download list	Shareware
Chrome Analyzer	Chrome	Cookies, history, download list, and bookmarks	Freeware
NetAnalysis	Internet Explorer, Firefox, Chrome, Safari, and Opera	History	Proprietary commercial
CacheBack	Internet Explorer, Firefox, Chrome, Safari, and Opera	Cookies and history	Freeware
Encase	Internet Explorer, Firefox, Safari, and Opera	Cookies, history, and bookmarks	Proprietary commercial
FTK	Internet Explorer, Firefox, and Opera	Cookies, history, and bookmarks	Proprietary commercial
HstEx	Platform independent	History	Proprietary commercial
Galleta	Platform independent	Cookies	Freeware

RUNNING WEB HISTORIAN

Web Historian is a powerful yet free tool that provides a wealth of information about a user's activity on the Internet. As of this writing, it is available for download at www.mandiant.com/resources/download/web-historian. Once it is installed on the investigator's computer, history files can be imported and analyzed, or a local profile can be analyzed. If installed on the target system, it can analyze all profiles present on the system. Additionally, it can analyze local files. If an image file is mounted on the system, you can essentially treat that system as a mapped drive.

Information found is stored in XML format. Therefore, it is not only viewable in Web Historian, but can be imported into a database application or into a spreadsheet.

Before scanning a system, configure the options to clarify what it is you are examining. Click on the Settings tab, and select from one of the three options (Figure 11.10):

- Scan my local system
- Profile folder:
- History file:

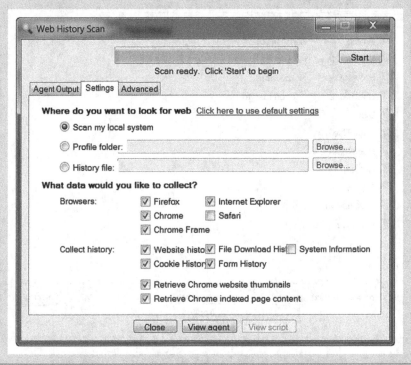

Figure 11.10 Web Historian settings

Continues

The first option will analyze every profile it finds on the system from which the executable is running. To analyze mapped drives, one of the other two options must be used. Profile folder requires that you browse to the folder where the profile is housed (which can be on the local machine or a network share). The same applies to the History file option. Then, click on the Start button in the upper right-hand corner of the screen. It can take a while to analyze a system with an extensive history, so be patient.

Once the scan is completed, the various filters configured in the application can help limit the viewable output to such records as fit into predefined parameters. In addition to the built-in filters, the application allows the user to build custom filters based on specific requirements. Some of the filter options just for Web history appear in Figure 11.11. By default, all options are selected. To narrow the search, deselect all options except for the one that interests you. For example, in a multiuser machine, it would be a good idea to sort by UserName. Or you might want to find out how many of your employees are visiting Monster.Com and submitting resumes. Filter by URL to do that.

Figure 11.11 A few of the filter options in Web Historian

Another valuable tool is the Website Profiler. Make sure the history scan has already been run and is loaded in Web Historian. Click on Tools. Website Profiler. Type in a domain name that you wish to analyze, and press Enter. The tool will tell you how many cookies have been downloaded from the site, provide a summary of all temporary files found from the site, and tell you how many users have visited it, how often it was visited, and how recently it was visited.

WEB SERVERS

On the server side, there may be multiple searches for an investigator to perform. A complex Web site will have a Web server application such as Apache as well as one or more Web-based applications. There may be chat logs to analyze as well as authentication logs.

HOW A WEB SERVER WORKS

When the client browser on a user's workstation makes a request to access any resource on the Internet, it sends an HTTP request to the Internet service provider (ISP). The ISP maintains a DNS server that examines the URL, extracts the domain name out of the address, and translates it to an IP address. The ISP then forwards the request to the IP address it found. This IP address is the physical address of the server hosting the Web site. This may or may not be an individual server. Web server applications are very I/O intensive, but not so very much processor intensive. Most companies that host Web sites for small to mid-sized companies use virtual machines to host each site. One physical server might host a hundred or more individual Web sites.

Accessing a Web server for investigative purposes is a lot more complex than getting into an individual computer. For the purposes of this chapter, it is assumed that the investigator has already successfully navigated the various hoops and legal snarls and now has access to the system. At this point in time, the biggest road block will be the fact that it will in all probability not be possible to bring down the server long enough to image it. And in most cases, the "server" will consist of a cluster of multiple servers with RAID arrays for drives—or perhaps a SAN. Therefore, one of two approaches must be taken.

It may be possible to directly access the server and work directly on the system. If this is the case, The Coroner's Toolkit—an open-source collection of forensic tools that includes a utility—can be used to analyze the data. In most cases, however, live acquisition will be the order of the day. As of this writing, very few forensic analysis tools are available to do live analysis remotely. Encase Enterprise is one tool that supports remote live analysis. From a Linux-based forensics system, PyFlag is a powerful utility that works with static images or live analysis. Lacking either capability, the investigator is likely to be reduced to acquiring the files targeted for analysis and making copies to be examined on a forensic workstation.

SERVER LOG FILES

Web servers store a significant number of files in various directories that keep track of different events that occur. These events include authentication success, authentication failure, IP addresses, connection history, and many others. Different applications use different formats for their log files. The two most popular servers are the Windows Web Server and Apache Web server systems.

Windows Log Files

Windows Web servers support the use of the following file formats (Technet 2005):

- **W3C**: ASCII format that allows customized properties. Time is recorded in Coordinated Universal Time (UTC), which is based on Greenwich Mean Time. Individual logged properties are separated by spaces.
- **IIS**: Fixed ASCII format that does not allow customization. Time is recorded as local time, based on the internal clock chip on the host device. Individual fields are comma delimited, making the file easy to export into a spreadsheet application.
- **NCSA** (Common Log): NCSA (National Center for Supercomputing Applications) uses a fixed ASCII format that does not allow customization. Time is recorded as local time, based on the internal clock chip on the host device. Individual fields are separated by spaces.
- **IIS ODBC**: ODBC (Open Database Connectivity) logging must be enabled before logs will be generated. A database must be configured to accept incoming data, and the database to be monitored must be configured. Since this function degrades server performance, it is not as frequently used.
- **BIN** (Centralized Binary): This method, used with IIS 5.1 and earlier, used binary data to store information and was able to log the activities of several Web sites at once.
- **XML**: XML (Extensible Markup Language) is a file format easily read by humans, but designed for moving data back and forth between applications.

Some specific log files to look for include

- **IIS Log Files**: These files are generally the most interesting to the investigator, as they contain information about all client requests against the Web server. By default, these files are located in the c:\%system%\system32\LogFiles\W3SVC1 directory. However, this location can be reconfigured by the administrator to reside anywhere on the system. The files have a conventional naming system of EXxxxxxx.log, where xxxxxx is a number generated by IIS.

- **IISMSID**: Logs Mobile Station Identifiers. A mobile station identifier is a number associated with a wireless service provider that identifies a particular unit on the network. This log is only present on a Microsoft Web server if the MSIDFILT or CLOGFILT functions are enabled.

- **HTTPERR**: HTTPERR logs record all invalid requests made to the Web server. These files are stored in the %systemroot%\System32\LogFiles\HTTPERR directory.

- **URLSCAN**: The URLSCAN tool is a utility that can be installed on a Microsoft Web server that allows the administrator to block specific HTTP requests. If the tool is installed on the Web server (and unless logging is disabled), a log file records all denied requests. By default the file is located in the directory %systemroot%\inetsrv\urlscan\logs.

Apache Log Files

Apache HTTP Server (currently version 2.2) uses the Common Log Format. As described above, the files are standard text files, readable in any text processing application. Fields are separated by spaces. The time is represented in local time, as reported by the device's clock chip, with an offset recorded for GMT. Two log files are of interest to the investigator:

- **Access Log**: On Unix/Linux systems, this file is called access_log. The default path to this file is /var/log/httpd/access_log on most distributions. It may also be located at /var/log/Apache2/access_log. On a Windows system, look for %systemroot%\System32\LogFiles\access.log. This file records all access requests processed by the server.

- **Error Log**: On Unix/Linux systems, this file is called error_log. The default path to this file is /var/logs/httpd/error_log on most distributions. It may also be located at /var/logs/Apache2/error_log. On a Windows system, the file name is error.log and is located in the %systemroot%\System32\LogFiles\directory. This file records any event that the system reports as an error. Entries may describe application errors or errors encountered in processing client requests.

Other log files located on an Apache server include the httpd.pid file, which records the process ID of an HTTP process. The Script log records the results of processing CGI scripts and is generally found only on test servers. The Rewrite log is used by developers for debugging. None of these files are particularly useful to the investigator.

PARSING LOG FILES

Comma-delimited or XML logs can be opened in a spreadsheet application. Even though these log files are human readable, to get the most information in the least time, the forensic investigator is going to want a more specialized tool. There are a wide variety options available.

Log Parser 2.2 is a tool distributed by Microsoft that reads most log file formats. As one might imagine, it only runs on Microsoft OSs. It is a command-line utility that not only extracts IIS log files, but also works with Event Viewer logs and SQL logs. Since it is a command-line utility, it is necessary for the user to be fully familiar with command syntax and the various modifiers that dictate how the utility works. Downloading and using Visual Log Parser from Serialcoder (currently found at http://visuallogparser.codeplex.com/) will relieve much of the pain. It is a GUI for the utility that allows the investigator to configure queries from simple-to-understand menus, and outputs results to easily read tables.

AWSTATS is an open-source log file for Web servers. The user can configure reports to show unique visitor lists, the results of error logs, and numerous other pieces of critical information. It works with IISW3C, NCSA, XML, and CLF.

A tool that is not precisely a parser but is very useful in conjunction with one is Webscavator. It takes the output of any parser that can generate CSV files and can generate graphs and charts using the data. Using this tool allows a person to visualize timelines, most frequently visited sites, and more. Most importantly, it allows the investigator to generate a timeline using the data collected.

ANALYZING LOG FILES

The server logs provide a large amount of information about any given HTTP transaction that the investigator can use in determining what happened and the order of events. While each type of Web server differs somewhat in how it records its log files, Microsoft Internet Information Service is fairly typical of most server logs. Table 11.4 lists the significant fields recorded in an IIS server log. It should be noted that since IIS uses W3C format, the content contained by the files may be customized by the Webmaster. Some of these fields may be absent.

Table 11.4 W3C Extended Log File Fields

Field	Description of Contents
date	Date of the activity
time	Time of the activity
c-ip	IP address reported by the client browser
cs-username	User name of account making the visit (if authenticated)
s-sitename	Name of ISP and specific instance number
s-computername	Name of the server on which the activity is occurring
s-ip	IP address of the server on which the activity is occurring
s-port	TCP port used to transfer data
cs-method	HTTP action requested
cs-uri-stem	Target resource of the requested action
cs-uri-query	Query string used
sc-status	HTTP status code
sc-win32-status	Windows status code
sc-bytes	Amount of data transmitted from server in bytes
cs-bytes	Amount of data received by server in bytes
time-taken	Amount of time required to process the requested action in milliseconds
cs-version	Version of the protocol employed by the client making the request
cs-host	Header name
cs(User-Agent)	Browser used by client in making the request
cs(Cookie)	Contents of any cookie transmitted or received during the transaction
cs(Referrer)	URL of the site that redirected the request to this server (if applicable)
sc-substatus	Substatus error code

The prefix of the field name determines the direction the data travels. The letter *c* indicates that the action resides solely on the client, while *s* indicates it is an exclusive server action. The letters *sc* indicate server to client, while *cs* indicates client to server.

Logs on a server get very large and are therefore rotated frequently. A typical scenario would be that the Webmaster is rotating logs every 24 hours. The old log file is renamed, using some naming convention selected by the administrator. In Apache, the file name is typically appended with a long number that basically represents the number of seconds that have passed between January 1, 1970, UTC and the instant the log file is created. For example, a few seconds ago, I ran an Epoch time conversion utility against the current time, and it read 1325787761.

Now it reads 1325787802, and so on and so forth. There is a Web site located at www.epochconverter.com/ that provides a handy Web tool that will convert those numbers into easily read time/date formats. If the investigator knows a specific time and date range for which the log files need to be analyzed, it is easy enough to use this method to narrow down the log files to those created during that time.

IIS approaches logging a little differently. The administrator can select *centralized login,* which allows for logging per server. With this option, a singularly large binary file is created that represents every site on the system. This may be advantageous if the Web server is internally hosted and only supports a small number of sites. ISPs will generally favor logging by site, which generates separate log files for each site hosted on the system. A commonly seen approach is to roll over log files daily. However, an enterprise site that gets a million hits a day can grow log files larger than a gigabyte before the day is through. On such servers, log rotation might be configured to roll over more frequently.

Prior to version 7.0, IIS file names were based on a base file name defined by the administrator when logging was initially configured with the time and date appended. For example, if the base file name was initially defined as IISLOGFILE, each file would be IISLOGFILE_*timestamp*.log. The timestamp was defined by the frequency of the rotation. A server configured to roll logs over every hour would use the syntax IISLOGFILE_yymmddhh.log. A daily log would eliminate the *hh* portion, while a weekly log would be IISLOG_yymmww.log. In 7.0 and later, instead of a preconfigured base file name, the first letters of the log file format are used, followed by a similarly defined timestamp. Table 11.5 shows common naming syntax for the different file formats (Microsoft 2008).

PROXY SERVERS

Many larger organizations employ **proxy** servers to separate their internal network from the outside world. Proxy servers serve two functions. With the appropriate software installed, they can serve as firewalls, keeping the outside world from accessing the internal network. They also act as a powerful Web cache that serves all users on the network.

Just like Web servers, proxy servers maintain libraries of log files that record activity. However, the proxy server records information regarding traffic specific to the network to which it is attached. In addition to history logs and user authentication logs, proxy server logs can also provide information on how much bandwidth each user utilized. If configured to do so, it can also keep track of how much time the server spent processing requests for each user it serviced. In an internal investigation, proxy server logs can identify attempts to access forbidden or undesirable Web sites.

Table 11.5 File Naming Conventions for IIS 7.0 Log Files

Log Interval	File Name Pattern
Microsoft IIS Log Format	
File size	inetsv*nn*.log
Hourly	in*yymmddhh*.log
Daily	in*yymmdd*.log
Weekly	in*yymmww*.log
Monthly	in*yymm*.log
NCSA Common Log File Format	
File size	ncsa*nn*.log
Hourly	nc*yymmddhh*.log
Daily	nc*yymmdd*.log
Weekly	nc*yymmww*.log
Monthly	nc*yymm*.log
W3C Extended Log File Format	
File size	extend*nn*.log
Hourly	ex*yymmddhh*.log
Daily	ex*yymmdd*.log
Weekly	ex*yymmww*.log
Monthly	ex*yymm*.log

Proxy log files exist in a variety of formats. One format common to Web servers is the W3C log file format. Servers configured to use this format can be analyzed with the same software used to analyze IIS Web servers. Other log file formats include

- Microsoft Web Proxy Server 2.0
- Squid
- Netscape Proxy
- Proxy[+]
- CCProxy
- CCProxy v2010

Different proxy software builds maintain different logs. Two common approaches are those of Microsoft (IIS) and those of Novell. A third one of which investigators should be aware is **Squid.** IS proxies use a logging scheme similar to that of IIS Web servers, so no further discussion is required.

NOVELL PROXY LOGS

Novell's BorderManager is capable of maintaining three types of logs. A fully configured proxy keeps a Common Log, an Indexed Log, and an Extended Log. The Common Log provides all of the basic information needed by an investigation. However, in order to generate the most complete reports, extended or indexed logs are desirable. It is possible to configure BorderManager to run without a log, but it is unlikely that any administrator would ever do this. Additionally, the destination of log files can be modified from those described in the following sections. This might be the case in large organizations where log files are frequently rotated and archived.

Common Log Files

Common files are typically maintained in the \ETC\PROXY\LOG\HTTP\ COMMON directory. The Common Log maintains the following fields:

- **IP Address:** The private IP address used by the machine accessing the BorderManager server.
- **Authenticated User Name:** User name of the individual accessing the Border-Manager server. The syntax of this entry makes use of full context (mgraves. mwgraves.com, where mgraves is the user ID and mwgraves.com is the domain). This entry is only included if authentication using the Single Sign-On (SSO) method (CLNTRUST.EXE) or Secure Socket Layer (SSL) method is configured.
- **Date:** The date on which the request was made.
- **Time:** The time (in local time) at which the request was made.
- **Time Zone:** The time zone configured on the server formatted as an offset from Greenwich Mean Time (for example, +0000).
- **HTTP Request:** HTTP code for the specific request being made in the individual transaction.
- **URL:** The URL of the site being accessed, including a fully qualified domain name along with the full path within the site for the file being accessed.
- **HTTP Version:** The version of HTTP employed by the client making the request.
- **Status Code:** The number that indicates the results of the client request. (See Table 11.6.)
- **File Size:** The size of the log file in bytes.

Table 11.6 HTTP Status Codes

Status Code	Supported by HTTP Version	Description
100	1.1	Continue
101	1.1	Switching Protocols
200	1.0, 1.1	OK
201	1.0, 1.1	Created
202	1.0, 1.1	Accepted
203	1.1	Nonauthoritative Information
204	1.1	No Content
205	1.1	Reset Content
206	1.1	Partial Content
300	1.1	Multiple Choices
301	1.0, 1.1	Moved Permanently
302	1.0.1	Moved Temporarily
303	1.1	See Other
304	1.0, 1.1	Not Modified
305	1.1	Use Proxy
307	1.1	Unused
308	1.1	Temporary Redirect
400	1.0, 1.1	Bad Request
401	1.0, 1.1	Unauthorized
402	1.1	Payment Required
403	1.0, 1.1	Forbidden
404	1.0, 1.1	Not Found
405	1.1	Method Not Allowed
406	1.1	Not Acceptable
407	1.1	Proxy Authentication Required
408	1.1	Request Timeout
409	1.1	Conflict
410	1.1	Gone
411	1.1	Length Required
412	1.1	Precondition Failed
413	1.1	Request Entity Too Long

Continues

Table 11.6   HTTP Status Codes—cont'd

Status Code	Supported by HTTP Version	Description
414	1.1	Request URI Too Long
415	1.1	Unsupported Media Type
416	1.1	Requested Range Not Satisfiable
417	1.1	Expectation Failed
500	1.0, 1.1	Internal Server Error
501	1.0, 1.1	Not Implemented
502	1.0, 1.1	Bad Gateway
503	1.0, 1.1	Service Unavailable
504	1.1	Gateway Timeout
505	1.1	HTTP Version Not Supported

Source: Williamson 2002.

Extended Log Files

The Extended Log contains all of the information stored in a Common Log, plus the following additional five fields:

- **Cached:** Indicates whether the URL was retrieved from cache or represents dynamic content. Possible values are: cache miss, cache hit, noncachable pattern (dynamic content).
- **[date-time]:** The date and time of the entry in local time, including the time zone offset relative to GMT.
- **c-ip:** The IP address of the requesting client.
- **cs-method:** The HTTP request type.
- **cs-uri:** The URL of the site being accessed represented as a fully qualified domain, with full path to the file.

The Extended Log files are stored in \ETC\PROXY\LOG\HTTP\EXTENDED. An administrator will generally select one type of log file.

Indexed Log Files

Indexed Log files are different from Common or Extended in that they are not stored as plain text. Either of the other two files can be viewed in Notepad or a similar plain text editor in a pinch. Indexed files are generated by a database engine based on Btrieve. Specialized tools are required for viewing or analyzing these files. Four tools provided by Novell for this purpose are

- NWAdmin
- ODBC
- CSAUDIT
- BUTIL

NWAdmin can export the file into ASCII format. So if the file is to be analyzed away from the server, this tool should be utilized first. Otherwise, a third-party tool might be useful.

SQUID

Squid is a Linux-based proxy server that is popular with many organizations. There are also Windows and OSX versions. The logging methodology is similar to all versions, and the following information is specific to the Linux version. Squid maintains three logs of significance:

- **Cache Log** (var/log/squid/cache.log): Squid stores error messages and information used for debugging in this file. This is useful for tracking failed authentication attempts.
- **Configuration Log** (/var/log/squid/squid.out): This file only exists when Squid is run from a built-in RunCache script. This file stores information about the Squid application and any fatal errors it has encountered.
- **Access Log** (/var/log/squid/access.log): This is the file most useful for forensic analysis. This contains records of all traffic back and forth between the client workstations and the Internet.

By default, Squid uses its own native format. If the administrator so desires, this can be changed to the Common Log Format.

TOOLS FOR ANALYZING PROXY LOGS

Common or Extended log files are based on plain text and can be viewed in a standard text editor. However, careful analysis of the files requires specialized tools. As mentioned, the Indexed file is in Btrieve format and requires conversions. Novell recommends WebTrends for this purpose (although it is also useful for a variety of other proxy servers). WebTrends reads any Novell Web server, firewall, or proxy server file and allows several layers of detailed analysis. Web activity can be divided between incoming and outgoing traffic. A standard, detailed summary report generated by the application provides information on

- General statistics
- Visited sites
- Top users
- Resources accessed
- Activity statistics
- Technical statistics

Another powerful tool, which can also be used for Web and application server analysis, is Sawmill. Sawmill can read virtually any log file format currently used. Its powerful tools include the ability to monitor multiple sites simultaneously, to generate reports on the fly from a running server, and much more. It also reports on penetration attempts and several other types of attack on the network. While not an inexpensive tool, its professional interface and results will make the investigator's job significantly easier.

CHAPTER REVIEW

1. Based on what you read in this chapter, explain why a cookie can show that a user has visited a specific site even if the browser history has been deleted.
2. Of all the information collected by a tool such as Web Historian, which field will tell you if a site popped up in a user's browser as a result of a redirect? What are some of the other fields of a temporary Internet file that Web Historian reads and reports that are of value?
3. Explain the concept of *knowledge of possession*. What are a couple of techniques an investigator can employ to demonstrate that a user knew that a particular file existed on her computer?
4. What are pop-up bombs, and how can they complicate an investigation?
5. How can server log files be used to corroborate evidence found on a suspect's computer?

CHAPTER EXERCISES

1. Download a copy of Web Historian, and run it against the Web history on a machine that has had Internet access for some time. Locate a Web site that

seems to get a lot of traffic, and run Website Profiler report against it. See if you can identify a specific user who has accessed the site. How many cookies were stored on the system by the site? How many temporary Internet files?

2. Using Web Historian, put together a list of every Web site visited by a specific user.

REFERENCES

ICANN. 2011. List of top level domains. http://data.iana.org/TLD/tlds-alpha-by-domain.txt (accessed December 23, 2011).

Technet. 2005. Log file formats in IIS. http://technet.microsoft.com/en-us/library/cc785886(WS.10).aspx (accessed January 3, 2011).

The State of Florida v. Casey Marie Anthony, Circuit Court, Fla. 9th Jud. Cir., Oct. 14, 2008.

The United States v. Tucker, 150 F. Supp. 2d 1263 (D. Utah 2001).

Williamson, M. 2002. Understanding Novell Border Manager's HTTP proxy logs. http://support.novell.com/techcenter/articles/ana20020102.html (accessed January 6, 2011).

SEARCHING THE NETWORK 12

In ancient civilizations, telecommunications consisted of a runner carrying a printed scroll from the general in the field to the emperor, extolling the successes of the campaign. A high-speed connection was available any time the courier was mounted on a horse. Modern technology has enabled trillions of riders to carry trillions of packages every day. And that is just on a medium-sized corporate network. When crimes are committed on the network, it is a greater challenge to find the culprit and enough presentable evidence to make a case. Instead of just one computer with two or three storage devices, the investigator now is faced with hundreds or even thousands of devices. Where does one begin to look? That is what this chapter is all about.

AN EAGLE'S EYE VIEW

Suppose for a minute that the president of a medium-sized corporation becomes convinced that one of his executives is about to move over to the competition. If that isn't bad enough, it is very likely that this woman is in the process of collecting as much information as she can to take with her to her new job. What is the target of the investigator's search for evidence?

The local area network will consist of several servers and most likely some form of network storage. E-mail communications will be managed by something along the lines of an Exchange server, and there will be Web access to examine. E-mail and the Internet are covered in detail in other chapters of this book, but that still leaves a vast area to search. Most networks of today have remote data centers and disaster recovery sites. Many of a company's applications are "in the cloud," meaning that the application—and very likely much of the company's data—is hosted and managed on the vendors network.

The application service provider (ASP) model allows venders to maintain much more control over their product. Instead of licensing the software, they can now sell the services provided by the software directly to the customer. This benefits the customer because the company sheds the responsibility of maintaining vast arrays of computers needed for the solution, along with the personnel needed to support it. It benefits the vendor because the result is recurring revenue in the form of annualized license fees, annual maintenance contracts, training, and many other sources of income. It becomes a nightmare for the forensics technician who now has multiple networks to consider when looking for data leaks.

INITIAL RESPONSE

The investigation model of a network investigation differs in no way from that of one involving individual computers. Only the processes and tools differ. Therefore, the first step in any network investigation is the first response. The first task is to assess the scope of the problem. And that assumes that a problem actually exists.

The first question to ask any potential victim is "What makes you think you have a problem?" In the example used in the previous section, it becomes necessary to ask the president why he is so convinced the woman is taking information from the corporate network. If he provides a technologically sound and logically coherent answer, there is reason to continue the questioning, and the forensics team should move forward. An answer reflecting little more than paranoid fear requires further triage before extensive resources are committed for a full investigation. If he simply says, "That's just the sort of thing she would do," it's probably not a good idea to book hotel rooms and make airline reservations for the investigative team just yet.

Ask to interview IT personnel, and request traffic logs for the time frame in question. Find out if there has been any evidence that the suspect has transferred files off site. Ways of determining this will be discussed later in the chapter. Ask if the suspect has logged onto the network at any unusual hours, if there has been any remote access activities, or if her e-mail has contained excessive numbers of attachments. If there is time, ask the company's IT staff to put a protocol sniffer on her network interface and look for unusual FTP traffic. Audit her access to the storage locations where the suspect data is housed, and find out if she's showing an inordinate interest in researching the company's history of late.

Assuming that there is sufficient incentive to proceed with the investigation, there is still some triage work to accomplish at this stage. Several questions need to be addressed.

What is the time frame in which the suspected activities occur? Was it an isolated incident involving a single attack or transfer of data? Or has it been an ongoing situation where data may have leaked out over an extended time? A little prodding might be in order here. If there is any possibility of negative publicity or embarrassment, a truthful answer might have to be pried out of executive management.

Are there any other people involved? Is she working alone on this, or does she have help? Even assuming she's going solo, if there are other people who are aware of her activity, it is possible that they might have information to share. Additionally, it is a good idea to find out whether or not she suspects she is being watched. If she has reason to believe that others are aware of her activities, she is likely to be much more cautious in her behavior.

What network resources are involved? Investigators are going to need to know where the evidence trail might exist. A detailed map of the network would be nice. With many organizations it will also be unlikely. However, any good IT team will be able to give the team a good schematic diagram of the network. What does the network use for storage? Are there any intelligent switches and routers that might have logs that would be useful to examine? Are there ASP systems involved that are going to require cooperation from outside technical staff (and political pressure)?

Is there any evidence that the suspect might be technically astute? If she has a decent understanding of the network and is familiar with the systems involved, then it is more likely that she will be trying to cover her tracks. If she is technically ignorant but is using sophisticated methods to obtain data, then there is evidence that someone else might be involved.

Is the network equipped with an intrusion detection system? If so, do the logs support evidence of any efforts to penetrate the network from the outside? Collect the logs from any such systems, along with proxy server logs, router and switch logs, and remote access server logs for the time frames involved. It's better to have them and not need them than to need them and not have them. Logs frequently get overwritten over time.

A critical part of the incident response plan is the ability to make certain decisions quickly. Should the team keep the impacted systems connected and active in an effort to identify the perpetrator? Is it more critical to protect sensitive data by either disconnecting or shutting down the targeted systems? Is it possible to conduct covert monitoring of the network connection without imposing unacceptable risk? None of these questions should be answered by the investigative team, but that team is going to need answers very quickly. An effective organization has a response plan in place long before an incident occurs. When this is the situation, response time is significantly faster and risks are reduced. A good response plan focuses on a number of objectives:

- Contact information for IT personnel, management, and digital forensic personnel is immediately available.
- Procedures are in place for analyzing the nature and the extent of an event.
- Tools are available and in place for collecting and preserving information associated with the event.
- Communications lines are available to the response team that won't be tapped by targets of investigation.
- A method exists for returning targeted systems to normal operation in the shortest time.
- A post-incident review will collect all the necessary facts into a conclusive report.
- Evidence collected will be safely stored, with appropriate chain of custody documented.

PROACTIVE COLLECTION OF EVIDENCE

There are two phases involved in collecting evidence. In the event of an investigation into ongoing activity, it is very likely that proactive collection of evidence while the activities are occurring will be feasible. Situations that would suggest such an approach include

- Current and ongoing intrusions
- When there is ongoing theft of data
- Misuse of company resources
- Suspicion of data export
- When internal systems may have been compromised
- When ascertaining whether malicious software has been embedded in the system
- In order to determine how the intrusion was accomplished

The second phase would be post-incident collection of evidence. This is the search for artifacts left over from the event. Virtually every investigation will involve some level of post-incident collection. This phase will be discussed later in the chapter.

In the previous section, the importance of collecting logs was mentioned. In addition to network logs, the user's local system is likely to be a source of potentially important, but temporary, evidence. If possible, get a snapshot of the suspect system. Depending on the time structure provided by the scope of the investigation, it might be possible to configure the user's machine and network connections to collect data that contains evidentiary value. Such tools can provide a plethora of information that will be very useful later in the investigation. Some of the items to consider include keyloggers, network auditing tools, and network capture tools. Note that many tools, including the keyloggers and certain types of network capture hardware, are considered to be a form of wiretap, as discussed next, and proper legal authorization must be acquired before putting them to use.

KEYLOGGERS

Keyloggers are either software or hardware devices that record keystrokes and output them as a continual string to a file. Using such a tool allows an investigator to collect passwords as well as record commands issued from the command line. Examples of this tool include Keyghost, which is a small module that plugs into the keyboard and stores up to two million keystrokes in flash memory. Keygrabber Wi-Fi by KeeLog collects up to 2GB worth of keystroke data and sends it to a preconfigured e-mail address. These are only two examples in a long list.

Software keystroke loggers require installation on the host computer and are more likely to be detected by an astute user. The application generally has a very small footprint and creates a plain text file that is store on the local computer or on a network location in a hidden read-only file. Some of the more advanced versions can even capture data that was not typed manually. For example, applications such as Computer Watchdog and KeyCapture don't simply capture keystrokes. They also record what applications were launched, what files were downloaded, and what file system resources were accessed during each capture session.

Keyloggers, whether software or hardware based, fall under the category of interception devices. This is based on a court decision that "interception occurs when a communication is captured or redirected in any way" (*U.S. v. Rodriguez* 1992). As such, their use is governed by federal and state law.

In the corporate environment, it generally will not be a problem to insert keystroke loggers into any computer system owned by the company. To be safe, the company should have each employee read and sign a standard policy document that defines what rights the company reserves in this regard. The existence of such a document goes a long way in protecting an organization from charges surrounding the invasion of privacy. *United States v. Simons* established that the presence of an established company policy, combined with a legitimate business interest in monitoring employee conduct, dispelled any perceived expectation of privacy (*U.S. v. Simons* 2000).

Different issues surround the tapping of private computers. In *United States v. Nicodema S. Scarfo, et al.*, the court held that the use of a keystroke logger did not violate the ECPA. However, in this case, the software was designed specifically to work only when the computer was not hooked up to the modem. The Fourth Amendment issues raised by the defense were denied by the court as well, stating that keyboard capture was not similar to a "blanket search" (Etzioni 2002).

It should also be noted that there are some exceptions to the laws. Naturally, any court order will allow the use of any interception device. The *consent exception* specifies that if any one party involved in a communications link is aware of and consents to the interception of the communication, other parties need not be informed (18 U.S.C. § 2511, 2008). The *Ordinary Course of Business* exception allows the interception of communications through any device used in the performance of day-to-day tasks. A common example of this is the recorded hold message people frequently hear that informs them that their call may be monitored for this or that reason.

SYSTEM AUDITING

Most network operating systems have some fairly sophisticated methods for auditing a wide variety of activities on many levels. This includes login activities for users and a variety of other functions. To enable auditing on a Windows server, do the following:

1. Open Administrative Tools. Local Security Settings.
2. Expand Local Policies (will open the window shown in Figure 12.1).
3. Select Audit Policy.
4. Select the events to be audited.

Audits can be based on success, failure, or both. Some critical activities to audit include

- Access to network objects, including NFS files and folders: This allows the administrator to keep track of who is trying to gain access to sensitive information.

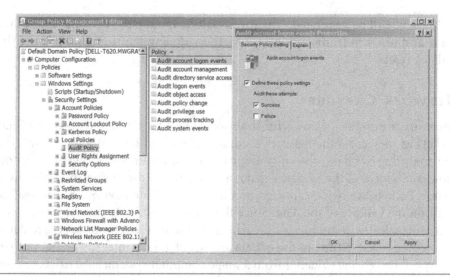

Figure 12.1 Enabling auditing events in Windows server

- Login attempts: Lets the administrator know when people are logging into the network.

- Modifications to user account security settings: If a user with appropriate rights is misusing his or her authority to change settings, this will uncover who is doing it and what changes are being made.

- Write access for program files: If unexpected processes are running on the server, this generates a log of when they are running and who the owner of the process is.

- Policy changes: Hackers may attempt to make policy changes to network servers in order to facilitate certain types of attack.

Before setting out to audit the network, a little planning is in order. Decide precisely what information needs to be collected in the process. Audit logs can grow quickly, and selecting unnecessary objects to track only exacerbates the situation. Archive the existing logs and clear them so a fresh slate appears. Keep the old ones so that any evidence of earlier activity is preserved.

Configure the system to audit system events as well. On Windows servers, tracking event messages with the 517 number allows the investigator to see if somebody has altered the actual audit logs. A 519 event indicates that an invalid remote procedure call was attempted on the system. If somebody attempts to change the system time in order to falsify MAC labels on files or e-mail messages, a 520 event will be generated. The investigator can take the time the change was made and use it to frame any suspect activity during the time between the first and last resets.

NETWORK CAPTURE

There are a number of powerful tools available that allow the capture of data packets as they cross the network medium. There can be problems in capturing and analyzing live data when it comes to generating admissible evidence. For one thing, the source of the evidence is not actually in the direct control of the investigator. Packets are being captured over an intermediate device. This brings into question the validity of the data. Since the source of the data cannot be packaged into a forensically sound image, it will be up to the investigator to be able to define the methods used in the capture of data and to defend the integrity of the findings.

When presenting evidence from a single computer system, hard drive, or other static device, it is possible to prepare a primary image of the data source and use copies for all subsequent analysis. Network analysis involves a lot of random data moving back and forth between multiple devices. The investigator must capture all that information, filter out the relevant information, and verify its authenticity.

Verifying Authenticity

Verifying authenticity is the hard part, because there are so many tools a hacker can use to cover his tracks. Additionally some perfectly legitimate processes confuse the legitimacy of network analysis. For example, proxy servers alter the source IP to keep it anonymous to the outside world. Onion routing is a secure transmission method that encrypts data in multiple layers and then bounces it over a series of specialized routers—the onion routers. Each router removes a single layer of encryption, reads the routing information assigned to it, and then strips off the routing information of packets before sending them along to the next router in the path. As such, none of the intermediary routers know the origin or the destination of a packet. Anonymous remailers are mail servers that take SMTP messages, read embedded code that tells them where to forward the message, and then alter the originating IP.

Other techniques are not so legitimate. IP spoofing software strips out information such as the IP address of the original client and replaces it with bogus information. DNS cache poisoning occurs whenever an attacker replaces the IP address of a legitimate machine on the network with that of a device under the attacker's control. After that, whenever the DNS server gets a request for the legitimate device, the request is forwarded to the hacker's machine.

All these techniques, along with dozens of others, make it difficult for the investigator to qualify the legitimacy of information gathered during a live capture. The investigator accomplishes this by using well-documented tools and techniques.

Identifying Traffic

The first step is to carefully identify all sources of network traffic being captured. Sources of network activity include

- Ethernet connections
- Wireless network connections (including Wi-Fi hotspots)
- Bluetooth devices
- Router interfaces
- Intranet addresses
- Internet addresses

Once the sources of data have been identified, a network sniffer, such as WireShark, CommView, or OmniPeek, is used to capture and analyze the data. (A Microsoft tool called Network Monitor can also be used; however, it has fewer forensic capabilities than dedicated applications.) Most investigations involve capturing data in a specific time frame, known as the *acquisition window*. Also, the acquisition will most likely be done on a single segment within the network. A 100MB segment functioning at full duplex (100% capacity) would require approximately 45GB of storage per hour of capture. Networks rarely operate at full capacity. Therefore, an external 2TB drive (approximately $150 at the time of this writing) would store more than 44 hours of capture.

For continuous monitoring of a full network, there are advanced hardware/ software turnkey solutions that have very powerful capabilities. A company called Endace manufactures an entire line of hardware solutions dedicated to network capture. One of these, EndaceExtreme, can do continuous capture over a 100GB network, storing capture data into volumes with up to 96TB capacity. Riverbed's Cascade Shark handles multiple interfaces up to 100GB with a maximum storage capacity of 32TB. Network Instruments' Observer is limited in capacity to the amount of storage available on the network. This makes the product extremely scalable because storage area network (SAN) or network attached storage (NAS) devices can be continuously added if necessary.

Archiving the results of continuous network monitoring can be very resource intensive. Most solutions are designed to flow data through the system. As storage capacity fills, older data is deleted from the beginning of the archive as newer data appends the file. In the course of an investigation, it is probable that the data capture for a specific acquisition window must be archived, hashed, and stored. For today's high-speed networks, the amount of space required for such an archive can be quite intimidating to smaller organizations. For example, a gigabit Ethernet working at 65% capacity generates about 81.25MB/sec of data. A 1TB hard disk would be able to store a little under 3.5 hours of network traffic. Table 12.1 lists storage requirements for several network scenarios.

Capturing network traffic solves two problems. Dynamic network traffic is difficult, if not impossible, to analyze forensically in real time. Additionally, the "image" in the network changes every few nanoseconds. A preserved stream of network traffic provides an accurate picture of everything that happened on the network medium during the acquisition window. Multiple examiners can analyze the data, knowing everybody involved is seeing the same thing.

At the same time, it represents a static image of a nonstatic event that occurred between multiple entities. In other words, the network capture collected all of the communications that occurred during that time between every device that was live on the network. Network protocols give a specific device the ability to "ignore" packets not intended for its attention. The investigator uses the tools at her disposal to sift through the collection of data looking for packets specific to a problem. A conversation between network stations can be analyzed. If necessary, timelines can be generated from the time stamps on the collected packets.

Tools such as Wireshark provide the ability to filter the collection of packets based on one or more criteria specified by the investigator. Boolean operators allow a range of options for each filter. For example, if a specific workstation is

Table 12.1   Storage Requirements for Network Capture

Connection Speed	Network Utilization	MB/sec	Acq. Window/TB
100MB	10%	1.25	222.2 hours
100MB	25%	3.125	88.9 hours
100MB	65%	8.125	34.2 hours
1GB	10%	12.5	22.2 hours
1GB	25%	31.25	8.9 hours
1GB	65%	81.25	3.42 hours
10GB	10%	125	2.2 hours
10GB	25%	312.5	.89 hours
10GB	65%	812.5	.34 hours

being monitored, the application can be asked to filter out all packets except those originating from or intended for a specific IP address. Individual sessions between two network entities can be isolated and studied.

Performing a Network Capture

Capturing network data isn't difficult. Any device with a network interface adapter that can work in **promiscuous mode** allows the investigator to perform this task. Typically a network interface card (NIC) filters out all packets on the wire intended for another destination, processing only those targeted for the local system. In promiscuous mode, the adapter will process every frame that passes the interface. Windows drivers typically do not have the ability to set the device to this mode. This is done in the settings of the software doing the network capture.

In the following examples, we will be using Wireshark (Figure 12.2) to capture and analyze a packet stream. The first thing is to tell Wireshark to work in promiscuous mode. There are a few other options that need to be configured,

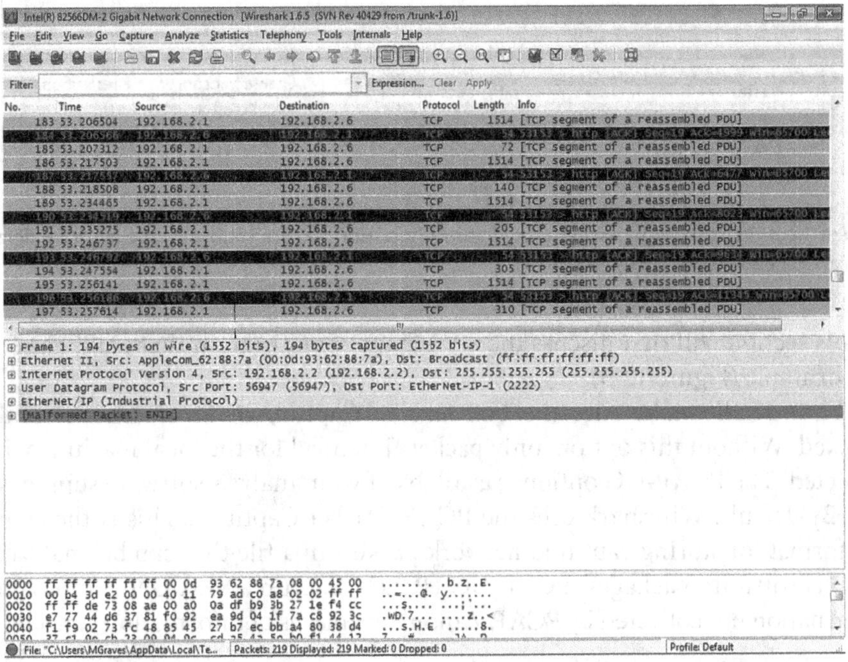

Figure 12.2 Wireshark is a very powerful open-source application that allows the investigator to perform network capture.

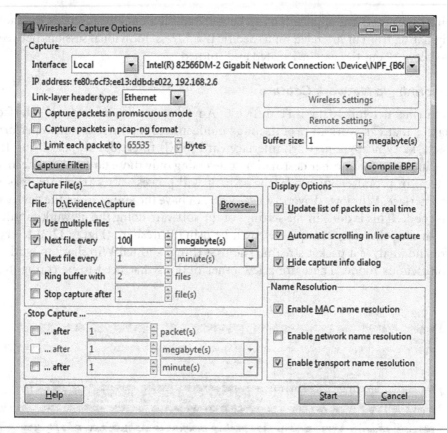

Figure 12.3 Wireshark has several configuration options. Promiscuous mode is set by default and rarely needs to be changed.

so this section will first discuss the Wireshark configuration that will be used for this example (Figure 12.3).

First of all, make sure the box labeled Capture in Promiscuous Mode is checked. Without this option, only packets intended for the local machine will be collected. The PCAP-NG option is available if your analysis software supports the file. By default, Wireshark uses the PCAP (Packet Capture). This is the standby file format for storing captured network packets in a file that can be analyzed by various software packages. PCAP-NG (Packet Capture, Next Generation) stores information not collected by PCAP. Among the pieces of information collected are

- Extended time stamp information
- Interface identification information

- A deeper set of capture statistics
- Name resolution information
- Any user comments that have been embedded

Two other settings that should be configured by the investigator appear in this window. The path to the directory where Wireshark should store the file needs to be configured. Otherwise, it will try to store it to the Wireshark directory on the drive where the application is installed. This might not be desirable if really huge files are to be collected or if the host drive is not likely to be available during later analysis.

If it is anticipated that the acquisition window is going to be large, it might be better to capture multiple files rather than a single large file. By default, Wireshark captures everything in a single file. In the example shown in Figure 12.3, the application is configured to start a new file every 100MB. This allows smaller files for analysis in the event of extended capture times.

Once the options are configured, it is time to start capturing data. One of the options for starting a capture is to click the Start button after configuring the options. Otherwise, the investigator can click Capture. Start (or CTRL + E). When enough data has been collected, click Capture. Stop (or press CTRL + E again). Wireshark's display is divided into two panels. The upper panel is called the *packet list pane* (A in Figure 12.4). In this window it is possible to scroll through every packet captured or view packets based on the application of any of the many filters available within Wireshark. The lower pane is the *packet details pane* (B in Figure 12.4). This shows the contents of whatever packet is highlighted in the packet list pane.

Now that the data has been collected, analysis consists of applying the appropriate filter to isolate only those packets relevant to the search. In Figure 12.5, Wireshark has been asked to show only packets that contain the IP address of 192.168.2.2. (Note that the host IP is 192.168.2.6.)

It is also possible to isolate a single conversation between two devices. This is referred to as **sessionizing.** A conversation is just what it sounds like—the exchange of packets between two devices in the course of completing a single communications session. Click on Statistics. Conversations and the window shown in Figure 12.5 will appear.

Select a specific conversation that is of particular interest, right-click on that selection, and select. In the example shown in Figure 12.5, the option to select a conversation including packets going in either direction between the two specific IP addresses in the selected conversation has been chosen. Other options include

- A → B: Only packets traveling from the selected source IP to the selected destination IP

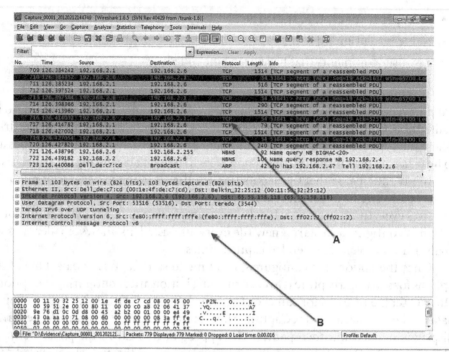

Figure 12.4 A is the Wireshark packet list pane, and B is the Wireshark packet details frame.

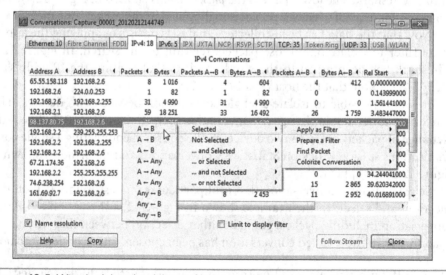

Figure 12.5 Wireshark has the ability to filter out only the packets relevant to a single conversation.

- A ← B: Only packets traveling from the selected destination IP to the selected source IP
- A ↔ Any: All packets moving from the source IP to any destination or any destination to the source IP
- A → Any: All packets moving from the source IP to any destination
- A ← Any: All packets moving from any destination to the source IP
- Any ↔ B: All packets moving in either direction between any destination and the IP identified as the destination in the selected conversation
- Any → B: All packets moving from any destination to the IP identified as the destination in the selected conversation
- Any ← B: All packets moving from the IP identified as the destination in the selected conversation to any destination

It should be quite evident by now that Wireshark is a very powerful tool for the network forensic investigator. Several entire volumes have been written on how to use Wireshark as a network diagnostics tool and as a forensics tool. A complete discussion would be beyond the scope of this book.

LIVE CONNECTION INFORMATION

If the system is currently logged on and running, there is a lot of information that may be useful that will disappear once the system is shut down. A small batch file can collect some of this vital information into a text file. The batch file is very short and can be run from a removable USB drive. Each command performs a specific function and outputs the results to a text file called netstats.txt. (Note that the batch file should be edited to point the text file to the drive letter specific to the removable USB drive on the local system. Additionally, batch files should always be created in a basic text editor, such as Notepad, and not with word processing tools that add formatting bytes.) The single bracket in the first line creates a new text file called netstats.txt. The following lines all contain double brackets, which append the existing file without overwriting any of the existing data within the file. The file is as follows:

```
time /T > netstats.txt
date /T >> netstats.txt
ipconfig /all >> netstats.txt
netstat >> netstats.txt
net user >> netstats.txt
net accounts >> netstats.txt
```

```
net start >> netstats.txt
net use >> netstats.txt
net session >> netstats.txt
net share >> netstats.txt
net file >> netstats.txt
```

The first two lines, as is obvious, record the time and date—*as configured on the system*. If the system time is different from the actual time, it needs to be independently documented. The third line pipes the complete TCP/IP configuration to the text file. The **netstat** command lists every network connection made to the system over the network adapter. Net user identifies what user ID was used to log onto the system. Net accounts is used to update the network accounts database and to modify password requirements. Without any parameters defined, the command spells out the password policy enforced on the system. The net use command is typically used to connect or disconnect the system to network resources. Used without any parameters, it will return a list of active network connections. Net sessions identifies any currently active sessions on the computer. (Note that this command can also be run from the command line to forcibly disconnect any untrustworthy sessions identified. The syntax for this command is net sessions \\computername/ delete.) Net share lists all of the shared resources on the local system. Net file displays all files on the local system currently opened by network clients. As with net session, the command can be used to forcibly close a file open on the system. The syntax is net file 2 /close (where 2 is the identifier of the file, as provided by a previous execution of the net file command).

POST-INCIDENT COLLECTION OF EVIDENCE

A great deal of evidence can be collected from a variety of sources after the event has transpired—assuming of course that it hasn't been overwritten or deleted. There will be a number of files that the investigator will want to acquire while the iron is still hot, so to speak. There is a wide variety of event and application logs that can be a gold mine of information. Additionally, the registry can potentially provide valuable details.

Network operating systems differ in how they collect logs. However, there is a great deal of consistency in what information is collected. It is beyond the scope of this book to cover every platform in detail. Since Windows networks represent the majority of those the investigator will see, this discussion will concentrate on the log files generated by a Windows Server operating system. The different log files generated by a Windows system include system event logs and text logs generated by different services and applications running on the server.

EVENT LOGS

Windows servers, by default, log a wide variety of events. What events are logged is a function of what version of Windows Server is running on the system. A glaring example is that versions prior to Windows 2003 Server did not enable security logging by default. An administrator had to proactively configure this feature, along what logging events to track, on the system. For the most part, all other logs are similar across versions. They can be configured by an administrator to log additional items. Three logs of significance to the investigator are the application log, system log, and security log.

Installation and uninstallation of different applications is logged in the *application log* (Figure 12.6). Additionally, significant events generated by individual applications will show up here. A good example of this is antivirus programs. They will frequently record the detection of suspected viruses here as well as in their own logs. All program updates will appear here as well. Looking in the application log can indicate when unauthorized software is installed on the system. If a user temporarily disables an application for any reason, this type of event is recorded.

The *system log* (Figure 12.7) records events specific to the day-to-day running of the system. One area of interest to an investigation might be the ability to show when system services are started or stopped. Specific times that these events occur appear here. Also, device drivers that are loaded on the fly (such as USB storage devices) will generate an event. This type of information can be used to confirm

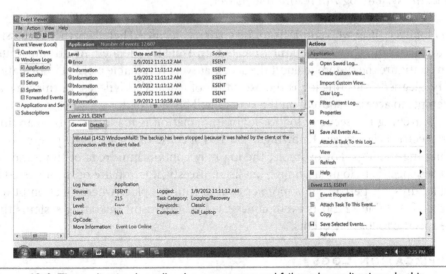

Figure 12.6 The application log talks about successes and failures by applications. In this example, Windows Mail failed because it was opened at a time when there was no network connection available.

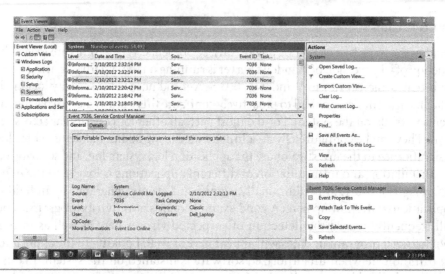

Figure 12.7 The system log records operating system events. This example is one of a successful event providing valuable information. Event viewer is reporting the precise time and date that a portable storage device was inserted into the system.

the presence of such devices and precisely what time (based on system time) they occurred. If the user tried to falsify the time of an action by changing the system time, the system log will record that as well.

The *security log* (Figure 12.8) is the investigator's playground. All login information for every user who connects to the system is recorded here, whether successful or unsuccessful. If a new account is created, an event is generated. An administrator can configure the system to audit file access as well. A valuable piece of information to be gleaned from this log is the execution of elevated privileges. In this way, all attempts to access resources on the system will be recorded.

Searching the security log for login information is made easier by searching for specific event types. Knowing event IDs specific to the event helps greatly in searching the logs. For example, the log may contain hundreds of thousands of entries specific to login attempts, but as an investigator you are only interested in log failures. Or perhaps, it is more critical to find the place where an attempt was successful. Table 12.2 lists event codes used by Microsoft operating systems that are specific to logging events.

APPLICATION LOGS

The operating system and many core applications, such as Exchange, SQL Server, and Internet Information Services, maintain relatively detailed histories of activity. Some

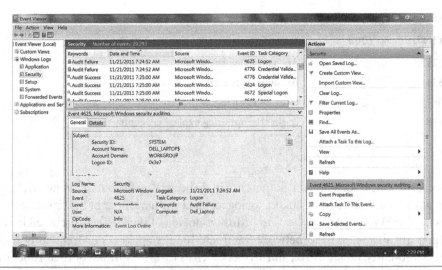

Figure 12.8 The security log tracks events specific to accounts and privileges. Here, Event Viewer reports a failed attempt by a system account to access a network location.

Table 12.2 Microsoft Logging Event IDs

Windows XP, 2000, 2003	Description
528	Successful login
529	Login failure due to bad User ID or password
530	Login failure due to a violation of time restrictions
531	Login failure resulting from a disabled account
532	Login failure resulting from an expired account
533	Login failure resulting from logging in from a restricted machine
534	Login failure due to user not being granted requested login type
535	Login failure resulting from an expired password
536	Login failure because the Netlogon component is not running
537	Login failure due to other unspecified reasons
538	User logged off
539	Logon failure because the account has been locked out
540	Successful network logon
551	User initiated logoff
552	Login attempt using explicit credentials

Continues

Table 12.2   Microsoft Logging Event IDs—cont'd

WIN7/Server2008	Description
4625	Account failed to log on
4634	Account logged off
4647	User initiated logoff
4648	Login attempt using explicit credentials

of these are in text format, while others are in dedicated log formats. Chapter 11, "Web Forensics," had a detailed discussion of log formats and a number of the significant log files used for Web-based applications. Most, if not all, of the log files discussed in that chapter are also relevant to network forensics. Today's applications frequently make use of Web-based architecture, and services such as IIS are required for their functionality. Activities relevant to such applications will be found there.

SQL Server is a database engine used by a large number of software products used in many industries. Somebody tapping into the corporate network is very likely in search of information. Information is generally found in the company databases. Three SQL logs of interest to the investigator are

- SQL Server Profiler Log: This file, named log.trc, in the %ProgramFiles%\ Microsoft SQL Server\MSSQL.1\MSSQL\LOG directory, maintains records of events related to database activity. It is generally analyzed through Microsoft's SQL Server Profiler tool.
- SQL Server Agent Log: This file records errors and warnings relevant to jobs and queries run against the database. This can indicate if somebody is making repeated efforts to access a database. It is called SQLAGENT.OUT and is located in the %ProgramFiles%\Microsoft SQL Server\MSSQL.1\ MSSQL\LOG directory.
- SQL Server Error Log: Typically, this file is used for troubleshooting SQL problems. However, since somebody hacking a system tends to create problems, this is a good place to find out if unusual activity related to the databases is going on. The file is named simply ERRORLOG and is located in the %Program-Files%\ Microsoft SQL Server\MSSQL.1MSSQL\LOG\ERRORLOG directory.

On a DNS server, the DNS logs can be of interest as well. The logs will tell the investigator what domains were queried from inside the network. The caveat here is that the administrator must have previously enabled DNS logging. This option is not enabled by default when DNS is configured. The DNS debug log file will be found in %systemroot%\System32\DNS\DNS.log. DNS logs can be read in a simple text editor. However, for more powerful search and analysis, one of the log file analysis tools discussed in Chapter 11 will be more appropriate.

Antivirus logs may contain information pointing to attempts to insert malware into the system. The activity logs are the files of interest. Typically, the manufacturer expects these files to be viewed from the client application. From a forensic standpoint, this is the least desirable method. Many of the log file parsers discussed in Chapter 11 will open files from common vendors, such as Norton or McAfee.

Locations of the files vary with the manufacturer and the version. The following is a list of file locations used by Symantec and McAfee. A popular antivirus software used by consumers is AVG Antivirus and has been included here as well.

- Symantec Antivirus Corporate Edition
  - WIN2000/XP2003: %SystemDrive%\Documents and Settings\All Users\Application Data\Symantec\Symantec AntiVirus Corporate Edition\7.5\Logs
  - WIN98/ME: %SystemDrive%\Program Files\Symantec_Client _Security\ Symantec AntiVirus\Logs
- McAfee Antivirus
  - Host Intrusion Files: C:\Documents and Settings\All Users\Application Data\McAfee\Host Intrusion Prevention\. Folder containing log files pertaining to attempted intrusions.
  - Desktop Protection Files: C:\Documents and Settings\All Users\Application Data\McAfee\DesktopProtection. Folder containing log files pertaining to local resources.
  - AccessProtectionLog.txt: C:\Documents and Settings\All Users\ Application Data\McAfee\DesktopProtection\ AccessProtectionLog.txt. Logs attempts to access protected resources.
  - BufferOverflowProtectionLog.txt: C:\Documents and Settings\All Users\Application Data\McAfee\DesktopProtection\BufferOverflow ProtectionLog.txt. Of little use to the investigator. Records events that result in buffer overflows.
  - EmailOnDeliveryLog.txt: C:\Documents and Settings\All Users\Application Data\McAfee\DesktopProtection\EmailOnDeliveryLog.txt. Records events triggered by scanning incoming e-mails and their attachments.
  - OnAccessScanLog.txt: C:\Documents and Settings\All Users\Application Data\McAfee\DesktopProtection\ OnAccessScanLog.txt. Records events

triggered when external objects such as file downloads or Web documents are accessed.

- AVG Antivirus
  - Message Queue: C:\Documents and Settings\%USER%\ Application Data\AVG7\QUEUE
  - Activity Log: C:\Documents and Settings\%USER%\ Application Data\ AVG7\Log\

ROUTER AND SWITCH FORENSICS

An important part of the network forensics report is the path data took in and out of the network. Routers and layer 3 switches all maintain important log files that can be used to trace traffic. Additionally, there is the possibility that volatile information may exist in the devices that will be of importance. Viewing or acquiring any of this information requires directly accessing the device. Therefore, a significant degree of cooperation is needed from the IT staff. Unless the investigator is specifically trained in the administration of these devices, it is recommended that the task of collecting information be left to the professional network administrator.

Following are a few rules for you (or the network administrator) to follow:

- If at all possible, access the device through the console. Do not access a router or switch over a network connection unless it is completely isolated.

- Enable logging on the terminal software used to engage the device *before* making the connection. This will record the console session, along with all commands issued throughout the process. With Hyperterm, this is done by selecting Transfer. Capture Text.

- Take screenshots of each activity run. Record actual time and router time for each activity (if there is a difference).

- Make a record of all volatile information, as this will not be retained after the session is completed.

Typically, routers use the Trivial File Transfer Protocol (TFTP) while others use the File Transfer Protocol (FTP). Many routers, including the Cisco brand that dominates the industry, support both protocols. Make sure that you understand which protocol is configured on the router and use the right one. It is not an acceptable practice to make any changes to the router configuration before or after collecting the information needed.

Information retrieved from routers comes in two forms. The *volatile* information is that which would be permanently lost if the device lost power. It is typically stored in active memory and not in flash RAM. However, there are some files stored in flash that are overwritten whenever an orderly shutdown occurs. Therefore, these files are considered volatile as well. *Nonvolatile* information is that which is permanently stored in flash memory. Powering the system down will not alter the contents of the files, nor erase them.

ROUTER INTERFACES

As mentioned in the previous section, a router should never be accessed across the network. There are ways of connecting to a router that are safe for the investigator, although they require direct access. The Console Port exists as a direct RJ-45 or serial connection (depending on the age and model of the router). Some Cisco models are RJ-45 (Figure 12.9) on one end and DB-9 serial on the other. TTY or auxiliary ports exist on some routers and are holdovers from the days of analog modems. These are most frequently DB-9 connectors as well, so more than just a visual examination will be required in order to interface with the device.

Connections over these interfaces are done with Telnet, which is a command-driven communications application. This of course requires that the investigator be familiar with Telnet commands. Telnet commands are executed from Microsoft's HyperTerminal (Figure 12.10). Many lower-end devices, such as those used for DSL or ISDN connections, interface with a server via a USB port.

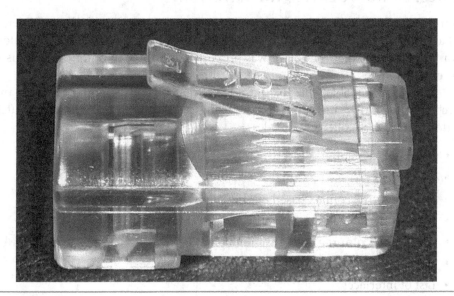

Figure 12.9 RJ-45 terminal

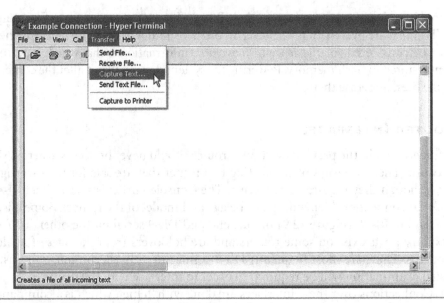

Figure 12.10 Telnet connection from HyperTerminal

COLLECTING VOLATILE INFORMATION

Rarely does the volatile information collected from routers provide direct evidence of an intrusion or a crime. What it does do is provide the framework to support (or argue) claims that the router was properly configured and not compromised by external forces.

Whenever possible, the volatile information should be copied to files and archived. Typically, this is possible by using the copy command on the router. Information to be collected includes

- Router OS version
- Router logs
- Time of initial contact based on the router's clock
- Copy of the startup configuration
- Copy of the running configuration
- Routing tables in memory
- List of interfaces
- Copy of the access lists

- Open sockets
- NAT translation tables

A good tool for collecting information from Cisco routers is the Cisco Router Evidence Extraction Disk (CREED), developed by Jesse Kornblum of the U.S. Air Force. The tool was designed as a bootable floppy diskette, so a laptop with a floppy disk drive (increasingly rare) or an external floppy drive will be needed. To use the tool, boot a laptop computer to the CREED disk. Connect the computer to the router, going from the serial port on the computer to the router's console port. Once the computer is completely booted, removed the CREED diskette and put in a blank MS-DOS formatted diskette. At the command prompt, type acquire. Log into the router (this will require the administrative password in order to enter privileged mode). The program will then run the following commands against the router and copy the results to a text file on the blank floppy diskette (Shaikh 2008):

```
# terminal length 0
# dir /all
# show clock detail
# show ntp
# show version
# show running-config
# show startup-config
# show reload
# show ip route
# show ip arp
# show users
# show logging
# show interfaces
# show ip interfaces
# show access-lists
# show tcp brief all
# show ip sockets
# show ip nat translations verbose
# show ip cache flow
# show ip cef
# show snmp users
# show snmp groups
# show clock detail
# exit
```

Another Cisco-specific tool is the Router Audit Tool, regretfully known as RAT. RAT is best used against the router by the network engineer, as it must be run against an established baseline. Having some knowledge of the network's infrastructure is necessary because the utility will interpret certain differences between the baseline and the running configuration to be vulnerabilities, when they are in fact intentionally configured parameters.

COLLECTING NONVOLATILE INFORMATION

Most routers have two places where nonvolatile information is stored. The flash RAM that has been discussed earlier is a place where data can be permanently stored. Typically, the router will have its operating system installed here. Nonvolatile Random Access Memory (NVRAM) is another repository of permanently stored information, as well as nonvolatile session information. An example of the latter is that on startup, the router copies the configuration data loaded into RAM to a file in NVRAM.

There are several commands to run against the router at this point. Again, the examples below are based on Cisco routers. Different OS versions will have varying commands, but all should have a similar command set. As mentioned when discussing the collection of volatile information, make sure that logging is enabled on the terminal software in use.

- `#show history`: This command displays the last ten commands issued to the router. The network administrator can determine if those were legitimately issued commands.

- `#copy startupconfig tftp`: The router will use the TFTP protocol to copy the permanently configured startup configuration from flash RAM to the TFTP server configured on the router. Compare this configuration to the running configuration collected from volatile memory to see if any changes have been made since the router was last started. Be very careful not to copy the running configuration to the startup configuration or vice versa before making copies. Doing so could potentially overwrite evidentiary material.

- `#dir slot 0`: This command displays a directory of files on the first flash disk.

- `#dir slot 1`: This command displays a directory of files on second flash disk (if available).

- `#show users`: This command displays a list of all users currently connected to the device.

Note that if any files are to be copied from nonvolatile memory to the evidence file directory, the `verify /md5` command should be run against the file before it is copied, and then an MD5 hashing utility run against the copy to verify the integrity of the file.

ANALYZING THE DATA

In itself, router data provides little meaningful information. What it does provide is corroboration for conclusions fueled by other evidence discovered in the course of investigation. For example, if it is important to establish that a particular user went to a specific Web site, the investigator can use the DNS logs to indicate that the user prompted a DNS query when he typed the URL into the browser's address bar. The router logs can pinpoint the time that a network connection was made to that address.

When looking for evidence of an outside attacker, router logs can provide information that proves certain events took place. A hacker trying to gain access to a secure network will go through several phases of an attack. The first step consists simply of information gathering. Much of the information about an organization's network is freely available. A WHOIS query can provide potential attackers with information about domain names, assigned IP address ranges, names of administrators, and a great deal more. Figure 12.11 is a WHOIS query of the author's Web site.

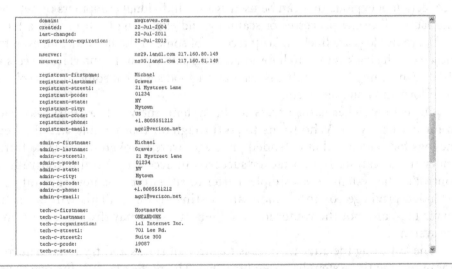

Figure 12.11 A WHOIS query of the author's Web site. For reasons of privacy, some information has been altered.

Far too often, information gathering is nontechnical and finding the artifacts left behind are beyond the means of the digital investigator. Much of the information used to penetrate the tightest security is gained through social engineering, and more often than one might expect, simple dumpster diving. People are often easily beguiled into handing out information over the telephone to callers posing as trusted vendors or customers. Employees have been known to carelessly discard sensitive materials without first destroying them. In most states, once that information hits the dumpster, it is free for the taking, and any expectation of privacy goes by the wayside. The Supreme Court decided in *California v. Greenwood* (1988) that articles left in trash disposal bins were readily accessible to all.

The next steps taken by the attacker involve probing the network for vulnerabilities. Tools such as NMAP can quickly scan a block of network addresses (for example, 192.168.2.1/24) looking for open, closed, or unfiltered (subject to firewall rules) TCP/IP ports. A secured router will detect such a scan and stop responding to the probe after a certain number of queries. However, the persistent hacker can simply script the application to try a few ports, wait a set number of milliseconds (or seconds or minutes), and try again. The investigator can find evidence of these attempts in the logs.

Once weaknesses have been found, the attacker now looks for ways to exploit them. Hackers have hundred of tools at their disposal, the same way artists have brushes and canvases of different variety. There is even a commercial suite of penetration tools available over the Internet called Metasploit. This package includes a collection of exploits that can be used against individual computers or network interfaces. Since the processes of scanning and exploiting both involve a lot of traffic, router logs are likely to keep records of some of the failures, and even the successes. The trick is to search for anomalous activity on the interface. Excessive UDP or incoming ICMP traffic is generally a good sign that somebody is collecting information on the system.

Once an attacker gains access to the system, she wants an easy way back in for her next visit. Who wants to go through all that trouble again? Check the logs for evidence that extended privileges were invoked in the time frame under investigation. If an attacker succeeds in accessing administrative-level control of the system, it is a simple matter to either create a new account with extended privileges or to promote an existing account. (This will be in the server logs, and not the router logs). Other attackers may drop a rootkit onto the system.

The last thing the attacker does is to cover all tracks and try to keep anyone from knowing the system has been breached. The perfect hack is the one that is never detected. A wide variety of antiforensic techniques are employed by hackers and by criminals to hide evidence, destroy evidence, or obfuscate evidence. This will be the subject of Chapter 15, "Fighting Antiforensics."

CHAPTER REVIEW

1. Why is it necessary to ascertain a particular time frame in which an incident occurred as part of the initial response procedure?

2. What information can you collect from a keylogger that would be difficult, if not impossible, to determine any other way?

3. Explain the difference between standard mode and promiscuous mode on a network interface card.

4. Two options for configuring a network sniffer are to capture data exchanged between two specific points and to capture data between one specific point and any other nod on the network. Explain why you would choose to use one mode over the other.

5. Since information extracted from router or switch interfaces do not provide specific evidence of a particular crime in most cases, what use is the information collected from those devices?

CHAPTER EXERCISES

1. Open the Event Viewer on a Windows-based computer, and select the application log. On the top menu, click Action. Filter current log.

   a. In the dialog box that opens, make sure that only Critical and Error are selected. Click OK. Make a note of what errors are reported, and copy down the Event ID for that message.

   b. Now use the tool to filter only by the ID you selected. To do this, copy the Event ID into the field labeled "Includes/Excludes Event IDs:"

   c. In your browser, browse to Microsoft's Technet site at http://technet. microsoft.com and do a search for Event ID xxxx, where the x's represent the number of the ID you located.

2. Download a copy of Wireshark (available at the time of this writing at www. wireshark.org/download.html). Install the application on your machine according to the instruction, and configure it to perform a capture of your IP address to anywhere. Spend some time looking at the different types of data you collect.

REFERENCES

California v. Greenwood, 486 U.S. 35, 39 (1988).

Etzioni, A. 2002. Implications of select new technology for individual rights and public safety. *Harvard Journal of Law and Technology* 15(2):280.

Shaikh, A. 2008. CREED (Cisco Router Extraction Disk). *Anish Shaikh's TechFactor.* www.anishshaikh.com/2008/03/creed-cisco-router-evidence-extraction.html (accessed February 20, 2012).

United States v. Rodriguez, 968 F.2d 130, 136 (2nd Cir. 1992).

United States v. Simons, 206 F.3d 392, 398 (4th Cir., Feb. 28, 2000).

EXCAVATING A CLOUD

The rapid emergence of *cloud computing* has added a few new challenges for the digital investigator. Just what is cloud computing? A good definition appears on Novell's Web site, which defines cloud computing as "a set of services and technologies that enable the delivery of computing services over the Internet in real time, allowing end users instant access to data and applications from any device with Internet access" (Novell 2011). A number of factors contribute to the complexity of identifying and extracting data relevant to an investigation where cloud computing is involved. To a very great extent, the technologies involved differ little from those discussed in the chapters on Web forensics and network forensics. But the approach can be a little different. A good place to begin would be a discussion of how cloud computing works and how it is used by corporations and individuals.

WHAT IS CLOUD COMPUTING?

There seems to be some general agreement among basic vendors regarding what cloud computing really is. For the purposes of this book, I turned to an authority on the subject. The National Institute of Standards and Technology (NIST—the folks who brought us forensic tool testing) published a paper called *The NIST Definition of Cloud Computing*. It states, "Cloud computing is a model for enabling ubiquitous, convenient, on-demand network access to a shared pool of configurable computing resources (e.g., networks, servers, storage, applications, and services) that can be rapidly provisioned and released with minimal management effort or service provider interaction" (Mell and Grance 2011). The authors define five essential characteristics of cloud computing:

- **On-demand service**: Computing capabilities, storage capacity, and availability are not limited by time or geography. All of these can be provisioned automatically without intervention from the service provider.

- **Broadband network access**: For multiple applications running on different platforms, it is necessary to have a standard interface over which traffic flows. It must be able to support both thick- and thin-client applications and be OS independent.

- **Resource pooling**: All available resources of the service provider should be readily available to all clients in a multitenant environment. This means that a single service provider (whether it be a server pool or a server/application combination) houses many tenants (clients sharing the architecture or running the software).

- **Elasticity**: Resources available to any given tenant can be scaled upward or downward as requirements change. This may be done manually or automatically. To the end users, the process must be completely transparent and require little or no intervention on their part.

- **Measured service**: Resource consumption must be monitored and reported accurately, assuring that the client does not pay for more services than are actually consumed. This monitoring must not impact on delivery or efficiency of service.

There are three service models as well, to be covered in the next section—Infrastructure as a Service (IaaS), Software as a Service (SaaS), and Platform as a Service (PaaS). Independent of the service model is the deployment model. NIST defines four deployment models:

- **Private cloud**: In this model, the infrastructure is constructed and managed for the exclusive benefit of a single entity. Within that entity multiple business units (or consumers) utilize the services provided. While the term "private" may imply direct ownership, this may not be the case. While the organization benefiting from the private cloud may indeed own the infrastructure, it is also possible to contract out these services to one of the commercial service providers who in turn manage an exclusive collection of hardware and software just for this one cloud. A single service provider might provide the same software application or infrastructure model to many clients, but each client is heterogeneously separated from the others.

- **Community cloud**: An organization consisting of a group of unified users with mutual interests band together and build their own cloud. An example of this would be an organization of realtors or a network of hospitals. The infrastructure might be owned and operated by one (or more) of the community members, or it might be contracted out to a third-party service provider.

- **Public cloud**: The public cloud is available to anyone who wants to subscribe to the services. Google and Amazon both provide large numbers of cloud-based applications and services to the general public. The cloud provider owns and operates the infrastructure. Not all public clouds are for-profit organizations. Libraries, government organizations, and such all operate public clouds.

- **Hybrid cloud**: Any two or all three of the above models can be effectively combined. Multiple cloud entities exist within a single larger cloud but are entwined by infrastructure or application architecture.

As you can see, cloud computing covers a lot of territory and entails multiple options for building systems and storing data. There is no one-stop shopping plaza for investigation techniques.

SHAPING THE CLOUD

But wait. Clouds don't have shape, do they? Aren't they amorphous objects, shifting every moment with the slightest breeze? To a certain extent, yes, but if that was 100% true, how would banks and publishers and sales organizations embed the foundations of their businesses in it? The fact is that the services provided are locked in place—it is the users that shift with time. Three primary forms of service are provided by companies offering "cloud computing" services. These are

- Infrastructure as a Service
- Software as a Service
- Platform as a Service

Each one of these services offers a different set of challenges, so a quick overview of how each works is in order. However, there are some commonalities between them. All cloud systems have a front end (the client computer) and a back end (database and application servers) connected by middleware. The middleware is the software running on the service provider's systems that acts as the traffic cop.

Since multiple clients are using a single (albeit extremely complex) system, the middleware also acts as the gatekeeper. The whole system is very much like the old time-sharing mainframes of old. When clients log onto the system, the meter starts running. When they log off, it stops. The server logs keep track of things like the amount of time utilized by the client, the volume of storage in use, and any other billable items. At the end of the month, the client gets an invoice for services used.

The real question to come into play—and the question most relevant to the digital investigator—is just how secure and accessible cloud data is. How does one get to the information stored, and how easily can unauthorized people access the information? And what happens to all the organization's precious data if the service provider gets taken over by a competitor, is nationalized by a newly hostile third-world government, or is a mile from ground zero after a nuclear attack?

The advantages are fairly straightforward. Cloud computing, as you will see, does have the potential of bringing costs down for an organization. Both hardware and software costs are more easily controlled and more easily monitored. Users can access their data from anywhere they can find an Internet connection. The service engineer on a road trip can log into the company network just as easily from the motel room as from the office cubicle. A powerful incentive, especially for the smaller organization, is that a significant amount of infrastructure is made available to each client.

INFRASTRUCTURE AS A SERVICE

Operating a server farm has never been cheap, and it's never been easy. Most large companies considered it a necessary evil, and many smaller organizations built networks a server at a time and worried later about how the architecture was coming together. Some organizations seemed to have it together better than others. As broadband became faster and more readily available, some of these companies began to lease out their infrastructure to companies who either couldn't afford to manage their own or simply chose not to.

A company who uses IaaS pays for the services, storage, and bandwidth that it actually uses. Capital expenditure on large numbers of servers, racks, storage devices, routers, switches, and so forth are drastically reduced. A company that outsources their infrastructure doesn't have to hire a team of network administrators. Their service provider does all that for them. The theory is that since a single provider acts as the server farm for a large number of customers, the costs are spread out.

The reality of the situation is that when Jones Associates, Inc., leases its infrastructure from MYIAAS.COM, it isn't leasing a bunch of physical computers. A concept called *virtualization* comes into play. A single, very powerful computer running a specialized operating system allows dozens (or even hundreds) of virtual machines (VMs) to run simultaneously on a single hardware platform (see Figure 13.1).

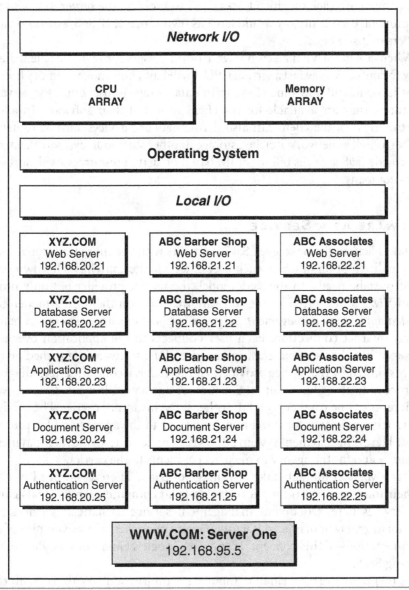

Network I/O

| CPU ARRAY | Memory ARRAY |

| Operating System |

| Local I/O |

| XYZ.COM Web Server 192.168.20.21 | ABC Barber Shop Web Server 192.168.21.21 | ABC Associates Web Server 192.168.22.21 |

| XYZ.COM Database Server 192.168.20.22 | ABC Barber Shop Database Server 192.168.21.22 | ABC Associates Database Server 192.168.22.22 |

| XYZ.COM Application Server 192.168.20.23 | ABC Barber Shop Application Server 192.168.21.23 | ABC Associates Application Server 192.168.22.23 |

| XYZ.COM Document Server 192.168.20.24 | ABC Barber Shop Document Server 192.168.21.24 | ABC Associates Document Server 192.168.22.24 |

| XYZ.COM Authentication Server 192.168.20.25 | ABC Barber Shop Authentication Server 192.168.21.25 | ABC Associates Authentication Server 192.168.22.25 |

| WWW.COM: Server One 192.168.95.5 |

Figure 13.1 Virtual machines are the secret to success for the IAAS provider.

Each VM runs its own copy of an operating system, loads its own set of drivers, and thinks it's the only game in town. To the administrator of a server (commonly referred to in virtualization as the *node*) running VMs, each machine is known as an *instance*. In Figure 13.1, you see an illustration of a single server hosting three client companies, each of which leases five instances on the server. In a real-world environment, each company would have its own range of IP addresses and varying numbers of instances.

When leasing a virtual computer from a service provider, a client has the ability to configure how fast a virtual CPU it will have, how much memory the server sees as its own, and how much long-term data storage to use. Once the servers are configured, they are available for the client to install their software. In addition to virtual servers, the client can also define network devices such as routers and switches as well as network attached storage or other storage arrays. Most companies that provide IaaS services bill monthly, based on actual resources used, sort of like the gas company.

SOFTWARE AS A SERVICE

SaaS takes IaaS to the next level. SaaS contrasts with the more traditional form of software distribution in which each user of a computer purchases his own copy of the software he needs. In the SaaS model, the service provider not only provides a set of VMs, it also provides the software that runs on them. In a model known as *hosted application management,* software applications are delivered in real time over an Internet connection. Each user connects to the application over a Web browser. When the user connects, an instance of the software is launched on one of the VMs hosted by the service provider. Figure 13.2 is a conceptualized diagram of the process. In this illustration, the insurance agency utilizes two SaaS providers. One accepts online payments and the other is the insurance carrier. The carrier has a dedicated application for providing quotations to the agency and for processing claims. The online payment system allows the end users to make their payments to the agency and for the agency to make its payments to the carrier.

Many vertical markets take advantage of SaaS. There is no need to configure their industry-specific applications on local computers. Individuals can also find services here. Document management services, financial services, automatic form generation, and contact management are just a few examples of many implementations of this concept. If you use Google's Gmail or Google Docs, you are using SaaS.

As mentioned earlier, cloud computing is multitenant. With SaaS, all clients will run a single version of the application with a single basic configuration. While

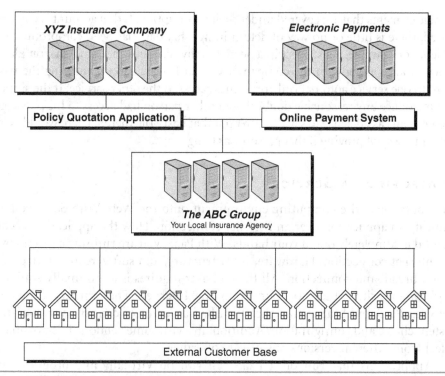

Figure 13.2 SaaS is frequently used by companies with industry-specific applications.

this is not always the case, the vast majority of SaaS providers also include data storage as part of their service package. Data generated by the application is stored remotely and delivered via the browser.

The advantages of SaaS make it understandable why so many organizations find it attractive—especially for complex proprietary applications related to specific business functions. Administration of the application is offloaded to the vendor. There is no need to train your own IT staff in a new application. Updates and patches are tested and deployed for you as they become available. Since everyone runs the same versions of the software, there is no need to worry about compatibility issues.

SaaS can vary in how it manages certain forms of data, depending on whether it is a public SaaS, such as a Google- or Amazon-provided service, or a private SaaS, such as a contact management solution provided to a vertical market. The public apps are most likely going to provide a single sign-on (SSO) form of security to an entire set of applications. Once signed in, the user can access any of the applications or data storage elements that are covered under their subscription. If that account is compromised, there is little or no way of determining what data has been compromised or added. For example, if a suspect in a pornography case subscribes to Amazon Elastic Block Storage along with the company's Virtual Private Cloud, knowing the password to one service automatically presumes access to the other service. If the suspect can introduce any reasonable doubt that another person had access to his password, then it is an easy defense to say, "I didn't put that nasty file there." There would be no authentic way of proving if that person was lying.

PLATFORM AS A SERVICE

PaaS puts the entire computing environment onto the Web. With SaaS, you are running an application over an Internet connection. How the application is configured is completely out of your hands. With PaaS, you are running a system over an Internet connection. Hardware, infrastructure, and software are all deployed over a broadband connection. All the end user requires is a minimally equipped workstation with which to connect to the Internet. The primary difference between PaaS and SaaS is that the client had a degree of control over operating system choice and configuration. Additionally, with some vendors, it is possible to select from different versions of software offerings.

Applications that run on a PaaS can run on virtually any programming language the developer chooses. If a clients are sufficiently sophisticated, they can choose whether their application should be programmed in C+++, Java, Perl, or whatever. From a service provider's standpoint, this means that each tenant exists in its own isolated little universe. As such, the client can exert a greater degree of control over security, availability, accessibility, and so forth.

Clients have more control over how information is stored and how logging is managed (assuming they have the expertise to do it). Logs can be configured to be stored on a third-party server or even sent back to their own local servers if the service provider allows for that. The advantage of doing this is that if hackers get into the system, they can't alter logs.

THE IMPLICATIONS OF CLOUD FORENSICS

When the digital investigator finds herself confronting a situation where the target of the investigation involves computing on the cloud, a new set of problems arise. Warrants issued by a court to search the computer systems of The Graves Group allow just that. She can search the devices owned and operated by The Graves Group.

A search of resources on the cloud can be performed to the extent that such a search is limited to cloud infrastructure leased and controlled by the object of the warrant and can be performed on or from devices owned and controlled by that entity. To put it more succinctly, that warrant would allow the forensic copying of each hard disk owned by the Graves Group. It would *not* allow the copying of hard disks owned and operated by the service provider. Since the resources of cloud computing generally exist on VMs, the conventional bit copy from sector 0 to the end of the disk cannot be performed. There is no physical disk to clone. What appears as Drive C on the VM is a chunk of disk space carved out of a much larger medium, such as a NAS or SAN.

Collecting data from a cloud environment poses some challenges. First of all, the preservation of data must be accomplished in a manner found acceptable by the jurisdiction of the court issuing the warrant. However, if the service provider is a company located in another country, the process of obtaining evidentiary materials from their machines must conform to their laws and regulations as well. So if The Graves Group is contracted with a company in India to provide an IaaS solution, obtaining any material related to the service that is not directly obtainable from a computer inside of The Graves Group would require getting permission from the national and local governments governing the service provider. For example, if part of the solution is a document management solution, documents found and archived from the client workstations would require only a U.S. court order. To obtain metadata from the servers would require approaching the foreign government.

Evidence must be collected without compromising its integrity. In the paragraph above, I mention the difference between collecting the document and the metadata. In many cases, the document is of little value without the metadata. It is the metadata that proves when it was created, opened, edited, or copied. A document that says "I robbed the Glendale Train. Signed, Michael Graves" looks very incriminating. However, my sworn enemy may have written the letter and slipped into my system in a Trojan horse. Metadata tells us who originally created the file and in many applications may show the identities of everyone who edited to it. While it is true that metadata can be manipulated, a digital document with no metadata is of virtually no value. Substantial amounts of supporting evidence must be provided in order to create value.

Additionally, the methods by which the investigating team collects the evidence must be reproducible. Another team should be able to come up with the same data and reach similar conclusions, even if they use a somewhat different approach to collecting evidence. My FTK forensics suite should not be obtaining significantly different results than your Encase tool kit.

The next few pages are going to discuss several critical questions the investigating team must address whenever their investigation takes them into the cloud.

- The structure of the cloud
- Technical aspects of cloud forensics
    - What types of data are stored by the service provider?
    - What logs are generated by the service provider, and where are they stored?
    - Where is it stored?
    - How is it accessed?
    - How is it possible to identify and capture the data required by the investigation?
- Evidentiary materials
    - Do the service provider's systems allow them to vouch for the authenticity of evidentiary material collected?
    - How does the team separate evidentiary materials from data that is irrelevant and possibly even protected?
    - Where is it stored?
    - How is it accessed?
    - How is it possible to identify and capture the data required by the investigation?
    - Does the service provider store the data in some proprietary format or platform that will require their involvement in data extraction and analysis?

Finding answers to these questions is not simply a technical hurdle. There are legal ramifications (as mentioned earlier) as well as organizational challenges. A digital investigation involving cloud resources will require a significant degree of collaboration between the client, the service provider, and law enforcement. As the subject of the investigation, the client may not be supportive of your efforts. The service provider is mostly concerned about the consequences of failing to comply with a court order. On the other hand, they are equally concerned about protecting the security, privacy, and integrity of their other clients. Since they are a multitenant service, this becomes quite a challenge.

The best way to approach this discussion will be to divide it into the technical aspects, the organizational aspects, and the legal aspects. As each topic circles around to the next, the overall picture should become increasingly clear.

THE STRUCTURE OF THE CLOUD

For cloud computing to work, the service provider must design and configure three basic models that apply to each client on the system (Armbrust et al. 2009). All three of these models must be considered in preparing for an investigation involving cloud resources.

- A computational model
- A storage model
- A communications model

Each of these models generates and stores data specific to its role. The location and type of data to be collected varies from one model to the next. How the data is accessed is also different from one tier to the next. Cloud structure can also be centralized or distributed. A centralized cloud has most or all of its infrastructure in one or more data centers. Failover or disaster recovery sites will be located in a different area for safety and security reasons, but will still be contained within the confines of one or more data centers. Distributed clouds are scattered among numerous locations across a wide geographical area and generally communicate via the peer-to-peer communications model discussed later in this section.

The Computational Model

The computational model has been touched on in this chapter already. The platform (PaaS, IaaS, or SaaS) has some impact on how each customer is configured on the host platform. However, a key ingredient to all platforms is virtualization. Another element to be considered is *elasticity*. As a client's needs increase or decrease, the provider needs to be able to increase or decrease the resources utilized accordingly, or the costs associated with maintaining the client are less easily controlled. Applications designed for cloud computing, as well as the hardware, must be able to scale up or down.

The Storage Model

Storage must be secure, scalable, and dependable. The clients must be assured that the information they store is only accessible by those they allow and not by those allowed by the service provider. As storage needs increase, the architecture needs to expand with those needs. Two options exist for scaling storage in any given environment. Block store storage models generally have a fixed amount of storage configured for the client. In order to increase or decrease this amount, the client submits a request and the service provider fulfills that request and adjusts their billing accordingly. Dynamic scaling grows or shrinks capacity as needs change. If a client has been utilizing an average of 20GB of storage over several months, then their virtual infrastructure will make a bit more than that available. When something comes along to suddenly change the capacity requirements, the client need take no action. The system will automatically adjust. So will the monthly bill.

Communications Model

All networks employ some model of communications. A *peer-to-peer* (P2P) network (Figure 13.3) treats every node on the network as an equal. A uniformly deployed protocol acts as a gatekeeper to make sure that one node doesn't hog all the network resources, and each node uses time-sharing to find communications time on the medium. A *client-server* network (Figure 13.4) utilizes one or more computers that act as controllers to the rest of the network. Clients must ask the server for access to resources. A cloud implementation will make use of

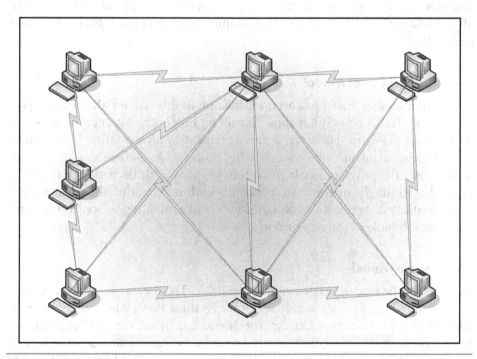

Figure 13.3 Peer-to-peer networking

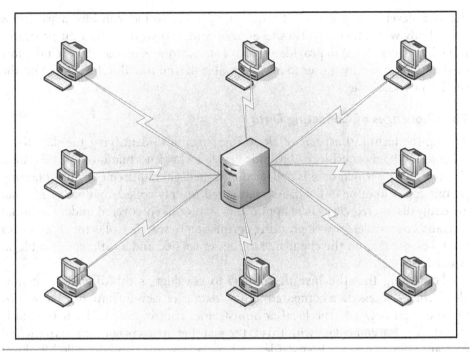

Figure 13.4 Client-server networking

one or both of these models within the infrastructure, and then combine virtual networking with the equation.

On a deeper level, you also have models based on the technology they employ. In the old days of telecommunications, modems could communicate in either simplex or duplex mode. Simplex meant that only one device could transmit at a time. One device in the conversation could not send until the other finished. With duplex communication, all devices on the network could transmit simultaneously (sort of). The communications protocols policed the medium and enforced a set of time-sharing regulations.

Within the infrastructure, there is generally a distinct separation between the computational and storage tiers. Depending on the needs of the clients, applications can be either *stateless* or *stateful*. A stateful computation model remembers the environment from one session to the next. For example, when a user opens Microsoft Word on her computer, the File menu remembers the last few files that were open. All configured options and settings follow the user's profile. That is an example of stateful computing. By default, a Web browser is stateless. It processes each request for a URL as if it were the first request ever made for that resource.

Browser developers get around what many users would consider a weakness (everybody wants their favorites to appear, after all) with application programming interfaces (APIs) to provide a sense of state. Storage, on the other hand, must be stateful in order for a user to always be able to find the files she's stored on the service provider's site.

The Challenges of Collecting Data

Among the technical aspects of cloud investigations, identifying the data to be collected is the most critical. Until it is decided what information must be found, the methods by which data is collected and the legal requirements for obtaining permission cannot be defined. As mentioned, simply collecting documents that are easily discovered via a client application is most likely covered under the initial warrant, court order, or writ granting permission to search. Collecting logs moves the investigator from the client side to the server side and a different set of legal issues arise.

Something that the investigator has to consider is the difference in how cloud clients access data compared to how data is retrieved from local networks. On the local network, the local administrators control how and where data is stored. Directly coincident with this is the fact that artifacts relevant to the actual customer data, such as deleted files and metadata, are also controlled by local administrators. In the cloud environment, method of access and locations of data are dictated by the service provider. While there will be a user interface for loading and viewing files stored on the cloud network, there is less likelihood that there will be a user interface for metadata, server logs, and other nondocument data useful to the investigator. Coordination with the service provider will be needed in order to gain access to such information, assuming that it remains on the servers to be extracted. Information regarding VM configuration, size and location of disk images, and VM file system metadata are examples of the type of information that falls under this classification.

It is highly unlikely that it will be possible to make a true forensic image of a physical disk. It is a virtual machine, and not a physical one. The disk drive consists of a file with a name along the lines of *myvm.vmdk*. It is very elastic in nature, and as long as it stays live, data is being added and deleted from the virtual system. Complicating matters is the fact that its "disk drives" are likely spread across multiple disks on a RAID array, mixed in with the drives of many other VMs. Capturing the physical disks of the server that hosts a VM would also entail capturing the data from other virtual systems on the machine. The risk of exposing the private information of nontargeted clients means that there would have to be very pointed reasons for capturing the entire disk before a judge would ever issue a warrant. However, it is possible to clone each individual VM managed by the client and treat the clone as a disk image.

The virtual image that represents the VM is replicable but is likely to require a completely separate court order. It is not technically the property of the client. As far as real-time monitoring of the service provider's network—you can almost forget about that. While the court may consider issuing a warrant for such activity in extenuating circumstances, the risk of privacy breach affecting other clients will be an obstacle to overcome. You can, however, monitor network activity across the virtual switches and interfaces. To do this, it would be necessary to install the network monitoring software or its agent onto the virtual device you plan to monitor.

Recovering deleted data from public cloud service providers is extremely difficult. With most cloud services, only the client holds the right to add or delete files. Once a file is deleted, the disk space it occupied is immediately made available to future write operations. The speed with which new data pours into the host arrays almost assures that in short order this disk space will be overwritten.

On Virtualization

As has been repeatedly mentioned, a key aspect of cloud computing is that the service provider is managing a multitenanted behemoth, and as an investigator, you are only privileged to search the resources of the tenant defined in the warrant or discovery order. You will be working within the confines of a complex, virtualized environment. It is also an environment that is configured to fulfill one of the promises made by the vendor to each client. That is the concept of "pay for what you use." A virtualized environment may be expanded or contracted to fit the current needs of the client. More critically, if capacity changes are sufficient to justify the effort, the environment may also be somewhat migratory. By that I mean that a client that needs a relatively small server with moderate horse power one day may experience sudden growth and find that they now need a multiprocessor server with four times as much memory. The service provider smiles and says, "No problem," and then moves the client's entire environment from one rack of servers to another. So much for searching slack space for deleted files.

VMs exist as *guests* on a host server. The server runs the *host operating system*, and each VM runs as an independent entity and operates its own *guest operating system*. The host OS and the guest OS don't need to be the same platform at all. A Linux box running Oracle's VirtualBox can support dozens of guest machines running Windows, Linux, or OSX. Do you have a specialty OS that you want to experiment with? Set up a VM, and install it there. Some commonly used VM server applications include the aforementioned VirtualBox, VMWare, and Microsoft Virtual Machine Manager. Individual users might be using Microsoft Virtual PC for smaller implementations. While there are certainly differences between the various products, they are similar enough to discuss as a unit.

Multiple VMs may be grouped together in a virtual network as a *team*. A team is a group of VMs that act as a multitier environment for a particular implementation. For example, a database server might be teamed with an application server and a storage server. Teaming allows all machines that are configured in a team to start up together, in a preconfigured boot order.

Not all files related to a VM are stored inside of the VM. The host has multiple files related to the configuration of the VM. There may also be a shared folder on the host that teamed VM access for mutually required data or configuration files. Whenever possible, try to capture the entire VM. As we will see later in the chapter, this is not always feasible.

FILES SPECIFIC TO THE VIRTUAL MACHINES

Naturally, it isn't just the user data that will be of interest. If possible, we would like to collect deleted data as well. Additionally, there will be log files and other system files that will help in building timelines, identifying user behavior, and so forth. A common commercial tool used for creating VMs is VMWare. On any given VMWare server, there are several files related to each VM (see Table 13.1). With VirtualBox, there is a single XML file for all configuration settings with an extension of .VBOX and a file for the virtual disk with a .VDI extension.

Table 13.1   VMWare Virtual Machine Files

Extension	Description
VMDK	A file that acts as the hard disk for the virtual machine (VM). This "disk" may be either a dynamic or fixed virtual disk. Dynamic disks start with a relatively small volume and are then allowed to grow to a preconfigured maximum size. Fixed disks do not change. Essential to capture.
VMEM	A backup of the VM's paging file. This file only exists on a running VM or on a VM that has at some point in time experienced a fatal error. May be useful.
VMSN	VMware snapshot files. A VMSN file records the state of a VM at the moment the snapshot is created. Of little forensic use.
VMSD	Metadata defining the snapshot. Of little forensic use.

Table 13.1 VMWare Virtual Machine Files—cont'd

Extension	Description
NVRAM	This is the file that stores the BIOS information for the VM. Of little forensic use.
VMX	Configuration file for the VM. Records such information as the operating system, disk and volume information, memory configuration, and so forth. Required for documentation purposes.
VMSS	Records the state of a suspended VM.
VMTM	This is the configuration file containing team data. VMs that are part of the team and boot order and start-sequence delay are configured here.
VMXF	If a VM is removed from a team, this configuration file remains.

UNDERSTANDING VIRTUAL NETWORKING

For all of the machines in a cloud to work together, they have to communicate with one another. Being virtual, they don't each have separate network adapters, and they don't connect directly to a switch. All of this, just like the machine, is done virtually. Virtual networking require a virtual adapter (simply called the VNIC from here on out) and a virtual switch (VS). Figure 13.5 is a virtual illustration of a virtual network.

A VNIC is treated no differently than a physical adapter. It is assigned a physical address (the MAC address, as it is called, from the fact that it runs on the Media Access Control layer of networking) and an IP address. Two configuration settings often required of physical adapters that a VNIC does not require are adapter speed settings and the communications model (duplex, simplex, etc.) The VNIC is configured as a device on the guest machine and managed the same way as any other NIC.

A VS is a little more complex than a VNIC, in that some of the configuration must be done when it is first created. A MAC layer forwarding engine is dependent upon what type of VNIC was configured on the various VMs. VLANs are another object that must be configured at creation time. A VLAN is a *virtual local area network*. Essentially, you are creating a virtual network within a virtual network. Many other features are similar to conventional switches. Various ports are configured to point to specific virtual devices on the network. When a packet arrives at the VS, it examines the packet's header for addressing information, finds the correct port, and forwards the packet out of that port. Each port is owned by a specific device, and only traffic intended for that device travels across the port.

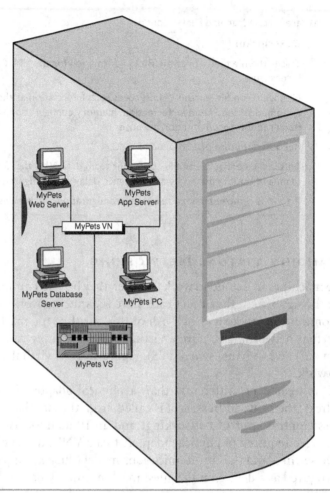

Figure 13.5 Virtual networks are built within the host server, the same way as virtual machines, complete with virtual NICs and virtual switches.

A key difference between a VS and a physical switch is that on any given virtual network on a single host, only one VS is required (or allowed, for that matter). In VMWare, a switch can have up to 1,016, and a given host can support up to 4,096, total ports distributed among all VSs installed on the host. Limitations are not published for Microsoft or VirtualBox.

VIRTUAL MACHINE SNAPSHOTS

A key attribute of VMs is that they can be "put to sleep" and revived to use later. A *snapshot* is a file that records the configuration and state of any given VM on a host. This is somewhat like putting a laptop computer into hibernation, except that unlike the laptop hibernation file, it isn't the contents of RAM that are stored. The snapshot contains the VM hardware configuration settings, network configuration, active state, and physical location of all virtual disks assigned to the VM, and (if the VM was running when the snapshot was made) the contents of VM memory. Initially, a snapshot file is not overly large. As more data is added to the hard disk, it becomes increasingly larger. In order to prevent snapshot files from becoming excessively large, VM management systems typically use a process called *differencing*. With differencing, each subsequent snapshot taken of a VM records only the changes that have been made to the VM since the last snapshot.

Using a snapshot to restore a VM carries the risk of deleting critical data. Going back to a snapshot permanently deletes any disk write operations that occurred in the interval since the snapshot was made. If an administrator inadvertently goes back to an earlier snapshot than the most recent, a significant amount of data can be destroyed.

TECHNICAL ASPECTS OF CLOUD FORENSICS

While the field of cloud forensics is relatively new, it employs a number of common techniques in its approach. Capturing a VM as an image is most certainly possible, with cooperation from the service provider. With VMWare, as well as some of the open-source VM managers, it is possible to capture the image and mount it as a drive image. FTK Imager will add a VM as an evidence item, and the investigator can use the usual tricks to search for evidence. Therefore, once an image is acquired, the process of examining it isn't much different than for a disk image. However, in a cloud environment, simply getting a single machine image may not be the total solution.

Insomuch as cloud forensics is still in its infancy, there are currently no sophisticated tools specific to the task. The same techniques of acquiring data in the various other forms of forensic acquisition will have to suffice. The challenges lie in collecting the data images to analyze. Both technical and legal hurdles prohibit going into a service provider's server farm and seizing a cluster of blades that hosts the VMs you want to search. The other clients whose VMs exist on that same cluster will take a dim view of that.

Live response is just as critical in the virtual environment as it is on physical machines. Perhaps it is even more important, since the virtual environment is more subject to change. Specialized tools need to be developed for capturing the memory image of a virtual server over a remote connection. For conventional data searches, such as e-discovery compliance or similar document searches, conventional tools are adequate.

The collection of artifacts will be done on both the client side and the service provider side. Client-side artifacts pose no problems any more complex than any other system search. The provider side is where it gets complex. The investigation team has to work with the provider to assure segregation of tenants. The problem faced here is that currently no tools available are really up to the task of identifying artifacts on a machine hosting multiple VMs. CPU and graphics processor caching is not segregated in such a way that you can simply copy the memory locations without pulling down information related to other tenants on the system.

Earlier in the chapter, I mentioned that one of the first questions to ask before starting to dig was what kinds of data was being sought along with where and how it would be stored. You also have to figure out how you are going to get at the data. In an SaaS environment, data files generated by the application will be stored in a data archive somewhere in the vendor's environment. However, it is also possible that copies of files might exist on the client machine as well. In PaaS or IaaS, you should assume some sort of stateful storage has been configured. You should *not* assume that all data stored in a cloud environment was generated by an application running on that cloud. Many services give control over the storage environment to the customer. So a virtual data warehouse designed to hold financial records might also be a convenient place to store illegal downloads.

The Types of Data Stored in a Cloud

The type of data you seek is very similar to what you would look for in any other investigation. You are looking for specific user files related to the case at hand. You are looking for deleted files that may be of interest, and you are looking for any temporary files created during the work process that generates user data. User data is generally relatively easy to map if you have the cooperation of the service provider. Their technical team will have configured the file structure used by the client. These are the people who can tell you specifically where each application used by a client stores its data. Therefore, one of the questions you ask the service provider early on is, For what services has this particular client contracted with your firm?

Understand the form in which the data resides as well. A document imaging system is likely to store documents in large cabinet files or folders (Figure 13.6). The file naming convention used by the application is unlikely to shed any light on the contents of each file. That information is maintained in metadata contained in separate database files (Figure 13.7).

In Figure 13.7, you see two pairs of files with .mdf extensions and two pairs with .ldf extensions. MDF stands for *master database file*. This file contains

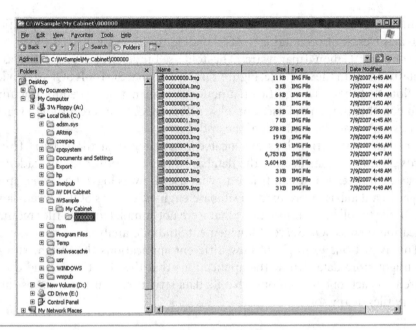

Figure 13.6 Files stored by document imaging systems use generic system-generated file names.

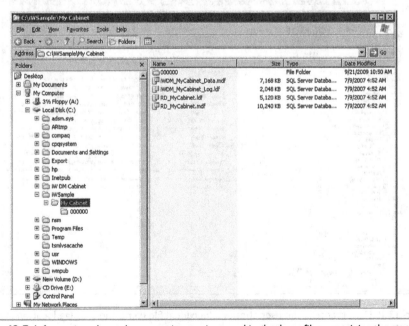

Figure 13.7 Information about document images is stored in database files containing the metadata.

information that tells the document imaging system how to find a specific file in the archives. It also contains MAC data. Figure 13.9 shows what the user sees when opening Canon Imageware. The folders, binders, and properties are all maintained within the .mdf file. Figure 13.8 shows what SysTools SQL MDF viewer sees. Note that there is a significant amount of information stored for documents and folders that the general user doesn't see. Figure 13.8 is a screenshot of what the user sees, based on the contents of the .mdf file.

Database transaction logs are located in the log data file (LDF). This file records all transactions against the database and any modifications made to the database. An investigator can find out what user ID was logged on when specific changes to a database were made. Database engines, such as SQL Server, can use the LDF file to roll back transactions that were not completed. LDF files require an application such as SQL Server Management Studio to analyze.

This is just one example of how different applications that might run on a PaaS might store data. Know the applications that the client runs, and do your research on each one to find out what its data structure is and if it stores supplementary files of any sort.

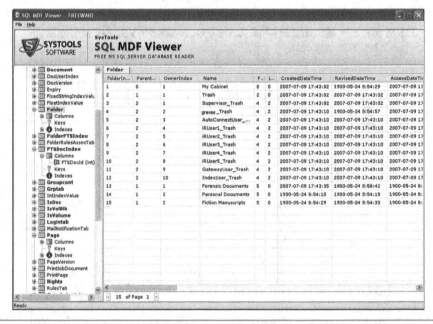

Figure 13.8 Data that tells the user about an individual file name and storage location is stored in the MDF file.

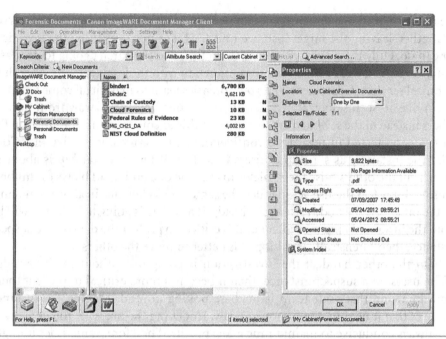

Figure 13.9 Data from the .mdf file fills in the screen that the user sees.

The Process of Capturing Virtual Machines

When there is no danger posed by having the client know that the investigation is in progress, and it is known what specific servers contain the information being sought, VMs managed by a client can be cloned and uploaded to a forensics server. This makes the forensics process no more complicated than any other digital investigation. An image of the VM, virtually identical to a disk image, is collected and analyzed.

Frequently the client must be kept out of the loop. Live data collection might be the focus of the investigation, and shutting down the VM is not an option. In a traditional forensics investigation, one of the first things the investigator does is to isolate the "crime scene" from any environment that can possibly contaminate it. The investigator has no control over the virtual environment of the host provider, so it must rely on cooperation with the vendor to accomplish this. As stated previously, the customer's services exist on the provider's network as an individual instance, and multiple instances exist on a single server or node.

Delport, Olivier, and Köhn (2011) propose that the solution to this dilemma is to isolate the instance in the service provider's environment. This means either moving the instance from one server to another or moving all other instances on the server to another, leaving the target instance intact. This is not something the investigator can do. Only the service provider can do this, and they aren't going to do it as a casual favor. You will need to work in conjunction with the legal team, the provider's technical services department, and your forensics team to make it all come together.

While it seems logically easier to move one instance away from several others instead of the several from one, there is this to consider. Each instance on the servers is protected in regards to confidentiality, integrity, and availability. Consider the instances as starship cruisers in a fleet. When one starship is about to launch, all the others raise their shields in case the one taking off blows to smithereens. VMs protect themselves in much the same way. When one instance is moving, all the others on the node raise their shields. If any data is going to be lost, it will be from the instance being moved. Since it is critical to protect the data on the suspect instance, then forensically speaking, it is better to move the others.

On the other hand, if the investigation is going on without the knowledge of the users on a suspect instance, then it becomes more critical to prevent them from knowing that your team is in there poking around. Moving the instance requires that it be shut down momentarily. Knocking the users off the network is not always conducive to maintaining a low profile. Therefore, sometimes it might be necessary to move the suspect instance, and other times it might be necessary to leave it in state and move all the others.

Instance relocation can be done manually or automatically. Manual relocation involves the administrators of the virtual network creating a new instance and ending the old one (or vice versa). This method allows virtual memory, virtual disks, and allocated memory to be copied to files and saved. The new instance is configured to have all of the same network resources as the old and then switched on. From a forensic standpoint, this method is preferable, in that a static image of the VM can be made and the image analyzed in conventional forensic software.

CONSTITUTIONAL ISSUES

Legal ramifications have been mentioned several times throughout the course of this chapter. This section will demonstrate just how confusing this issue is. As with any other issues covered by this book, a forensic investigation into the cloud must meet all constitutional criteria when the government is involved and all legal standards imposed by legislation in private enquiries. Essentially, the rights of the individual don't change just because the computing platform moved from the living room to the Internet. However, the doorways through which the data must pass, as well as the halls in which it resides, differ greatly. Accordingly, the methods by which data is excavated changes as well. This section will deal with some Fourth and Fifth Amendment issues specific to cloud computing. Just as the technology of cloud computing offers new challenges on the technical side, the arguments posed by the technology are convoluting the legal side.

FOURTH AMENDMENT ISSUES OF CLOUD COMPUTING

To review some issues covered in Chapter 3, "Search Warrants and Subpoenas," you will recall that a very formidable foe of the prosecutor was the exclusionary rule. If evidence is obtained in a manner inconsistent with constitutional dogma or legislative rule, then it doesn't exist. You can have thousands of graphic images of child pornography that it is easy to prove came from the defendant's computer. However, if the defense can convince the court that the computer was seized illegally or that the search was in any way inappropriate, those images will be inadmissible. That is the basic tenet of the Fourth Amendment.

Several questions are considered by the court when deciding whether evidence is admissible. This was covered in Chapter 3, but to review, those questions include

- Was the search legal?
- Did the individual have a reasonable expectation of privacy?
- Did the individual knowingly expose private information to the public?

If the evidence presented passes through all three filters intact, it is considered admissible. The courts try to interpret these issues using existing case law as much as possible, using analogies such as the closed container rule applied to hard disks. After all, it is quite obvious that in today's digital world, a man's computer is his castle. What happens when the "castle" is shared with two dozen others on a single drive array in a server farm two thousand miles away? Where do the castle walls stand?

When can an investigator search the castle? As we saw in Chapter 3, the personal computers and hard disks of defendants were vigorously protected under Fourth Amendment law. When it came to cloud computing, the walls started to blur. The Electronic Stored Communications Act (ESCA) of 1986 exposed one limitation to these walls long before cloud computing was imagined. Under this legislation, a court can order an ISP to turn over any e-mails or electronic records that have resided on an external server for more than 180 days (ESCA 1986), *without notifying the owner of those files*. That was all fine and good when it was assumed that records left on a public server that long could be essentially considered abandoned. However, with cloud computing, the client is using public servers as the permanent storage mechanism. Any person with a subscription more than 180 days old is subject to having the older files grabbed for any reason, without the need of the investigator having a warrant.

When it comes to the concept of "reasonable expectation of privacy," the courts have been friendlier to prosecutors than defendants in some regards. A case used frequently as a precedent for granting access to remotely stored electronic data is *U.S. v. Miller* (1976). Here, the courts declared that the defendant had no reasonable expectation of privacy regarding his bank records because by revealing his affairs to another entity (in this case, the defendant's bank), he assumed the risk that such information would be vulnerable and made available to government scrutiny. The same philosophy has been applied to acquiring telephone records as well.

Intentional use of cloud services really blurs the lines when it comes to whether or not the individual has intentionally exposed information to the public. Cloud services are generally considered public utilities, in some cases, even where a private cloud has been configured. Applications and operating systems designed with cloud computing in mind, such as Google Chrome and Google Apps, store calendars, notes, documents, images, and contact information on public servers. A reasonable expectation of privacy is implied by the fact that the user is required to enter a user ID and password in order to access this information. However, the ground rules of the ESCA also apply. Which takes precedence?

Applications such as Facebook allow the users to set the configuration on their personal page to allow their "friends" to edit the page, which enables lively exchanges of ideas, resources, and insults. In allowing external edits, the user has essentially given up all expectation of privacy. They are not only saying, "Come in and look," but they are also saying, "Add your own illegal content while you're in here." At what point does the account owner give up responsibility for content?

The courts more recently took a proactive step in the direction of the individual user rights in *State v. Bellar*. In this case, images of child pornography were discovered on a suspect's computer. Justice Edmonds, in writing the decision, specifically targeted cloud computing when he wrote, "I suspect that most citizens would regard that data as no less confidential or private because it was stored on a server owned by someone else" (*State v. Bellar* 2009).

It is clear that there is a substantial amount of work to be done before there is clarity on the legal issues of a cloud search. With courts disagreeing with one another, it is not surprising that law enforcement is confused. The legal issues are as new as the technologies when it comes to the cloud, and it is essential that legal counsel be obtained whenever there is doubt about direction. When in doubt, get a warrant.

FIFTH AMENDMENT ISSUES OF CLOUD COMPUTING

The other constitutional battleground involving the cloud will be over passwords. Accessing a suspect's data and applications in the cloud will require knowing the user ID and password in virtually every case. Is forcing the surrender of a password in violation of the Fifth Amendment?

In *re Boucher*, the court stated that production of a password might be deemed self-incriminatory if it was the production of the password that induced the incrimination. In the decision, the judges wrote, "A password, like a combination, is in the suspect's mind, and is therefore testimonial and beyond the reach of the grand jury subpoena" (*re Boucher* 2009). However, the same court also allowed the inclusion of the evidence obtained because the knowledge of what existed on the hard drive existed before the search was initiated. The court ordered that the production of an unencrypted hard disk did not infringe on the suspect's rights.

This concept was revisited in *U.S. v. Fricosu* (2012). Government prosecutors argued that the password used to encrypt a hard drive was a token and thereby not necessarily protected under the Fifth Amendment. The defense argued that since the password was something contained within the defendant's mind and not a physical entity, forcing her to divulge the password would infringe upon her rights. The Tenth U.S. District Court of Appeals took an end around in this case. The judge did not order Fricosu to divulge her password but did order her to turn over an unencrypted copy of the hard disk for examination. It is very likely that this case will be appealed and may eventually wind up in the Supreme Court, as it poses significant questions regarding the relevance of the Fifth Amendment in the digital age.

The arguments center on whether a password is considered to be a "key," which is a physical thing and covered under the Fourth Amendment, or more akin to the combination to a safe. *Doe v. United States* (1988) tackled the role of combinations to safes long before passwords to encrypted drives were an issue. In this seminal case, the Supreme Court stated that a suspect might be "forced to surrender a key to a strongbox containing incriminating documents" but not "compelled to reveal the combination to a wall safe." This puts the password as a combination securely into the purview of the Fifth Amendment. The criminal who locks away all trace of sin with a key can be forced to give it up. The one who uses a combination lock can keep it a secret for a long time. It is an argument that is likely to go on for several years.

CHAPTER REVIEW

1. What are the three forms of service offered by cloud computing? Briefly describe each one in terms of form and function.

2. When a warrant is issued to search the computer systems of a particular entity, it generally specifies what forms of hardware are to be searched and the location of that hardware. Why is that impossible if the target of the warrant employs cloud computing? How can this problem be overcome?

3. Briefly describe the concept of *virtualization*. How is it relevant to the concept of digital forensics?

4. A suspect in a particular case employs an enterprise-level document imaging system to manage his files. The files all carry file names such as 003224.img. What are some other files managed by the system that will help isolate and identify these files?

5. Describe the process of capturing a virtual machine. How is it different than acquiring a conventional disk image? How is it similar? What are some factors that must be considered before you even begin?

CHAPTER EXERCISES

1. Browse to Amazon Web Services (currently at http://aws.amazon.com/) and examine their services offered. Which services are IaaS, which are SaaS, and which are PaaS?

2. Look up the case *Metro-Goldwyn-Mayer Studios Inc. v. Grokster, Ltd.,* and consider the following. Grokster and StreamCast were held liable for copyright infringement, simply on the merit that they provided the software that made the storage, search, and distribution of copyrighted materials possible. Briefly discuss how this decision could potentially affect companies who offer SaaS services.

REFERENCES

Armbrust et al. 2009. *Above the clouds: A Berkeley view of cloud computing.* http://x-integrate.de/x-in-cms.nsf/id/DE_Von_Regenmachern_und_ Wolkenbruechen_-_Impact_2009_Nachlese/$file/abovetheclouds.pdf (accessed May 23, 2012).

Delport, W., M. Olivier, and M. Köhn. 2011. *Isolating a cloud instance for a digital forensic investigation.* http://icsa.cs.up.ac.za/issa/2011/Proceedings/Research/ Delport_Olivier_Kohn.pdf (accessed May 14, 2012).

Doe v. United States, 487 U.S. 201, 210 (1988).

Electronic Stored Communications Act of 1986. Pub. L. 99–508, 100 Stat. 1848.

Mell, P., and T. Grance. 2011. *The NIST definition of cloud computing.* Special Publication 800-145. http://csrc.nist.gov/publications/nistpubs/800-145/SP800-145.pdf (accessed May 1, 2012).

Novell. 2011. Cloud computing: What is the cloud? www.novell.com/communities/node/13328/cloud-computing-what-is-the-cloud (accessed May 7, 2012).

re Boucher, 2007 WL 4246473 (Nov. 29, 2009).

State v. Bellar, 050230673; A129493. Multnomah County Court (2009).

United States v. Fricosu, No. 10-cr-00509-REB-02 (Jan. 23, 2012).

United States v. Miller, 425 U.S. 435, 443 (1976).

MOBILE DEVICE FORENSICS 14

Mobile devices (cell phones in particular) are integral to today's society and can be a crucial part of a forensic case. It is important to have an understanding of what challenges an investigator may face when it comes to mobile devices.

This chapter visits what types of data are stored on most cell phones and where this data can be found. It also reviews what types of tools there are to assist with cell phone forensics, whether they be hardware or software based. Demonstrating a few cell phone forensic tools, this chapter reviews acquisition and analysis of data. The chapter wraps up by looking at a few legal case studies where cell phones were pertinent to the investigation.

Due to the extremely wide variety of devices on the market and the differences in how these devices are acquired, this chapter provides only a review of the techniques for mobile device forensics. It will be less "hands-on," as it is unlikely that the tools and devices will be available to the average reader.

CHALLENGES OF MOBILE DEVICE FORENSICS

There is no greater challenge to a digital investigator than mobile forensics. Mobile devices have much of the same capabilities as a fully functional computer system, such as gaming, photography, messaging, and the ability to send multimedia, but it fits in a pocket.

The ease of use of functionality that mobile applications provide allows for a treasure trove of data for an investigator, but mobile device forensics lacks the tools that are available for computer forensics, and the requirements are often more strenuous. Compare acquiring a Windows machine to a cell phone at a corporation.

The investigator may receive instruction to acquire a computer for forensics. Let's assume the computer has been shut down or the requestor has properly ensured the machine stay "live" until told otherwise. After receiving the computer, the investigator would be able to do an acquisition using any court-recognized forensic tool (EnCase, iLook, Helix, etc.). If the computer has disk encryption software, the investigator would need the encryption key to decrypt the software or use a module device with a choice of acquisition software. The examiner then acquires the system. After these steps are complete, the investigator has an original copy of the computer that is "bagged and tagged" and a working copy of the computer in which to work from. Simple enough.

When it comes to mobile forensics, there are similar steps in acquisition and analysis, but these come with caveats when analyzing the device. Later we will review some of the steps needed to go through an acquisition of a mobile device, but here are a few things to ponder: What if the mobile device is issued by the company and password protected, but the suspect did not sign a waiver form to state that the mobile device could be analyzed at the company's discretion? Even worse, what if it was a personal mobile device, but might have company data on it? These are simple questions, but the ramifications of these simple questions need to be addressed before attempting to even begin to examine a mobile device.

How Cell Phones Work

Understanding the process of how cell phones work will help you understand where data can be found during an investigation. Cell phones are full-duplex devices, which means two people can speak at the same time. A half-duplex device, such as a walkie-talkie or CB radio, allows only one person to speak at a time. And while half-duplex devices have an estimated communication distance of one to five miles, a cell phone user can speak to someone across the globe, as long as the battery stays alive. The magic that allows this distance for a cell phone user is cellular towers and a well-crafted network.

Cellular Towers

A major cell phone carrier receives a certain amount of frequencies to use. These frequencies are split up between the cells, which are usually ten square miles in area. Since both the cell phones and cell phone towers utilize a low bandwidth,

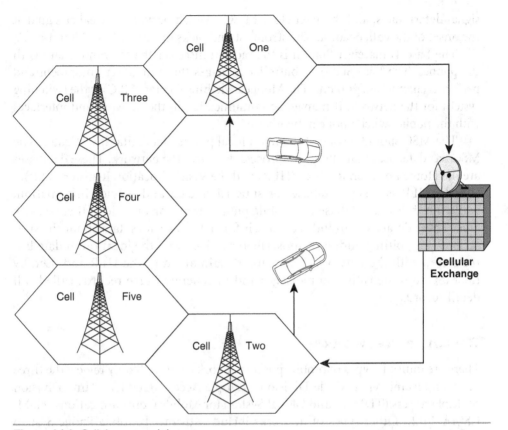

Figure 14.1 Cellular network layout

the cell phone frequencies can be reutilized within a nonadjacent cell, causing no interference. Referring to Figure 14.1, a cell phone user in Cell One can be on the same frequency as that of a user in Cell Two, but not that of Cell Three.

When a cell phone caller dials a person who is utilizing a landline, the process is simple. The cell phone call goes to the base tower, which is then sent to a receiver, which is then transmitted to a landline. Making a call to a cell phone from a cell phone is basically the same principle. The caller makes a cell phone call, which is picked up by the base tower closest to them, which goes to the receiver, to the landline system, and then to the receiver on the cell phone tower that is closest to the receiving cell phone. From there, the signal is transmitted to the tower and subsequently relayed to the target cell phone.

A cell phone call is held by the tower closest to the person making a call (the closer to the tower, the stronger the signal). As the caller moves out of range, the signal deteriorates, and the next closest tower, which provided a weaker signal at the onset of the call, becomes the strongest and picks up the call as a "hand-off."

The Base Transceiver Station is the radio transceiver that communicates with the phones. The Base Station Controller manages the transceiver equipment and performs channel assignment. The Mobile Switching Center (MSC) is the switching system for the network. It manages communication in the network and interfaces with the public switch phone network.

The MSC should be one of the main focal points of a digital investigator. The MSC has databases that allow it to process data over the network. These databases are the Home Location Register (HLR) and the Visitor Location Register (VLR).

The HLR is a key database for subscriber data and service information, while the VLR is a database for mobile phones roaming outside of their service area. These databases provide account information, such as data about the subscriber (e.g., billing address), subscribed services, and the location update last registered with the network. This data is maintained in the HLR and used by the MSC to route calls and messages and to generate usage records called call detail records.

CELLULAR NETWORKS

There are multiple types of mobile phone networks, but we'll only review the three most important types: Code Division Multiple Access (CDMA), Time Division Multiple Access (TDMA), and Global System for Mobile Communications (GSM; GSMA 2012). Other types of networks include Advanced Mobile Phone System (AMPS), Integrated Digital Enhanced Network (iDEN), and Universal Mobile Telecommunications System (UMTS).

CDMA is a technology designed by Qualcomm that transmits multiple signals spread across an entire bandwidth. As each signal reaches its destination, it gets decoded at the receiving end. The key part to CDMA is that it shares bandwidth with other CDMA users, utilizing a shared frequency spectrum, but it is based on a code. Instead of focusing on different frequencies, CDMA focuses on these codes to distinguish between stations, or users. The receiving tower knows what one mobile user's code and channel is and can differentiate between other mobile users. It is the same concept as "the cocktail effect." While at a social gathering, there are many people speaking all at once. Instead of missing your conversation from all the others occurring at the same time, you know which conversation to listen for, just like the base tower receiver would.

TDMA is very similar to CDMA in that it utilizes a spectrum sharing technology, but it is based on time. The spectrum is broken into three time slots, which allow multiple users to communicate without interruption. Utilizing the example from before, there would be one person speaking at the cocktail party at a time. They would then stop to allow another person to speak, and so on.

TDMA technology is incorporated into the more advanced GSM technology. GSM is currently the world's most widely used technology. One of the reasons for this popularity is that GSM network sharing essentially eradicates most roaming for cell phone users. Another huge advantage for GSM is that the mobile devices utilize a **SIM** card, which we will discuss later in the chapter.

TRIANGULATION (TRILATERATION)

Thanks to the Pythagorean theorem, a cell phone can be triangulated in close proximity using cell tower triangulation, or it can be located using a more focused approach like GPS. The Global Positioning System (GPS) is used to track cell phone locations, and most current models have built-in GPS capability. According to the National Coordination Office for Space-Based Positioning, Navigation, and Timing (2012), there are 31 operational GPS satellites, of which 24 are assured to be activated at any given time.

To locate a cell phone's exact location, GPS communicates with three satellites near the phone's position, which is determined by the cell phone's GPS receiver. The satellites form three circles, and where they intersect is where the phone is located.

A cell phone is triangulated by cell phone towers, rather than satellites (Cloudetal 2011). Just as satellites can triangulate a mobile device, three cell phone towers communicate with a cell phone to determine its location. The first tower calculates the distance to the phone using the strength of the signal. We can draw a circle along which the phone can exist anywhere along the periphery (Figure 14.2). With the first tower, we estimate the distance from the tower to the cell phone at one mile.

A second tower calculates distance on the basis of signal strength and comes up with a distance of one and a half miles. Where the distances overlap between the first and second towers, we have a likely position for the cell phone. This narrows the position of the cell phone down to two possible locations (Figure 14.3).

Now a third tower is used to calculate distance. This time the signal strength tells the towers the cell phone is 1.7 miles away. The circle for the third tower is drawn and the location is locked down (Figure 14.4).

When a tower sends a ping to a cell phone, the distance can be calculated by the lag time it takes to get a ping back from the cell phone. This is similar to how bats use echoes to determine their distance from nearby objects.

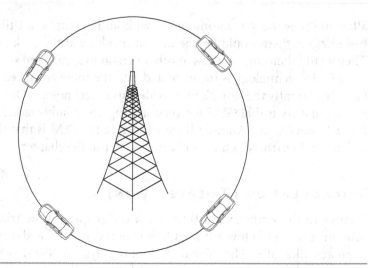

Figure 14.2 Triangulation distance (1 mile)

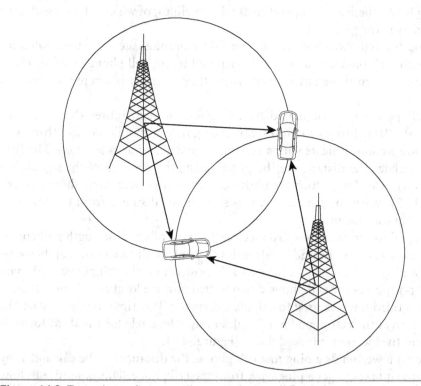

Figure 14.3 Triangulation distance with a second tower (1.5 miles)

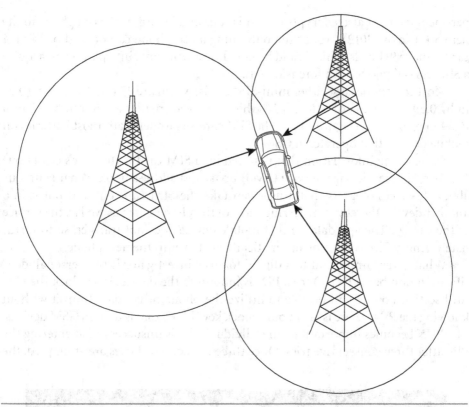

Figure 14.4 Triangulation distance with a third tower (1.7 miles)

DATA STORAGE ON CELL PHONES

There is a plethora of data that can be found on a mobile device, but you have to know where to look. The phone could contain pieces of physical hardware that retain this data, and not knowing the internals could cause future problems. The investigator must understand that there is pertinent data in identification numbers that may or may not be easily seen inside the phone, and there are data chips that allow network communications to occur. We'll go over some of the more important data areas, but the investigator should obtain all information about a particular mobile device by searching the manufacturer's Web site.

MEMORY

The Subscriber Identity Module (SIM) card is very important to understand as it not only stores vital information about the cell phone, the user, and some pertinent data but also encrypts transmissions and identifies the cell phone to the network (Kayne 2012). About the only thing a cell phone can do without a SIM card is make 911 calls. This should be noted, as it will come into play if you acquire a SIMless cell phone with forensic tools.

Most cell phones use either mini-SIM cards, which are 25 mm by 15 mm (0.98 in by 0.59 in), or micro-SIM cards, which are even smaller at 15 mm by 12 mm (0.59 in by 0.47 in) (Figure 14.5). The SIM card sits underneath most batteries on mobile devices that operate on GSM.

Some of the information that is stored on a SIM card is the user's cell phone number, Simple Message Service (SMS) texts, and address book. What is unique about this technology is that a user can take the SIM card out and put it into another device, thereby transferring most of the phone's data as well as the service of the carrier. The app data on that mobile device does not transfer, so unfortunately, Angry Birds does not automatically port over to the new phone.

What is very important to a digital forensic investigator is the personal identification number (PIN). Once a PIN is input into the device, it will lock the SIM card so that no one will be able to utilize the phone or get data from it without knowing the PIN. There is also a pin unlock key (PUK) that is used in GSM devices. The PUK becomes important to an individual who is unsuccessful at entering the PIN after three consecutive tries. Once three unsuccessful tries are attempted, the

Figure 14.5 SIM card

SIM card will lock and will require the service provider to provide the PUK to unlock the SIM card. The service provider will ask for the Integrated Circuit Chip Identifier (ICCID) located on the SIM for verification before it provides the PUK.

It is critical to know that if an individual attempts ten unsuccessful tries at unlocking a PIN, one of two things will happen: The SIM becomes permanently blocked, or if the device is corporate owned and managed by an enterprise server, the cell phone might be configured to be overwritten. It should also be noted that within the cellular configuration settings, an automatic wipe after ten attempts can be set by the owner.

While the SIM has some storage capability (128KB in some instances), it is not the only storage on a cell phone. There is both read-only memory (ROM) and random access memory (RAM). The ROM will hold the operating system (OS) of the device, while the RAM is volatile and can disappear without proper power. Just as in traditional computer forensics, if the investigator wants to acquire the memory of the operating system, it is best that the system have a power source. This can be a major issue with cell phones because there are many types and many different power requirements to contend with.

While this chapter will not go into great detail about operating systems on cell phones, be aware that the OS in ROM that an investigator would expect may not be the one that is there. For example, just because a cell phone appears to be a Droid does not mean it will be configured with an Android OS. This is because an OS can be replaced on a cell phone.

DEVICE INFO

Not only can the SIM and ICCID number be found printed on the cell phone label, but there is other useful information about the phone as well. There is both the electronic serial number (ESN) and the mobile equipment identifier (MEID), and the International Mobile Equipment Identity (IMEI). The ESN and MEID numbers are specific to each CDMA phone, and they are the unique identifiers to the CDMA network. The IMEI number is specific to GSM phones. These numbers can be thought of as a mobile device's "social security" number.

The ESN of a cell phone is a unique number that is used by the switching office to check the validity of the call (Mobiledia 2012). An MEID holds the same functionality as does an ESN for identifying the cell phone to the CDMA network, but it doesn't have the limitations of ESN. In 2005, there was a shortage of ESN numbers because ESN is based on 32 bits, with only 4 billion unique numbers. The MEID utilizes 56 bits, and that gives millions of times as many unique numbers as ESN.

Another way to retrieve the MEID is to key in *#06# on the mobile device. If the device is a Motorola phone, the MEID can be retrieved by the sequence #, *, Menu, and then the right arrow key. If the mobile device is an iPhone, just go to Settings, General, and About. The MEID is a hexadecimal number and can be readily found by viewing the first digits that begin with A–F.

IMEI is similar to the MEID number in that it will identify the mobile device to the network. This number can be utilized to have the device blocked should it be lost or stolen. This number is printed in the battery compartment (Figure 14.6).

The IMEI number has a total of 15 numeric digits and has a few different purposes. The first eight digits are the Type Allocation Code (TAC). These numbers indicate the phone's model and where it was made. The next sequence of six digits is the serial number of the device. The last digit is the checksum number.

Before moving on to discuss forensic methodology of acquiring cell phones, it goes without saying that that all information that is found on a device label can be

Figure 14.6 IMEI number

tampered with. A nefarious individual can remove the label, alter it with a permanent marker, or just scratch the information off the phone, making it hard to find the correct information.

There are many other ways to find out what the device is or to whom it belongs. Just as with computer forensics, an investigator has to utilize all tools available and search for information. Some of the information can be retrieved by looking at the power cord of the device, which may be specific to a particular model of a phone. An obvious search around the general area may reveal other peripherals that attach to the device, including computer systems that can be forensically searched. As a last resort, utilizing the cell phone's number in a reverse-lookup on the internet may reveal the owner.

ACQUISITION AND STORAGE

During acquisition of the cell phone (if powered on), the investigator must notate the phone's date and time while being able to compare that time to another clock. The USNO navy clock is an accurate option (http://tycho.usno.navy.mil/).

It is also suggested that the investigator take notes on all device information available that is easily viewable while it is powered on. If the device is powered off, then the phone's battery source can be removed to view all device info.

While there are multiple tools, both free and off-the-shelf products, this chapter focuses on products that can be purchased. The main reason we focus on these off-the-shelf products is that they have been tested, and there is no need to go through a full-blown validation process (although in-house testing is still recommended). The risk of having evidence declared inadmissible by the court might possibly be increased by utilizing free tools if the evidence cannot be validated. The standards of evidence authentication defined in *Daubert v. Merrel Dow Pharmaceuticals* (1933) most certainly apply to evidence extracted from mobile devices.

HARDWARE

One advantage we now have as investigators is the plethora of hardware-based tools available for mobile device acquisitions. One of the challenges is keeping the phone from being able to communicate over the mobile network during the investigation. After a mobile device is seized in a search incident to arrest (SITA), if it is powered on and communicating on the mobile network, there exists the possibility that it might be remotely tampered with or even wiped. There are many signal-jamming hardware devices available, and we review a few more popular devices.

Faraday Enclosures

As can be ascertained, the Faraday name is relational to keeping unwanted signals, or interference, out of an enclosure (Faraday Cage 2012). The Faraday bag, which is a radio frequency isolation device, is very similar in design to that of a freezer bag, but much more secure (Figure 14.7). One aspect of the Faraday bag that cannot be viewed in Figure 14.7 is that there are two sealing strips to ensure the bag completely prohibits communication.

It is important to note that the incident responder that secures the mobile device should ensure that there is a power source to attach to the mobile phone before putting it in a Faraday bag. The reason for this overzealous behavior is that with the mobile device powered on, it will continue to attempt to communicate with the cell towers. If the mobile device is powered on and does not have a battery pack connected to it, if it has no possible connection, the battery will drain much quicker than a phone that can communicate with a cell tower.

While having a Faraday bag is nice, it will not guarantee that the device will not make communication with a cell tower if there is any opening on the bag. A good example of this is when the mobile device is examined. If the investigator

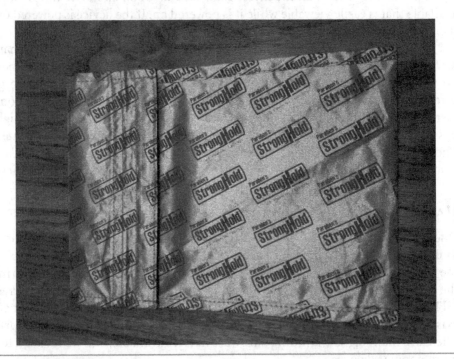

Figure 14.7 Paraben's Faraday bag

opens the bag ever so slightly to connect a data cable to the mobile device, then the cable can act as a strong antenna.

Prior to inserting the mobile device into a Faraday bag, the incident responder can put a portable charging device on the mobile phone. There are multiple instant charging devices available like Cellboost, Turbocharge, and Energizer. The premise behind these chargers is to give emergency power to the mobile user (incident responder) prior to the mobile device losing all of its charge. These instant charging devices are very similar to plugging the device into an AC outlet, but the phone works on more of an emergency mode.

The way to get around the dilemma of not being able to do analysis work on the mobile device securely is by utilizing a Faraday pouch or a Faraday box. Paraben's StrongHold Pouch is one device that an investigator can utilize. Using this pouch, the investigator first inserts the powered-on mobile device into the secure enclosure. The investigator then inserts the mobile device's data cable, which then connects to a shielded data connector inside the pouch. There is a connection on the back of the pouch that allows the investigator to connect the mobile device to a computer system.

Should the incident responder team need an enclosure that prohibits network signals and can hold multiple personnel, the next logical device would be a Faraday tent. This tent is very similar in concept to either a Faraday bag or a pouch; it is just more grandeur in scale. As working in these enclosures can become extremely hot, some of these tents include signal shielding for ventilation. What is practical about these signal enclosures is that they are portable and come in a variety of sizes. Some of them come in either single- or dual-layer protection.

CHANGING PHONE SETTINGS TO BLOCK COMMUNICATION

While it is almost always a bad idea for an investigator to change any settings on a mobile device they are examining, sometimes utilizing the operating system to perform forensic work may be a necessary evil. However, if any changes are made to a suspect device (mobile or otherwise), the investigator must document in great detail every step taken.

Setting a phone to airplane mode is one way to keep the device from communicating with the network. This setting prohibits the sending or receiving of text messages, e-mails, and phone calls and was intended to prevent communication during flight. This setting is common on most cell phones today.

Again, extreme care should be taken when making any device setting changes, and they need to be notated.

Screen Capture Devices

Screen capture devices document an investigator's every move. They can be very handy at times, especially when there is a need for a video log of all activities that are completed on a mobile device. There are multiple providers of screen capture devices. Two of these are Paraben's Project-A-Phone and the Eclipse screen capture device.

It is best if these pieces of hardware are used within a Faraday enclosure. If that is not possible, on a GSM phone, the investigator will need to determine whether to remove a SIM card so that no data transmission to the cell network occurs.

As stated earlier, when doing work with digital forensics there is a need to have extremely well-written notes to depict what work was done and how it was completed. Phone projection devices satisfy those requirements. These devices create case files, hash the video file, and also allow case notes to be added during examination into the software.

Image Extraction Devices

Cellebrite has proven to be one of the more popular mobile forensic companies around, providing products that focus on acquiring physical (bitwise) as well as logical images. Two of the flagship products that Cellebrite has to offer are the ever-popular Universal Forensic Extraction Device (UFED) and the Chinex device. Both devices also have the ability to obtain deleted data because of their physical extraction abilities.

The UFED device works on more than 1,600 different mobile devices. It captures all available mobile data (address book, SMS messages, pictures, videos, and call logs). The mobile device connects to the UFED by one of multiple available data cables, Bluetooth, or infrared. Once the device is recognized by the UFED, the investigator has the choice of which data retrieval options to pursue. Extracted data can be stored on an SD Card, a USB storage device, or the investigator's computer.

One of the more prominent features of the UFED device is that it has the ability to clone SIM cards. This is a very useful feature for an investigator when there is no SIM card present in the phone or when the examiner does not want the mobile device to communicate with the GSM cell network.

As discussed earlier in the chapter, another problem investigators experience in the field is a locked PIN on a mobile device they are examining. With UFED, the investigator can choose to extract a password instead of extracting phone data, cloning the SIM card, or using any other UFED feature. It must be noted that there is a completely different process that an investigator would go through when extracting passwords from a cell phone. After choosing the Extract Passcode option and continuing through the UFED menu for the type of device being worked on, the investigator can determine if the passcode is extracted to a USB device, SD Card, PC, or Display. The display option allows the investigator to view the passcode on the UFED device.

The Chinex device is an add-on device that plugs into the UFED. Like the UFED device, Chinex is geared toward the extraction of physical and logical images, but it is centered on Chinese chipset (MTK and Spreadtrum)-based devices. The Chinex device can perform extractions on thousands of different mobile devices.

SOFTWARE

After the investigator has extracted the data, it can be viewed in reporting software. Reporting software has many different analysis features built in, including viewing the data in hexadecimal mode. The report view contains information about the acquisition from the mobile device, along with MD5 hashes of the data. For example, it would indicate whether the picture that was captured from the mobile device has a hash value associated with that specific file.

There are many different mobile device software tools available to an examiner, like Paraben's mobile Device Seizure or BlackLight from BlackBag technologies, and they all perform different functions. Some investigative software is great for e-mail extraction, while another tool may be best suited for registry pulls. The focus of investigators when purchasing software is having a good idea of what mobile devices they will likely encounter during their investigation.

REMOVING MOISTURE FROM A CELL PHONE

There have been numerous cases in which a suspect threw a mobile device into a body of water to destroy evidence. The iPhone has four water indicators on the inside of the phone that turn pink if the device is submerged in water (The Full Signal 2012).

When an investigator discovers that a phone has been in water, the number one priority is to ensure the device does not stay powered on; unless, of course, there is a need for that risk. There is a Save-A-Phone product sold by Paraben that absorbs moisture from a mobile device, allowing for a safer power-up. Another option would be to set the mobile device in a bag of salt, allowing the salt to absorb the moisture. Another method that works is putting the phone in a sandwich bag that has packets of silica gel inside. In all cases it is recommended that the investigator allow the phone to dry for 3 to 5 days. Afterward, the investigator should examine the phone for any moisture that could be hidden, before turning on the device.

LEGAL ASPECTS OF MOBILE DEVICE FORENSICS

Cell phone technology has posed some interesting problems for the courts as well as the investigator. Courts have had a difficult time establishing precedents for a variety of questions regarding the legality of evidence extracted from cell phones. Legal issues include

- The legality of the search
- The integrity of the evidence extracted
- The validity of the evidence extracted
- The relevance of the evidence extracted

Because so much information can be stored in a cell phone, investigators frequently look at the device as a gold mine filled with smoking guns. As we've seen, the contents of a cell phone can include photographs, deleted text messages, GPS information showing where the device has been, contact information, and call logs. The issue the courts have had to face is when it is legal to search a phone and whether certain evidence stored on the phone might be considered either protected or exempt. Just as an example, Newitz (2007) pointed out that Mobile Phone Manager had been used by law enforcement agencies nationwide to collect cell phone evidence for two years before the developers (Oxygen Forensic) released a version that generated hash values of data images before and after capture. Before that, it was a crapshoot whether the data captured could be considered "tamperproof."

THE LEGALITY OF A CELL PHONE SEARCH

Search and seizure laws regarding cell phones differ in whether the target of the search is protected by the Constitution or by regulatory law. Any time law enforcement or a government agency is involved, the constitutional rights of the person being searched come into play. In situations involving civil law, the legal issues can become more convoluted and might be governed by any one (or more) of several different privacy laws.

Legal Issues Facing Law Enforcement

Early case law involving cell phones was directly impacted by a court decision handed down not too long before mobile telephones became commonly available to the public. In *The United States v. Ortiz* (1996), the Seventh Federal Circuit ruled that law enforcement could legally search a person's pager. The assumption guiding the decision was that any new pages issued from the time of the incident to the moment at which a warrant could be obtained could potentially overwrite valuable evidence.

Cell phones are considered the property of the person in possession until proven otherwise. As such, a random search or seizure of the device would constitute a breach of the owner's Fourth Amendment rights. Two situations exist that can allow a judge to deem evidence obtained by law enforcement without a warrant to be admissible. These are the incident to search and the exigent circumstances exceptions. There is a history of the courts generally accepting both of these exceptions in criminal cases.

U.S. v. Finley (2007) decided in favor of the government regarding the right of law enforcement to search a cell phone seized at the time of the arrest. (This same case will be examined later in this chapter regarding the rights of a private individual when using a corporate telephone.) In this incident, the cell phone of the suspect was removed from his possession at the time of arrest and incriminating evidence was found. The key point in this decision was that the cell phone was in his possession and within his reach.

An exigent circumstances exception is likely to be granted whenever law enforcement can demonstrate that there is a strong likelihood that a crime is in the process of being committed or that safety to life and limb is at risk. However, the argument that critical evidence is at risk of being destroyed if the device remained in the possession of the suspect may not always hold water. There has been a leaning toward citing *U.S. v. Salgado* (1986) in recent cases. In this decision, Judge William Campbell wrote, "A mere possibility that evidence will be destroyed—a possibility that exists any time a drug dealer is arrested outside of his home or other place of (illicit) business—is not enough. Otherwise the requirement of a warrant would have little meaning in the investigation of drug crimes." This suggests that other mitigating conditions must support a search and seizure based on exigent circumstances.

In the case of *Salgado*, the conviction was upheld because the government could demonstrate that there was a near certainty that evidence would be destroyed. Conversely, in *U.S. v. Young* (2006), the decision read, "This Court finds that exigent circumstances existed because the evidence could be lost if not retrieved immediately without the benefit of a search warrant." Such contradictory messages from the court are precisely why legal counsel should be involved in all searches. To be safe, always assume that a warrant is needed.

Legal Issues in Civil Cases

Think back to a comment I made in the previous section. A cell phone is considered to be the property of the person in possession until proven otherwise. This can have a direct impact on civil litigation as well. A person who is assigned a company-issued cell phone is the person in possession, but not necessarily the legal owner. Somehow the rights of the individual must be balanced by the rights of the owner. Generally speaking, in the presence of an official company policy regarding cell phone usage, the policy dictates what rights the user has. If the policy states that the company reserves the right to monitor or search the phone, then the individual would have an uphill battle in pursuing claims in the event of a search.

In *City of Ontario, California v. Quon* (2008), the issue revolved around a mobile phone issued to an employee for official use. When Quon became the target of an internal investigation involving sexually explicit messages being transmitted from his phone, the city confiscated and searched his phone. He argued that since the city was a government entity, he was protected by the Fourth Amendment and that even though he did not own the phone, a warrant was required to seize it. The Supreme Court disagreed. Since this was a government related case, how does this relate to civil issues?

It boils down to a statement made by Justice Scalia in the decision *O'Connor v. Ortega*, 480 U.S. 709: "Government searches to retrieve work-related materials or to investigate violations of workplace rules—searches of the sort that are regarded as reasonable and normal in the private employer context—do not violate the Fourth Amendment."

The general interpretation of this rule is that if the company owns the cell phone, a search by the employer is legal. The secondary interpretation is that even when conducted by the government, a search within the context of the workplace, targeting workplace malfeasance, is acceptable.

CHAPTER REVIEW

1. Explain triangulation and why it would be useful to law enforcement.

2. The PIN and the PUK are two different codes that are significant to the investigator. Explain what they are. How are they related? How are they different?

3. Why is it important to have a device such as a Faraday bag available when transporting cell phones as evidence?

4. Lacking a Faraday bag, what is another way to prevent the device from connecting to external devices (assuming the option is available on that particular phone)? What precautions must the investigator take before using this method?

5. Under what circumstances might it be considered acceptable to seize a cell phone without the benefit of a warrant?

CHAPTER EXERCISES

1. Look up *U.S. v. Finley* (2007) and review the decision. What mitigating circumstances led to the court deciding that the evidence obtained by government agents was admissible, in spite of the fact that no warrant had been obtained?

2. Go online and research at least two different companies that manufacture hardware designed for capturing cell phone data. Put together a short list of each one's benefits and each one's limitations. Choose one for your own use, and explain why you chose that particular model.

REFERENCES

City of Ontario, CA v. Quon, 08-1332 (2010).

Cloudetal. 2011. Triangulation: Fun time with maths. www.cloudetal.com/triangulation-fun-time-with-maths (accessed May 29, 2012).

Daubert v. Merrell Dow Pharmaceuticals, Inc., 509 U.S. 579, 589 (1993).

Faraday Cage. 2012. Faraday cage. www.faradaycage.org/ (accessed June 2, 2012).

GSMA. 2012. GSM. www.gsma.com/aboutus/gsm-technology/gsm/ (accessed June 1, 2012).

Kayne, R. 2012. What is a SIM Card? www.wisegeek.com/what-is-a-sim-card.htm (accessed May 29, 2012).

Mobiledia. 2012. Electronic Serial Number (ESN). www.mobiledia.com/glossary/95.html (accessed May 29, 2012).

National Coordination Office for Space-Based Positioning, Navigation, and Timing. 2012. Official U.S. Government information about the Global Positioning System (GPS) and related topics. www.gps.gov/systems/gps/space/ (accessed Dec. 29, 2012).

Newitz, A. 2007. Courts cast wary eye on evidence gleaned from cell phones. Wired.com. www.wired.com/politics/law/news/2007/05/cellphone_forensics (accessed May 15, 2012).

The Full Signal. n.d. How to dry out a water-damaged iPhone. www.knowyourcell.com/apple/apple-iphone/iphone-guides/357471/how_to_dry_out_a_waterdamaged_iphone.html (accessed June 6, 2012).

U.S. v. Finley, 477 F.3d 250 (2007).

United States v. Ortiz, 84 F.3d 977 65 (1996).

United States v. Salgado, 807 F.2d 603 (1986).

United States v. Young, 2006 U.S. Dist. (2006).

15

FIGHTING ANTIFORENSICS

One problem the archaeologist rarely deals with is having the civilization under study deliberately hiding evidence of their existence. That is something the digital investigator faces on a regular basis. People who operate computers with malicious intent frequently understand that their activities can be traced and will go to great lengths to cover their tracks. Common roadblocks to the investigator include secure deletion of data, hiding of data, and booby traps that destroy data or systems when certain events are triggered. If the intent of an action or procedure is to hamper the efforts of a computer investigation, it can be considered **antiforensics.** Kessler (2007) lists four categories of antiforensic behavior:

- Artifact destruction
- Data hiding
- Trail obfuscation
- Attacks against forensic tools

The first part of this chapter will cover actions to take when data is overwritten so completely that no conventional methods will permit recovery. This does not mean merely erasing files. A suspect may well leave the file intact, but erase metadata that the investigator may need to reconstruct events. This book will refer to these concepts generically as artifact destruction. After this will follow a discussion of different ways in which users can hide data on a storage device.

As with everything else discussed in this book, it is best if the actions described in this chapter be performed against a forensic image of the system being examined. If the forensic image can be mounted as a file system, that is the best way to work. Paraben Software's free utility P2 Explorer is a tool that performs this trick. The latest version as of this writing is ver. 3.1. It is capable of mounting Paraben's own Forensic Replicator images. It also mounts Encase, Safeback, SMART, FTK, and DD images as well.

ARTIFACT DESTRUCTION

The most common form of destruction is file deletion. Incriminating evidence is removed from the drive, and efforts are made to prevent an investigator from restoring that information. This destruction could be files, records from databases, e-mail messages, or calendar entries. If the reader has learned nothing else from this book, she should at least understand that simply deleting a file initially doesn't do anything to remove the actual data. This was discussed in some detail in Chapter 8, "Finding Lost Files." Astute criminals are as aware of this as any investigator and will take the extra effort necessary to wipe the data along with the file entries.

Literally hundreds of utilities exist that overwrite the media surfaces in order to discourage the recovery of deleted files. Most of these operate by recording a string of 0s over the clusters that hosted the file, erasing them, writing a string of 1s, and repeating the process numerous times. Some utilities write random strings of 1s and 0s. Recovering actual data after a wipe utility has been used is feasible using highly specialized hardware and software, but for the typical investigator, it isn't possible.

That isn't to say that the investigator cannot prove that the file once existed. It also doesn't mean that other versions or artifacts of the file won't still exist on the media. The Windows registry can be a source of information regarding previously opened files. Also, as discussed in Chapter 8, file system metadata may still contain entries to the file. Additionally, many applications constantly create temporary files that are deleted whenever the file is closed by the application. This deleted temporary file may well be recoverable.

EXTRACTING HISTORY FROM THE WINDOWS REGISTRY

On Windows systems a search of the registry can be quite educational. Several different registry entries list the most recently used (MRU) files, even if the files have been deleted. Figure 15.1 shows the Windows registry listing the last several files opened by an application.

Several MRU lists are accessible in the registry. Not all are called MRU or even include the letters in the name. The example in Figure 15.1 shows a hive entry entitled Recent File List. Most applications maintain an MRU, and the OS keeps several as well. Start with HKEY_USERS. Each user with an account on the system will have a subhive with their preferences. The registry will not list users by name, but rather have a lengthy numerical identifier called the *Security Identifier* (SID), with several clusters of numbers separated by hyphens. The shorter user IDs under HKEY_USERS represent default accounts. These are S-1-5-18 (the local system account), S-1-5-19 (the local service account), and S-1-5-20 (the network service account). These rarely have information relevant to the investigation.

Following these numbers will be one or more numbers beginning with S-1-5-21, followed by a long string of numbers. These represent actual user accounts, past and present. In an organization where one computer might be used by several users, each user who logs on will automatically generate a hive in the registry for their account. This is where all the user-specific preferences and properties are maintained. If working under orders to target a specific user, it will be necessary to identify which subkey belongs to that user. In order to do this, open the folder called Volatile Environment. The user name is listed in plain text in this location.

Now under that folder, open the HKEY_USERS > Software hive. Each application that is installed is listed here. Note also that applications that were uninstalled will continue to be represented by a folder in this hive unless the

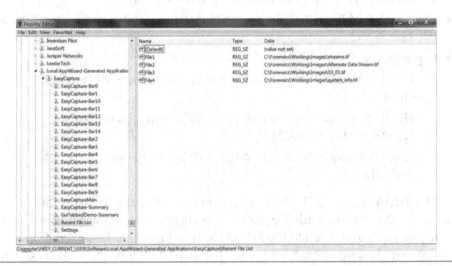

Figure 15.1 The registry stores lists of recently used files, even if those files have been deleted.

user took specific action to remove the folder. This can be introduced as evidence of previous applications if desirable. Some places to look for various applications (and this is an abbreviated list) include the following:

- Adobe Acrobat (Reader or Professional): HCKU/Adobe/Acrobat Reader/ {version number}/AVGeneral/cRecentFiles
- Internet Explorer: HCKU/Microsoft/Internet Explorer/TypedURLs
- Microsoft Access: HCKU/Microsoft/Office/(version)/Access/File MRU
- Microsoft Excel: HCKU/Microsoft/Office/(version)/Excel/File MRU
- Microsoft Excel: HCKU/Microsoft/Office/(version)/Excel/Place MRU
- Microsoft Management Console: HCKU/Microsoft/Microsoft Management Console/Recent File List
- Microsoft Publisher: HCKU/Microsoft/Office/(version)/Common/Publisher/ File MRU
- Microsoft Publisher: HCKU/Microsoft/Office/(version)/Publisher/ File MRU
- Microsoft Word: HCKU/Microsoft/Office/(version)/Word/File MRU
- Microsoft Word: HCKU/Microsoft/Office/(version)/Word/Place MRU
- Offline Files Use: Microsoft/Office/Offline/Files
- Roxio Photo Suite: HCKU/PhotoSuite(ver)/RoxioPhotoSuite/MRUFiles
- Softland doPDF: HCKU/Softland/doPDF/doPDF v(x)/
- TechSmith SnagIt: HCKU/TechSmith/SnagIt/(ver. no.)/SnagItEditor/Recent File List
- Explorer:
    - HKCU\Microsoft\Windows\CurrentVersion\Explorer\ComDlg32\ OpenSaveMRU
    - HKCU\Software\Microsoft\Windows\CurrentVersion\Explorer\ ComDlg32\LastVisitedMRU
    - HKCU\Software\Microsoft\Windows\CurrentVersion\Explorer\ RecentDocs

The HKEY_CURRENT_USER hive contains all of this information as it is relevant to the user currently logged in. In reality, it is merely a symbolic link to the registry hive associated to the SID of the user logged in. However, if imaging a live system, be sure to examine the CURRENT-USER area in the same general locations.

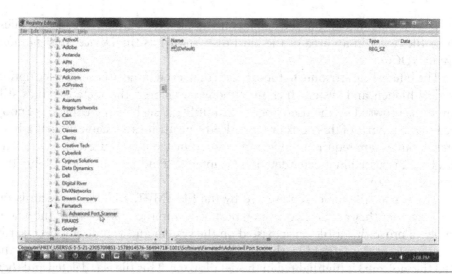

Figure 15.2 Applications no longer installed on a system might still have registry entries associated to them.

The registry can also provide evidence that applications that do not currently reside on the system once did. HKEY_CURRENT_USER > Software records all software installed by that user. Even applications that have been removed are likely to retain folders, as the uninstall process of Windows is imprecise at best. The view of the registry seen in Figure 15.2 shows a long list of applications. The Advanced Port Scanner highlighted is not currently installed on the machine being examined. However, the fact that it was once present might be relevant to the investigation at hand.

Manually searching the registry is a time-consuming and imprecise method for analysis. Most of the forensic suites offer some form of registry analysis as a function of their package. Access Data's FTK allows live capture of registry entries loaded in memory as well. Paraben's P2 Commander has a built-in registry analysis tool as well.

A very handy tool for the investigator is RegRipper by Harlen Carvey. This open-source tool will create reports that incorporate many of the MRU lists described earlier from a GUI. A command-line version of the utility offers even more utility to the person willing to take the time to learn the various triggers to manipulate the command. RegRipper is *not* designed to run against a live machine. Run this utility only against forensic images of machines.

FILE SYSTEM METADATA

Every time a file is created or deleted on a computer, today's operating systems log that event. These logs are not easily readable or even accessible to the average user.

On a Windows system, the metadata consists of several hidden, read-only files. These files exist in an area of the hard disk known as the *Device Configuration Overlay* (DCO).

The interesting attribute to these files is that, even if the user selects the option to view hidden and system files in Windows Explorer, the metadata files still cannot be browsed by the user. Specialized utilities, such as the Directory Snoop used in other parts of this book or the disk editing utilities available in virtually all forensic suites, are required to view file system metadata (Figure 15.3). Metadata files were discussed in greater detail in Chapter 8, "Finding Lost Files." Table 15.1 provides a recap.

The master file table, represented by the file $MFT, still retains records for files long after they are deleted, even if dumped from the recycle bin. If the goal is simply to prove that a file once existed on the system and you do not necessarily have to present the actual file, this might be a good approach. In Figure 15.4, the MP3 file tao1.mp3 is highlighted in the details pane. This file was deleted and then wiped for the purposes of this exercise. (It was, however, backed up on another drive because the song is just *too* good to lose!)

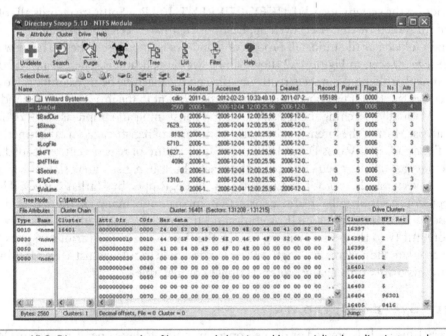

Figure 15.3 File system metadata files can only be viewed by specialized applications, such as Directory Snoop, shown here.

Table 15.1   NTFS Metafiles

File Number	File Name	Description
1	$MFT	Live master file tables for the file system
2	$MFTMirr	Snapshot of the MFT used for system recovery
3	$LogFile	File of all file transaction logs currently recorded by the system
4	$Volume	Volume attributes, such as volume name, size, and FS version
5	$AttrDef	Definitions table for file system and user-defined file attributes
6	.(dot)	Root directory of the file system
7	$Bitmap	Bitmap listing of allocated clusters within the file system
8	$Boot	On a bootable volume, contains the bootstrap code
9	$BadClus	Maps bad clusters found during disk scans
10	$Secure	File system security and access control attributes
11	$UpCase	Cross-matches uppercase to lowercase to eliminate case-sensitivity in file names
12	$Extend	Directory of optional extensions
13-16	UNDEFINED	Bookmarks created by developers for future files
17	$Extend\$Quota	When user storage quotas are enforced, identifies each user's quota
18	$Extend\$ObjID	Object identifier attributes, such as link tracking and index root
19	$Extend\$Reparse	Stores definitions for symbolic links to file system resources
20	$Extend\$UsnJrnl	Stores log changes for the NTFS journaling system

A string search for the characters TAO1 across all clusters, including slack space, also revealed an entry for the file in Media Player's current database. We learn that the file is a Flamenco piece by Tao Ruspoli. Because it exists as an entry in Media Player's database, we also know that the existence of the file was known by at least one user, and that the file has been manipulated. This relates back to the discussion in Chapter 11, "Web Forensics," regarding points the prosecutor needs to prove in order to establish culpability.

We now have more information about the file than when we started. And yet the file no longer exists on the computer.

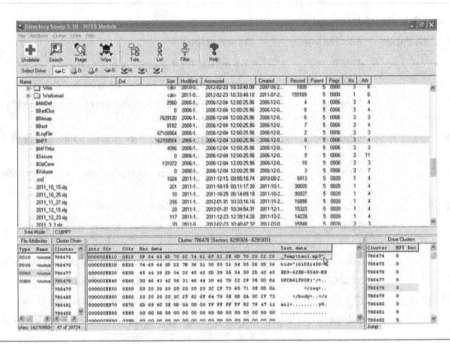

Figure 15.4 A search of a file name being sought by an investigator finds an entry in the MFT that reveals that it once existed on the computer.

Microsoft makes a utility called nfi, which is part of the original Windows 2000 debugging tool kit. The nfi utility extracts information about the NTFS file structure and outputs it in humanly readable form. (As of this writing, the tool-kit is still available for download at http://support.microsoft.com/kb/253066.) To use the tool, open a command prompt (as administrator), and type the command nfi c > MFT.txt. It takes a while to process the file, especially on a large hard drive.

A few notes about the tool are in order. The command works on a single volume at a time. The command nfi c runs the tool against the C drive. Do not use the :\ suffix, as that will only output the MFT information relating to the root directory. If you want the entire file system of the drive, you type *only* the letter. The trigger > MFT.txt pipes the output to a text file called MFT.txt in the directory from which the utility is run. If you want to output to a different drive and directory, you must type the full path to that location. For example, nfi c > F:\Evidence\ CASE001\MFTDRIVEC.TXT creates a text file called MFTDRIVEC on my thumb drive in the CASE001 subdirectory of my evidence folder. The results look like those seen in Figure 15.5. Here we see a logical link left behind by the mystical TAO1.MP3.

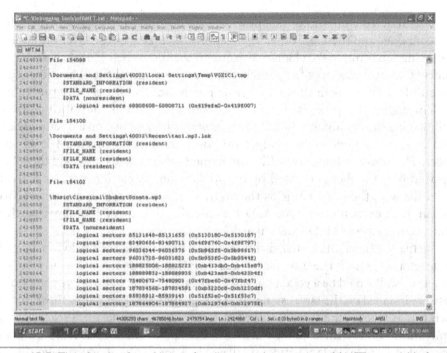

Figure 15.5 The nfi utility from Microsoft will output the contents of $MFT in readable form.

EXAMINING TEMPORARY FILES

One feature most appreciated by computer users the world over is the magical ability to "do over." If a writer makes a mistake in his forensics book, it is a simple matter of clicking the Undo button and the error goes away. How is that possible if the change has already been made in the file?

Microsoft Word is a good example of an application that relies heavily on temporary files. Temporary files are helpful not just for the purposes of editing but also because they can speed up performance and protect data integrity (Microsoft 2010). There are four default temporary files that Word creates when the application is started.

A file named ~wrf0000.temp is a DOS-based file that acts as a pointer to reserve four file handles within the operating system. A scratch file, named ~mfxxxx.tmp (where the x's are replaced by a number generated by the application), becomes the target for the first round of edits. Two additional temporary files are created at startup that are a bit more complicated. One is a *transacted compound file* with the name of ~dftxxx.tmp (where the x's are replaced by a number generated by the application), and the other is a *direct compound file* called ~wrf0001.tmp.

A transacted compound file allows the application to store a document into this container and then lets other applications, such as a spreadsheet program or a drawing program, make changes directly to the file. When the file is saved, the contents of the temporary file get merged with the original file. The direct compound file is a document file that is created with each Save As or Save function.

Throughout the process of creating a document, Word is constantly automatically saving the document. Still, if the user works for an hour on a document and then decides that none of the changes are worth keeping, the original file remains intact. The autosave temporary files are named ~wraxxxx.wbk (where the x's are replaced by a number generated by the application) in earlier versions of Word and a file with the same name as the original. Later versions of the autorecover file carry an extension of .asd. ASD files are likely to carry file names such as "Autorecover save of MyDocument.asd."

Virtually all applications that feature autosave functionality or a redo function will create temporary files. There are far too many applications on the market to attempt a complete list. It would be a good policy of every investigation to do an inventory of all software installed on the target system and systematically research how those that are likely to affect the investigation generate temporary files. Also note that version changes sometimes result in changes to the extensions of temporary files. Table 15.2 contains an abbreviated list of important temporary files to look for during an investigation.

It is possible to recover deleted files from unallocated space using standard file carving techniques described in Chapter 8, "Finding Lost Files." Slack space in clusters that are partially overwritten may contain text or file metadata that can be useful as well. Therefore do not restrict the search for temporary files to those viewable in the file system.

HIDING DATA ON THE SYSTEM

Centuries ago, when the Roman generals wanted to send a secret message and time permitted, they would shave the messenger's head, tattoo the message onto the scalp, and then wait for the hair to grow back before sending the message along the way. Needless to say, this was not the preferred method for emergency communications. So they also found methods to hide messages inside of seemingly innocuous texts, encoding the data or finding interesting places on the messenger's body to hide the message capsule.

Today's computer criminals have easier ways of hiding data. The term **dark data** is used to describe files and other information that are misplaced, concealed,

Table 15.2 Temporary Files

Application	Version	Naming Convention	Description
Microsoft Word	2000 up	~wraxxx.wbk	Backup file
Microsoft Word	2000 up	filename.asd	Autorecover file
Microsoft Word	2000 up	~wrfxxx.tmp	Bookmark file
Microsoft Word	2000 up	~mfxxx.tmp	Scratch file
Microsoft Word	2000 up	~dtf.xxxx.tmp	Transacted document files
Microsoft Word	2000 up	~wrf.xxxx.tmp	Compound document files
Microsoft Excel	2000 up	Random name, no extension	Deleted when file is saved
Microsoft PowerPoint	2000 up	pptxxxx.tmp	In user's TEMP directory
Microsoft Visio	All	~$$filename.~vsd	Usually in same directory as drawing
OpenOffice Calc	All	*.stc	In %user%/backup directory
OpenOffice Writer	All	*.bak	In %user%/backup directory
Photoshop	All	Photoshop tempxxx	No extension
WordPerfect	All	Wp{filename}.bkl	Extension numbers versions

or otherwise missing. Data can be hidden within the various components of the structure of the OS. Places to hide data are called the **warrens** (not warrants, as in "get one before you search," but rather warrens, as in "where a bunny hides when you let the dogs out"), where data hides from predators. Just like rabbits have warrens, so do digital criminals.

Many manufacturers have a hidden partition where system information such as BIOS and device configuration data are stored. This is called the **Host Protected Area** (HPA). The HPA does not show up in typical file system browsers such as Windows Explorer or the Linux file browsers. Another hidden area of the hard disk is the DCO described in the previous section. Lastly, certain advanced utilities allow the user to manage slack space as though it were a separate file system.

HPA/DCO Data Hiding

Many people have information that does not need to be regularly accessed, but cannot be forgotten. Perhaps the documents are critical, but read only under rare circumstances. The criminal often needs to keep this information from ever being found.

By using partitioning software to change the size of the HPA, a relatively large amount of data can be stored. The HPA is relatively small, comparatively speaking. Typically, it is under 100MB for most systems, but can be 10GB or larger. The size of the HPA depends on how the manufacturer intended the partition to be used. For example, some models of Fujitsu Siemens computers store a complete OS image on a 10GB HPA.

There are tools that allow the size of the HPA to be modified by the end user. The legitimate use for these utilities is that they allow a manufacturer to use different models of hard disk and have them all consistently read the same apparent size to end users. Two of these tools are HDAT2 and MHDD. Once the HPA partition has been modified, disk editing utilities can be used to copy the desired data into that partition.

Copying the HPA is not a major problem for forensic duplication utilities. Even the venerable DD utility can copy hidden partitions. In order to search the partition, data carving utilities such as Scalpel can find common file formats. String searches using strings in Windows or GREP in Linux or Unix can locate specific text passages.

Hiding Data in the Slack

The concept of file slack has already been discussed in multiple places within this book. Here is another area where it comes into play. Covert utilities, such as Slacker from the Metasploit suite, can manage slack space as if it were a separate and hidden file system. A directory containing a large number of files, each of which contain only a byte or two of data, is created as a repository. Slacker then uses this, along with any other slack space available on the system, to create *ghost partitions*. Ghost partitions work for the OS in the same way as any other partition, with one key difference. Conventional file browsing utilities cannot detect them.

So how does the owner of the partition access it if it cannot be detected? Generally, a small executable program (such as Slacker) that can exist anywhere on the system launches a shell that manages the ghost partition as if it were a separate file system. The file can be innocently named and even appear to be one of the standard OS system files. Only those "in the know" are aware of what program to launch. This is one place where the analysis of the registry may show some light. Check for recently run programs and program hives that appear out of place. Something like Slacker is unlikely to create much of a footprint, so external evidence might suggest the possibility of a ghost partition. Do all the legitimate hidden partitions and system partitions add to up the right size for the hard disk that hosts them all? A 2TB disk that only reports 1.5TB of partitions is a logical candidate for a drive with ghost partitions.

Take note if a disk appears to have an inordinate number of partitions. The process of partitioning disks creates another form of disk slack known as *partition slack*. The area between the end of any logical partition and the end of the block of sectors assigned to the partition can be relatively significant. It is not accessible to the file system, but it can be used by Slacker to increase the size of the hidden volume it creates.

Storing Data in Bad Clusters

The $BadClus metadata file is actually an artifact left over from the days of early hard drive technology. Current hard disks have the capability of managing bad sectors built into the firmware and do not depend on the OS for such functionality. The hard disk has a reserved space of spare sectors at the end of the drive. When the drive detects a questionable sector, it marks it as bad, moves the data to a new sector and releases a spare from the reserve supply. In the old days, the OS detected bad sectors and moved the data, and in this metadata file, the file system identified the sector by its geometrical location.

Hiding data using a disk editor such as Directory Snoop or WinHex, a user could conceivably edit the $BadClus file to include the sectors of a file she is trying to hide. This is a theoretical method discussed in a lot of the literature, but one that is rarely (if ever) found in the field. The reason for this is that in addition to editing the $BadClus metafile, it is also necessary to alter the $Bitmap metafile in order to mark the clusters as either available or unavailable. There are far too many other methods of hiding data that are easier and less detectable.

It's easy enough to detect if a perpetrator has successfully used bad clusters to hide data. Virtually any system in use today will contain $BadClus metafiles with a size of zero bytes. If the file exhibits a value of other than zero, you should copy the clusters defined in this metafile into a file system file for examination.

Hiding Data in the Registry

There has already been a lot of discussion about using the registry to find evidence. Now it is time to consider it as a place to hide evidence intentionally. To understand how this is done, it is necessary to understand a little about the registry's structure.

Every key within the registry has three components. The name is obviously what identifies the key, but is unfortunately not always the best way to find a key. The maximum size of a key name is 255 characters. Many key names are generated by the OS and consist of 32-bit or 64-bit values. It is not exactly intuitive for the investigator to understand that the key labeled {0AFACED1-E838-11D1-9187-B532F1E9575D} defines a specific property for Windows Explorer. Nothing in that name is something that is going to jump right out as a logical search string. Looking for Explorer.exe did find it.

A second component of the key is its type. Here is where the investigator gets interested. There is a fairly wide variety of key types, and any given type can be used for different purposes. The maximum size for a key, including name, value, and data is 64KB. While this does not sound like a lot, up to 70 pages of ASCII text can be stored in less space than that. Table 15.3 lists the different key types and the kind of data that can be stored in each one.

Table 15.3   Registry Key Types

Data Type	Name	Description
REG_BINARY	Binary Value	Raw binary data. This is generally unreadable to humans and can be viewed in Registry Editor in hexadecimal format.
REG_DWORD	DWORD Value	Data represented by a number that is 4 bytes long (a 32-bit integer). Could be used for storing telephone numbers or other numerical data.
REG_EXPAND_SZ	Expandable String Value	A variable-length data string. This type of data is the type likely to be used to conceal data.
REG_MULTI_SZ	Multistring Value	Values that contain lists or multiple values in a form that people can read are generally this type. Entries are separated by spaces, commas, or other marks. Another area of interest to the case.
REG_SZ	String Value	A fixed-length text string. Good for telephone numbers.
REG_RESOURCE_ LIST	Binary Value	A collection of nested arrays that store a resource list used by a hardware device driver or one of the physical devices it controls. This information is collected by Windows during the installation of the device.

Table 15.3 Registry Key Types—cont'd

Data Type	Name	Description
REG_RESOURCE_ REQUIREMENTS_LIST	Binary Value	A series of nested arrays that stores a list of possible hardware resources that a device is capable of using.
REG_FULL_RESOURCE_ DESCRIPTOR	Binary Value	A series of nested arrays that stores a complete list of resources used by a physical hardware device.
REG_NONE	None	Data without any particular type. Virtually any type of user data can be stored here.
REG_LINK	Link	A string (in Unicode) that defines a symbolic link.
REG_QWORD	QWORD Value	Data represented as a 64-bit integer.

Source: Microsoft 2008.

The final element of the registry key is the data within the key. In the Registry Editor (type `regedit` in the Run line) keys are viewed, edited, and created. There are also utilities that can generate registry entries that are imported into the registry as .reg files. Creating new hives and keys is simple and straightforward. In Figure 15.6, I have created a Software entry called Bubba's Revenge.

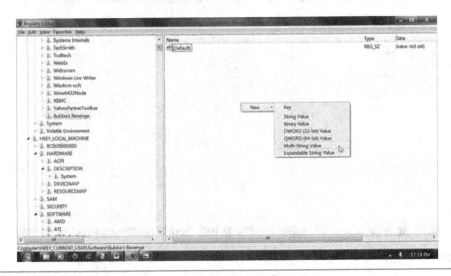

Figure 15.6 It is a simple matter to create new keys in the registry.

Now in order to create a key inside of the entry, it is a simple matter of right-clicking anywhere in the details pane and then selecting the data type of your new key. I've selected a multistring value here. In the next step, I named the key Recipes and subsequently copied the entire contents of one of this book's chapters into the value data (Figure 15.7).

Finding this data won't be quite as easy as it may seem. In this particular example, the name of the key makes it stand out. But what if I named the key {0AFACED1-E838-11D1-9187-B532F1E9575D}? Still, it is not an impossible task.

Microsoft distributes a free utility called LogParser (current version is 2.2). This powerful command line utility can read registry entries as well as log files. It allows the investigator to run SQL queries against the live registry or against static files from a disk image. It is also possible to examine the registry of any computer that can be reached on the network. The output is extracted from the fields listed in Table 15.4.

It should be noted that since the registry is a very large database, a little care is in order when executing commands. While it is beyond the scope of this book to provide detailed instructions in how to use LogParser, a few pointers are in order. The syntax of a basic query is all one line:

```
LogParser "SELECT * INTO reg.csv FROM HKCU" -i:REG -o:CSV
```

This simple query creates a database of the entire Current User hive of the registry in comma-delimited text and stores it as a file called reg.csv. Since there

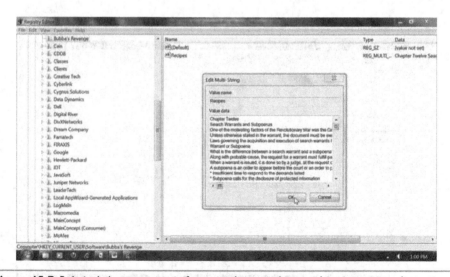

Figure 15.7 Relatively large amounts of text can be stored in a multistring registry key.

Table 15.4 Registry Field Values

Name	Type	Description
ComputerName	STRING	Name of the computer from where the registry value was extracted
Path	STRING	Complete path to the registry key containing this value
KeyName	STRING	Name of the registry key containing this value
ValueName	STRING	Name of the registry value
ValueType	STRING	Type of data held within the specific key
Value	STRING	ASCII values of data contained in key
LastWriteTime	TIMESTAMP	Time and date when value was last modified

were no additional parameters specified, the file landed in the C:\Program Files\ Log Parser 2.2 directory.

An attempt to load the file in its entirety directly into Excel results in an error message that reports that the file did not completely load. The reason for this is that there are far too many rows generated by this command. A useful utility to own is Notepad++ (currently available at http://notepad-plus-plus.org/). This is a replacement for the Windows Notepad utility that has the capacity to load substantially larger files. After loading the output file generated by the computer, Notepad++ demonstrated that it contained 95,421 lines, each of which translates into an Excel row.

Excel has a limitation of 65,536 rows. In order to load the entire output file, it is necessary to split the file into multiple sections, all of which contain fewer than 65,536 lines. The end result is a file that looks like the one displayed in Figure 15.8.

Now the extracted data can be analyzed using any of Excel's tools. For example, the LastWriteTime field can be sorted in ascending value, and all the rows that fall between certain dates moved to a new worksheet. Now only values that were altered during that time period are available for subsequent searches.

It is also possible to prefilter by a range of dates. However, since it is likely that other registry analysis will be done, a full output file is desirable.

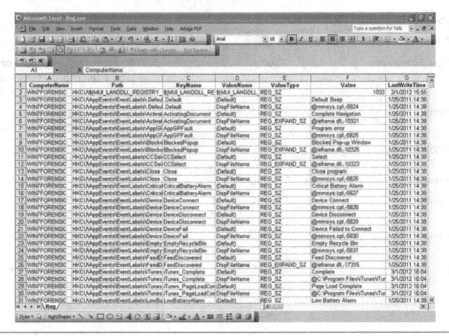

Figure 15.8 Data from Log Parser 2.2 can be output into CSV and subsequently opened in Excel.

HIDING DATA AND APPLICATIONS IN ALTERNATE DATA STREAMS

For Windows users using NTFS, a common approach to hiding a small executable program such as Slacker is to add it as an **alternate data stream** (ADS) to a legitimate file. An ADS is very much like an attribute to a file. It does not show up in the directory structure. It adds nothing to the file size, and it goes wherever the file goes. If you delete a file with an ADS, you delete the ADS.

Once an ADS has been attached to a file, the correct file name looks something like filename.txt:alternatestream. A simple directory command will only show the file called filename.txt.

Unlike the other hiding techniques described in this section, there are no special tools involved and only minimal computer expertise is required. As an example, let's put the Microsoft Calc application into a simple text file called Streams.txt:

1. Open a command console.
2. Create an empty text file called Streams.txt. Right-click on the desired target folder in Windows Explorer, and select New › Text file and name it Streams. In this example, the path will be C:\AA_Temp.

3. From the command prompt, type the following command (Note that the *complete* path to the executable and to the target file are required):

`C:\Windows\System32\calc.exe > C:\AA_Temp\ streams.txt:calc`

4. To run the executable from the text file, type the following command:

`START c:\AA_Temp\streams.txt:calc.exe`

The results will look like the image in Figure 15.10. Needless to say, the actual start command in use will vary, depending on the path where the streamed file is located. In Figure 15.9, the file has been moved to the Assets directory, and the command modified accordingly. Files hidden in data streams can be launched from shortcuts, from scripts, or from a RUN key in the registry.

Now let us examine the streams.txt file in Directory Snoop. If you look closely at Figure 15.10 where the cursor points, it will be clear that there are two data

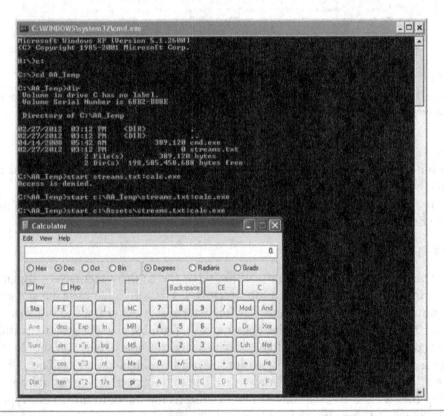

Figure 15.9 Alternate data streams allow executable programs to be hidden in seemingly benign files.

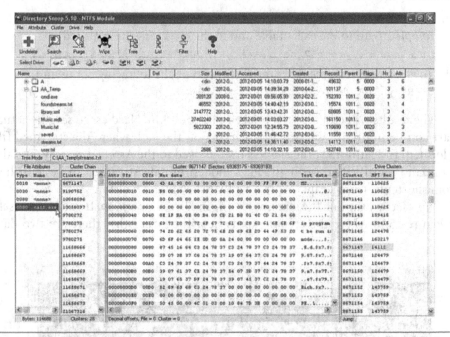

Figure 15.10 Alternate data streams show up as an extra data attribute in disk editors such as Directory Snoop.

attributes applied to the file. The second is named calc.exe. Of course, in this situation, we knew precisely where to look.

To find hidden streams files, the **streams** utility in the SYSINTERNALS suite is the best solution. To find all ADS pointers on the system, the command is

```
Streams -s c:\
```

The -s trigger tells the command to search the C: drive recursively, digging down into all the directories and subdirectories. The search will reveal a surprising number of files with alternate streams attached. Most are not to be worried about. Many files, especially the ones named "thumbs," have a stream named "encryptable." This is as is should be . . . and a fine example of why you should *not* use the other option in the utility to automatically delete all streams. Those files with a ":SummaryInformation" stream are also to be expected. You should not be seeing files with .exe extensions or any extensions for standard document types, such as .doc, .tif, .jpg, and so forth.

COVERT DATA

Other methods of hiding data involve putting it out there in plain sight for everybody to see. **Covert** dark data is intentionally concealed dark data. Two common methods of concealing data are encryption and steganography. Technically speaking, one of these methods isn't really a form of hiding. Encryption of data leaves it in place, but unreadable to anyone except the one who has the encryption key. Steganography is a little trickier. This is a method of placing data into existing files that everyone sees and assumes are innocent.

ENCRYPTION

NTFS 5.0, as part of its structure, includes the Encrypting File System (EFS). EFS provides encryption/decryption services within the operating system using a combination of the *Data Encryption Standard eXORed* (DESX) and a public key exchange. The most recent incarnation of this feature is known as BitLocker Drive Encryption.

Methods of Encryption

Accessing an encrypted drive in BitLocker is accomplished in one of three ways. First, the user may have simply assigned a password to the encrypted file or folder. Second, it can be configured to work with a Smart card. Smart cards are plastic security cards with a built-in computer chip. To access the encrypted drive, a card reader must be installed on the computer. The user swipes the card and gains access. An associated personal identification number (PIN) must be entered as well. The third way involves using the login credentials of the user to authenticate encryption and decryption. When the user logs on, his or her credentials are passed on to the security engine of the OS and provide the encryption key.

When the third method is used, EFS is transparent to the user. The user's private key is stored as part of their profile. A public key is maintained in the OS so that a recovery agent can access the encrypted files if necessary. The recovery agent is an individual (usually an administrator) whose permissions extend to that of accessing encryption keys.

For an investigator, encryption poses a unique set of challenges. For one thing, encrypted drives and folders will be password protected. Despite what the prime time crime shows will have you believe, cracking a password is not a simple process. Additionally, the suspect is likely to be protected by a variety of laws and even the Fifth Amendment of the Constitution. You might have a warrant to examine her computer, but the warrant does not put her under any obligation to give you her encryption password. If there is any reason to suspect that a computer might be encrypted, and it has been left on—*do not turn it off.* There are two optional paths to proceed with the investigation when this happens. Which path you choose should be the result of a conversation with legal counsel (if possible) and any investigating officers involved.

Option one involves performing a live capture of the system. Perform as thorough a live response investigation as is made possible by your resources while operating within the constraints of your warrant or other authorization. Get a live capture of memory, and collect as much information from the hard disk as possible. Document each and every step you take along the way. Any live data capture is going to have consequences (remember Locard's principle from Chapter 6, "First Response and the Digital Investigator"). You will be making changes to the system. There will be somebody somewhere along the way pointing the finger at investigative procedure at every opportunity. Try not to give them any opportunities.

Option two is to transport the computer, while running, back to the lab for analysis. This is why one of the devices listed in the portable tool kit is a battery backup that will keep the system powered.

Cracking Encryption Passwords

A more likely scenario is that the investigator is going to need to acquire the encryption password prior to continuing the search. The obvious first step is to ask the user to give it to you. If you ask, there is a remote possibility the user will give you the password. If you never ask, there is a 100% possibility they won't.

The next attempt should be an effort to guess the password. Operating systems and company policies require far more complex password requirements than they did just a few years ago. A common password requirement for organizations is a combination of uppercase and lowercase letters, combined with numbers and special characters. Most users have a hard time keeping up with all the password rules and look for easy ways to remember their passwords. One commonly found password is the user's e-mail address.

Dictionary words with the rules in place are common. An example of this would be C@m3ra—a short but complex alliteration of the word "camera." According to a study by Kuo et al. (2006), 11% of the passwords studied were cracked using a dictionary of 1.2 million words. The fastest I ever guessed another user's password was when the person's cubicle was decorated with old cameras and several black and white photographs he had taken. On the sixth try, the string Ph0t0grapher got me into the system. Rarely is it that easy.

Another method—which makes a password harder for investigators to guess and much more difficult for password-cracking software to resolve—is the use of mnemonics. An example of this technique is the password IluvmyK1tty. I love my kitty, too, but I'm not going to use that as a password. The same study cited above found that only 4% of passwords using mnemonics were successfully cracked.

The most likely approach that most investigators will take is to use a software-based password cracking solution. Virtually all of the forensic suites ship with at least one variation of password attacking software. Some stand-alone programs include such hacker favorites as John the Ripper, Cain and Abel, or Crack. These tools attack the problem in two ways.

The fastest of the two ways, when it works, is to use a standard dictionary. The software tests each word in the dictionary against the targeted user account. Various permutations of each word are tested, including changing the case of each letter, substituting letters for commonly used character replacements or numbers for letters (such as @ for a and 1 for i). If this fails, then the application will revert to a brute-force attack. In this method, every possible character is tried against every possible position in a password. This is incredibly time-consuming, even for today's fastest supercomputers. For example, a password encrypted with a 56-bit key yields 72,057,594,037,927,936 possible password combinations. Tests performed by Nobis (2011) showed that a computer equipped with a 3.2GHz 64-bit multicore processor could test approximately 4,366,723 combinations per second. His calculations suggested that if every possible combination had to be tested, it would take 58 years to find the password.

Most cases need to be solved more quickly than that. Therefore, algorithms have been created to provide "short cuts." One of these methods is to use frequency. Generally speaking, certain characters appear far more frequently than others. As a general principle, the at sign (@) appears in a very high percentage of passwords. This is partially because it serves as a character replacement for the letter A, and also because it is part of an e-mail address. As mentioned before, e-mail addresses are frequently used.

Most of the more advanced password crackers make use of **rainbow tables** (which are an offshoot of *Hellman tables*). Since the OS does not store passwords as text but rather as hashed strings, it makes sense that comparing a table of known hash strings against those found in specific areas of the system would be faster than brute force attacks.

Hellman tables were created by Martin Hellman in 1980. In this method, every character is hashed in all of the current algorithms and the values stored in a table. Then, combinations of two characters are hashed, combinations of three, and on up the ladder. When cracking a password, the hash values are compared against possible password combinations. While this method dramatically speeds up the process of cracking passwords, it is extremely memory intensive.

The problem with Hellman tables is that there is a lot of redundant processing as different tables are loaded and unloaded into memory. Rainbow tables are sorted into columns, with each column representing the results of a different method of reducing the hash values. This greatly reduces the number of redundant processing cycles the computer is forced to generate.

There are several sources for downloading rainbow tables. A great deal of care is in order regarding the source selected. Rainbow tables are a favorite place for hackers to hide malicious software. You don't want the tools you select for fighting crime to be the ones criminals use for fighting you.

STEGANOGRAPHY

The word **steganography** is derived from the Greek word *steganos,* meaning impregnable or impenetrable. Archaeologists have found examples of steganography dating back as far as 475 BC. General Pausanias was recalled from the field by way of a graphic image made from wax on wood. Beneath the wax were the written orders to return (Molin 2005). In 1462, Johannes Trithemius authored a book entitled *Steganographia.*

Computer files offer a marvelous platform for hiding data. Virtually any file can be used, but files that are typically compressed are the best ones for the purpose. Image files and music files are the most commonly used, but the wise investigator does not limit the search to just those files. PDFs, document files, and databases also offer a lot of slack space for hiding peripheral data. Since image files are far and away the most commonly used, the following discussion will be based on piggybacking data onto a digital image.

Steganography Methodology

Compression can be accomplished in two manners. **Lossless** compression does not allow any pixels to be left behind. Every byte of compressed data is restored when the file is uncompressed. **Lossy** compression assumes that a few missing or a few incorrect bytes won't do that much harm. Unless, of course, that compressed file happens to be carting around the extra load of a top-secret phone book. Then, losing bytes is a bad thing. Therefore, lossless compression methods are preferred for the purposes of steganography. Lossless image files include .BMP, .TIF, and .GIF files. Lossless music files include .RAW, .MSC, and .WAV; .JPEG images and MP3 music files all involve a degree of data loss, although there are methods of hiding data in these files as well.

Embedding data in a stego file involves the creation of two files. The first, called the *cover file* or *carrier*, is a seemingly innocuous image. The second file, called the *message*, is the data to be hidden. Specialized software combines the two files into a single file known as the *stegoimage*. Along with the message, a digital code is included for unlocking the files and separating them. This is the *stegokey*. Generally speaking, most steganographic applications use a simple password for the key, but that password can be as complex as the user wants it to be.

Three ways exist for inserting the data into the image. *Least significant bit* (LSB) insertion allows the stego application to store three bits of data into each pixel of a 24-bit image. A typical ASCII character will accordingly be spread across three pixels. A 24-bit 1280 × 768 image has 983,040 pixels and therefore could conceal 2,949,120 bits—about what one would need to store a 360KB file. This has minimal impact on the appearance of the image file, because typically the bits being replaced are spread across the three primary colors. Instead of each color being defined by 8 bits, it is defined by 7 bits. Adding the three bits of data to the pixel alters the color of each one very slightly. Therefore, a slight loss of contrast or color saturation may result, but without having an unaltered image to compare with, who's to know? Eight-bit images can be used, but the amount of data that can be stored is significantly less and the alterations to image quality are more easily noticed. Compressing the file can destroy the embedded information.

Masking and filtering steganography is restricted to 24-bit color and gray-scale images. It basically consists of a hidden watermark embedded in the image. A good example of this technique would be a one-page list of names and phone numbers. This list could be hidden as a watermark or as an invisible secondary layer on a dark image, such as a black cat in a pile of coal at midnight. By adjusting the luminosity of the secondary layer, the text becomes visible. Compressing the file has little or no impact on the hidden message.

Algorithms and transformation is a method that allows the cover file to be manipulated, edited, and changed to a certain extent without negatively impacting the message. *Redundant pattern encoding* breaks the message file up into smaller bits and scatters pieces of it throughout the cover file. This technique minimizes the impact of minor image edits or compression. This technique has opened the door to embedding data into JPEGS. *Encrypt and scatter* also breaks the message up, but encrypts each piece before embedding it into the cover file.

Steganography Tools

More complex steganography tools can split the message up and embed it in multiple files. Most tools offer this option. However, there are three things to consider regarding the technique. If one of the cover files goes missing, the embedded data is lost. If one of the cover files gets corrupted or subjected to excessive manipulation, the data is lost. Getting the message back requires that the carrier files be processed in the correct order. These points can be considered a threat or a security feature, depending on how you employ it. Splitting a critical file up into multiple files and sending it by way of multiple carriers reduces the threat that intercepting the file compromises the message. Unfortunately, so does accidentally losing one.

Tools used for creating steganography include (Johnson 2011)

- Hermetic Stego
- JP Hide and Seek
- Open Stego
- OpenPuff
- Red JPEG
- Steganographic Laboratory
- Steganography Studio
- StegoDOS
- STools
- White Noise Storm

This is not an all-inclusive list and readers should assume that many other tools exist that might cross their paths. Johnson (2011) lists over 100 different applications purported to enable steganography. For the following explanation of the process of hiding images, Hermetic Stego was used to hide one of the chapters from this book into a screenshot of the product.

When the program is first launched, a window similar to the one shown in Figure 15.11 will appear. The file with data to be hidden is the desired message. The Input Images folder is the directory that contains a list of potential bitmap images that can be used for hiding the data. The Stego images folder is the target directory where the combined file will be located. To identify the key for unlocking the message from the carrier, click "Specify key" and type in the selected key—preferably something a little less easy to guess than the one in the figure. Click "Hide the data," and you now have a stegoimage.

The interesting thing about the process is that since the message is replacing existing bytes in the image file, the size of the file doesn't change (Figure 15.12). The hash values will change. The existence of two identical files with different hashes suggests that the files need a closer examination.

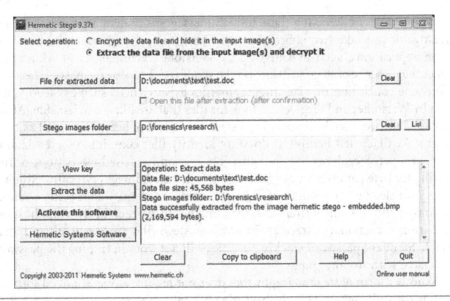

Figure 15.11 Hiding data using steganography tools could hardly be easier.

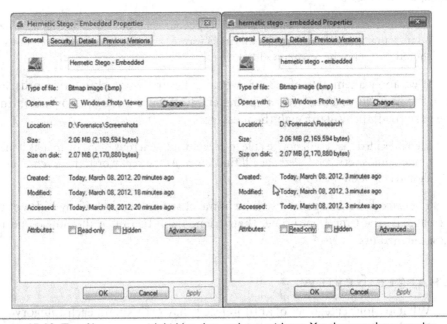

Figure 15.12 Two files—one with hidden data and one without. Yet they are the same size.

The process of detecting these hidden messages is known as *steganalysis*. The investigator can take two approaches to determining if steganography is at play. Some applications, such as Gargoyle by Wetstone Technologies or Maresware, detect the presence of stego software on the system. If the software exists, it becomes a foregone conclusion that steganography files exist. Others, such as Stego Watch (also by Wetstone) and StegDetect, look for files that are likely carriers. StegAlyzer AS can detect registry keys specific to steganography applications as well as other program artifacts left behind. It does not identify files containing secret data. Its sister product, Stegalyzer SS, does that job. It examines the byte pattern of files looking for byte patterns—or *signatures*—left that stegoimages typically exhibit.

As Kessler (2011) points out, it is one thing to identify that a file contains steganography. It's an entirely different matter to extract it. Two applications that utilize a dictionary attack against known stego files are Stegbreak and Stego Watch. Standard password cracking utilities will not work in finding the password associated with steganography.

Another form of steganography that does not require any specialized software at all is the **null cipher.** This simple little trick takes a seemingly innocuous message and embeds a completely different message within by using a predefined pattern or template. Somebody who knows the pattern can translate the real message. Consider this message:

> I have decided that I will not be able to accept your generous offer. Be that as it may, home sounds very good. Perhaps I'll find a way. At the very worst, the seven of us should go out on the town tonight.

If we apply a template of 4,8,4,8, we take the first word, skip four words, and take the next word. Then after skipping eight, we have our next word. Continue the pattern all the way through the message.

> I have decided that I will not be able to accept your generous offer. Be that as it may, home sounds very good. Perhaps I'll find a way. At the very worst, the seven of us should go out on the town tonight.

The encoded message is "I will be home at seven tonight." If my kids got the message, by the time I get home, their friends will be out of the house and the mess cleaned up.

CHAPTER REVIEW

1. What are four categories of antiforensic behavior? Explain each category briefly.

2. The HKEY_USERS hive of the registry can offer several clues as to what has gone on with a computer. How do the MRUs of the registry aid in an investigation? What do software keys potentially tell you?

3. Temporary files can be a gold mine of information in many situations. Describe several different forms of temporary file that might be of use to the investigator. What types of information, aside from the raw data they contain, can these files provide?

4. The registry can be used to hide data by creating fake registry keys. What type of key is best used for storing data? Potentially how much data can be stored?

5. Describe the concept of alternate data streams. What are they? How can they be used to hide information? How do you detect them?

CHAPTER EXERCISES

1. Download and install the Stream utility from the SysInternals Web site. (As of this writing, it can be found at http://technet.microsoft.com/en-us/ sysinternals/bb897440.aspx). Run the utility against your computer, and take a look at the different files you find that contain alternate data streams. Using the instructions found earlier in the chapter, embed a small application into a music file. Run the utility again, and see what there is to see.

2. Open a Microsoft Word document, and do a few minor edits. Wait a few minutes until the first autosave occurs. Now do the unthinkable. Unplug the machine without shutting down. Reboot and see if you can find the temporary files created by Word. (Hint: Make use of MAC attributes in a search, using a utility such as Directory Snoop.)

REFERENCES

Johnson, N. 2011. Steganography software. www.jjtc.com/ Steganography/tools. html (accessed March 9, 2011).

Kessler, G. 2011. An overview of steganography for the computer forensics examiner. www.garykessler.net/ library/ fsc_stego.html (accessed March 9, 2010).

Kessler, G. 2007. Antiforensics and the digital investigator. *Proceedings of the Fifth Australian Digital Forensics Conference.* http://ro.ecu.edu.au/cgi/viewcontent. cgi?article=1000&context=adf&sei-edir=1&referer=http%3A%2F%2Fs

cholar.google.com%2Fscholar% 3Fq%3Dantiforensics%26hl%3Den%2
6as_sdt%3D1%252C22%26as_sdtp%3Don#search=%22antiforensics%22
(accessed February 22, 2012).

Kuo, C., S. Romanosky, and L. Cranor. 2006. *Human selection of mnemonic phrase-based passwords.* Pittsburgh: Carnegie Mellon University, Institute for Software Research.

Microsoft. 2008. Windows registry information for the advanced user. *Technet.* http://support.microsoft.com/ kb/256986 (accessed February 23, 2012).

Microsoft. 2010. Description of how Word creates temporary files. *Technet.* http://support.microsoft.com/kb/211632 (accessed February 23, 2012).

Molin, R. 2005. *Codes: The guide to secrecy from modern to ancient times.* Boca Raton: Chapman & Hall.

Nobis, J. 2011. *Rainbow tables: Past, present, and future.* Presented at the DFW Security Professionals. http://insomnia.quelrod.net/docs/dfwitsecpro_2011-03_frt.pdf (accessed March 7, 2012).

LITIGATION AND ELECTRONIC DISCOVERY

Much of the discussion in this book so far has treated evidence as though it were to be presented in a criminal investigation. Digital detectives employed by a corporation are more likely to spend the majority of their time involved in civil litigation than in criminal action. In any legal case, one of the first steps taken is for both sides to meet and discuss what evidence is relevant to the proceedings and come to an agreement on how the information controlled by each litigant will be made available to the other party. The presentation of all documents relevant to a case is a process known as *discovery*. In virtually every case filed in U.S. courts today, the presentation of electronic documents is crucial to success or failure. This is electronic discovery, or as it is more commonly referred to, *e-discovery*.

Consider a few statistics, and it will become clear just how critical a good discovery strategy really is. According to the Association of Corporate Counsel, a third of 485 companies responding to their survey reported e-discovery was a key component in 70% or more of their cases. More than half indicated that over 90% of their cases involved electronic documents. Only 5% indicated that they had not been involved in e-discovery (Association of Corporate Counsel 2010).

With increasing emphasis on sanctions against organizations that fail to properly comply with an e-discovery motion, it is more critical than ever that IT staffs and legal departments have a solid understanding of the processes and requirements involved. This chapter will discuss the anatomy and function of an e-discovery motion and outline the steps an organization will take in order to comply.

WHAT IS E-DISCOVERY?

In the old days (about ten years ago), when a lawsuit was filed, lawyers from both sides got together and debated over what kinds of paper records each side would have to produce. Virtually all records existed primarily in hard copy. Computer systems were used as a means of facilitating work. They were not the primary repository for records. Acres of file cabinets that could be navigated by only a select few housed a company's records.

In today's corporate world, the paper record is the "backup." The real world exists inside of silicon-based life forms known as computers. The document search of today does not look for letters—it searches e-mail records. The file cabinets consist of a database-driven engine that sorts documents based on metadata. Those documents might be scattered across a global network made up of thousands of computers. Finding all of the documents related to a singular event is now more challenging than ever. Dozens of different versions of the same document might exist, with only minor variations between some of them. In some cases, similarly named document may have no more resemblance than the name they were given. As long ago as 2003, experts were estimating that as much as 95% of information generated by a corporate entity never appeared in printed form (Lyman and Varian 2003).

The courts and the legislatures have responded to changing technology. The Federal Rules of Civil Procedure (FRCP), Rule 34, defines the role of electronic documentation in civil procedure where evidence exists only in electronic form. In this section of code, the definition for the term document is revised to include documents and electronically stored information, and calls for respondents to provide that information in readable form (Committee on the Judiciary 2008). Simply put, e-discovery is the preservation, identification, and production of all documentary evidence related to a specific piece of litigation.

A ROADMAP OF E-DISCOVERY

E-discovery begins long before there is ever a scent of a lawsuit. Company policies, such as document retention and deletion policies, e-mail rules and retention, and so forth, all play into discovery. Many companies rush to destroy incriminating evidence as soon as there is anticipation of litigation, although some recent penalties have certainly provided negative incentive for such behavior. Sanctions include having the court issue a default judgment against the offending party or forcing that party to pay attorney's fees. Additionally, the court can order the violating party to pay compensation to the victim. This will be discussed in more detail later in the chapter.

While every case carries with it unique situations, it is safe to say that the majority of discovery requests will follow a certain order. Figure 16.1 illustrates the Electronic Discovery Reference Model (EDRM), developed by the group of the same name. The EDRM represents nine steps in six phases that most cases will go through from beginning to end.

It is no coincidence that the discovery model so closely resembles the forensic investigation model presented in Chapter 1, "The Anatomy of a Digital Investigation." To summarize the model, the individual steps are

1. Information management
2. Identification
3. Collection
4. Preservation
5. Processing

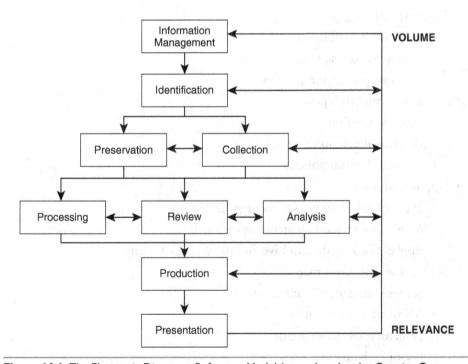

Figure 16.1 The Electronic Discovery Reference Model (reproduced under Creative Commons Attribution, based on EDRM 2010)

6. Review

7. Analysis

8. Production

9. Presentation

The next few pages will provide additional detail for each step.

INFORMATION MANAGEMENT

Information management is the one step of the discovery model that occurs long before litigation is ever contemplated. Every organization should have established policies in place that determine the basic rules of information control. This information should be included in a detailed document, two copies of which should exist. The first should be a general document that can be made available to members of the public that may have a need to know, but that does not include sensitive information such as passwords and Directory Services (including Active Directory) information. Several aspects of this policy should be included:

- Document storage policies
  - Designated custodians
  - Controlled storage locations
  - Data loss prevention policies
- Document retention policies
  - Retention period
  - Document deletion policies
  - E-mail retention policies
- Application map
  - Types of documents used by organization
  - Applications used to generate documents
  - Applications used to archive and manage documents
- Network architecture map
  - Server names and IP addresses
  - AN volume information
  - Directory Services schema
  - Backup schema
  - DR architecture

An organization with detailed documentation going into litigation is better protected in several ways. The forensic investigator is likely to spend far less time searching for documents. Knowing what applications and operating systems are in use facilitates recovering deleted data. In the event critical data proves to be unrecoverable, being able to represent that the information was deleted in accordance with defined policy makes it easier to defend accusations of **spoliation**.

IDENTIFICATION

Today's corporate network contains more information than a team of humans could ever hope to sort through in several lifetimes if forced to read each page of documentation individually. Because of the extreme volume of data to be searched and due to the sensitive nature of much of that information, there are several steps involved in identifying the data to be produced. Consider the identification process to occur in two stages. The first stage consists of critical decisions to be made before anyone touches the hardware. The second stage occurs during the search.

Pre-search Processes

One of the first steps in litigation, as defined by FRCP, is disclosure. Rule 26f of the act states that all parties of litigation will agree to a conference to discuss the nature of the claim and the possibilities of settlement and to develop a discovery plan. During this conference, representatives for each party will discuss the following issues:

- The nature of information determined to be discoverable
- Names and contact information of all parties likely to possess discoverable information
- Details to take into consideration for a suitable discovery plan of action:
  - The timing of initial discovery
  - The scope of discovery
  - Issues regarding disclosure of information
  - The form of production of discoverable information
  - Limitations of discovery
  - Claims of privilege
  - A procedure for invoking privilege on documents identified during discovery

- The scope of documentation each disclosing party has in possession that supports its claim or its defenses
- Witnesses expected to present testimony

Once the scope of the search has been agreed upon by both legal teams, it is time to start planning for data acquisition. If it has not already been done, a **litigation hold** must be placed on all data hosted by the target network or devices. A litigation hold, sometimes known as a preservation order or a hold order, is a directive ordering the party to suspend all document deletion or destruction. Under litigation hold, information must be retained in its exact form, with no alteration.

The duty to preserve is defined by two parameters: trigger and scope. The trigger is a point in time at which a party is legally under an obligation to preserve evidence. The scope refers to the types of materials that must be preserved pursuant to this obligation. The trigger is that magical moment when there is reasonable anticipation of litigation.

What constitutes reasonable anticipation? This question was addressed in two Florida cases. *Hagopian v. Publix Supermarkets, Inc.* (2001) involved a situation where evidence was collected in an accident case before there was anticipation of a lawsuit. No lawsuit was filed for several years, and in the meantime, the evidence was discarded. The court found Publix to be guilty of spoliation because, after making the effort to preserve evidence, they allowed it to be destroyed.

Royal & Sunallaiance a/s/o R.R. & L. R. Corp, Inc. v. Lauderdale Marine Center (2004) took the discussion to the next step. In this case, a Florida judge stated that mere anticipation of litigation does not automatically establish the necessity to preserve evidence. Evidence of a fire was discarded, and yet the courts stated that there was no reasonable expectation of legal action. The difference between the two cases, as explained by the court, was that Publix had collected the evidence, expecting a lawsuit, and then destroyed it. In Lauderdale Marine, the destroyed material was collected merely as part of a routine investigation with no effort to preserve it as evidence. No explanation was offered as to how one should determine intent to preserve.

In *Zubulake v. UBS Warburg* in 2003, the court had a different opinion. The court issued a decision in this trial that the defendant should have known as much as six months prior to a lawsuit being filed that the plaintiff was likely to sue. As such, they were required to preserve evidence. Additionally, the court noted that UBS Warburg destroyed the evidence in violation of its own published retention policy.

Spencer (2006) noted several events that can lead the courts to determine that spoliation occurred. One of these events is the destruction of any document in violation of an existing statute. The example he uses is that of personnel records.

Such records should be retained for either one year beyond when the record was made, or one year beyond such time as an action was taken using the record, whichever comes later. Early destruction is spoliation. A second form of violation is more obvious. If documents are destroyed in direct violation of a litigation hold order, the spoliation has occurred. The final example is the violation of a court order. Beyond these obvious violations, courts have the ability to issue sanctions any time there is evidence that a party destroyed evidence with the intent of preventing the court from ever seeing it.

The obvious conclusion is that the instant there is a whiff of litigation in the air, a litigation hold should be immediately imposed that prevents any documents from being deleted. As a digital investigator, it is your job to locate and identify any evidence that documents have been deleted pertaining to the investigation at hand. The inherent problem is that there has been no clear definition for a good retention policy for documents and document types. The only thing that is really clear is that if your organization has a published policy, and it violates its own policy, it is very likely to face sanctions if the court determines that it is guilty of spoliation.

Search Processes

Once both parties are in agreement on the scope of the discovery request, it falls on the legal team and document management specialists to identify what documents fulfill the criteria defined in the request. This is the process of data mapping. Identifying individual items of data is not always as easy as it sounds. Many people are likely to have been involved in the case. Any one of them may have created, modified, or copied documents relevant to the case. It is a virtual certainty that e-mails will be a search target as well as written documents, images, and possibly sound clips. An organized approach is required for success.

The first thing to do is develop a strategy. Just like a good general doesn't go into battle without a detailed plan, neither should the digital investigator. Before the first computer is turned on (figuratively speaking), several details should be considered:

- Identify stakeholders. Who all is likely to be involved in this case, beyond those named in the complaint?
  - Corporate legal
  - Outside legal
  - IT/records management
  - Employees and their managers
  - HR personnel

- Determine what document and data types are relevant. Aside from standard text documents and e-mails, are there images or sound files needed? How are relevant records from databases to be separated from protected or privileged records? In what format are files to be presented?
- Identify any data custodians who would have control over the data. This might include IT personnel or office managers as well as the stakeholders.
- Identify all data repositories where information might be held:
    - Local disks
    - SAN
    - Servers
    - Portable storage
    - Employees' personal hardware
    - Retired systems
    - Disaster recovery systems
    - Tape backups
    - Optical disks
    - Internet storage locations
- Prepare a list of key contacts, including outside counsel, IT personnel for the opposite team, and any third-party service providers that might be involved.
- Locate and prepare copies of all corporate documentation relevant to the investigation. This might include employee manuals, DR plans, backup/recovery strategies, and document/e-mail retention policies.
- Assign a time frame to use as a search parameter.
- Analyze the discovery request to assemble a qualified list of key words to use in a keyword search.

A proactive company already has much of this information in place. It is just a matter of collecting it all into a unified structure. Once this has been completed, the process of data mapping is finished. A document should be prepared and signed by both parties acknowledging the parameters of the search as defined in this phase. The team is now ready to begin the document recovery.

COLLECTION

Data collection is undoubtedly the most challenging (and probably the most fun) part of the process. It will not be as easy as having someone present the team with a list of files to locate. More likely, the request will bounce back and forth between parties several times before it is considered specific enough to be accomplished and yet generic enough to cover all bases. The initial request may be for "all documents, files, messages, and transactions related to Acme Industries." The refined order might read "all electronic information related to real estate transactions between Acme Industries and Ima Landlord between January 1, 2010, and January 1, 2011." If Ima Landlord is a real estate broker, even the more specific request may be refined even further.

Not every relevant document is going to have a file name clearly identifying it as relevant (an e-mail stored as a message file might have a file name such as *RE Tuesday Meeting.msg*). Content searching utilities are in order, and if they are to be used successfully, careful consideration must be given to what search strings to employ.

Data searches cannot be conducted randomly. The e-discovery team needs to plan out the collection strategy very carefully, decide on a specific method by which data will be collected, and then document every step of the collection process. Evidence that is collected must be packaged in the manner agreed upon by all parties, and a chain of custody maintained for all materials collected throughout the course of the investigation.

Using Search Strings

Careful selection of text strings to use in a keyword search will determine the success or failure of the search. As Justice Peck points out in *William A. Gross. Constr. Assocs., Inc. v. Am. Mfrs. Mut. Ins. Co.* (2009), a request that is too loosely defined will result in a collection of materials substantially larger than is required and result in undue burden on the producing party. Conversely, a search that is too restrictive in nature is likely to miss critical evidence.

Koutrika et al. (2009) point out that any data search is basically a quest to find one or more "entities." The entity is a document or file that meets a specific set of requirements. Yet any given entity can be accurately described in a number of ways. For example, searching for a digital image of storm damage caused by Katrina can result in different degrees of success, depending on your selection of search criteria.

Typing in "Katrina NEAR JPG" in Yahoo can be most disappointing. On Google, the request on one particular day resulted in over 28 million hits. While many of those hits were relevant images, it also offered links to a vast collection of images that would land the average employee in HR if they were ever displayed in an office cubicle. Adding the words "Storm Damage" to the search string narrows the results to 104,000 hits, and (for the first several pages, anyway) none of them feature scantily clad females. While this example is Web-centric, the same principle holds when searching any document collection.

In view of all this, is it ever possible to know whether a particular search has resulted in finding everything that is relevant? Of course not. However, as long as an organization can demonstrate that it made a good faith effort to retrieve and present all requested materials and can document the process used to collect those materials—and as long as that organization has done all it can to prevent the loss of any material it possesses—then they should be safe from sanctions. In *SafeCard Services, Inc. v. SEC* (1991), the court stated, "mere speculation that as yet uncovered documents may exist does not undermine the finding that the agency conducted a reasonable search." Their job may not be finished, because opposing counsel may redefine how they want the search to be accomplished using a set of keywords of their own. But the possibilities of legal repercussions are minimized.

Forms of Data

The job of data collection would be much easier if everything requested existed in a uniform time-space continuum. However, data exists in a wide variety of locations, including some that are typically inaccessible to the average user. Zubulake (2003) identified two primary categories of data, each of which is further divided into subcategories. Each form of data gets increasingly distant from the user interface (see Figure 16.2).

The first category is **accessible data.** This is any information readily retrieved by the average user. There are three subcategories of accessible data. *Active on-line data* consists of information stored on installed media, such as the hard disk, that is easily accessible via the file system. *Near-line data* exists on user media, such as rewritable CDs or DVDs, external USB drives, and such. *Off-line storage* or archives hold information that is not directly stored or read from local drives. This would include network storage locations, Internet storage services, and so forth. Off-line storage may be directly linked to the computer system via logical mappings, such as mapped drives, or it may require logging into separate systems.

The second category is **inaccessible data.** The most commonly requested subcategory of inaccessible data is the information stored on backup tapes. While, technically speaking, data found on tapes is not truly inaccessible, the degree of difficulty in locating specific information on a tape allows it to fall into this category. Accessing backup data requires that the tapes be restored to active systems or that the backup software used to create them be used to search for files. Backup tapes are very time-consuming and costly to search. Even more difficult is the second subcategory of erased, fragmented, or damaged data. Recovery of this

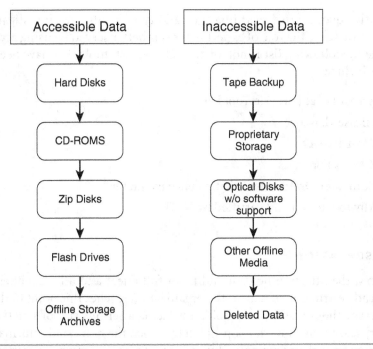

Figure 16.2 Data falls into different subcategories of either accessible or inaccessible data.

form of data requires specialized tools and people with specialized skills. This is where the forensic specialists are called upon for their services.

Data Collection Tools

Most of the tools that will be discussed in Chapter 18, "Tools of the Digital Investigator," are as relevant to the litigation support professional as they are to the forensic specialist. The basic goal is the same. Find existing target files as quickly as possible and locate as many deleted files as possible. On a corporate network it is hardly likely that an investigator will be asked to provide a forensic copy of a SAN. Therefore, live searches are the order of the day. It is possible that certain individual computers or storage devices might need to be imaged, and therefore, the tool kit needs to contain the appropriate utilities.

Great care must be taken in the selection of these tools. The courts have recognized a relatively small collection of hardware devices and software utilities that are considered acceptable for extraction, analysis, and presentation of evidence. While it is not forbidden to use tools not on this list, doing so is likely to result in

extensive questioning regarding the validity of results. An investigator not prepared to assume the role of expert witness is better served by using accepted tools.
While the following list is not an all-inclusive list, tools that have been proven in
court include

- Access Data: Forensic Tool Kit
- Encase eDiscovery
- Pro-Discover
- X-Ways Forensics
- Computer Online Forensic Evidence Extractor
- Any tool tested and certified by NIST

PRESERVATION

By now, the litigation hold should be in full effect and all personnel notified to
suspend destruction of data. If the organization reaches this point in the discovery
process without instituting a hold, it is facing a serious risk of sanction. The discovery team must now develop a plan by which the requested information will be
collected, stored, and prepared for delivery. This is not simply a matter of copying
files to media.

Files must be presented exactly as they exist on the host system. Additionally,
on the vast majority of networked systems today, files will exist in multiple locations, and possibly in multiple versions. While it is unlikely that several identical
copies are desirable, there is a good chance that different versions or iterations
of a file might be required. Develop a plan of action that includes de-duplicating
(deduping) files to minimize the quantity of data collected while still presenting
what is required (see side bar entitled "Duplicates versus Near Duplicates").

Larger organizations employ some form of document management system
for managing *electronically stored information* (ESI). These systems store metadata
separately from the files. The metadata is critical for establishing audit trails and
time lines. Most discovery orders will require that the metadata be preserved. It is
also possible that dedicated software might be required for presenting information
in a readable format.

Determine how data selected for review is going to be stored. There is increasing emphasis on the use of online document reviews in litigation (to be described
in more detail later in this chapter). If this is the method selected, the site must
be prepared, accounts configured, and security established before the first byte of
data is copied from the source media.

If physical media is to be used, the form, format, and density of media must be agreed upon in advance. Whenever possible, new media should be employed. If existing drives must be used, then it is essential that they be wiped with a Department of Defense (DOD) certified data wiping utility and reformatted prior to use.

DUPLICATES VERSUS NEAR DUPLICATES

A problem that every e-discovery project encounters is the existence of files that are virtually identical, but not exact duplicates of one another. Examples of such files would be evolutionary versions of a file, a PDF version of a Microsoft Word document, partial files recovered from slack space, or a TIF file of a scanned document. The conventional method for identifying duplicate files is to use a utility that compares the hash of different files. This method has the problem that even the minutest change will drastically alter the hash of a file. Figure 16.3 shows the results of a text file that had a single character changed from capital to lowercase.

Finding exact duplicates is good because getting rid of them eliminates dead weight. Finding near duplicates is good because you can find altered documents, build a timeline of the evolution of a document, or find remnants of destroyed files in the unallocated space of a hard disk. However, finding near duplicates can be very tedious and time consuming without some form of automation.

A technique called *context triggered piecewise hashing* (CTPH) allows this magic to be performed on a system (Kornblum 2006). CTPH uses an algorithm

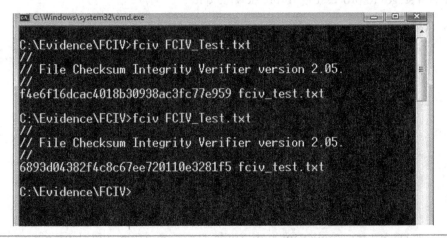

Figure 16.3 Changing a single character in a Word document completely alters the hash of the file.

that calculates the hash of smaller blocks of the file rather than the entire file. This is called *rolling hash*. File similarity is calculated by measuring the number of data blocks that are identical. Kornblum used this algorithm in a utility called ssdeep.

By itself, ssdeep can compare individual files and report if they are near duplicate or not. The Forensic Tool Kit by Access Data Corporation uses ssdeep as its fuzzy hashing algorithm, but builds on it to allow full-directory searches. Encase by Guidance Software and X-Ways Forensics both have near-duplicate detection capabilities, but it is unclear what underlying technology is used, as the companies are protective of their intellectual property.

PROCESSING, REVIEW, AND ANALYSIS

The next three steps are going to be the most labor intensive, and possibly the most scrutinized after the collection techniques used. In a complex case inside of a large organization, the search process very likely generated a massive volume of data to be processed, reviewed, and analyzed. Only a relatively small percentage of that material is going to end up as evidentiary material. The court simply does not want to see several million pages of evidence. Only evidence that is directly incriminating or exculpatory is going to be allowed.

Processing

The processing stage is where the weeding-out process is accomplished. There are several stages to processing and reviewing data:

- Assessment
    - Assign roles and responsibilities to team members.
    - Determine what data archives need to be searched.
        - What type of media is involved?
        - What tools are required for searching the types of data targeted?
    - Decide on the target format and media to be used for the collection.
    - Establish the processing steps that will be used.
    - Determine what possible problems the team might face in extracting data streams.
    - Define the criteria for "acceptable" data.
    - Determine a policy for audit trails, error reporting, and chain of custody.
    - Establish a credible and measurable measure of success.

- Preparation
  - Convert any legacy data formats into a format readable by all parties.
  - Restore any relevant backups to live systems.
  - Run a deduping utility against the data set to eliminate excess baggage.
    - Some of the network duplication detection utilities are not considered forensically sound.
    - Some of the more advanced applications detect near duplicates as well as duplicates.
  - Identify and extract any cabinet files or e-mail PO box files.
  - Run a text indexing utility against each archive to identify possible data sources.
- Selection and review
  - Eliminate identical duplicates.
  - Review near duplicates to ascertain relevancy.
  - Work with the legal team to identify protected data.
  - Determine the feasibility of running a concept extraction utility against the archives (see sidebar "Concept Extraction at Work").

CONCEPT EXTRACTION AT WORK

A significant part of the job of the e-discovery specialist is identifying documents identified in the request (responding documents) and also information that is protected from disclosure to the opposing party (privileged documents). Wading through several terabytes of corporate data to find the exact collection of data to present is tedious and time consuming. Fortunately, technology can help in this regard as well.

Deshpande et al. (2000) described a technique of software-assisted discovery that mines relevant data out of mountains of generic bits and bytes. The authors define two categories of search functions that assist with the sorting. The first category is a set of focus items that target the type of information sought. Focus categories look for specific types of behavior. An investigation into corporate malfeasance might target documents or e-mails with content-specific terms related to legal terminology. Terms such as *contract, litigation, legal, attorney,* and so forth are examples. Next, the search focuses on filter categories. Items such as private communications, corporate documents, and so forth constitute filter categories.

Continues

A typical Boolean search brings up every piece of information that meets the criteria defined. Concept extraction software compares the focus and filter categories to relevant topics and identifies documents specific to the search. Well-designed concept extraction utilities recognize that a paper about elephants is not relevant when looking for proof that evidence was hidden in the culprit's trunk. Artificial intelligence algorithms work with rules of language processing to bring up only relevant documents.

Tools that employ concept extraction are not common, and they are not cheap. One example is ZyLab eDiscovery. The text mining capabilities of this package include linguistic analysis, content clustering, concept and pattern extraction, and even e-mail chain analysis. Kazeon Systems' Analysis and Review package provides similar capabilities.

Review

In larger litigation events, data will be presented in a *rolling review*. This is a process by which data is produced in incremental stages, rather than all at once. There are two advantages to this method. First of all, it lets the technical staff working on data extraction to identify and resolve any ghosts in the machine. Unwieldy search strings or poorly defined objectives are usually picked up early on. It's better to figure out the problems before inflicting them on the entire project as a whole. Second, data review by postproduction personnel (doctors and lawyers and such) can begin before all production is complete. Meeting difficult deadlines is made easier this way.

Another form of review that is becoming increasingly popular is the online review. In this format, all documents from both sides are stored on a mutually accessible platform with controlled access. Documents must be checked out for review and checked back in when the session is completed. Audit logs are maintained to verify times and dates of access. Typically, an online review is useful when there are large amounts of data to be reviewed by several people. The online platform helps reduce costs and (if properly configured) increase security. There are several concerns that need to be addressed if the parties agree on using online review as a platform.

How will the data be viewed? If documents are to be viewed in native format, do both parties have all the necessary applications required to open the files? A critical consideration is making sure that the data is online all the time when either party requires it. As a security precaution, it may be decided that only certain "windows" of time are available for review. The Web host might open access to the data from 9:00 a.m. to 5:00 p.m., and then lock it down to prohibit after hours access.

Speaking of security, who is in charge of that critical element? Typically, a third-party service provider will be selected to host the data, and it falls upon the third party to provide security. This third party may be an entity agreed upon by the two primary litigants, or it may be one assigned by the court. Once that has been decided, the service provide must assure that the confidentiality and privacy of all data is maintained at all times. To that extent, there must be some agreement on how privileged information will be redacted from documents put up for review.

Once the review has been completed, it is essential that all information be handled in the manner dictated by the court. It is likely that the review, along with all of the audit logs generated in its lifetime, will be archived for possible use in future appeals. If this is the last leg of the journey, it is likely that the data will be ordered destroyed. It is up to both parties to verify proper disposition of data.

Analysis

Analysis occurs in two stages of the discovery process. Initially, the team must perform an analysis of the data archive to determine what to search. Once that decision has been made, it becomes necessary to decide what to produce. Not everything that the recovery team finds is going to be used in litigation. As mentioned earlier, duplicate files can be eliminated during the review process. Near duplicates must be analyzed and a decision made as to whether the differences are sufficient to qualify each document as a separate item. Therefore, near duplicates must be moved into the next phase. Each document retained for possible presentation will eventually be analyzed to ascertain whether it is truly relevant or whether it might contain privileged information. Any preliminary screening at this stage will reduce later efforts.

During analysis, the team will collect an inventory of all information collected. A detailed chain of custody for each document archive must be created and maintained. Lists of all document sources complete with network or computer location, the name of the data custodian, and any information relevant to the retrieval of the data must be assembled. This would include such information as what tools were used to retrieve the information, whether the information had to be extracted through less than conventional methods (data carving, tape backup recovery, etc.), and the name of the technician who retrieved the data.

During this time, the team needs to maintain certain metrics. These metrics would include information such as

- Percentage of requested data collected
- Percentage from each custodian collected
- Percentage of requested data that was not found (or not retrievable)
- Total number of items collected

- Total number of items per custodian collected
- Overall volume (in bytes)
- What data was collected by what technician

Identify each tool used in collection, and be prepared to describe how it was used. It may be necessary to defend the techniques used by each member of the team. Opposing counsel will leverage any weakness they can find to fray the seams in your presentation.

PRODUCTION AND PRESENTATION

The final stages of the e-discovery process involve packaging the information the investigators uncover into a usable bundle. Data is preserved in the agreed-upon format and storage schema and delivered in the manner determined during the initial conference. This may be bundles of CDs, boxes of printed documents (highly unlikely these days), or with increasing frequency in an online forum for review.

During the initial conference, the form of data production will have been determined. Presentation of data in native format means that the potential viewer of the information must have the proper software installed on the review computer. For example, an Excel spreadsheet in native format can only be opened in Excel or an Excel viewer. In order to see embedded code, Excel will be required. An example of non-native production would be if Excel documents were printed out in PDF format. In this format, only the information entered into the spreadsheet can be viewed. The formulae used to calculate values are not visible, and macros cannot be examined. Generally speaking, native format is the desirable option.

Near native format is a desirable option in certain cases. E-mails extracted from e-mail servers may be presented in MSG or EML format. Databases are typically too cumbersome to present in their entirety, and doing so would most likely expose protected information along with the discoverable data. The discovery team will work with the legal team and business managers to determine what records need to be produced and what the best production format is going to be.

Documents stored in document management systems are usually managed by the application that stores the document and not by the one that created it. As such, the document management software is most likely going to have numerous indexing and management files that control the information, while the information itself is stored in a condensed archive. Figure 16.4 illustrates the file structure of a typical document management application.

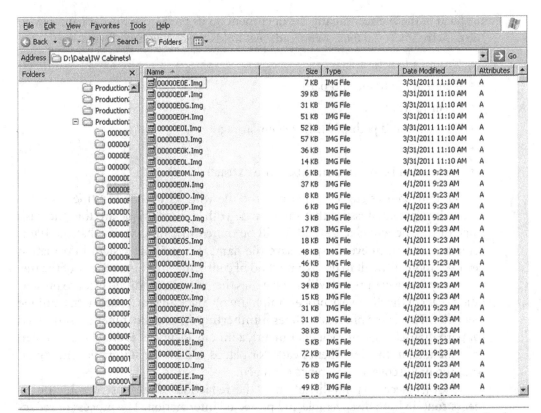

Figure 16.4 Document management applications store massive amounts of information about the documents they manage in separate index files. Each folder holds hundreds of documents, and the database files maintain the metadata.

The second phase of analysis begins now. The team wants to present the minimum amount of information that will satisfy the discovery order. Each document will be examined by the legal team and business group to determine relevance and privilege level. In extreme cases, it might be necessary to examine particularly incriminating documents for authenticity. A study of the metadata may be able to determine if a document was subjected to additional editing since its creation. Speaking of metadata, here is where it becomes necessary to package it for presentation.

It will be necessary to prove authenticity of each document that is selected for presentation. A simple MD5 or SHA-1 hash of the file is a generally acceptable method of proving that two copies of a file are identical. Once files are produced, an auditable chain of custody must be maintained. Generally, the best way to track specific documents is to create a unique identifier for each file. That identifier and the hash of the file accompany the document on its path from the data archives to the courtroom. A database or spreadsheet holds the following information:

- Unique identifier
- Original file name and path
- Hash value of file
- File name and path of file in review storage
- Type of file
- Technician ID of team member who extracted file

Some references suggest renaming the file with its unique identifier as a file name. Two potential issues that might arise with this technique are that the hash value of the file will change, and it will be more difficult to verify that the file is actually identical in every aspect save file name. Second, file system information becomes more difficult to use as a method of confirming the authenticity of the file.

Every discovery project will involve files that must be modified prior to presentation. Part of the discovery process might involve labeling each page with a unique identifier. This is the process of **Bates numbering.** As each document is processed (or perhaps each page of each document), a unique identifier is attached. This can be embedded in the document header or placed as a visible stamp, depending on what the prediscovery conference arranged.

Another necessary modification is the redaction. Many discoverable documents contain both discoverable and protected information. The process of **redaction** is simply a method of blocking protected information in a document before releasing it. This is usually not possible in native format. Documents that must be redacted will be converted to an image file, with the protected information blocked. This is the digital equivalent of blocking out letters on a page with a black marker.

Simply blocking the visible text with a black rectangle does not completely hide the information. The hidden data remains in the document and can be extracted by a knowledgeable person. The black marker is simply a graphical overlay that exists coincidentally with the text. To effectively redact a document, you must first create a valid copy of the original data. It is certainly not a good idea to permanently alter the only copy of a document. Next, it is necessary to make sure that no metadata exists within the document that contains protected information. For example, it might be necessary to conceal the identity of an individual, but that individual was the creator of a document. The document's creator is identified in the metadata.

Other pieces of information that can be identified from metadata include user information of those who may have edited the document, to whom the software is registered, dates of creation and editing of the file, and the file path to where the file was originally stored. If the user happened to use any of the custom fields available to most software packagers, there is a wide array of information that might be extracted.

CONCLUSION

As long and as detailed as this chapter may seem, it really only scratches the surface of the complexity of electronic discovery. In truth, the subject deserves a dedicated book of its own. In most cases, the forensic investigator is only going to play a limited role in the process. Still, the more he or she knows about the subject, the easier the task will be for everyone concerned.

CHAPTER REVIEW

1. What is the significance of Rule 26f in the Federal Rules of Civil Procedure? How does it impact on a civil case?

2. Under what circumstances would it be advisable to issue a litigation hold in a corporate environment? Who all should be affected by such a hold?

3. Explain two circumstances that would constitute "spoliation" in the eyes of the court, should evidentiary material conveniently disappear. What is a mitigating circumstance that might convince the court to overlook the destruction of critical evidence?

4. Differentiate between *near-line* data and *inaccessible* data. Where does *offline storage* fit into the equation?

5. Several sources cite the review of potential data as being the most expensive aspect of the e-discovery process. Explain why this is the case.

CHAPTER EXERCISES

1. Locate at least one civil case that involved spoliation, and describe what happened in that case. Were there any sanctions imposed? If so, what were they, and if not, why was the destruction of evidence overlooked?

2. Go on line and find three examples of an enterprise-level document management system. Read what the vendors say about their products in regards to e-discover and regulatory compliance. Can you think of why the two concepts might be related?

REFERENCES

Association of Corporate Counsel. 2010. *Civil litigation survey of the chief legal officers and general counsel.* University of Denver, Association of Corporate Counsel. Denver: Institute for the Advancement of the American Legal System.

Committee on the Judiciary. 2008. The federal rules of civil procedure. www.law.cornell.edu/rules/fcrp (accessed May 12, 2011).

Deshpande, M., J. Srivasta, R. Cooley, and P. Tan. 2000. Web usage mining: Discovery and applications of usage patterns from Web data. *ACM SIGKDD Explorations Newsletter* 1(2).

EDRM. 2010. The electronic directory reference model. www.erdm.net/archives/2998 (accessed May 13, 2011).

Hagopian v. Publix Supermarkets, Inc., 788 So.2d 1088 (2001).

Kornblum, J. 2006. Identifying almost identical files using context triggered piecewise hashing. *Digital Investigation.* www.dfrws.org/2006/proceedings/12-Kornblum.pdf (accessed June 6, 2011).

Koutrika, G., Z. Zadeh, and H. Garcia-Molina. 2009. CourseCloud: Summarizing and refining keyword searches over structured data. Presented at Microsoft's Extending Database Technology. http://academic.research.microsoft.com/Paper/4706513.aspx (accessed November 30, 2010).

Lyman, P., and H. Varian. 2003. *How much information?* www.sims.berkeley.edu/research/projects/how-much-info-2003/printable_report.pdf (accessed May 12, 2011).

Royal & Sunallaiance a/s/o R.R. & L. R. Corp, Inc. v. Lauderdale Marine Center, 877 So 2d 843 (Fla. 4th DCA 2004).

SafeCard Services, Inc. v. SEC, 288 U.S. App. D.C. 324, 926 F.2d 1197, 1201 (D.C. Cir. 1991).

Spencer, B. 2006. The preservation obligation: Regulating and sanctioning pre-litigation spoliation in federal court. *Fordham Law Review* 79:17–18.

William A. Gross. Constr. Assocs., Inc. v. Am. Mfrs. Mut. Ins. Co., 256 F.R.D. 134 (S.D.N.Y. 2009).

Zubulake v. UBS Warburg, 220 F.R.D 212 (S.D.N.Y 2003).

CASE MANAGEMENT AND REPORT WRITING

The ancient Egyptians took their case documentation very seriously. The Abbot Papyrus is one of the earliest examples of an investigation being documented by the officials assigned to the case. Ramses IX ordered an investigation into tomb robberies that plagued the kingdom. The method by which the ancient Egyptian investigators approached their subject is made very clear. And obviously a permanent document was created to record the findings, or we wouldn't know about it today. There were no computers involved, but the precedent remains intact.

As the title infers, there are two different but related subjects covered in this chapter. Properly managing a case minimizes the duplication of efforts and maximizes the return on time and money invested. The concept of documentation is one that has emerged many times throughout the course of this book. Here is where the various forms of documentation that will be prepared in the course of an investigation will be examined. Failure to efficiently manage a case and failure to prepare adequate documentation are both likely to have the same result—failure.

MANAGING A CASE

The least desirable component of any investigation to many professionals is the administrative aspects of preparing, executing, and presenting a specific case. Still, without this aspect, an investigation will quickly become disorganized and inefficient. Additionally, many investigations that wind their way into the courts take many years to go through the process. A gentleman I interviewed in the process of completing my graduate degree told me of a case that was just going to an appeal that he started 12 years earlier. To be able to accurately report the results of a digital investigation that long after the actual events occurred—whether it is criminal, civil, or internal in nature—requires attention to detail.

In Chapter 1, "The Anatomy of a Digital Investigation," we discussed the investigative model. Several papers have been written on different *frameworks* that can be applied to the investigative process. A framework is simply a method by which a case can be broken down into segments and each segment managed as a separate entity. Each of these approaches takes the investigative model (or some variation on the theme) into consideration and breaks a case down into phases in which each component of the model is addressed. Most of the defined frameworks are similar in nature and vary mostly in philosophical approach.

The Department of Justice model is a four-phase process that is evidence driven. The phases consist of collection, examination, analysis, and reporting. Preparation is assumed, and presentation is integrated into the reporting process (U.S. DOJ 2004).

Kruse and Heiser (2001) simplify an investigation into three steps, also evidence driven. Those phases are acquiring the evidence, authenticating the evidence, and analyzing the data. The assumption is that preparation and reporting are not in integral part of the investigative process.

The one that I personally find appealing is an objective-based framework proposed by Beebe and Clark (2005). It suggests that each investigation be divided into three stages (Figure 17.1), with each stage subsequently divided into phases. Stages are sequential and dependent on the completion of its predecessor before it can be initiated. An investigation cannot begin until preparation is complete, and it is impossible to present findings until the investigation is finished. The one

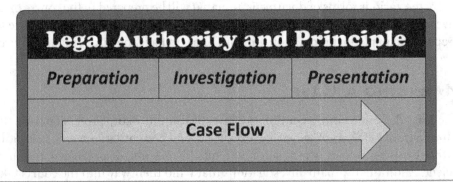

Figure 17.1 The objective-based framework consists of three stages.

overlapping principle that ties all the stages together is the correct interpretation and application of law.

Interestingly enough, each stage can be further broken down into these same three stages. There is a preparation, investigation, and presentation stage for each preparation, investigation, and presentation you do.

THE PREPARATION STAGE

The preparation stage is done outside of the general scope of any specific investigation. This is the part where the organization or the investigative team sets the groundwork to be prepared for the any of the disasters that will inevitably occur. Organizations preparing for internal investigations have different priorities—and therefore will prepare somewhat differently—than a criminal investigation team. Still, there is a significant amount of overlap.

Whether setting up an internal forensics division for a large corporation or a new team for a law enforcement agency, the preparation stage is a lot of work in itself. Starting a new endeavor of this nature would be the subject of an entire book, but it will be covered in some detail in Chapter 21, "The Business of Digital Forensics." Getting the necessary approvals and lining up the appropriate personnel is the preparation stage for the preparation stage.

The types of threats that an organization faces or that a team is equipped to handle need to be identified, quantified, and documented. Just like a bank responding to regulatory requirements, a group preparing for digital investigation capacity needs to develop an information retention policy and plan. What information must be collected, how will it be securely stored, and when the time comes to get rid of it, how can it be securely destroyed?

Develop your technical capabilities, and know precisely what they are and, more important, what the limitations are. During this part of the first stage, it will be important to engage everyone involved with the process to analyze what requirements are needed and to make sure that the resources are available to fulfill those requirements. An investigation team with nobody trained in cell phone capture and analysis, and that does not have the apparatus and software for performing such tasks, is in no position to accept responsibility for an investigation where cell phones are paramount to the investigation.

Create, distribute, and enforce strict policies and plans for each stage of an investigation. Don't reinvent the wheel with each new project. There should be specific incident response plans with flexibility to deal with live response as well as static capture. A strict file-naming convention for evidence files should be enforced from the beginning. Many software products create default file names that will make no sense to a user six months down the road. Every computer file should clearly relate to the case for which it was generated. Evidence handling procedures, chain of custody reporting, documentation standards, and reporting protocol must be predefined and understood by everyone on the team.

Everyone on the team should have specific roles and assignments. It goes without saying that they need to be properly trained to perform their jobs, but ongoing refresher training must be part of the mix.

Acquiring facilities is a critical part of the preparation phase. Imagine the confusion that would result from a first-response team arriving at the office with a half dozen computers and several pieces of media that need immediate analysis and the workstations are all being used by the administrative staff to process payroll. How much fun will it be to capture a 750GB hard disk and find out that your 1TB host storage is still full from the last job? Evidence handling and storage is a critical part of facilities management. It is critical that your team be able to demonstrate that all evidentiary materials were safe and secure and free from tampering the entire time they were in your possession.

Know in advance who you can consult regarding legal issues. Develop working relationships with several vendors who specialize in your type of products and services. You never know when you might need a couple of 2TB drives drop-shipped to a field site or need to subcontract a service you can't provide. Have emergency contact information available for all personnel and know who controls your budget and what your budget limitations are. You cannot begin your first investigation until all of the above is in place, but you have at least completed the investigation phase of preparation.

Equally important is that all of the above be clearly documented and available in a location easily accessible to key personnel. Ensure that all necessary information for submitting business change requests and project control forms has been collected. The policies that are generated during this phase, as well as contact information, should be posted where all the relevant people can find it. If just the division manager knows all this information, who will be able to take over when she steps out in front of a bus?

THE INVESTIGATION STAGE

When an actual case lands in the department's hands, it will be time to start the investigation stage, because all of the preparatory steps have already been taken. A case is initiated through some form of alert. Either the manager of a department suspects an intrusion or some form of malfeasance, or a warrant has been issued for the search and seizure of digital devices.

Preparing for the investigation stage is generally straightforward. Most of the commercial forensic suites automate much of the process of documentation, but there is still some preliminary thinking involved. This is where the file-name conventions mentioned earlier come into play. Access Data's *Forensic Tool Kit* (Figure 17.2) is a good example of a suite with automated documentation.

Triage

Depending on the type of situation and the severity, there might be several options for proceeding. Working with everybody involved in the investigation, it will be necessary to establish priorities. This is similar to the triage that doctors do on the battlefield. Dress the worst wounds first. In a situation involving large networks or

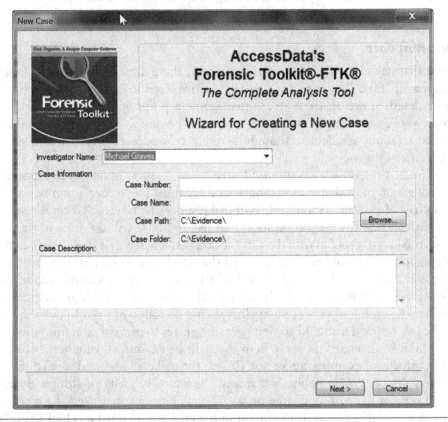

Figure 17.2 The first step in any investigation is beginning the case documentation. Most forensic suites help by automating this process.

very sensitive information, it is very likely that protecting the data carries a higher priority than collecting evidence. Cutting an active hacker off from a database of credit card information may be deemed more important that backtracing the connection to identify the culprit. A list of priorities might evolve from asking these questions:

- Is there potential risk of injury or death?
- Does either activity or inactivity lead to loss or serious damage to infrastructure?
- Is the private information of customers or employees at risk?
- Is there a significant risk of financial loss?
- Is identifying the culprit a high enough priority to introduce any of the above risks?

First Response

Once dispatched to the scene of the incident, there are certain rules to follow. Chapter 6, "First Response and the Digital Investigator," covers most of this in more detail. However, from a case-management point of view, it is essential to create a solid foundation that the remainder of the case will rest upon. It is always best to treat any incident as though it were a crime scene, even if it is a simple internal investigation.

The first response team will need to make an assessment of how to proceed in the collection of evidence. A response strategy must be decided upon before the first piece of evidence is touched. Will live response be needed? Generally speaking, unless there is a clear indication that live response will do more harm than good, it is best to proceed with the assumption that it will be. Regardless of whether live response is conducted or not, record the active state of each device examined as it is initially found. Is it on or off? If it is on, is it in screensaver mode? Are other forensic investigators involved? If so, there may be a degree of cooperation involved regarding whether fingerprints should be collected prior to live response or the live responder should go first, wearing gloves to prevent contamination.

Make an inventory of every item that will be examined, whether it is being taken off-site for examination or not. Collect the make, model, and serial numbers of each device. Where applicable, record the stated capacity of storage devices. Make note of the battery charge on any portable device that needs to be transported, especially if it needs to remain in the on position until it is looked at. For any items being transported, begin the chain of custody immediately and have someone with authority sign off on the time and date that the item was released and to whom it was released. That person must also sign or initial the chain of custody report. Every time the item changes hands, record the event, including exact times and dates, identifying who handed it off and who received it.

Crime Scene Management

While not every investigation strictly involves criminal activity, it is best if the investigation team approaches each incident as though it did. That way, in the event that criminal activity is uncovered, the evidence won't already be inadmissible because of bungling on your team's part. Carrier (2003) identifies the following phases to crime scene management:

- *Crime Scene Preservation:* Secure the scene, and detain any witnesses. If physical violence has occurred, tend to any injured people. If the suspect is present, detain that person.

- *Crime Scene Survey:* Don't do anything that might spoil evidence. If anything must be moved, carefully avoid any contact that could potentially damage existing fingerprints and be sure that you don't add your own. Take note of all people who are on the scene at the time of arrival. Identify anything that is clearly evidentiary in nature, and secure it.

- *Crime Scene Documentation:* Photograph and, if possible, make a video survey of the scene. Any materials that are collected as evidence must be carefully documented as described in the previous section of this chapter. It is essential to work with any other forensic teams during this phase to assure that the preservation of your evidence doesn't have a negative impact on the ability of others to do their jobs. Fingerprints from the keyboard may need to be collected before you attempt live response activities.

- *Crime Scene Search:* Look for additional evidence that may be concealed. In most "real" crime scenes, the forensic team breaks down the area into grids and goes over every square inch with the proverbial fine-tooth comb. In an initial response involving civil claims or internal investigations, it is likely that this part of the search will not occur. Still, it is important for your team to find things such as slips of paper with possible passwords, thumb drives tucked into drawers, notes about Web sites, or file names that the suspect may have jotted down by hand. Nearly everybody writes things down, even when using a computer.

- *Crime Scene Reconstruction:* Once again, this phase may not be necessary in anything but an actual crime scene. However, it is commonplace for forensic teams to try to analyze the location and position of various items at the scene to determine how things might have occurred. From a computer operator's point of view, this might include details such as what side of the computer the mouse is located (is the suspect right-handed or left-handed?), whether the computer display was configured for a sight-impaired person, and so forth.

Lab Preparation

While the response team is working their magic, there is a lot of work that can be done at the lab as well. There must be a single repository for all files generated during the investigation. While it is preferable that new media be used for storing files, existing disks and platters may be used as long as they are subjected to a DOD-approved wipe process to eliminate any possibility of cross-talk from a previous investigation. If this is the path taken, document the process of preparing media for case files.

Figure out how much storage will be needed for all the forensic images that will be prepared—and then allow for about twice that capacity. Forensic investigations are probably more susceptible to scope creep than any other project. Identify the personnel who will be assigned to the project, and make the appropriate assignments. Most importantly, make sure that all legal authority required to initiate the investigation is in place. If it is a criminal investigation, have the warrant in hand.

For an internal investigation, you need to make sure not only that you have written authorization but that the authorization is issued by somebody who actually has that authority. I was once involved in a situation where a manager authorized the search of several corporate computers in order to assess the damage caused by a disgruntled employee. Only as fate would have it, that manager had not cleared his decision with executive management. The damage control that followed that event was extensive.

Evidence Handling

The method by which evidentiary materials are transported from one site to another is a critical aspect of the investigation stage. Any external or environmental condition that damages the data hurts the investigation. Any suggestion that such conditions may have existed hurts the credibility of the results. Some suggestions for transporting digital evidence include

- Use antistatic bags for anything that holds magnetically stored information.
- Use Faraday bags for transporting wireless devices.
- If a battery-operated device is still in the on position, try to keep it powered up.

- Don't let magnetic media or circuit boards come in contact with any surfaces that may be statically charged.

- Keep magnetic media away from loudspeakers, heated car seats, radios, or any other device that may emanate electromagnetic radiation.

- If there is reason to transport monitors, make sure the screen is protected from possible impact. Find out if other forensic teams are going to need fingerprints.

- Don't let evidentiary materials be exposed to temperature extremes.

- If unplugging devices such as hard disks from enclosures, take extreme care not to damage connectors.

- Don't let any evidence get wet, dirty, or dropped.

If any of the aforementioned events do occur, document when, where, and how it happened. Report anything that may have caused such an incident to occur. Try to assess any possible impact it may have had on the authenticity or reliability of any evidence that might be obtained from the affected device.

For any materials transported off-site for examination, document where and how these items are to be stored while in the possession of the investigation team. Any time an item is checked in or out of the evidence locker, the transaction *must* be recorded in the chain of custody log. Additionally, anytime an item changes hands, that transfer must be recorded. Any break in the chain that the opposition can find will cast doubt on any evidence returned by that device. Storage must be secure and monitored. Larger organizations most likely will have a locked facility with controlled access. This type of control is mandatory for the storage of evidence used in a criminal investigation.

In addition to security, there are several other aspects of the storage environment that must be considered. Temperature and humidity should be carefully controlled. Too much or too little of either one can damage circuits or corrupt data under the right conditions. The environment should be as static free as possible. There are commercially available antistatic floor mats and counter mats that help out in this regard. A permanent facility can be designed to include Faraday shielding in the walls to prevent outside connections to be made with wireless devices stored within. There needs to be sufficient space in the storage facility to allow the evidence from multiple cases to coexist without any possibility that they will become comingled.

Evidence Examination

Once the examination of the evidence actually begins, the documentation and reporting become an integral part of the investigation. The examination starts with a hypothesis, and the goal of the investigation is to prove or disprove that hypothesis. Generally speaking, the hypothesis is presented for you. If the assignment is to look for pirated music on a server, the hypothesis is that somebody has intentionally acquired the illegal material and deliberately stored it.

Each examination must be conducted using the correct tool for the job. Just like you are not supposed to use a bigger wrench as a hammer, you don't use Windows Explorer to make forensic copies. As pointed out in previous chapters, record what tool was used for each process and document each step taken, along with the time and date it occurred. Work only from copies of the data. Never do anything that can alter, damage, or destroy the original. Every time a new copy is made, hash the copy and compare the values. Make sure you're working with an identical copy. Always remember that you are not just looking for incriminating evidence. As an investigator, you do not take sides. Look carefully for any exculpatory evidence as well.

While analyzing the results of the examination, follow all the same rules. Keep accurate records, because these reports will be the presentation that results from this stage of the investigation.

Throughout the course of the investigation, the team should have regular meetings. Each member of the team should be aware of what the other members are doing. Information found by one person might be the clue that helps another find the way. Brainstorming sessions and general rap sessions where people compare results do a lot for keeping a case moving along. These meetings also help out later on in the presentation stage when one or more members are called upon to testify.

THE PRESENTATION STAGE

The final act of any investigation is presenting the results. A final report accomplishes two things. First of all, it clearly explains what was found during the examination of the evidence. Remember that it isn't the job of the investigation team to interpret results—only to present them. A photograph may appear to be pornographic in nature to you and your team, but a jury may not agree. Therefore your report does not list 107 pornographic images. It lists 107 graphic images of people doing whatever it is they are doing in the photograph. A detailed description of a murder might read like evidence of a crime to most people, but in the final tally, it may simply be a chapter out of the suspect's next novel.

The second aspect of the report is to prove that the evidence is what you say it is and that the methods you used to obtain that evidence were valid procedures and performed in an acceptable manner. Using the pirated music hypothesis described above, the investigation should be able to prove these key points:

- Music downloads do exist on the system.
- No exculpatory evidence indicates that the songs were obtained legally.
- The evidence points to an individual or individuals who were responsible for copying the files to the system.
- No other evidence was found linking any other individuals to the files.

If the additional allegation was made that file-sharing was taking place, there would need to be evidence collected that pointed to that as well. Network packet capture, logs showing network connections with suspect devices, and so forth could point to data transfer between two points.

There always exists the possibility that one or more investigators will be called upon to testify at a hearing or a trial. If that happens, whoever will be performing this onerous duty must be completely familiar with the case in its entirety. Remember those meetings I discussed in the previous section. This is one very good reason why they are important.

WRITING REPORTS

Writing reports is probably the least favorite part of any investigator's job. The resistance becomes exacerbated when multiple investigators are involved. The final report can be a voluminous manuscript and require the cooperative effort of several people.

CONTENTS OF A REPORTING PACKAGE

In actuality, there are several documents that comprise the final report:

- The original request for an investigation to be conducted
- Copies of any authorizations issued (there may be several)
- An inventory of all devices touched by the investigative team
- A chain of custody report for any device seized by the team
- All case logs generated by members of the team
- All case notes maintained by members of the team
- Photographs and/or videos taken by the first-response team
- The final report of the investigation team

The final report is likely to be the most voluminous. It will contain summaries of much of the information listed in the preceding list. Additionally, it will contain a detailed description of the investigation as well as any conclusions derived from the process. Information contained in the final report will include, at a minimum, the following pieces of information:

- An identification of the reporting agency or individual
- The name of the person directly submitting the request
- The date of submission
- Any case numbers assigned by both the reporting agency and the internal team
- The date that the case was accepted for review
- The names of investigators assigned to the case
- A detailed report submitted by the first-response team (if applicable)
- A list of all items examined described by manufacturer, make, model, serial number, and capacity (if applicable)
- Descriptions of each step taken in the course of the investigation, including
  - Name of investigator conducting the procedure
  - Tool used for each procedure
  - Times and dates marking the beginning and end of each procedure
  - Specific parameters for any given procedure (such as search strings employed, header and footer information used in data-carving procedures, etc.)
  - The results of each procedure (if no results obtained, indicate this in the report)
- Conclusions arrived at by the team

Textual material within the report must be factual with no expression of opinion about what the result may mean in terms of innocence or guilt. That is the job of the jury to decide such matters.

STRUCTURE OF A FORENSIC REPORT

There are as many different variations on the "template" for a final forensic report as there are agencies and companies doing the reporting. Various places on the Web offer templates for download, some which come at a significant cost. Essentially, every organization will eventually have to prepare their own template based on work flow and the categories of investigation in which they specialize. There are some uniform components that will be a part of any report. Without them, the report would be incomplete.

The Case Summary

In the case summary, the basic information about the situation is briefly described. What happened to lead to an investigation being launched? If this was a news story, the basic questions would be Who, What, When, and Where. The How and Why will hopefully become a part of your summary.

Who reported the incident? Who all is involved? Provide a list of every individual that is involved in the case, starting with who filed the report, all the way to the names of the people conducting the investigation.

Record when the incident was reported. Was the report filed immediately upon discovery? If not, when was the incident first discovered? Record the date that your team accepted responsibility for conducting the investigation. If there is a significant lapse, explain why this occurred. People are going to want to know why, if the event occurred on January 1, you didn't start looking into it until August 1.

What happened? Is criminal activity suspected, or is this in internal investigation into possible employee malfeasance? Here is where you will indicate if you are looking for contraband, for breaches of security policy, evidence of theft, or whatever the cause for concern might happen to be.

Where did it occur? Is the incident isolated to a single workstation, or is it a network event?

Acquisition and Preparation

Next, the report goes into the steps taken in preparing the devices and media for examination and how the examination of the materials was conducted. This section of the final report summarizes the details that are in the various examinations logs that were collected along the way. It is not necessary to be quite as detailed here, but it is important that no steps be left out. The reader can be referred to the examination logs for intimate details.

Details that should be included are

- Any actions taken prior to evidence acquisition (such as photographic records, forensic examinations by other departments, etc.)
- How the media where forensic copies were stored was prepared, including what tools were used to sanitize the media
- File names and before/after hash values of disk images examined

- Tools that were used for making images
- Individual steps that were taken during each process

Include times and dates that evidence items were handled and when they were returned to evidence storage. It is essential that everything in the report can be corroborated by the chain of evidence logs and any other documents filed.

Findings

The findings section is not a place for coming to conclusions. This is only where the results of the various tests, examinations, and procedures are reported. As with the preparation stage, it is necessary to document what tools were used and what steps were taken, but the reader can be sent to the examination logs for a blow-by-blow description.

The process used in any given file search should be described, including such details as command-line triggers used to refine the search, search strings used, Boolean operators used, and so forth. Rather than list each and every file found during the search, a summary of findings, including the number and types of files found, is in order. For example, it would be appropriate to say "256 image files were discovered, 128 of which were JPEGs, 39 of which were TIFs, and the remainder were PNG files." If appropriate, a complete listing of files, complete with file name, path, and MAC data can be recorded in an appendix attached to the final report.

The results of an Internet search would include a listing of any Web sites visited by users on the target system, organized by user. A timeline of Internet activity should be provided as a graphic as well as in tabular format.

E-mail searches should be treated similarly to file searches with some notable exceptions. Individual messages may have trouble standing alone as evidentiary material unless the content contains a real "smoking gun." In general, e-mails need to be processed and presented in such a way as to provide the entire chain of messages, with each TO and FROM entry intact. It is important to be able to identify which message may have been the initial carrier for specific attachments.

Report Conclusion

The summary is where the investigative team presents its interpretation of the facts. The "how" and "why" parts of the story are filled in (although "why" is rarely an issue in most investigations). As has been stated numerous times, it is not appropriate to hypothesize guilt or innocence of any party. The goal of the investigation is to excavate and present evidence, incriminatory or exculpatory, directly relevant to the complaint issued when the case was first handed over.

At this point, the writer of the report may need to do more than present facts about what was found. For example, as part of the evidence it may be that the examiner discovered log entries indicating that SQL records were accessed by a specific user ID and that a particular sequence of database events was initiated as a result of that access. The general reader is not likely to understand how this implicates the user or exactly what it is that the evidence suggests they were doing. An explanation of why this is relevant is necessary.

Additionally, some steps taken by the investigation team may not seem relevant or logical. An examination of Exchange Server logs reveals a lot to a professional, but the average person won't even know they exist. Likewise, an analysis of the Windows Registry can be very revealing, but the investigator may need to explain exactly what was being sought and how the registry holds the key to finding it.

As with all other sections in this report, the expression of opinions should be reserved. However, this is the one place in the report where a professional opinion might be required. For example, the evidence might point to the possibility that the user employed antiforensic tools to obfuscate evidence. However, there is nothing remaining on the system to prove such tools were used. It would be appropriate to explain why such an opinion was reached and how it affects the other evidence that was actually found and presented as part of the investigative process.

The conclusion should tie all other sections together. The final report should indicate that the investigation was thorough and complete. If a report leaves the reader asking more questions than are answered, there exists a distinct possibility that the investigation was not completed as well as it might have been.

CHAPTER REVIEW

1. Describe several aspects of the preparation phase of digital investigation. What types of tasks can be accomplished before an assignment is ever received? What tasks in this phase are specific to a particular assignment?

2. How would you describe the triage process used by a first response digital investigation team? What type of issues are considered, and what are the priorities?

3. Brian Carrier defines five phases of crime scene management. What are those phases, and how do they relate to digital forensics?

4. What impact can poor evidence handling have on whether or not the courts consider digital evidence admissible in court? What document records how evidence is handled as it moves from one stage of the investigation to another?

5. Describe the contents of a final case report package. Be as thorough as possible.

CHAPTER EXERCISES

1. Using your favorite word processing application, put together your own template for an evidence chain of custody. Use the description in this chapter as a guide.

2. Based on what you have learned in this chapter, put together a list of files that will be generated by the investigative team throughout the course of an investigation. Decide on a file-naming convention, and itemize the list of files you will create.

REFERENCES

Beebe, N., and J. Clark. 2005. A hierarchical, objectives-based framework for the digital investigations process. *Digital Investigation* 2(2):3–10.

Carrier, B. 2003. Getting physical with the digital investigation process. *International Journal of Digital Evidence* 2(2):2–3.

Kruse, W. G., and J. G. Heiser. 2001. *Computer forensics. Incident response essentials.* Boston: Addison-Wesley.

U.S. DOJ. 2004. *Electronic crime scene investigation: A guide for first responders.* Washington, DC: U.S. Department of Justice.

TOOLS OF THE
DIGITAL INVESTIGATOR

In order to excavate the data of a digital device, you will need to have access to certain tools. Some of these tools are software applications, some are devices specific to the field, and others are general devices used by many occupations. This chapter is not intended to be a tutorial on how to use each device, but rather more of a shopping list for the person starting a new We Be Forensics and Stuff location. Looking on the bright side: some of the software tools are free, so they don't damage the wallet.

SOFTWARE TOOLS

Software tools can be broken down into three basic categories:

- Utilities built into the OS
- Open-source applications
- Commercial applications and suites

As you might imagine, each of these applications will perform specific functions. In order to make full use of a particular product, you will need to practice with it quite a bit before trying to use it in the field. Don't expect to be able to dive in and use a command-line utility for the first time in your life while having the chief of detectives hanging over your shoulder.

In addition to the software categories, software tools can be broken down into functional categories as well. A good toolkit will have a utility or application that will work on the following levels:

- Physical media capture and analysis
  - Data capture
  - File system analysis
  - Media management
- Memory capture and examination
- Application analysis
- Network capture and analysis

DATA ABSTRACTION LAYERS

Before you can begin to understand how a tool works against a file or file system, you have to have a basic understanding of how data is interpreted by a machine. A realization that evades even some advanced computer users is the fact that everything you see, hear, and do on a computer system is a result of *abstraction*. Nothing you see is real. The term abstract means literally *difficult to understand*. For the vast majority of the human race, this definition applies perfectly to any computer code ever written. On the most basic level, every bit of information stored on a computer system—whether it be a text file, a photograph of an orange, or a Shubert Symphony—exists as a stream of 0s and 1s. Since people don't communicate in binary, it is up to the programmers of the world to create tools that convert that stream of bits into a usable structure. In most cases, there is a series of steps that any given file goes through before it is humanly accessible. These steps are known as *abstraction layers*. The abstraction layer is an application interface that the computer applies to a data stream to convert it into another format. As data moves down the layers from the user to the CPU, it must get more and more specific, until it eventually can be processed in a series of commands.

An example of an abstraction layer is a simple text editor. Computers have long employed a series of *character sets* that are readable symbols that represent binary data as readable information. One common character set is the American Standard Code for Information Interchange (ASCII). ASCII takes a standard character, such as a letter, a number, or a punctuation mark, and represents it as a stream of data eight bits long. The lowercase letter *a* is represented in ASCII as 0110 0001. Capital B is 0100 0010 and a lowercase *d* is 0110 0100. The lowercase letters o and y are 0110 1111 and 0111 1001, respectively. Now, when reprimanding your son, are you more likely to say he is a "Bad Boy" or that he is a "0100 0010 0110 0001 0110 0100 0100 0010 0110 1111 0111 1001"?

A simple text editor takes that string of bits, applies a few simple rules, and outputs the characters we know and love. Figure 18.1 abstractly illustrates that concept.

File systems use abstraction layers in order to translate a very complex collection of binary data into the lovely little file cabinet analogy with which we've all grown accustomed. In Figure 18.2, you see the familiar Windows Explorer screen with its folder icons and easy to navigate interface. The F drive shows up with a listing of directories and file folders contained within. Therefore, that's all there is to see, right?

Electrical Charge

-+--++-+-++-+--+-++---++-++-+----++---+-++--+-+-++-++--

Binary

0100110101101001011000110110100001100001011001010110100

ASCII

ABC

Figure 18.1 Data moves through several abstraction layers to get from raw binary data into a usable format.

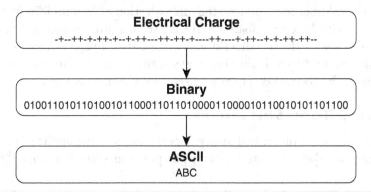

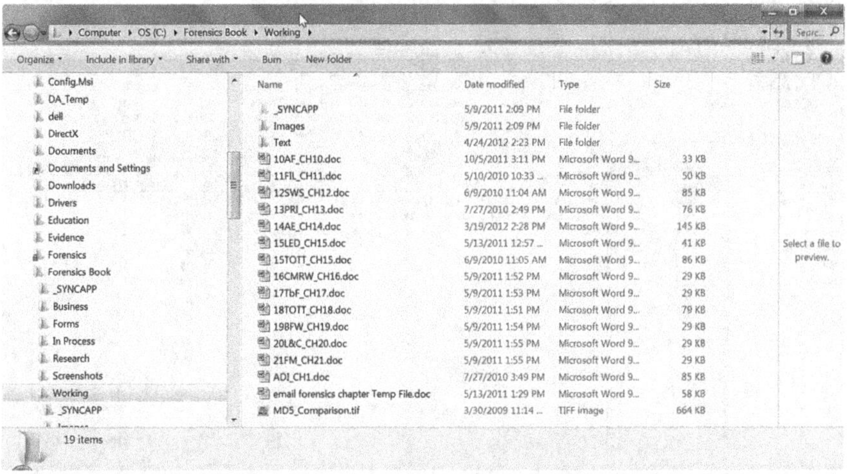

Figure 18.2 Windows Explorer provides a user-friendly interface for viewing the file structure of a storage device.

Figure 18.3 strips away several abstraction layers and shows the root directory of the F drive in hexadecimal. Aside from the fact that it's not very user friendly, this view also shows data that is used by the system and is all but useless to the average user. Figure 18.4 moves up a step in the abstraction layers, showing the file structure once again in the file cabinet analogy. However, this utility displays entries in the file allocation tables for directories and files that have been deleted.

So how does this relate to the digital archaeologist? That depends on the format of your data source. If you work from a forensic image, you may or may not be able to *mount* the volume, depending on the sophistication of your tool. To mount a volume is to load its directory tables into the OS so that utilities such as Explorer can work their magic on the metadata stored within. If an image cannot be mounted, it is nothing more than a single, very long stream of bits. The software tools of the trade provide the abstraction layers necessary for viewing data in a useful manner.

SOFTWARE TOOL SUITABILITY

Before settling on an individual utility to perform a specific application, there are some things to take into consideration. The previous section discussed how data

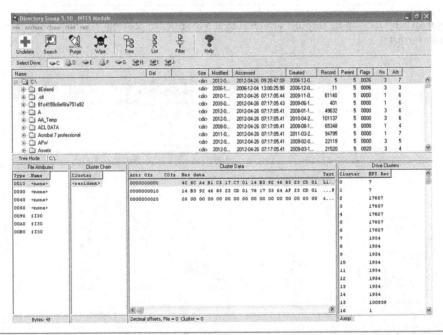

Figure 18.3 Actual directory entries aren't quite as friendly as Windows Explorer would have you believe.

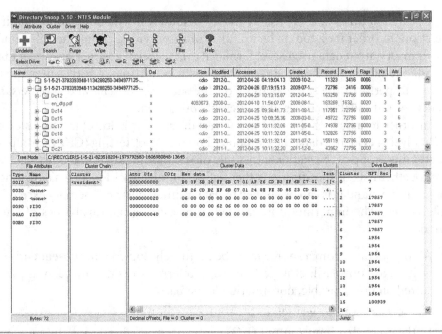

Figure 18.4 More powerful browsing tools, such as Directory Snoop, can display deleted entries alongside of live data entries.

moves through layers of abstraction to get from stored digital code into readable format. Abstraction layers will either be lossless layers or they will be lossy layers. Lossless layers will make no changes to information as it moves up the levels of abstraction. What you start with is what you end with. With lossy algorithms, a certain amount of interpretation of data goes on.

How accurately an application performs this interpretation will dictate its utility as a forensic tool. An OS application such as Windows Explorer will be lossless. Most hex editors are lossless as well. Network capture utilities and intrusion detection systems are looking for patterns in data and can be open to interpretation. Incorrect interpretation leads to error. Therefore, they are considered lossy tools.

In the vast majority of cases, the forensic analyst will not be using OS utilities. Third-party utilities and applications can be measured by

- Accuracy
- Verification capabilities
- Consistency
- Usability

If a tool is missing even one of these attributes, it isn't suitable for forensic detection. In order for a tool to be useful, it must provide a comprehensible interface, it must output data in a useful format at every level of abstraction, and it must provide the same results on the same set of data every time. Another user should be able to perform the same analysis on the same set of data and see the same results, even if the user comes to a different conclusion.

In order to assure that a tool meets certain standards for obtaining, storing, and analyzing evidence data, the Computer Forensic Tool Testing (CFTT) group—a functioning group of the National Institute of Standards and Technology (NIST)—puts together lists of specifications that define a usable tool for forensic investigations. Similar standards can be applied to data mining tools and memory extraction tools as well. The important criteria used in measuring the capabilities of a tool include

- All digital data from a source must be accurately copied and subsequently written to nonvolatile storage. This copy, referred to as the image, must be stored on non-erasable, non-rewritable media.
- No new data can be written to the source medium.
- In the event that input/output (I/O) errors occur while reading the source data, a predefined value must be written to the corresponding locations in the target image. The utility must log the type of error and the memory address range in which the error occurred.
- There must be a documented procedure, with the steps performed duly recorded, along with the results obtained, detailing the hardware and software resources that it uses to read the source data.
- In the event that the destination medium is of a larger capacity than the source, the start and end locations of source data must be clearly and accurately recorded within the destination image.
- Should the destination medium be of smaller capacity than the source, the application must notify the user. Then it will either abort the acquisition or copy as much data as possible into the destination. Details of the event must be documented.

If a particular utility is used during the course of an investigation that does not meet NIST requirements, an opposing attorney or a judge may insist that the evidence collected by that tool be declared inadmissible. That is not to say that such tools cannot be used. You may simply have to defend your choice and provide solid evidence that the information you gathered is accurate. If your tools can pass the scrutiny of the four tests of the *Daubert Process,* then it is likely that the judge will accept the evidence produced by your procedures. The Daubert Process asks four questions:

- Can the evidence presented be or has it been tested empirically, and can it be falsified?
- Has the approach or technique been the subject of peer review and publication?
- Is the technique generally accepted within the scientific or professional community?
- Does the technique or procedure contain a high known or potential rate of error?

Why is it called the Daubert Process? This is because the rules were defined in a case entitled *Daubert v. Merrell Dow Pharmaceuticals* presented before the U.S. Supreme Court in 1993. In this case the court laid out the opinion that has since provided the guidelines for determining the validity of expert witnesses, which would include scientists and computer professionals.

OS UTILITIES

In the real world, there are many different operating systems in use, and you certainly face the possibility that you will encounter all of them at least once in your life. However, it's likely that over 99% of the computers you encounter will run one of the basic three:

- Windows
- Linux
- Macintosh OSX

It's possible that you will encounter Macintosh OS9 and Unix as well. Unix is similar enough to Linux that most of the utilities will be the same. OS9 is not similar to OSX in several respects, but in many cases, the same utilities are available for both OS9 and OSX.

Windows

Since Microsoft Windows is far and away the most popular operating system in existence, it shouldn't come as much of a surprise that there are more utilities available to support it. There is also an impressive number of utilities packaged into the system. Others are available for download on their Technet site (currently located at http://technet.microsoft.com/en-us/bb403698.aspx). Some of these utilities are fairly handy for extracting hidden information and helping you find a user's foot-prints in the digital sand. The ones discussed here are

- Regedit
- Event Viewer
- SysInternals

Regedit The registry is a set of configuration files that tells a Microsoft OS how to run. For the most part, the registry is best left alone. Most configuration changes can be made in the OS within different applets or fields, which were discussed in Chapter 9, "Document Analysis." However, once in a while, it is necessary for a technician to manually edit entries in the registry. This is done through a command-line utility called *regedit*. Later versions of Windows also included regedt32. Regedit was included in the first version of WIN95 as a 16-bit registry editor and has been included in every version of Windows released since that date. As its name implies, regedt32 is a 32-bit editor.

The registry editor is not accessed through any shortcut. It is a command-line item, although it can also be accessed from the Start menu. To open regedit, click Start. Run and type `regedit` into the command field. A screen like the one in Figure 18.5 will open.

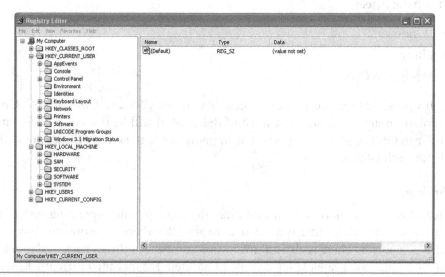

Figure 18.5 The Windows REGEDIT utility

Regedit also keeps track of some of the things Windows has done recently. It is through the registry that MS Word knows what files to list in the Recent Files list on the File menu. One thing it can give you is a list of files recently opened on a computer, even if the user has cleared their recent history. Assuming a user is technically savvy enough to clear the history after deleting files, there are a number of settings that retain historical data. Chapter 7, "Data Acquisition," discussed this in more detail.

Event Viewer Microsoft's Event Viewer utility is used more for network forensics than for excavation. It is included in all Microsoft OS versions since Windows 2000. Several logs keep track of different types of incident, recording them as informational events, warnings, or errors. Three logs of interest to us are the Application, Security, and System logs. While not as useful as the registry editor, Event Viewer can tell you about things such as failed logon attempts, access denials, and write attempts to removable storage.

In Figure 18.6, you can see all three of the icons indicating the severity of an event. The lowercase i indicates an informational event. Nothing bad happened; Windows just thought you should know. The triangle with the exclamation point is a warning. Windows didn't like something it saw, but whatever it was wasn't enough to set off

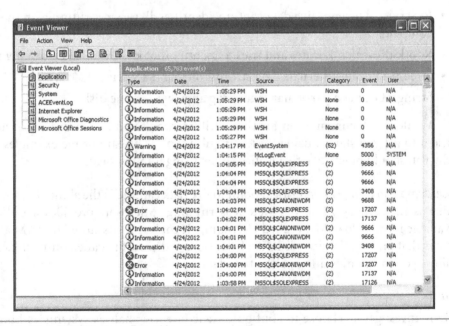

Figure 18.6 The Windows Event Viewer

the major alarms. The circle with an X through the middle is an error. These are the messages that indicate something is wrong and deserves your attention.

SysInternals   The SysInternals suite of utilities distributed by Microsoft offers some very powerful tools. All together, there are over 60 utilities (and counting) included, and they are available as a free download from Microsoft. (And you thought Microsoft never gave *anything* away for free!) Of those, only a small number are of use to the forensics professional:

- Autoruns: Identifies every process configured to start automatically when Windows loads.
- EFSDump: Shows what accounts are authorized to access an encrypted file.
- PendMoves: Lists all files that have been tagged for removal on the next reboot. This may help prevent the loss of files from a running file system configured to autodestruct on the next boot.
- PSFile: Identifies files open on the computer, including those being accessed remotely. Useful during live capture.
- PSList: During a live data capture, identifies all processes running on the computer.
- PSService: During a live data capture, identifies all services running on the computer.
- RootkitRevealer: Locates and tries to identify root kits installed on a system.
- Streams: Locates alternate data streams on an NFTS drive.
- Strings: Locates a particular text string anywhere on the disk.

While the documentation for these utilities won't win any awards, it is sufficient to get you started using these very nice tools. They are prime examples of why you should practice with a utility before using it in the field.

Userdump and Dumpchk   A critical point to live data capture is the ability to record what is in memory while the system is running. Microsoft provides a utility, available for free download, called Userdump. It copies all bits stored in RAM and stores that information in a disk file. Later on, another utility called dumpchk.exe allows you to examine and analyze that data.

Linux

Many investigators choose to configure their forensic analysis systems as Linux boxes for a variety of reasons. Many of the utilities used by Linux can work on Windows and Macintosh computers. The reverse can't be said of those two machines. Also, there is a wide variety of software available through open source for a Linux box. The interesting thing about the Linux OS is that everything connects to the system as an installable package. Distribution packs include a large collection of various applications and utilities, but if you need something different, it's easy enough to add. Some of the following utilities are likely to be included in whatever Linux distribution a user chooses to install. Others might need to be downloaded and installed separately.

Disk Dump (DD) The seemingly simple Disk Dump utility carries a lot more power than any of the integrated Microsoft utilities. It creates a direct copy of a disk by copying block by block or bit by bit. (In UNIX-type file systems, a block is the equivalent of a cluster.) DD can do simple backups, directly clone a hard disk, or create a bit-by-bit image of a disk. An impressive variety of command-line switches allows a knowledgeable user to strictly manage the way data is copied.

The key word here is knowledgeable. Since it is a command-line utility running on a UNIX-based OS, getting things wrong in the syntax can be disastrous. For example, if you get the source and the target disk in the wrong order when typing the command, you will overwrite the data disk with a blank one. This might not be the worst thing to happen to you in your life, but if it is a critical evidence disk, it might be the worst to happen in your career. Chapter 7 provided a full section on acquiring a forensic image using this utility.

GREP GREP is a command-line utility that works as long as you know the name and extension of the file you wish to recover. Primarily targeted at text files, GREP can be used to recover binary files using the –a trigger.

Linux Disk Editor (LDE) If you require the ability to view the actual contents of the disk, Linux Disk Editor is one utility to use. It allows editing as well, but that activity goes against the grain of what the investigator is trying to do. It works with the ext2 and ext2fs file systems as well as minix and xiafs. In addition, it provides rudimentary support for FAT and NFTS as a hex editor. Using the –recoverable trigger, this utility can locate inodes that contain recoverable data.

PhotoRec Primarily designed to recover digital image files from memory sticks, this utility can also be used to recover document files, PDFs, and audio files from other media such as hard disks and CD-ROMs. It works over FAT, NTFS, HFS, ext3, and ext3. Document formats it can recover include Microsoft Word, Open Office, XML, MS Works, and several others. Altogether the developer's site lists over a hundred different file formats it can recover. Its unique claim to fame is that it can ignore the file system and carve data directly off the disk surface.

Macintosh OSX

Like Linux, the OSX OS used by Macintosh (Mac) computers is loosely based on Unix. Therefore, it isn't surprising that some of the utilities are the same, only different. As with Linux, the file system used by Macs is a journaling system and self-maintained.|Therefore, recovering deleted files is not as easy (and frequently not possible). However, it's an easier system to hide stuff in. Some of these utilities will help.

GREP The Macintosh version of the GREP command-line utility searches files or directories, looking for specific text strings. A wide variety of triggers lets the user control how the command behaves. A good feature is the -text trigger that allows a binary file to be processed as text. It can look for patterns of text as well as fixed strings.

HEAD HEAD is another command-line utility. If you suspect you have a file that has been renamed to disguise the contents, you can use this nifty little program to view the first few lines of the program. The default is ten lines, but the -count trigger allows you to specify how many lines to display. To make the utility even handier, more than one file can be processed at a time. In this case, the output results are preceded with a text string identifying the file name.

Finder Finder is the OSX equivalent to Windows Explorer. It searches the disk for files based on user search parameters. Like Windows Explorer, Finder searches file contents as well as file table information. With Finder, this is a default behavior. If you type in *Doberman*, it first searches the HFS file tables and then searches file contents, finally displaying every file that contains that particular string anywhere in the directory name, file name, or within the file itself.

Spotlight Spotlight is an offshoot of finder. It takes advantage of the services of another OSX feature known as the *Metadata Server* and lets the user perform selection-based searches. Unlike Finder, which uses indexes of file names and of text, Spotlight uses indexes created from *metadata* stored by various files on the system.

Metadata is information embedded within a file that provides information about the file. As you will see in several places throughout this book, metadata plays an important role in tracing footsteps and in identifying critical information. The Metadata Server is a service running on OSX that scans each file on the system as it is added and indexes that information. Chapter 9, "Document Analysis," covers metadata in much greater detail.

COMMERCIAL APPLICATIONS AND SUITES

Most professional computer archaeologists are going to take advantage of one of the dedicated suites of applications available. There are a number of these suites available, and since most are somewhat expensive, you should know what you need your applications to do before you invest. The courts are fairly strict about how data is extracted, archived, and analyzed. The suites automate most of the functions required to meet legal standards and eliminate much of the "grunt labor" involved in the process.

Suites

A forensic suite is a unified collection of utilities that provide a wide variety of functions. Most also include automated reporting capabilities. At a bare minimum, a good forensics suite includes a forensic imaging utility, data search and recovery functions, and a hash generator. The better ones can search slack space and unallocated space, and even scrub the file tables for latent entries. The ones worth looking into are

- Windows
  - AccessData
  - Guidance Software
  - Paraben
  - X-Ways Forensics/Investigator
- Linux
  - The Sleuth Kit
  - FCCU Forensic Boot CD
  - Forensic or Rescue Kit (FoRK)

These vary in the number and variety of tools included, and some have more powerful reporting functions. Since it isn't the role of this book to act as sales counselor, refer to the various companies for more details.

Applications

For the investigator who elects to pick and choose individual utilities, most of the same companies that offer suites offer one or more dedicated applications or utilities as well. In addition to the ones listed above, a number of companies specialized in dedicated utilities. The following tools perform powerful functions:

- AccessData
  - EDiscovery: Provides a systematic approach for preparing a system for e-discovery
  - SilentRunner: Monitors network traffic and performs pattern and content analysis
- Guidance Software
  - Encase Forensics: Performs file system analysis, data searches, and common reporting
  - Neutrino: Portable device data acquisition
- Paraben
  - P2 Commander: Analyzes e-mail, chat logs, and file systems
  - Forensic Replicator: Provides a forensically sound copy of the data source
  - Decryption Collection: Cracks up to 35 types of file encryption password
  - Lockdown: Write-protects a device for analysis
- Pinpoint Labs
  - SafeCopy: Provides a forensically sound copy of the data source without altering metadata
  - Metadiscover: Searches files for metadata fields and provides a detailed report
  - PG Pinpoint: Confirms identity of known file types by comparing hash values
- X-Ways
  - WinHex: Provides file system analysis, data recovery, and disk editing
  - Capture: Provides a forensically sound image of data
  - Trace: Deciphers browser activity

OPEN-SOURCE APPLICATIONS AND UTILITIES

There is a plethora of freeware and shareware utilities available that perform functions useful to the investigator. A bit of caution is in order here in that if your investigation is headed for court, the lawyers and judge are going to look very carefully at the tools you use to extract and examine data. Specifically, they will be looking at an applications target function, its documented reliability, and exactly how you used the tool to arrive at your conclusions.

That does not mean that the courts will disallow information extracted by these tools. Simply make sure that you are well versed in what a particular utility does and that you use it as intended. In particular, there are some powerful tools that help in analyzing a file system, extracting data, and tracing computer activity.

I've listed a few personal favorites here, along with a short description of their function. Freeware means that you never pay a royalty fee, and shareware means that after a designated trial period you are expected to pay a clearly defined registration fee for continued use.

- Pinpoint Tools by Pivotal Guidance
  - Safecopy: Freeware that copies data without altering metadata.
  - Metaviewer: Freeware that extracts metadata from MS Office documents.
  - Hash: Freeware that creates hash values of any file or image.
  - Filematch: Freeware that identifies duplicate files in a volume.
- Runtime
  - Disk Explorer for NTFS: Shareware (with a nominal fee to register) that allows you to examine the contents of a disk on a very granular level. You can view MFT entries, boot records, partition entries, and file contents, copying all contents (including slack space) to a file for recovery.
  - Disk Explorer for FAT: Same as Disk Explorer for NTFS (with a nominal fee to register), but is used for FAT12, FAT16, and FAT32 formatted drives.
  - DriveImageXL: Freeware intended for individual use. It is a file copy utility and is not used for forensic images.
  - Captain Nemo: Shareware (with a nominal fee to register) that allows you to mount an NT, Linux, or Novell drive image on a Windows based computer.
  - DriveLook: Freeware utility that allows you to search a data source for suspect content.
- Disk Investigator: Freeware that allows you to search a data source sector by sector. It can undelete files that were removed from Recycle Bin as long as they haven't been overwritten.
- Directory Snoop: Shareware (with a nominal fee to register) that acts as a powerful ally to the investigator that examines hard disks, removable media,

flash drives, and camera cards. It can view MFT and file table entries and even identify names of files that once existed on the drive, but were deleted and even wiped. Raw cluster data can be copied and saved to a file.

- Winhex: A freeware version of the Winhex tool mentioned in the previous section is available from http://winhex.en.softonic.com/. The nice thing about Winhex is that it can be used to examine any form of data, regardless of the host file system.

WORKING WITH "COURT-APPROVED" TOOLS

A lot of ink and digital space gets devoted to what constitutes a court-approved tool. In fact, while there are several instances of a court accepting a tool because it has been used successfully in previous case history, our judicial system is not actively involved in the testing and approval of forensic tools. Additionally, just because a judge in one case accepted the results of a tool as evidence in court, there is no guarantee that another judge will follow suit. This might possibly explain why the majority of first-page Web hits for the search "Court Approved Forensic Tool" are sites sponsored by manufacturers of forensic tools.

Any legitimate tool used in a forensically sound manner will produce forensically sound results, just like any sufficiently sharp saw will cut wood. The key question therefore is not "What tools does the court approve?" Rather it is "How can I convince the court to approve the evidence produced by the tools I use?" In the final act, it will be the investigator, testifying from the stand, who delivers the presentation that must convince judge and jury. In order to do that, the investigator must do these things:

- Use tools that are generally accepted throughout the industry.
- Understand precisely how those tools work.
- Demonstrate that the tools were used in a professional, sound manner.
- Document which tool was used for every step in the investigative process.

WHAT TOOLS ARE ACCEPTED IN THE INDUSTRY?

If the idea was to produce a 700-page book here, we could simply put together a list of every piece of software or hardware ever used in the process of a digital investigation and have our page count. The list is seemingly endless. The purpose of this discussion is to determine what makes a tool acceptable.

In 2004, the National Institute of Justice established the Computer Forensics Tool Testing (CFTT) program. According to their Web site (NIJ 2012), the purpose of this program is to

- Streamline the process of testing digital forensics tools.
- Provide unbiased standards for testing digital forensics tools.
- Provide manufacturers with feedback for improvements.
- Aid law enforcement agencies in making better informed purchasing decisions.
- Increase understanding among law enforcement of the different tools and their respective capabilities.
- Provide a methodology for testing that can be replicated by other law enforcement officials.

The program does not just test software and hardware tools. It also concentrates on developing testing methods, testing criteria and sample data sets for testing tools that other organizations can use in the development of new tools or the testing of existing ones.

Over the ensuing years, over a hundred different products have passed through CFTT. All of the commercial forensic suites have had various components tested. In addition, a large number of open-source and freeware applications have passed muster. Making use of a product that has passed CFTT examination is a good first step in assuring that your evidence will be admissible.

It is not sufficient, however, to assume that since the tool used to image the drive came right off of CFTT's approved list that all will be well. The investigator must also be able to verify that a sound and tested version of the product was used. For example, launching a memory capture utility directly on a compromised machine opens the door for the argument that the tool was affected by code on the machine. A brand-new write-protection device that has not been tested prior to first use to confirm its capabilities can be challenged. Know your tools and never stop testing them. This is where the sample data sets and test criteria developed by CFTT come in handy.

UNDERSTANDING HOW THE TOOLS WORK

When presenting evidence from the witness stand, an investigator is going to play one of two roles. If called as a material witness, the investigator will be fielding questions pertaining to what actions were taken, how they were taken, and what results were obtained. Only facts will be accepted as answers.

Opinions are unlikely to be solicited, and unsolicited opinions are unlikely to be welcome. As an expert witness, opinions *might* be requested. However, they are only going to be accepted as long as the witness can back up her opinion with fact.

In either case, it is probable that since the jury is filled with mostly lay people who have no technical expertise in digital forensics, an investigator will probably be asked to explain how the tools performed the task claimed. For example, opposing counsel may want to know how you can be so sure that in the process of capturing live memory, you didn't insert new data into the mix. To adequately answer that question, you need to know exactly what the memory footprint of the tool you used is and, if possible, what address range it occupied in the system during the capture.

Always test any new tool against a known data set in order to get a good idea of the tool's reliability and functional limitations. Any time that a tool gets upgraded or reinstalled, it is critical that the tests be run again and the results compared. If you have not tested a piece of software against a known data set, you can never be sure that it is working exactly as it should against the unknown. More importantly, you cannot successfully argue the validity of your results against a hostile cross-examination.

DEMONSTRATING SOUND USE

Here we go back to the consistent mantra heard throughout this book. Document *everything* that you do. At the beginning of any investigation, regardless of how large or small it might be, a **case log** must be started. Various pieces of documentation will be collected and attached to this log as the case progresses. See Chapter 17, "Case Management and Report Writing," for a detailed discussion on documentation.

In situations where multiple computer systems are involved, it is a good idea to keep a separate case log for each system. This minimizes the possibility that actions taken on one system will not be confused with those taken on another. Additionally, an activity log must be kept for each piece of media analyzed, detailing each action taken against the media, the tools used to analyze it, and each step taken during the course of analysis.

Document the exact time each step was initiated and the exact time at which it was completed. When making a forensic copy of original media, calculate hash values in both MD5 and SHA256 algorithms. After the copy is completed, perform the same calculations on the copy. They should match. If not, recalculate the hash on the original. If it has changed, there is something wrong with either your

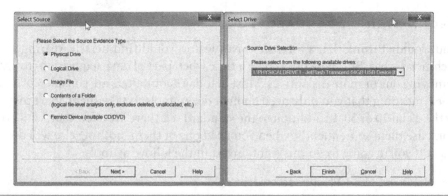

Figure 18.7 Various options are available when making a disk image using FTK Imager.

software or (more likely) your write-protection device is not functioning properly. (Remember the part about testing everything before you begin?)

Both the original and the initial copy will now be stored in a secure location. Make a second copy for processing. Once again, calculate the hash values and make sure they match. You should have recorded in your activity log the times and dates begun and completed for each of these steps.

As you progress through the examination of the device, as each tool is employed, describe each step you take and record the times and durations as before. If there is any variable involved, such as triggers to command-line tools or optional settings, those must be recorded as well. Figure 18.7 shows an example of different options available when making a disk image with FTK Imager.

HARDWARE TOOLS

Not everything the investigator does deals with code. There are several pieces of equipment that are absolutely necessary for the success of an investigation. This section offers a brief overview of the following tools:

- Technician's standard toolkit
- Write-protect interfaces
- External storage units
- Forensics workstations

While a detailed explanation of how to use each of these tools is beyond the scope of this book, it is essential to introduce you to their form and function.

TECHNICIAN'S STANDARD TOOLKIT

You wouldn't think that a forensics investigator would find herself wearing a PC technician's hat. But there does come a time when part of data acquisition involves removing one or more disk drives. Most of today's computers are considered "tool-free," meaning that you only need about a dozen tools to take them apart instead of the usual 20 or 30. In addition to the standard set, there are a few that, while you don't use them so frequently, when you need one of them, nothing else will do the trick. If you're going to do this right, invest in the following tools:

- No. 0 and No. 1 Phillips screwdrivers
- 1/8-inch, 1/4-inch, and 3/16-inch flat screwdrivers
- T7, T10, and T15 Torx screwdrivers
- 3/16-inch and 1/4-inch nut drivers
- 3-claw part grip
- Tweezers
- 5-inch needle nose pliers
- Reverse-action tweezers
- A plastic scribe

The screwdrivers and nut drivers should be self-explanatory. They are for removing and replacing screws when going inside a computer system. The claw grip and tweezers are for picking up the screws you will inevitably drop into the computer while working. If you've never used reverse-action tweezers, then you don't fully appreciate how useful they are. They open when you squeeze and clamp down when you release. With this useful tool, you don't have to maintain your grip while you work. The scribe is useful for opening plastic cases without damaging them. Many of these tools are shown in Figure 18.8, and a good set can be inexpensive.

WRITE-PROTECT INTERFACES

In order to make a forensically sound copy of a device, it is *essential* that you not allow new data to be written to the source media. To do so would cause two problems. From an investigatory standpoint, writing new data to the medium could possibly overwrite evidence that exists in slack space, deleted files, or unallocated clusters. (This was discussed in further detail in Chapter 7, "Data Acquisition.") From a legal standpoint, if the source image is different in any way than the

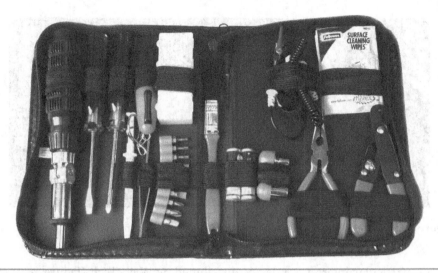

Figure 18.8 A usable technician's toolkit need not be expensive. This one was under $20 at a local office supply store.

acquired image, as evidenced by the hash values of each one, then unless you can satisfactorily explain the difference, your procedure and results can be called into question by the opposition.

Several companies make devices that allow data extraction and prevent data from traveling from the target system to the source medium. Devices range from simple interfaces that permit only unidirectional data transfer to fancy disk duplicators that allow several drives to be imaged at once. They are available for a variety of interfaces, and it is likely that you will need more than one device in order to image the different systems you will encounter over time. There are too many of these devices to mention each one. Among the more prominent (in alphabetical order) are

- Advanced Test Products: Write-protect interfaces
- Digital Intelligence: Write-protect interfaces
- Forensic Computers, Inc.: Write-protect interfaces and forensic disk duplicators
- Forensic PC: Write-protect interfaces and forensic disk duplicators plus memory card duplicators
- Guidance Software: Write-protect interfaces
- Intelligent Computer Systems: Write-protect interfaces and forensic disk duplicators

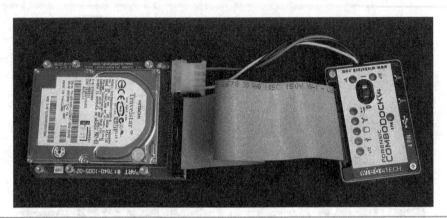

Figure 18.9 Write-protecting the source disk is essential in obtaining a forensic image.

Of particular interest is a device distributed by WiebeTech (Figure 18.9) that includes interfaces for IDE, SATA, and SCSI all in one kit.

EXTERNAL STORAGE UNITS

If working in the field, you will need a verifiable repository for the target image to reside after capture. In addition, if doing live data capture, you need a place other than the local hard disk to point the data. You can't choose local disk storage for a memory dump because you might overwrite valuable evidence, and you will also alter the source image before you even acquire it!

There are three basic external storage units that should be part of your arsenal. A USB thumb drive is good for memory captures as well as creating documentation as you work. For creating non-rewritable images, a good DVD recorder is necessary. And for creating a forensic image of a larger device, make sure you have available an external hard disk.

As of this writing, it is possible to get eSATA devices that store up to 16TB of data, if you don't mind carting around a large device. For imaging single drives, a 1TB external drive with a Firewire interface is available for under $200.00. Before using external hard disks for a forensic image, make sure you are familiar with the laws and regulations pertaining to the case with which you are involved.

FORENSICS WORKSTATIONS

Most forensics labs have one or more dedicated systems used only for investigative work. In addition, they will have field units configured from high-end laptops.

These are the forensic workstations. For the most part, the workstation is simply a more powerful personal computer equipped with a few extra accessories. Because of the nature of its task, a workstation features

- Multiprocessor capability: Most current processors are multicore. This helps immensely, but the addition of a second processor greatly speeds up the machine.
- Extra memory: If running a 32-bit OS, install 4GB of RAM. A 64-bit OS should have at least 8GB.
- Disk capacity: In addition to the primary disk running the OS and system applications, there should be one or more hard disks configured to accept target images. SATA drives of up to 2TB are currently available which allow large target images.
- Hot-swappable hard disk bays: These disk bays allow you to install a source disk into a caddy and mount it on the workstation without dismantling the workstation.
- External SATA connectors allow the investigator to connect SATA drives via an easily accessible port.
- External SCSI connectors allow the connection of SCSI devices.
- Memory card readers are necessary for reading flash memory.
- ZIP disk drives are not as commonly seen, but still occasionally appear.
- Built-in write-protect devices: For USB, Firewire, SATA, IDE, and SCSI.
- Multiple-monitor capability: Having multiple monitors is a luxury, but one you will quickly grow to appreciate as you work with multiple browsers and run applications simultaneously.

The same rules apply to the field workstation as do the lab station. The only difference is that the majority of the accoutrements will be externally connected devices and you will "field-dress" your system at the scene.

BUILDING A FORENSICS WORKSTATION

An organization with a staff of hardware technicians might find it more economical to build a forensics workstation than to purchase one preconfigured. This is especially true if you expect to run Linux and use open-source applications such as Sleuth. This process does presume that the person doing the building already has a strong background in PC hardware support. For more information on building systems from scratch, see *PC Hardware Maintenance and Repair* (Graves 2001). The next chapter covers this subject in detail.

The hardest part of building a workstation from scratch is sourcing some of the unique components used in its construction. The construction is simple assembly and configuration. Keep in mind that your workstation has some specific requirements:

- It must support IDE, SCSI, and SATA busses (write protected).
- Hardware disk duplication is necessary (write protected).
- Hot-swappable drive bays are needed.
- It must have network connectivity.
- It has to reside behind a powerful firewall.
- It should be able to read all standard memory card formats.
- The BIOS should support booting remote images.

From a software standpoint, you need to be able to read from any file system. All graphics file formats need to be readable. Installed applications must be able to collect evidence in a fashion recognized by the courts.

NONTECHNICAL TOOLS

Not all of the necessary tools needed by the investigator are targeted to the geek. Some essential accessories under any other circumstances might well qualify as toys for grownups. However, since you need them to do your job, not only do you have an excuse for buying them, but your tax accountant might even be able to claim them as deductions on your next return. Some of the other devices won't be quite so fun to own, but if you don't have them, you'll regret it. These devices include

- A laptop computer
- A digital camera\video recorder
- A digital audio recorder
- A Faraday shield
- Antistatic bags
- Presslock evidence bags
- Adhesive labels and a felt-tipped pen

Happy shopping.

LAPTOP COMPUTER

It would probably be best if you decide what forensics software you intend to use before sinking money into a laptop. The OS dictates what software you can run. If you know you're going to use a Windows-based application, then buying an Apple laptop is probably a poor choice. Most of the Intel-based laptops (including Apple) can be reconfigured to run Linux. Some brands, including Dell and HP, will ship a laptop with Linux preinstalled. Therefore, if you plan to run The Sleuth Kit or the Forensics Research Kit, these would be the logical choice.

Make sure you get a full-featured notebook—preferably one that will allow you to add an optional docking station. A field computer for the forensics analyst needs to be able to hook up to a wide variety of devices, including proprietary I/O devices, external storage units, and so forth. Most of the so-called "netbooks" fall short in these capabilities. They also don't allow you to install sufficient RAM. As of this writing, the top-of-the-line netbooks feature 2GB of RAM. Get a notebook with at least 4GB. The nice thing about a current model of notebook is that I don't have to caution you to make sure that it comes equipped with USB or FireWire. They all do.

What you *do* have to watch for is the ability to add an optical disk. An internal disk is best for field work because you have to use it all the time. An external accessory drive is usable, but quickly becomes a pain.

DIGITAL CAMERA/VIDEO RECORDER

Two years ago, it would have been more difficult to combine cameras and video recorders. You could get a digital camera that did short video clips, or a video camera that offered a still option. But the clips were too short to be useful on the digital camera, and the stills offered by video cameras were of insufficient resolution to offer decent detail. All of that has changed.

To make the specifications for a digital camera/recorder make sense, you have to understand a few basic principles. Digital images are measured in pixels per inch (ppi) if viewed on a display and in dots per inch (dpi) if printed on paper. To be useful, a still image should be printed to 8.5" x 11" and have a *minimum* of 240dpi. To get this sort of resolution from the tiny imaging sensor (usually a charge-coupled device, CCD), you need a camera rated as 3 megapixel (MP) or better. Virtually all still cameras on the market do that these days. But most are limited to a maximum of 15-second video clips.

The purpose of a video camera in the field is so that you can do a 360-degree sweep of the scene as you initially find it. This will require far more than the

15-second clips offered by still cameras. So your best bet for professional work is a digital video camera that offers the ability to make 3MP still images. Fortunately, there is a fairly wide variety of those on the market, and many of them sell for well under a thousand dollars. You're not looking for the best in creative imaging here. Field records are not going to make you the next Steven Spielberg. The basics will do just fine. Look for a rugged camera, because it will get bounced around in and out of car trunks and desk drawers a lot.

DIGITAL AUDIO RECORDER

The digital audio recorder is one device that you can get by without as long as you're the type of person who takes detailed (and readable) notes in the field or are willing to stop everything you're doing once every 60 seconds or so to type your observations into your notebook computer. Someone like me, however, has trouble reading his hen-scratching ten minutes after it lands on the paper. And since I type 126 mistakes per minute, the audio recorder is, for me anyway, the way to go.

You don't need anything super expensive or elaborate. You just need something that does high-quality voice recordings. A sensitive microphone is nice, because you might find it necessary to set the device down in one place and have it pick up your voice as you walk around the room. Most video cameras offer reasonably good audio quality, but are a bit inconvenient to use when working at a computer or interviewing a witness. A separate recorder will pay for itself in short order simply in reduced frustration.

FARADAY SHIELD

A Faraday shield is an enclosure made from conductive material that blocks electromagnetic waves. It is named after the physicist Michael Faraday, who made the first one back in 1836. Any electrical field surrounding the enclosure is intercepted by the conductive exterior and drawn away from anything enclosed. The enclosure can be anything from a small bag just big enough to transport a cell phone to entire rooms in which several people can work at once. The idea is that as long as the device resides inside of a Faraday shield, nobody can tap into it using wireless technology and alter the digital contents.

ANTISTATIC BAGS

Most computer devices are far more sensitive to *electrostatic discharge* (ESD) than most people realize. Electrostatic discharge is that tiny spark that jumps from your finger to the door after walking across a carpet. Five thousand volts of ESD is enough to damage one of the chips used in a computer system. It takes as much as *fifty* thousand volts for you to feel it. Several companies make bags that you can use to transport digital devices that protect anything within from ESD. Always pack electronic devices in antistatic bags. If it is a wireless device, place the ESD-protected device into a Faraday shield for transport.

PRESSLOCK EVIDENCE BAGS

For smaller pieces of evidence that are not particularly sensitive to electromagnetic or electrostatic energy, a simpler storage and transport container is suitable. The standard presslock bags you buy for sandwiches work quite well for floppy disks, Zip disks, thumb drives, and other small devices you find on the scene. It is easy to apply a label to them, and they keep dust and moisture away from whatever is stored within.

ADHESIVE LABELS AND A FELT-TIPPED PEN

Label *everything* that you acquire from the scene. Label it with permanent ink, but in a way that does not permanently deface the object being identified. For this reason, it is important to select the type of label that uses nonresidue adhesive. Avery makes a label that they identify with the number 8160 that is a good size for the purpose. Any other brand will do as long as it is nonresidue. The marker needs to be a fine-tipped marker that writes in indelible ink. Black is best, but any dark color will do.

CHAPTER REVIEW

1. Explain the concept of *abstraction layers*. What are they? How does an understanding of the concept assist in designing and testing forensic tools? What do the terms *lossy* and *lossless* mean in this regard?

2. What are the four standards against which a tool is measured in regards to suitability for forensic use? How much impact does the failure of one measurement have on the usability of the tool?

3. Explain the value of the Windows Event Viewer to the forensic analysis. What are the significant logs it generates, and how can they be used in analyzing data?

4. In spite of their expense, there are a few significant advantages to using one of the commercially available suites as a standard in your investigative process. What are these advantages?

5. Why are write-protect interfaces so significant to the investigator? How are they used?

CHAPTER EXERCISES

1. Go online and research as much information about three forensic suites as you can find. Put together a spreadsheet that compares the various costs of using each suite, what tools each one offers, what standards they support, and what proprietary methods they employ. Then find out which, if any, of these tools have been tested by the National Institute of Science and Technology. Based on what you have discovered, which of these suites would you select for a new practice just getting started?

2. Using the same process as in the previous exercise, do the same level of research on at least two different forensic hardware toolkits.

REFERENCES

Graves, M. 2001. *PC hardware maintenance and repair.* Albany, NY: Prompt Publications.

NIJ. 2012. CFTT project overview. www.cftt.nist.gov/project_overview.htm (accessed August 16, 2012).

Building a Forensic Workstation

The civilizations of ancient times did not have huge factories churning out products at the rate of a few hundred thousand per day. If a particular tool was needed, the appropriate craftsman was called upon to make it. While it is true that there are several different commercially available models from which a forensic department can select its systems, it is also quite possible—and far more economical—for an organization with some moderately skilled hardware technicians to build the systems on their own. In this chapter, I will define what makes up a *forensic workstation*. From there, I will describe some of the most popular commercially available products, and then go on to discuss the components that go into making a system from scratch, and what to think about when selecting each part.

A cautionary note is in order here. This chapter is targeted for PC hardware technicians and presupposes that the reader has a working knowledge of computer hardware. There is neither time nor space in this volume to explain every term used in this chapter. Several good volumes on computer hardware exist, including two by this author. Among these are *The A+ Guide to PC Hardware Maintenance and Repair* (Graves 2006) and Scott Mueller's (2012) *Upgrading and Repairing PCs*, which receives annual updates.

Which brings up the next thorn in the side of any PC designer. This chapter will speak of processor speeds, memory capacity, rotational speed, and the like. By the time this book sees print, what was state of the art at the time I wrote these words is trailing technology when you read it. Keep that in mind, and recognize that it is the concepts that matter and not the specifications.

WHAT IS A FORENSIC WORKSTATION?

At the heart, a forensic workstation is just a more powerful computer. There are a few other differences that set this machine apart from the glorified word processor that sits on most people's desks. There are three major factors to address when setting up any machine to perform digital investigations—power, security, and the accessibility and authenticity of data. It isn't just the hardware that dictates how well these factors will be addressed either. Your choice of an operating system has a significant impact on all of the above.

COMPUTER POWER

Systems that are dedicated to forensic investigations need to be significantly more powerful than those used for conventional office applications. The tasks performed by this system involve extremely complex searches of very large data sets. Trying to crack an encryption password can involve billions of trial and error attempts. A lot of CPU power and vast amounts of memory will dramatically speed up the effort.

Significant amounts of hard disk space are required for image files, temporary files, and the more complex applications run by the digital detective. A typical forensic workstation does not have a single hard disk, but will likely contain an array of several. Details about the individual components that go into the making of a workstation are covered in the second half of this chapter.

COMPUTER SECURITY

A lot of the work that is done by the forensics team is of a nature that its findings are likely to get somebody in trouble—perhaps significant amounts of trouble. Therefore, it stands to reason that if that someone can find out who is looking into their activities, they might try to put a stop to it. Forensics labs are typically in secure environments to start with. Gaining physical access to the machines should be as difficult as possible without making it inaccessible to the forensics team.

Network security is another issue. It is a good policy for the forensic stations to be on their own subnet, isolated from the rest of the corporate network. There should be no Internet access directly to these computers. If Internet access is deemed necessary for the forensic network, it should be through a secure firewall.

Operating system security is similar to any other system. A good antivirus product needs to be updated regularly. Additional precautions should be regularly taken. Scan each system regularly to see if a rootkit has made its way into the system.

ACCESSIBILITY AND AUTHENTICITY OF DATA

Accessibility and authenticity is an arena where the forensic workstation differs greatly from most other desktop computers. Due to the wide variety of data sources the system must be able to access, the I/O subsystem must be substantially beefed up. Additionally, it is necessary to assure that original evidence is not overwritten by processes in the investigative procedure. To do this, there must be some mechanism in place that write-protects the device being copied.

On many systems, the BIOS can be configured to write-protect certain ports. Since BIOS is a function of the system board, your selection of this component should factor in this capability. Another method of write-protecting specific types of components is to use a third-party controller board instead of an on-board controller built into the system board. This is something that will be discussed in greater detail later in the chapter.

COMMERCIALLY AVAILABLE FORENSIC WORKSTATIONS

While this book is not intended to be a promotional guide for specific products, this is an area in which there are relatively few options. Therefore, I will try to describe the features available in each one without intending or inferring any preference of one brand over the other. I do not have extensive hands-on experience with every brand. Some brands that will be discussed in this section include Digital Intelligence, Forensic Computers, and Tritech Forensics.

Each of these manufacturers features a line of products, and it is outside of the scope of this book to attempt a complete review. The following represents only a sampling of products available at the time of this writing. This is a very volatile industry, and by the time you are reading this, it is likely that the offerings will be different.

DIGITAL INTELLIGENCE

Digital Intelligence is the home of FRED and FREDDIE. FRED is an acronym of Forensic Recovery of Evidence Device, while FREDDIE is Forensic Recovery of Evidence Device Diminutive Interrogation Equipment. FRED is available as FRED, FRED DX, FRED SR, and FRED-L. Each of these models is available in multiple configurations. FREDDIE is a portable field machine designed for a first responder or field investigator.

FRED

FRED can be had as a basic model or two DX models, one with a single RAID array and one with dual RAID arrays. RAID stands for Redundant Array of Independent Disks and can contain anywhere from two to dozens of hard disks. In FRED's case, each array contains five individual disk drives. All configurations include write-protected ports for IDE drives, SATA, and SCSI drives.

A device unique to FRED is the UltraBay. This device occupies the top 20% of the tower and provides external connections for a wide variety of devices. Write-protected ports can be switched between conventional read/write to write-protect mode by way of keypad controls. Additional ports allow USB, FireWire, and eSATA devices to connect to the system in either mode.

A built-in imaging shelf allows bare hard disks to be installed in hot-swappable bays. A push of a button opens the tray, and a hard disk is easily inserted. Both power and data buses are configured in such a way that the drive (regardless of form factor) plugs right in without fighting with a lot of cables. The system has two shock-mounted SATA bays that also support IDE drives, and an additional four hot-swap bays that support IDE or SATA drives.

For reading digital media, a forensic media card reader provides write-protected access to virtually every type of memory card currently manufactured. As with the drive connectors, any of these ports can be switched between read/write and write-protect with a few keystrokes.

USB support includes all versions from 3.0 down. There are six 3.0/2.0 ports and eleven 2.0/1.x ports. Of these, one each is write-protect only. One 400Mb/s FireWire port connects from the back of the system. Three 800Mb/s FireWire ports are also available, two from the back and one out of the UltraBay.

On the standard FRED, there are two hard disks included. A 300GB hard disk hosts the OS and the forensic software, while a 1.5TB disk holds the data. The RAID-equipped models feature a 150GB OS/Application disk and a 1.5TB data disk. As configured, the array is not populated. It can be configured with between two and five SATA or SAS drives connected to an Adaptec 8-port RAID controller in RAID 0 (a striped array for fastest performance). Since the controller supports 2TB drives, this allows up to 10TB of storage for large forensic images. The dual-raid offers another drive set up to 10TB.

The buyer has two different processor options for any of these systems. The lowest priced option includes an Intel i7 quad-core processor and 6GB of triple channel DDR. It can be upgraded to 24GB. The dual-Xeon option boasts two quad-core Xeon processors and ships with 12GB of RAM. This option allows the user to install as much as 144GB of RAM for extremely memory hungry operations.

All FRED models ship with Windows 7 and Windows 98SE configured as a dual-boot system. A full forensic distribution package of SuSE Linux is included on DVD. Additional software that ships with the system includes

- DriveSpy (a DOS shell for forensic applications)
- Image (a DOS shell for creating forensic images)
- PDWipe (a disk wiping utility that exceeded DoD specifications for data security)
- PDBlock (a DOS utility for write-protecting hard disk drives) and PART (a DOS partitioning utility)

The SR model of FRED adds enhanced processing and I/O as well as more robust networking capabilities. It is the equivalent of the dual-Xeon DX with dual gigabit Ethernet controllers. Expansion slots are all PCIe, and each of the processors is equipped with a dedicated memory bank. This is the equivalent of having six memory channels.

FREDDIE

FREDDIE is an integrated device that has some of the aspects of a portable computer (without the sleek form factor of a laptop) and some of the aspects of a full-sized workstation. It isn't exactly a lightweight—the base model comes in at around 55 pounds. However, the investigator will not feel like a lot of shortcuts were taken in the design.

The unit is equipped with the same UltraBay as is featured in the lab machines. The computer is powered with a 3.2GHz quad-core processor and ships with 12GB of triple-channel memory. A 300GB 10,000 rpm SATA drive hosts the OS and applications, while a 1.5TB 7,200 rpm drive acts as a repository for data. It has two shock-mounted SATA drive bays for attaching additional drives. Seven SATA connections on the rear of the computer allow for connecting a large number of externally mounted drives. Eleven USB and two FireWire ports provide connectivity to external peripheral devices. The Digital Intelligence Forensic Media Card Reader ships as an accessory device for connecting virtually every form of flash memory device currently (or historically) in production. Write-protection exists for every form of media.

As with the full sized models, FREDDIE is configured to dual-boot from either Windows 7 Ultimate 64-bit or Windows 98SE. Optionally, a SuSE Linux DVD allows for a Linux configuration to be built. All of the same software that ships with FRED also ships with FREDDIE.

FORENSIC COMPUTERS

Forensic Computers offers a line of 11 lab systems and 6 portable field systems. Their base model lab system is a full tower with a heavy compliment of WiebeTech components. Bay one is occupied with a WiebeTech Forensic Labdock. This is a write-protected I/O interface that allows USB, IDE, and SATA devices to be connected over an external interface. Beneath it is a Wiebetech RTX100H-INT trayless SATA dock for hot-swapping SATA devices. The third bay is occupied by a hardware-based encryption device by Dataport. The fourth bay hosts a Blu-ray DVD-ROM burner. Two hard disks compliment the system. A 300GB drive acts as the OS/Application drive. A 1TB internal SATA drive functions as data storage. The OS that ships with the unit is Windows 7 Ultimate, 64-bit.

Each model of the line gets progressively more powerful and feature laden until you reach the Forensic IV. This is a dual-Xeon machine with 24GB of RAM and a pair of 2.4GHz quad-core Xeon processors. A Tableau Forensic Bridge is built into the top bay and is designed to interface with virtually every type of hard disk made over the past several years. Everything from 1.8" IDE drives to solid-state SATA drives and even SCSI can hook up to this device.

As of this writing, a complete listing for Forensic Computers' offerings includes

- Forensic Tower
- Forensic Tower 6-core
- Forensic Tower IISE
- Forensic Tower III Core i7
- Forensic Tower III Dual Xeon
- Forensic Tower IV Core i7
- Forensic Tower IV Dual Xeon
- Forensic Analysis Workstation I
- Forensic Analysis Workstation II
- The Ultimate Forensic Machine
- Forensic Analysis SE—Rackmount

In addition to the lab machines, the company also manufactures a line of portable field machines. Their Airlite series differ from other companies' portable offerings in that the basic machine possesses a form factor of a standard laptop computer, as opposed to the "lunch box with drive bays" approach seen elsewhere. The rest of the kit is an extensive accessory package that connects to the laptop via USB or FireWire ports. The forensic accessories are all part of the Tableau line distributed by Access Data.

TRITECH FORENSICS

Tritech Forensics does not offer a wide or versatile line of workstations, but the one it offers is a viable option with somewhat lower cost than its competition. It is available with a choice of processors. The Intel 3.2GHz processor is listed as a six core. The AMD offering is an eight-core processor. Either way, the machine ships with 16GB of RAM.

Its storage is configured with three physical drives. The first is a high-speed 128GB solid-state drive. The OS/Application drive is a 450GB 10,000 rpm SATA drive. Data is stored on a 3TB 7,200 rpm drive. Forensic connections are made through a Tableau bridge similar to the one offered by Forensic Computers. It ships with Windows 7 Ultimate, 64-bit.

BUILDING A FORENSIC WORKSTATION FROM SCRATCH

An organization that maintains a computer support staff may be equipped to build its own forensic workstations at a substantial savings in cost. Two approaches can be taken in tackling this challenge. One way is to purchase a base computer model that has the power specifications desired and build it up by adding components specific to the task. The other way is to start from scratch, building from raw components. Either way, careful selection of products can save a lot of time and reduce headaches later on down the road.

THE HARDWARE OF A FORENSIC WORKSTATION

As mentioned earlier, a key difference between the machine we're building and a standard desktop computer is power. Power is such a relative term, isn't it? Not so much so when discussing the machine that is going to look for invisible needles in 2TB haystacks. Most of the processes that forensic applications perform are processor intensive to the extreme and will eat up as much memory as you can possibly throw at them.

Operating systems that support large memory addresses (i.e., 64-bit vs. 32-bit) and that support more than one multicore processor are possible base candidates for a forensic workstation. In the case of the forensic workstation, power is also meant in a quite literal sense. Insomuch as the system is likely to be operating a larger number of components simultaneously, a hefty power supply is essential.

A Suitable Enclosure

The enclosure requirements for the workstation are based on a number of factors. There are two questions to ask before selecting this component: Is it desirable to connect many peripherals and source drives directly to the system? Does the IT infrastructure require rack-mounted devices or blade servers? If a lot of peripherals are going to be connected directly to the system, the enclosure needs to feature sufficient drives bays—both internal and external—to fill the needs, and it (along with the system board) must allow for sufficient expansion slots.

The power supply is frequently an integral part of the enclosure, although there are some manufacturers that sell the two components separately. If the power supply ships with the enclosure, make sure that it is the right type to work with the intended system board and that it has sufficient power connectors and can provide enough power to light up all the devices that will eventually become a part of the system. A computer that will be powering several PCIe expansion cards, a dozen disk drives, and several other devices is not going to last very long with a small power supply. For the purposes of this project, 650 W is a minimum, and 850 W is a good starting point.

In the first paragraph of this section, I mentioned that there would be both internal and external bays for disk drives. Due to the nature of the forensic investigation, hard disks are going to be added and removed on a regular basis, unless the organization intends to invest in a dedicated forensic disk imaging device (which is the best approach to take, by the way.) Therefore, external bays are more critical than internal bays. An enclosure that features hot-swappable drive bays in abundance is the best approach to take. There is still a need for internal bays. At the minimum, two internal bays are necessary, and for reasons I will discuss later, three or even four are better.

A lab that does not own a dedicated imaging system will have a particular need for hot-swap bays. At least two drive bays should be configured to be able to hot-swap both IDE and SATA drives. While current models of desktop computers all ship with SATA drives, there are still many millions of computers in the real world that operate from IDE drives.

Processor Power

It isn't necessarily raw speed that makes a good CPU, although it is certainly true that you can't really have one that is too fast! The ability to process several threads of code and work on multiple tasks simultaneously is a more critical talent for the CPU to possess. Additionally, a faster *front side bus* makes a better performer as well. The front side bus is the electronic communications path between the CPU and the rest of the components in the system. Therefore, while a 3.02GHz processor sounds much faster than a 2.5GHz processor, a larger view might be in order. The 2.5GHz quad-core processor with the 1,033Mhz front side bus may do many things faster than the 3.02GHz dual-core processor with an 800MHz front side bus.

The logic behind that reasoning is actually quite simple. A machine that can work on 4 questions at a time will answer 16 questions in four cycles. The machine that only addresses 2 at a time requires eight cycles. Assuming that speed was the only factor considered (which you cannot really do), then the quad-core finished the task in 0.0000000016 second, while the 3.02GHz required 0.0000000026 ticks. In those terms, that doesn't sound like much. But realize that the 2.5GHz was 1.6 times faster than the 3.02GHz *for this task.*

How does the front-side bus come into play? It determines how many times per second the results of calculation by the CPU can be sent to RAM or other parts of the system. When the CPU can't dump its results, it stays idle until it can. Think of it as a conveyor belt. If the bottling machine is putting out 200 bottles per minute, but the packager only gets 100 out, what happens? Either the bottles get dumped, or hopefully, the bottling machine waits for the queue to empty.

Most of today's modern processors are *multicore.* What this basically means is that the designers built them to be the equivalent of two or more CPUs on the same chip. Each core can run processes separately from its counterparts as long as the operating system supports such a trick. Linux distributions since the release of the 2.0 kernel have all supported multiple processors. Windows has supported multiprocessor systems since the release of Windows 2000. Anything new you purchase is going to support multiple processors.

Currently there are two major players in the CPU field. Intel and Advanced Micro Devices (AMD) have been competing heavily on this playing field for several decades. As much as either company will disagree with this statement, neither company makes a "better" processor than the other. Each one may do certain things better than the other, but that's about it.

As of this writing, the Intel line of processors offers up to four cores per processor, each core capable of processing two threads simultaneously. AMD recently released a CPU boasting eight cores. It is questionable whether or not it will actually be faster than the Intel quad cores, because with the AMD CPU, each core only processes a single thread.

Computer Memory

When looking at memory specifications, it isn't hard to become a little dazed by all the terminology. There is DDR, DDR2, DDR3, and then the vendor throws out the term RDRAM to mix things up a little more. DDR simply means dual data rate, and the numbers that follow indicate the generation. The technical details could take up several pages, but it boils down to the fact that each generation is capable of processing more instructions on every clock cycle. RDRAM stands for Rambus Dynamic Random Access Memory and is a completely different technology. If your system board requires Rambus memory, it will say so in the technical specifications.

Memory and CPU go hand in hand. The later generations of CPU take the later generation of memory. Each CPU has a front-side bus speed, as discussed in the previous section. The memory must have the same bus speed to communicate with the CPU efficiently. It only makes sense. Among the various versions of DDR, there is a degree of backward compatibility. But going backwards slows down the rest of the system to keep up with the older memory. This sort of defeats the purpose of building a super-powered machine to solve our cases more rapidly. When building a machine, use the latest proven technology.

How much memory do you need? Ideally, you will populate the system with as much memory as it will support. This is dependent on both the system board used to build the workstation and the operating system used to run it. There will be a discussion of OS considerations later in the chapter, but in general, a 32-bit OS will support up to 4GB of RAM, while the newer 64-bit versions support much more. Build a 64-bit system, and dual-boot to a 32-bit OS if necessary. Forensic suites are memory hogs, and you need as much as you can get. For example, Access Data recommends 2GB of RAM per processor core. So a quad-core machine needs 8GB. A dual-processor quad-core needs 16GB.

Most of the multicore processors support *dual-channel* memory. Quad-core processors support four-channel memory. This means that if there are two threads running on a dual-core or four threads on a quad-core, each thread can have its own dedicated memory channel. (Quad-core processors also use dual channel memory, but will either require two pairs of memory chips or will "time-share" a single pair of chips. Obviously, the latter option will impair performance slightly.) This greatly reduces the number of processor cycles required to process each command. So essentially, you can speed up the system by correctly configuring your RAM in BIOS.

Memory should be purchased and installed in identical configurations. Mismatched memory sticks are a common source of memory errors and blue-screened operating systems. At the very least, each chip populating a single channel must be identical. Ideally, all memory modules in the system should match.

System Boards

The system board (or motherboard, as it is often called) is the most critical element in the mix. This component determines what kind of CPU you can use, what types and how much memory you can install, how many peripherals can be connected, and what type of peripheral support is provided. Some of this is a function of the BIOS, and some is a function of the physical form factor.

The system board and the enclosure are going to be married for life, so they must be a compatible mix. The form factor needs to match for both systems. A Micro ATX board is not going to be suitable for a full-sized tower case. The reverse won't even be possible. Additionally, the power connector must be able to mate with the power supply. As long as the enclosure and system board match, there should be no problem here.

Choice of processor is critical here as well. There will be one crop of boards to choose from that will support Intel processors and another selection for AMD processors. There is no intercompatibility. If you purchase an AMD processor and a board that supports Intel chips, one or the other is going back to the vendor. So decide on your CPU and system board at the same time. If it has been decided to use multiple processors, then the playing field will be significantly reduced. There are far fewer dual-processor options in the build-your-own market.

This early in the game, you might not have a solid idea of how much memory you want to install. But it's time to start thinking about it. While there will likely be a healthy supply of motherboards long into the foreseeable future, getting a board with all the features you will need for a forensic workstation can be more challenging. A quick review of a popular hardware vendor disclosed 88 Intel-based boards that supported only two DIMM modules and only two that allowed up to 12 modules. Manufacturers clearly are targeting the hobbyist and the mass-production users. That's where the majority of their income lies. Far fewer computers are built that require substantial amounts of memory.

The amount of memory on a single module is known as its *density*. DDR3 is currently available in up to 16GB packages. So in theory, one could assume that a board with eight slots could support 128GB of RAM. Unfortunately, in that regard one could easily assume wrong. Not all chipsets support the 16GB memory module. In some cases, the 16GB module will work, but will be recognized as an 8GB module. In other case, the system will refuse to boot. So it is imperative to make sure that your selection of system board not only supports the number of memory modules you plan on installing, but also the density of those modules.

The number and types of expansion slots must be considered as well. PCI Express (PCIe) is the current standard of slot architecture. There are several incarnations of this slot. PCIe 3.0 is the fastest form and is backwardly compatible with earlier versions, so purchasing a board that only supports this version won't hurt. (As of this writing, PCIe 4.0 is in development, but not yet released.)

There are also three different slot types. PCIe x1 is a very short slot that is used for devices that require low voltage and minimal data transfer rates. Sound cards and network interface cards frequently find their homes here. PCIe x4 is a longer slot. It will accept PCIe x1 devices as well. Some disk controller cards are designed to this standard. The PCIe x16 is the most commonly seen slot. It accepts both of the other standards as well and allows the highest data transfer rates and the highest voltages.

The vast majority of boards listed by the vendor reviewed supported three or fewer PCIe slots. Five products listed offered five or more PCIe 3.0 slots, while 14 products offered five or more PCIe 2.0 slots.

Permanent Hard Disks

The amount of long-term fixed storage is also a critical factor to consider. In the next section, I will discuss adding capabilities for hot-swapping or direct-connecting hard disks that are the subject of investigation. For maximum performance, adequate permanent storage is required as well. If you recall from the earlier section on commercially available forensic workstations, every single model offered featured a separate OS/Application drive and data drive. There are two reasons for this.

Reason number one is performance related. When hard disks are operational, they have several read/write heads mounted on arms that flick back and forth across the surface of the drive, looking for commands and data. All the arms are attached, so they have to move together. If the same disk is used for both data and applications, those arms are going to be jumping around faster than eighth-graders at a prom. To exacerbate matters, the OS is the first thing to go onto the hard disk, so it occupies all the space near the spindle of the drive. Data goes on last, so it would be along the center or outer tracks. The arm would move inward to get a command, outward to execute it, and so on and so forth. Reason number two is security. You can't write-protect the OS.

Therefore, it is good to have a hard disk large enough to support the OS. Many investigators like to have a dual-boot system that allows them the boot to either Windows or Linux, or perhaps to an older version of Windows. Additionally, this drive will host all of the forensic applications that get installed to disk. Typically, smaller disks perform better than larger ones, so it's a good idea to get the smallest disk that will adequately host the suite of forensic software and other utilities that are required. Always assume that several new applications are going to surface that will be needed.

A full forensic distribution of Red Hat Fedora is slightly under 3GB. A full installation of Windows 7 Ultimate, 64-bit is around a gigabyte. Forensic suites vary greatly, from just a few megabytes for The Sleuth Kit, which is primarily command-line drive, to over 3GB. Still, any way you look at it, 250GB is ample space for the OS drive. A fast drive is in order. A 10,000 rpm SATA or SAS is recommended. Several manufacturers now make 15,000 rpm drives.

The data drive must be much larger. Keep in mind that it is likely to be wiped and reformatted frequently, so brands with a good reputation for durability are the theme to follow. For the most part, some form of network attached storage or other external storage will likely be used as image libraries for evidence material. However, while an image is being processed, a copy will most likely be moved to the data drive of the forensic machine. Make it a big drive. As it was with the OS drive, speed is a virtue—although it is not quite as critical. A 7,200 rpm drive will suffice, although if the budget allows, the 10,000 rpm drive is better. The problem you may encounter here is that, as of this writing, the largest drive boasting this speed was 600GB. Most investigators do not consider this to be sufficiently large to serve as a data drive.

For ultimate speed and durability, there is no match for the solid-state drive. These devices have no moving parts, and access times for commands and data are significantly faster than conventional magnetic drives. Also, data deleted from solid-state drives is much more difficult to recover. However, as with the drives featuring higher rpms, there is a significant size limitation for solid-state drives. Pure solid-state drives peak out at around 256GB. Hybrid drives are available that integrate a solid-state drive with a magnetic disk drive. They allow for more space than pure solid state, but at a sacrifice in performance. Still, they are somewhat faster than purely magnetic drives.

Hot-Swap Bays

In the section on enclosures, the importance of having one or more hot-swap bays was discussed. Now is the time to explore that concept a little further. The hot-swap bay allows drives to be added to a computer system on the fly, without shutting down and restarting the system. They act somewhat like other removable media, except that they allow the investigator to take a suspect drive from a computer and add it to the forensic workstation without an exhaustive installation procedure.

In order to make forensically sound copies from target images, it is necessary to assure that the evidence device be fully protected from any write commands sent its way. Commercially available hot swap bays offer no write protection. They rely on a drive controller built into the system board or installed in one of the expansion slots on the system board. Such interfaces are designed with the idea that users generally *want* to copy data to their hard disks, and write-protection is not a standard feature.

There are a select few companies who offer solutions for this dilemma. Tableau (from Guidance Software) offers a line of controllers that install in one or more 5.25" drive bays and provide a write-protected interface to which hot-swap bays can connect. Some of the models also support external USB and FireWire interfaces. Table 19.1 lists four of the options available for building forensically sound solutions, along with the interfaces provided by each model.

To install these devices, Tableau connects to the drive controller in the system, and the data cable from the hot-swap bays connects to Tableau. Drives that are inserted into hot-swap bays controlled by Tableau are automatically detected, and the user is prompted to specify whether the device should be write-protected or mounted in read/write mode.

The two top of the line systems also feature connections for standard cables used by IDE, SCSI, and SATA drives. A 4-prong Molex power connector provides electrical current. This allows drives to be connected to the units even if there are no hot-swap bays available on the system. These devices can be part of a build-your-own configuration or can be installed into any commercially available computer system.

Write-Protected I/O

Hard disks are not the only media types to be examined during an investigation. Memory cards are becoming more common, and there is a wide variety of types. In the previous section, a Tableau device listed provides FireWire and USB ports

Table 19.1   Tableau Write Protection Devices

Model	IDE	SATA	SCSI	USB	FireWire
T34589is[a]	Yes	Yes	Yes	Yes	Yes
T3458is	Yes	Yes	Yes	Yes	No
T35is	Yes	Yes	No	No	No
T335	Yes	Yes	No	No	No

[a] As of this writing, the T34589is is only available with a Digital Intelligence FRED or FREDDIE system. It is included here for comparison purposes only.

that can be set to write protect. An external memory card reader can be attached to one of these ports for making forensically sound copies of memory cards. There is a good selection of external readers that are rated "forensically sound." To save space, it might be preferable to have a bay-mounted reader.

There are fewer companies who make such a product. Atech Flash Technology makes a 15-in-1 media card that reads all current varieties of CompactFlash, Secure Digital, Memory Stick, and xD Picture Card formats. It is a read-only device that fits into a standard drive bay and is powered from the PC's power supply. It hooks up to an internal USB 2.0 connection. In order to facilitate installing the device into a system with only a single internal USB connector, it ships with a Y-connector. Another convenient feature is that it has an external USB 2.0 connection for adding external devices.

Addonics makes a similar model that also reads MicroDrive devices. While the Atech only supports Windows systems, the Addonics device can also be installed on a Linux box (kernel 2.4 or higher). This makes it a better solution for building dual-boot systems.

Note that neither of the internal devices described above have been tested by NIST. Their usefulness is implied only by the fact that they can be switched from Read/Write to Read Only mode. Before using these devices in an actual investigation, it is important that you perform rigorous tests in your own environment.

Input/Output

Another obstacle that the forensic workstation must overcome is that of allowing easy access to I/O ports, such as USB and FireWire. Most computers have one or two front-mounted USB ports. Only a few models have FireWire at all, and those that do have the connections on the rear (except certain Macintosh models, which have front-panel FireWire).

Having a good selection of I/O ports conveniently mounted on the front of the enclosure, where they are easily accessible, is a very desirable feature. Fortunately, several companies manufacture I/O front panels that mount in an external drive bay. Two options to consider are by Vantec and Syba. Both occupy a 5.25" drive bay.

The Vantec features four USB 2.0 connectors and four FireWire 400 connectors (two are 4-pin and two are 6-pin). Additionally, an eSATA connector allows SATA devices to be connected on the fly. In order to utilize the FireWire capability, the system board must have that feature built in, or an expansion card must be installed that supports FireWire. Syba's unit is similar, but only has one each of the different FireWire connectors.

These devices are not intended to be write-protected devices. They are only designed to connect external peripherals. Therefore, if a forensically sound image is the reason for connecting a device, it is important to use one of the write-blocking accessories discussed in Chapter 18.

THE SOFTWARE OF A FORENSICS WORKSTATION

Investigations cannot be run on hardware alone. There needs to be an operating system (OS), and there needs to be several applications installed. Since the dedicated forensics software is covered in Chapter 18, "Tools of the Digital Investigator," I will not go over it in detail here. However, it is important that you know the minimum requirements of the software you intend to use before building a workstation. It could be a little frustrating to build a single-CPU computer with 4GB of RAM only to find that you need dual CPUs and 8GB. In addition to forensics software, there are some productivity suites and other applications that will be needed.

Operating Systems

Just because the investigative team will be looking at systems with multiple operating systems, that does not mean they need machines running them all. Most forensic tools can capture data regardless of the target OS. But they will only run on a specific host OS. The majority of systems will run on Windows operating systems. A network server will be running one of the various Windows Server applications. The forensic workstation will run Windows 7 (Windows 8 was released toward the conclusion of writing this book, but too soon to be available for any significant testing.).

Windows 7 is available in several different *builds* (versions of a version, if you will). The least expensive of these is Windows 7 Home, which is inadequate for our purposes. Window 7 Professional will do anything the forensics professional truly needs. If there is some reason to need extended multimedia features, Windows 7 Ultimate is only a few dollars more. Either of these versions is available in both 32-bit and 64-bit versions. This is based on your selection of a CPU in the previous section. The 32-bit OS will run on a 64-bit CPU, but not vice versa. It is highly recommended that you plan for 64-bit operation across the board.

The other viable alternative for a forensic workstation is Linux. In fact, I highly recommend that at least one of the forensic workstations in your lab be a Linux box. There are several utilities unique to Linux that have been mentioned in the course of this book that are valuable additions to the forensic arsenal.

Linux comes in a variety of distributions. All of them essentially run on the same core. This means that it doesn't really matter if you choose Fedora, SuSE, or any of the other popular distribution packages. In fact, most of the major Linux distributors offer either a Security distribution or a Forensic distribution. Either would make a good start toward building your lab machine.

Application Software

Report writing, generating illustrations, and communications are all critical elements of everyone's work. With the right software, all of these tasks are greatly facilitated. We are all familiar with Microsoft Office and how valuable it is to professional productivity. If the budget allows, Office is a great product. However, there are alternatives that work just as well.

OpenOffice is a suite of applications that is freely available from Apache Systems, available in versions to run on Windows, Linux, or OSX. It includes a word processor that contains most (if not all) of the features found in the Microsoft product. Its word processing application is fully compatible with other word processors on the market and has a full range of formatting, template, and automation functions. A spreadsheet application is included that exceeds Microsoft's in many respects. Formulae can be entered in human language without knowing a lot of programming functionality or code. Hundreds of templates make creating individualized spreadsheets such as invoices or payroll statements easy. A relational database is included that allows you to build standalone data processing applications, including inventory, case logging, and so forth. For users who need a presentation program similar to PowerPoint, the OpenOffice Impress should impress. It does everything PowerPoint does and is completely compatible. While not as user friendly as the other applications in the suite, OpenOffice Draw is still a powerful illustration too. A leaner and less resource-intensive version of OpenOffice—OpenOffice Portable—might be a good choice for laptop computers. It can run from a USB removable drive.

In the Linux environment, KOffice is very similar to OpenOffice in every regard. It even adds a utility for generating mathematical formulae (something I'm sure every forensic investigator is bound to need). Macintosh users might find the NeoOffice a good choice. However, since this product is based on OpenOffice, there is little reason not to go with OpenOffice to start with.

Processing digital images requires a specialized application of its own. For years the industry standard for digital imaging has been Adobe Photoshop (current version as of this writing is CS6). Versions are available for Macintosh and Windows users. It remains the standard-bearer, and for serious photographers, there is little that competes with it. One serious competitor is Optics Pro (its current version is 7.0). It is also available for Macintosh and Windows platforms and has many similar features as Photoshop. A freeware program that is very powerful and available for Macintosh, Windows, and Linux is GIMP (an acronym for Graphics Image Manipulator Program). While the program does have a fairly steep learning curve, it is every bit as powerful as either of the other options mentioned.

CHAPTER REVIEW

1. Summarize the minimal collection of components one will need to build a basic computer system. What additional (or different) components might be needed to turn that basic system into a viable forensic workstation?

2. Aside from raw speed, what other features of a microprocessor have an impact on the chip's overall performance?

3. List the different factors a designer must consider when selecting what type of memory to use when building a system. Assume that the system board has been predetermined and cannot be changed by the designer.

4. What is the advantage of using hot-swap bays in building a system? Why is this component of particular interest to the digital investigator?

5. Explain the difference between 32-bit and 64-bit operating systems. What are some things to consider when settling on an OS for your workstation? What is one way of avoiding having to decide?

CHAPTER EXERCISES

1. Find an online computer parts supplier (Newegg, Tiger Direct, and Directron are some good examples), and put together a shopping list for your forensic workstation. Make two lists. One will be your dream station where cost is no object, and the other will be the one your boss will actually approve—based on cost/performance/capability comparisons.

2. Find a PC that you can use for this project. It need not be anything more than a desktop PC bought from a surplus store or a retired office computer. A 1.2GHz processor and a gigabyte of RAM are all that you will need. Download a copy of Fedora Linux (the latest version). Now install the basic forensic tools. At a minimum, install The Sleuth Kit, Autopsy, and OpenOffice.

REFERENCES

Graves, M. 2006. *The A+ Guide to PC hardware maintenance and repair.* Clifton Park: Thomson/Delmar Publishing.

Mueller, S. 2012. *Upgrading and repairing PCs.* Indianapolis: Que Publishing.

LICENSING AND CERTIFICATION

There is a battle being fought in the field of digital forensics, and many of the practitioners aren't even aware that they are an object of the fight. A number of prominent individuals and organizations in the industry have been calling on a set policy regarding certifications. Are they needed? Are they even valuable?

Another obstacle that investigators face in many states is the bureaucratic process of licensing. While not a national issue, there are many states that require independent forensic investigators to obtain licenses to practice their trade. In some states, it is necessary to become a licensed private investigator. This chapter will not be the all-consuming answer readers might hope for, because—for the time being, anyway—there are no answers carved in stone for us to dig up and interpret. What will be covered here is a summary of what to watch for. Since different states have different laws, take care to be specific in your area.

DIGITAL FORENSIC CERTIFICATION

For several years now, there have been calls for a standardized approach to certifying professionals in the area of digital forensics. Meyers and Rogers (2004) took an academic approach to the argument in an article published in the *International Journal of Digital Evidence*. Their stance was that in order to provide standard levels of excellence in the practice, a uniform certification program should focus on three areas:

- Admissibility of evidence
- Standards and certifications
- Analysis and preservation

Assuming that everyone who possessed a certification was able to demonstrate a minimum level of competency in each of these areas, the assumption is that questions about the validity of the investigation process would be significantly reduced and hopefully become a thing of the past. The argument will continue, and in the meantime, we must go on with our work. So for now, this chapter will examine some of the current certification programs and discuss how each might be of significance to the forensic profession.

The certifications fall into two basic categories: vendor neutral and vendor specific. There is a certain value to each type. Vendor-neutral certifications concentrate on concepts that do not vary, regardless of what brand of software or equipment is being used. Vendor-specific certifications test the candidate's proficiency in using a particular device or product.

VENDOR-NEUTRAL CERTIFICATION PROGRAMS

Virtually every professional field has at least one certification program that tests professional qualifications. For example, the CompTIA A+ certification program evaluates the abilities of candidates to perform as computer hardware and desktop operating system technicians. Many organizations hiring help desk and desktop support personnel look for an A+ certification in the candidate's resume. Several organizations have stepped up to offer varying levels of certification in digital forensics. The ones discussed here are

- Global Information Assurance Certification (GIAC)
- Certified Digital Forensic Examiner (CDFE)
- Digital Forensics Certification Board (DFCB)
- International Society of Forensic Computer Examiners (ISFCE)
- Mobil Forensics Certified Examiner (MFCE)

Some of these organizations and programs offer multiple certification options. If so, the different programs will be discussed briefly.

Global Information Assurance Certification (GIAC)

GIAC offers three different certification programs for the digital forensics professional. Two of those certifications are targeted toward the type of investigations discussed in this book and will be covered in this section. The third, while not directly relevant, may be of some interest. The first of their two forensic certification is the GIAC Certified Forensic Examiner (GCFE). It is targeted toward individuals who perform basic search-and-seizure tasks and electronic discovery. The GIAC Certified Forensic Analyst (GCFA) focuses on a candidate's ability to collect and analyze data from Windows and Linux computer systems in a forensic manner. It is more suitable for law enforcement or civil computer examination positions. The third exam, the GIAC Reverse Engineering Malware program, tests the applicant's ability to examine the code of malicious software and back-trace its origin. This exam is beyond the scope of this book

GIAC certifications are acquired by demonstrating a level of professional experience in the field of choice and by passing one or more certification exams. There is no specific training requirement for the exams, although training is offered through the SANS (System Engineering, Networking, and Security) Institute at a charge. There is also a fee for taking the exams.

GCFA

Targeted at professionals working in information security who have an occasional need to perform forensic examinations of computers, GCFA is not quite as intensive as its GIAC brethren. Do not make the mistake of thinking that makes it an easy exam. To obtain the certification, the candidate must pass a proctored exam consisting of 115 questions. There is a 3-hour time limit for completing the exam, and a 69% or higher score is required to pass. Each candidate will be presented questions from seven different objective domains (Table 20.1), with equal emphasis on each domain (GIAC 2012a).

GCFE

The GCFE testing program concentrates on incident response, incident investigation, and intrusion analysis. To acquire the certification, a candidate must pass an examination consisting of 115 computer-delivered questions. Three hours are allowed for completion of the exam, and a passing grade of 71% is required. There are a number of exam objectives (Table 20.2) that will be covered (GIAC 2012b).

Table 20.1   Objectives of the GCFA Certification Program

Exam Certification Objectives	Certification Objective Outcome Statement
Acquiring and Analyzing Volatile Data	The candidate will demonstrate an understanding of how to acquire and analyze local and remote volatile evidence during an intrusion.
Analyzing Timelines	The candidate will demonstrate an understanding of creating and analyzing a timeline using file system, artifacts, and other available means and be able to use that timeline to analyze temporal events on the computer system around a specific time or artifact.
Data Layer Examination	The candidate will demonstrate an understanding of how to analyze and recover evidence from the file system and data layer on major file systems.
Digital Forensic Investigation Methodology	The candidate will demonstrate a fundamental understanding of the forensic process, methodology, common legal guidelines, documentation, and the common duties of a Digital Forensic Analyst and Incident Responder.
Digital Forensics and Incident Response	The candidate will demonstrate an understanding of how to properly acquire, validate, and analyze evidence on systems across the enterprise during the incident response identification and containment phases.
Forensic Intrusion Analysis	The candidate will demonstrate the ability to apply methodology to perform forensic analysis during an intrusion investigation.
Metadata and File Name Layers	The candidate will demonstrate an understanding of how to analyze and recover evidence from the metadata and file name layers on major file systems.

Table 20.2   Objectives of the GCFE Certification Program

Exam Certification Objectives	Certification Objective Outcome Statement
Browser Forensics	The individual will demonstrate a solid understanding of Browser Forensics
Digital Forensics Fundamentals	The candidate will demonstrate an understanding of forensic methodology, key forensics concepts, and identifying types of evidence on current Windows operating systems.
Evidence Acquisition, Preparation, and Preservation	The candidate will demonstrate understanding of evidence chain-of-custody and integrity, E-discovery concepts, evidence acquisition and preservation, and the tools and techniques used by computer forensic examiners.

Table 20.2 Objectives of the GCFE Certification Program—cont'd

Exam Certification Objectives	Certification Objective Outcome Statement
File and Program Activity Analysis	The candidate will demonstrate an understanding of how the Windows registry, file metadata, memory, and file system artifacts can be used to trace user activities on suspect systems.
Log Analysis	The candidate will demonstrate an understanding of the purpose of the various types of Windows event, service, and application logs, and the types of information they can provide.
System and Device Profiling and Analysis	The candidate will demonstrate an understanding of the Windows registry structure, and how to profile Windows systems and removable devices.
User Communications Analysis	The candidate will demonstrate an understanding of forensic examination of user communication applications and methods, including host-based and mobile e-mail applications, instant messaging, and other software and Internet-based user communication applications.

CERTIFIED DIGITAL FORENSIC EXAMINER (CDFE)

The CDFE is one of several information technology certifications administered by the Information Assurance Certification Review Board (IACRB). Since it is the only program administered by this organization that targets digital forensics, it is the only one to be covered in this chapter.

CDFE tests a candidate's basic understanding of digital forensics. The examination covers both the technical (or "hard skills" as IACRB calls it) and nontechnical ("soft skills") aspects of digital investigation. Soft skills would include topics such as the legal issues facing the forensic investigator and the basics of documentation.

IACRB (2012) lists nine knowledge domains that are tested with roughly equal emphasis on each:

- Law, ethics, and legal issues
- The investigation process
- Computer forensic tools
- Hard disk evidence recovery and integrity

- Digital device recovery and integrity
- File system forensics
- Evidence analysis and correlation
- Evidence recovery of Windows-based systems
- Network and volatile memory forensics
- Report writing

The exam consists of two parts. In order to progress to the second phase of the exam, the candidate must pass the first phase. The first phase consists of a multiple-choice exam built dynamically from a master bank of questions. The candidate is presented with 50 questions, and there is a 2-hour time limit for completing the examination.

Once the candidate has passed the multiple-choice exam, he moves on to the practical exam. A mockup of an authentic forensics case must be analyzed, based on a scenario presented in the case. The examinee has 60 days to create forensic images, analyze the data extracted, and present a formal report that would hold up as evidence in court.

DIGITAL FORENSICS CERTIFICATION BOARD (DFCB)

Of the certification processes covered in this chapter, the DFCB is probably the most rigorous. The two certifications offered by DFCB are the Digital Forensics Certified Practitioner and the Digital Forensics Certified Associate (DFCB 2012). To apply for either certification, a person must already have significant experience in the field of digital forensics to even begin the certification process. A candidate must be able to demonstrate a cumulative level of experience derived by totaling points from the following factors. The DFCB candidate must demonstrate that at least two of the years of experience claimed must have come within the last three years. Requirements are as follows:

- Cumulative work experience (five years minimum) as a manager supervising digital forensic professionals, as a digital forensic professional, or from any other professional discipline in which digital investigation is a part
- Minimum education of an Associate's degree, with additional credit given for higher degree levels and the number of credits earned in a digital forensics platform

- Additional training from sources such as vendor-sponsored classes, education-for-profit enterprises, and such
- Other related professional certifications
- Other professional experience

To get a more detailed explanation of the process, go to www.dfcb.org/dfcbapplication/login/AssessmentForm.aspx and complete the assessment form. Keep in mind that this is simply the assessment to determine if a candidate is eligible to start the process of DFCB certification. After DFCB completes the assessment, a $100.00 exam fee is required. Once the applicant has been accepted as a candidate, a $250.00 exam fee must be paid.

At this point the candidate is scheduled to take the exam in the next cycle. Exams are administered in the last seven days of every quarter. While waiting, the candidate must submit to a background check administered by a third party. If the candidate passes the exam and the background check, the experience and education claimed in the original assessment form with be verified. Once all of these steps are completed successfully, the person is registered as a DFCB-certified professional.

The exam contains questions derived from seven knowledge domains, some of which are subdivided into subdomains. It is not essential that the candidate be an expert in any one of the domains, but must show general proficiency in all seven. The domains, along with subdomains, are

- Legal
- Ethics
- Storage media
  - Acquisition
  - Examination analysis
- Mobile and embedded devices
  - Acquisition
  - Examination analysis
- Network forensics
  - Acquisition
  - Examination analysis
- Program and software forensics
- Quality assurance, control, and management

INTERNATIONAL SOCIETY OF FORENSIC COMPUTER EXAMINERS (ISFCE)

The ISFCE administers the Certified Computer Examiner (CCE) certification program. The goal of the program is to provide an equitable and vendor-neutral process of verifying the competency of people professing to be digital forensic specialists (ISFCE 2012). In addition to passing a rigorous examination, the candidate also undergoes a background check and application process conducted by the society.

While the process purports to be vendor neutral, it does not ignore the necessity of understanding how software tools do the job they do. The examinee is expected to have a fundamental knowledge of how to use the right tools for the job and to be aware of the capabilities of the various products on the market, both commercial and open source.

To be accepted into the certification process, candidates must demonstrate that they have either completed an authorized CCE Boot Camp Training program, provide proof that they have a minimum of 18 months of verifiable professional experience in conducting digital investigations, or present documentation of a program of self-study approved by the ISFCE board.

Once approved, the candidates begin the testing process, which consists of multiple phases. First, they must pass an online written examination with a score of 70% or higher. If an individual fails the first time, a single retake is allowed. A second failure results in expulsion from the program without an option to reapply.

After passing the written exam, the practical aspect of assessment begins. The candidate is assigned an individual assessor and is given the first of several practical projects. Each project consists of a disk image that the candidate downloads, processes, and analyzes. They have a 90-day time limit to complete each practical exercise, write a detailed report, and submit it to the assessor. Only one opportunity is provided to successfully complete each project. The projects are scored and averaged. An average score of 80% is required for passing the practical portion of the exam.

MOBILE FORENSICS CERTIFIED EXAMINER (MFCE)

The MFCE program is administered by Mobile Forensics, Inc. (MFI). The program recognizes the fact that there is a wide variety of software and hardware tools available to the investigator, and as such concentrates on the process rather than the tool. The certification process is a combination of written exams and practical application of knowledge through the completion of projects. While MFI does offer courses to candidates, it is not a requirement that a person attend these courses as a prerequisite to admission to the certification program as long as the candidate can demonstrate that he or she has successfully completed both a basic and an advanced course in cellular phone data extraction and pass a basic proficiency exam with a score of 85% or higher (MFI 2012).

Once accepted into the program, the examinee will complete six projects and undergo a final examination. Each project makes up 10% of the final score, and the final exam is worth 40%. The candidate must complete each project inside of 14 days, with a score of 100%. The final exam requires a grade of 85% or higher to pass.

Once the testing process is completed, the candidate enters a peer/supervisory review stage. During this phase of the certification process, it is necessary to conduct a minimum of four mobile phone examinations for the organization where the individual is employed. The peer or supervisor assigned to conduct the review will document each case investigated by the candidate and submit a report to MFI. Upon completion of four satisfactory analyses, the examinee will be awarded certification.

VENDOR-SPECIFIC CERTIFICATION PROGRAMS

The complexity of commercial forensic products gets greater every year. Failing to properly utilize a product almost certainly invalidates the results. It is not surprising that many of the major players in the field offer their own certification programs to test the users' proficiency. Many of these programs are internationally recognized. There are fees associated with each of the programs, and most require that you demonstrate a minimal level of formal training as well as experience. While there are literally dozens of privately administered programs, there are only a few that I will discuss here:

- Guidance Software
- Access Data
- Paraben

While there are numerous other programs, these three are commonly cited in interviews and online job descriptions.

GUIDANCE SOFTWARE

Guidance Software's Encase forensic suites were cited by PRNewswire as a clear market leader (PRNewswire 2011). Whether this is accurate or not, it is certain that the product is a powerful force in the industry. 2011 revenues were up over 12% from the previous year in spite of a challenging economic environment. The company offers two certification programs: the Encase Certified Examiner (ENCE) and the Encase Certified eDiscovery Practitioner (ENCEP).

ENCE

The ENCE certification is targeted toward forensic computer examiners in both the public and private sectors. It tests the applicant's proficiency in performing forensic examinations using the Encase suite of software. In order to apply for certification, an individual must either undergo 64 hours of authorized forensic training (college credits, generic forensic certification programs, etc.) or be able to document 12 months of professional computer forensic experience (Guidance 2012b).

Testing is done in two phases. Phase I is a written exam. The candidate must achieve a score of 80% or higher in order to pass. Those who pass will progress into Phase II, which is the practical exam. Here, the person is given a set of media to examine and has two months in which to complete the analysis and submit a written report. Phase II requires a score of 85% or higher to pass.

ENCEP

Individuals whose professional responsibilities primarily involve electronic discovery will be better served by pursuing the ENCEP certification. Much of the material covered on the exam overlaps that of ENCE, but is targeted more toward civil litigation and the recovery of materials requested in a discovery motion. As with the ENCE, the exam consists of two phases: written and practical (Guidance 2012a).

The written exam consists of 100 questions drawn from a pool of questions. The candidate must score 80% or higher in order to pass. The practical is somewhat less rigorous than that of the ENCE. For the ENCEP, Phase II consists of a series of scenarios presented in an online environment. Each candidate is allotted 3.5 hours to complete all of the assigned scenarios. A passing score of 80% is required.

ACCESSDATA

AccessData may lag behind Guidance in market share, but according to Business Wire, is growing faster and rapidly catching up (Business Wire 2009). Of the commercial certifications surveyed, AccessData offers more individual programs than its competitors. There are a total of five programs:

- Summation Certified Enduser (SCE)
- Summation Certified Case Manager (SCCM)
- Summation Certified Administrator (SCA)
- AccessData Certified Examiner (ACE)
- AccessData Mobile Examiner (AME)

The first three certifications are not targeted toward forensic examiners and will not be discussed. The last two are targeted toward specific digital forensic practices.

ACE

The ACE certification is targeted toward the investigator who works primarily in computer and networking environments. It evaluates the candidate's proficiency in using AccessData's Forensic Tool Kit for these investigations. The exam is purely practical and requires that the examinee have access to a computer that has a licensed version of FTK and other AccessData software installed. Once accepted into the program, a candidate is sent an image file to process. Once the work on the image file is completed, the user logs onto a Web site provided by AccessData and answers a set of questions based on the image file processed. There are no prerequisites regarding education or professional experience.

AME

Mobile forensic investigators are better served by pursuing the AME certification. This certification measures a candidates proficiency in using AccessData Mobile Phone Examiner Plus to process portable devices. The testing procedure is identical to that of ACE, and there are no prerequisite requirement for being accepted into the program.

PARABEN

Paraben Corporation offers two different certification programs. The Paraben Certified Forensic Examiner (PCFE) program is targeted toward computer and network forensic professionals using Paraben P2 Commander software, while the Paraben Certified Mobile Examiner (PCME) concentrates on the investigation of portable devices. All Paraben certifications require that the candidate sign a statement agreeing to abide by Paraben's code of ethics.

PCFE

Before a person is admitted to the PCFE certification process, he or she must meet both educational and profession experience requirements (Paraben 2012a). First, it is necessary to complete and pass the P2 Commander Level One class or a qualified equivalent. As of this writing, qualified equivalents had only been recently introduced and none were listed. Second, the examiner must complete and pass P2 Commander Level Two. There are no substitutes for this requirement. Information on registering for either of these classes can be found at www. paraben-training.com/pcfe.html.

The user must also demonstrate and document a minimum of six months professional experience as a digital investigator in any field. Verification can come in the form of a signed statement from a supervisor or previous employer.

Once accepted, the candidate enters a two-phase testing program. The first phase is a proctored online written exam. After passing the written exam, there are four practical assignments to complete. These all involve the examination of forensic images from FAT, NTFS, or ext file systems. All exams, both written and practical, must be passed with a score of 80% or higher.

PCME

Mobile examiners can demonstrate their prowess by obtaining the PCME certification. This program assesses a candidate's ability to examine portable devices. Prerequisites for acceptance are both educational and experiential. Educational requirements are to pass Mobile Level 1—Mobile Forensics Fundamentals (or an approved equivalent), Mobile Level 2—Advanced Smartphone and Tablet Forensics, and Mobile Level 3—Cellular GPS Signal Analysis. As with the PCFE program, there were currently no equivalent classes listed. Additionally, the candidate must provide documentation of at least six months of experience examining mobile devices.

Once accepted into the program, the candidate must pass a proctored written exam and four practical exams. All exams must be passed with a score of 80% or higher.

DIGITAL FORENSIC LICENSING REQUIREMENTS

While not obtaining a certification can keep you from getting a job, not getting the proper licenses can get you in trouble. As of this writing there is no licensing requirement on a national level. However, many states have specific licensing requirements for those who wish to open a private practice performing digital investigation. Unfortunately, there is currently no national registry of individual state requirements.

The majority of states that maintain licensing requirements for this profession treat it as though the digital investigator is a private investigator. Some states maintain a separate licensing procedure for digital investigators.

Kessler International conducted a survey in 2008 reviewing the licensing requirements of all 50 states (Kessler 2012). Questionnaires were sent to various state agencies and the results compiled. Only four states failed to respond. The results can be reviewed at www.investigation.com/surveymap/surveymap.asp. Three states reported having no licensing requirements: Colorado, Idaho, and South Dakota. Alabama, Alaska, and Wyoming do not have general statewide requirements, but enforce licensing requirements in certain cities. Delaware and Rhode Island specifically exempt digital investigators from Private Investigator licensing requirements.

If this isn't confusing enough, even within states that maintain licensing programs, there are some municipalities that have their own requirements as well. Insomuch as laws can change at the drop of a governor, it would be wise to check with your specific state and locality to determine what the specific requirements in your area might be.

Unlike realtor, bar, or medical licenses, there is little or no reciprocity between states regarding licenses. If you know for certain that you will be practicing in more than one state, it will be necessary to comply with the requirements of each state.

Licensing requirements vary from state to state as well. Some states require minimum educational levels in the field, in-state testing, or some other apparatus by which qualifications can be documented. Other states simply require a background check and a fee. Some of the licensing requirements even mandate firearm training because the requirement is a subset of the private investigator's license.

The disparity in requirements from state to state prompted the American Bar Association to publish an open letter requesting that licensing for digital investigators and electronic discovery agencies be abolished (ABA 2008). Lack of standards complicated the issue of applying precedents from one state court to similar cases being tried in other states. But for now, the issue of licensing remains one of the most convoluted legal issues an individual or organization faces.

CHAPTER REVIEW

1. What are three areas of competency that a good certification program evaluates? What different categories of certification program exist?

2. What are two programs that are available from GIAC? How do they differ from one another, both in scope and in requirements?

3. The CDFE tests both *hard skills* and *soft skills*. Define each of these terms, and give some examples of each.

4. What certification programs does Guidance Software offer? Which one is targeted for the entry-level examiner, and which is more advanced?

5. Why is it difficult to ascertain whether your state license to practice digital forensics will be recognized in another state? How can you find out for sure?

CHAPTER EXERCISES

1. Find three different training providers for different digital forensic certifications. List the classes they offer, and estimate the cost of final certification.

2. Write a couple of paragraphs listing your own state's requirements for licensing, should you desire to become a private digital forensic investigator.

REFERENCES

ABA. 2008. Report to the House of Delegates, Recommendation. www.abavideonews. org/ABA531/pdf/hod_resolutions/301.pdf (accessed April 13, 2012).

BusinessWire. 2009. AccessData[R] becomes fastest growing digital forensics software company. www.thefreelibrary.com/AccessData%5bR%5d+Becomes+ Fastest+Growing+Digital+Forensics+Software...-a0196137341 (accessed April 15, 2012).

DFCB. 2012. Digital Forensics Certification Board. www.dfcb.org/certification. html (accessed April 13, 2012).

GIAC. 2012a. Certification: GFCA. www.giac.org/certification/certified-forensic-analyst-gcfa (accessed April 13, 2012).

GIAC. 2012b. Certification: GFCE. www.giac.org/certification/certified-forensic-examiner-gcfe (accessed April 13, 2012).

Guidance. 2012a. Encase Certified eDiscovery Practitioner. www.guidancesoftware. com/computer-forensics-training-encep-certification.htm (accessed April 15, 2012).

Guidance. 2012b. EnCE Certification Program. www.guidancesoftware.com/computer-forensics-training-ence-certification.htm (accessed April 15, 2012).

IACRB. 2012. Certified Computer Forensics Examiner (CCFE). www.iacertification.org/ccfe_certified_ computer_ forensics_examiner.html (accessed April 13, 2012).

ISFCE. 2012. CCE Certification. www.isfce.com/certification.htm (accessed April 13, 2012).

Kessler International. 2012. Computer forensics and forensic accounting licensing survey. www.investigation.com/surveymap/surveymap.asp (accessed April 12, 2012).

Meyers, M., and M. Rogers. 2004. Computer forensics: The need for standardization and certification. *International Journal of Digital Evidence* 3(2):2.

MFI. 2012. Mobile Forensics Certified Examiner Program. www.mfce.us/ (accessed April 13, 2012).

Paraben. 2012. PCFE: Paraben Certified Forensic Examiner. www.paraben-training.com/pcfe.html (accessed April 15, 2012).

PRNewswire. 2011. Guidance Software and KPMG LLP announce alliance to provide customers with a comprehensive eDiscovery service offering. www.prnewswire.com/ news-releases/guidance-software-and-kpmg-llp-announce-alliance-to-provide-customers-with-a-comprehensive-ediscovery-service-offering-78413337.html (accessed April 13, 2012).

THE BUSINESS OF
DIGITAL FORENSICS

One of the lessons a field archaeologist learns early on is that in order to remain in the field, it is necessary to find funding for each project. Since archaeology is rarely a profit center (not if it's being done legally, anyway), funding must be acquired from sources outside of revenue.

This is true of a large majority of forensic centers as well. While digital forensic can be a very profitable endeavor, a large percentage of people who read this book are more likely to find themselves in the employ of a law enforcement organization or a corporation that is bringing forensics in-house. This chapter will cover four basic topics regarding the business aspects of a digital forensics organization:

- Starting a new forensics organization
- Maintaining an organization
- Generating revenue
- Obtaining an organizational certification

Not all of these topics will be applicable to every organization. Law enforcement is unlikely to generate much revenue. Likewise, it is unlikely that smaller law enforcement organizations and corporate departments will have the financial backing or the incentive to pursue certification for their team.

STARTING A NEW FORENSICS ORGANIZATION

Whether the seeds of a new division are planted in a local law enforcement facility or by the CIO of a regional bank, the vast majority of new departments begin with the question, "Can we save money by doing this ourselves?" In some cases, the question is about making money and not saving it, but the core concept remains the same. The startup phase can be considered to consist of two stages. In the initial planning stage, the powers that be brainstorm over the pros and cons of having their own shop. If the pros outweigh the cons, the initial planning stage moves into logistical planning stage.

DO WE BUILD OUR OWN SHOP?

The question of do we build our own shop isn't as easily answered as one might think. While financial considerations are certainly a significant aspect of this decision, there are also issues of privacy, communications, and competitive edge. Cetina and Mihail (2007) identify several factors to consider when approaching the decision:

- **Relative advantage:** What is to be gained by the new offering? The implementation of an internal e-discovery/forensics division with properly trained personnel will reduce the organization's reliance on third-party services in situations where current staff is not up to the task. Eliminating third-party access to private or privileged information significantly reduces the organization's exposure to threat. More importantly, the risks of noncompliance or unsatisfactory response resulting from reliance on improperly trained personnel will be significantly reduced.

- **Compatibility:** Having internal staff members who know the needs, the processes, and the structure of the organization means that document searches and investigations can be completed in shorter time periods. Outside contractors spend many hours of otherwise productive time familiarizing themselves with the environment, connecting with the right people, and other preparatory tasks. Internal staff will only have to familiarize themselves with the current situation. Additionally, the organization can rest assured that the staff members are familiar with the infrastructure of the information systems and with the regulations that apply. An outside contractor whose last job was working with hospital systems will have to be diligent to make sure that banking regulations are followed.

- **Marketing testability:** This is one area where some imagination might be required to apply Cetina and Mihail's factors to an internal division.

However, it can still be done. By assessing the type of information stored in the organization's file systems along with the past history of incident response, it is possible to apply third-party fees to a time and materials estimate for the value of having internal staff manage those incidents.

- **Communication:** When assessing a new product, the focus is on communicating the advantages of the product to potential customers. Existing customers are easier prospects because they are already familiar (and hopefully comfortable) with the organization's products and services. Communication is equally critical to a new department such as the one being proposed. Regulatory agencies will be interested in learning that the organization is voluntarily assuming these responsibilities. Legal issues caused by improper procedure will be dramatically reduced. Risks of penalty will be lower.

A factor not mentioned by Cetina and Mihail is that of preplanning. Internalizing all aspects of e-discovery and forensic services assures that complete control is maintained by the organization. Accomplishing this task will likely result in the side effect of the forensic team implementing processes and automated data collection tasks regarding computer usage and file system access. In the event of a discovery motion or requirement for investigatory services, the response time will be considerably faster and the process of collection information will be faster. Figure 21.1 illustrates a somewhat tongue-in-cheek flowchart for making this critical decision.

In addition to the obvious benefits, Rowlingson (2004) notes that when an organization makes the effort to create a forensic department, the effort acts as a deterrent to internal fraud. It demonstrates a commitment by executive management to take internal security very seriously. It will only take one or two successful

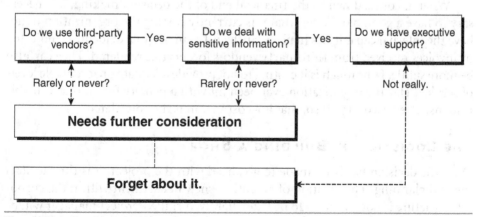

Figure 21.1 Should we build our own?

adventures by the new division for awareness of the organization's new abilities to permeate the corporation.

Part of the planning stage consists of analyzing the scope of services to be offered. A law enforcement agency will be looking to extract criminal evidence from suspect computers, networks, and portable devices. A regional bank will be more interested in assuming e-discovery processes and assuming the ability to take on the responsibility of internal investigations. Ascertaining the type of work to be assumed by the entity will have a direct impact on the costs of establishing and maintaining the organization over time.

It should also be considered that there is a certain amount of risk involved in creating any new organizational entity. Success or failure depends on the organization's ability to identify and mitigate those risks. Those specific to an expansion such as a new security division carry some unique problems:

- The right people in the wrong job
- Failure to provide sufficient training for personnel
- Not positioning the division for the greatest effectiveness
- Insufficient planning
- Insufficient funding
- Failure by management to "buy in"

Each of these risks will be discussed. It must be assumed that no single risk factor is of greater or of lesser import than any of the others. Consider them as threads of a single piece of fabric. When one begins to fray, the entire structure is in danger of unraveling.

When it comes down to the financial end of the decision making, it is necessary to have a good handle on what it is currently costing the organization to not have the internal capabilities in place. Such costs can be quite evident, as indicated by invoices received from third-party vendors for services rendered. They can also be more subtle. How much is it costing to not provide adequate or acceptable levels of service? Has the organization ever been hit with a penalty for an unacceptable response to e-discovery? If so, that is a cost that must be considered.

THE LOGISTICS OF BUILDING A SHOP

Once the decision has been made to go ahead with the project, it is time to start the real planning. The creation of an entirely new department within the corporate structure is not a venture to be taken lightly. A skilled project manager will be necessary to oversee the process, or the department will fail before it ever takes on its first case. Kerzner (2004) points out that the addition of a new department significantly alters the corporate structure and, as such, also alters corporate culture. In a corporate environment, the simple addition of a department such as this will change the way employees think about security.

This does not have to be a negative thing. Part of the planning process must include some method by which corporate employees are introduced to the new department. If it is presented as another "Big Brother" entity that threatens their livelihood, people are likely to respond in a negative manner.

Wiles and Reyes (2007) identify four aspects of operation for which a forensics department must plan:

- Business operations
- Technology operations
- Scientific practice
- Artistic expression

Business operational planning is a part of logistical planning. Its core services must be strictly defined by executive management, and the department manager must understand and abide by the decisions made here. Conversely, decisions made by management should not adversely impact on the ability of the department to perform its duties. A budget must be planned that is sufficient for department operation, and the manager must work within that budget. Policies developed by executive management must not negatively impact on the ability of the department to protect the organization.

Technology operations for a forensics department are somewhat different than for conventional information technology departments. Specialized equipment is needed and must be budgeted (this is covered in a later section of this chapter). The technology available to the criminal evolves on a daily basis. The technology made available to the department must keep up, or the advantage will tip decidedly in favor of the criminal. Regular refresher training for personnel will be a necessity. While this is technically an aspect of maintaining the organization and not planning it, if this ongoing cost isn't considered up front, executive management may well decide to drop the project after it is completed.

Acquiring, analyzing, and storing digital evidence requires specialized facilities as well. Secure data storage, secure physical storage, and at least one room isolated from wireless and cell phone signals will be required. Secure telephone lines, alarm systems, dry fire suppression systems, and structural renovation all must be considered.

Scientific practice may superficially appear to be similar to technology, but while the two concepts are interdependent, they are not the same thing. Scientific practice is the ability of department personnel to perform their tasks in a manner that is consistent with accepted forensic practice, is repeatable and verifiable, and is consistently objective. To the corporate department, this reduces the risk that their work will negatively impact the ability to pursue criminal prosecution at a later date. To the law enforcement agency, it is a critical element from the outset. To this end, the hardware and software selected play a significant role. More importantly, the talent and skills of personnel selected must be considered. Executive management plays a key role in this regard with the policies they define regarding operational management of the department.

Regarding the last element of Wiles and Reyes' list, one may not immediately think of a digital forensics practice as being an artistic venue. Still, intuition and creativity play as big a role as technology when it comes to analyzing the data collected during an investigation. In most situations, the approach taken by an investigator to locate and extract data is an expression of artistic ability. While there is little, if anything, that the project manager can to do plan for this aspect of the department, there is a great deal that executive management can do. Their decisions regarding personnel selection and the degree of control they exert over operations will have a direct impact.

ESTIMATING THE COSTS OF STARTUP

The initial costs for launching the department will consist primarily of equipment and software acquisition. Another significant expense comes from infrastructure costs associated with the remodeling of office space to accommodate a secure forensic environment and outfitting the office for day to day functionality. This includes network and IT infrastructure necessary for operation. Even though many of these items will exist in inventory, it is still necessary to account for their costs.

The next few pages of this chapter are derived from an actual project on which I worked as a consultant. Please note that while specific brands of equipment and software were used in generating these estimates, it is not my intent, nor the intent of this book, to suggest they are the best solutions. They simply happen to be the ones selected by this particular client. For reasons of privacy, the client's identity is not revealed, but the costs and products listed are derived from the final report as delivered to the CIO of the company. (Certain proprietary software that could conceivably help identify the client has been removed.) Keep in mind that dollar amounts listed in the tables are those in effect at the time of that effort. Since computer and software costs are such a volatile ingredient, it should be assumed that your actual costs will vary.

Hardware Acquisition

The tasks taken on by a forensics/digital discovery team are unique to the organization and require specialized equipment and software. While the general workstation used by staff for routine tasks can be drawn from a standard desktop image, the investigator workstations have specialized requirements. Likewise, there are some specific software requirements unique to the department. These initial costs are outlined in Table 21.1.

Table 21.1 Hardware Costs

Product	Qty	Unit Price	Net Price	Description
Investigator workstations	3	$2,900.00	$8,700.00 [a]	Dell Precision T5500, 12GB RAM, 1TB hard disk for processing images collected by forensic workstations
IW monitors	3	$420.00	$1,260.00 [a]	Dell 22". 25dp flat panel display
Office Computers	5	$800.00	$4,000.00 [a]	Dell OptiPlex 780, 4GB RAM, 1TB hard disk, 20" flat panel display
Forensic workstations	2	$8,000.00	$16,000.00 [b]	Digital Intelligence FREDDIE workstations for creating forensic captures
Acquisition workstations	2	$2,900.00	$5,800.00 [a]	Prevents the forensic workstations from being tied up for extensive periods of time while imaging media
WiebeTech Forensic Field Kit	3	$800.00	$2,400.00 [c]	For working cases in the field requiring forensic data capture
Investigator laptop computers	3	$1,400.00	$4,200.00 [a]	For working cases in the field
Twister box	2	$255.00	$510.00 [d]	Interfaces with many types of cell phone
Cell phone analyzer with dongle	2	$1,300.00	$2,600.00 [d]	Collects and analyses data from cell phones
Dell PowerVault NX300 (3.6TB, expandable to 7.2TB SAS)	1	$7,100.00	$7,100.00 [a]	3.6TB Intelligent SAN device, expandable to 14TB, which is to be off the main network for storing and archiving case files

Continues

Table 21.1   Hardware Costs—cont'd

Product	Qty	Unit Price	Net Price	Description
McAfee DLP 16GB encrypted flash drives	5	$235.00	$1,175.00 [e]	Allows moving data between outside network and lab network with auditing
Spare 600GB SAS hot-swap disks	6	$545.00	$3,270.00 [f]	Storage of live case data during investigations
Cisco 2901 security bundle	1	$1,700.00	$1,700.00 [e]	Secure router for interfacing network computer to Internet service provider
Cisco Catalyst 2955 managed switch	2	$1,450.00	$2,900.00 [e]	Layer 3 intelligent switch for connecting office and lab networks
		Subtotal	**$61,615.00**	

[a] Dell, Inc. (2011)
[b] Digital Intelligence (2011)
[c] Wiebetech (2011)
[d] BK Forensics (2011)
[e] Cost Central (2011)
[f] New Egg Electronics (2011)

Hardware requirements are relatively significant for the equipment used for forensic tasks. The workstations will perform processor-intensive and RAM-intensive tasks, and a slow machine with insufficient memory will be a handicap. Large amounts of secure storage are required. Evidence storage can be on the network SAN as long as adequate security is configured. Note that in Table 21.1, there are investigator workstations and forensic workstations. The investigator workstations are the computers on which employees will perform routine tasks, whereas the forensic workstations are specific to capturing and analyzing evidentiary material.

All costs were based on the premise that there would be five employees initially assigned to the department. It should be assumed that these numbers must be adjusted for variations in head count.

Software Acquisition

The workflow of a forensic department requires the services of several specialized applications as well as conventional office productivity applications. The forensic software selected for this project, shown in Table 21.2, was identified based on its ability to perform functions required by both the forensic investigator and by an electronic discovery specialist. However, to get maximum benefit out of the product,

Table 21.2 Software Costs

Product	Qty	Unit Price	Net Price	Description
McAfee Total Protection	11	$75.00	$825.00 [a]	Network protection for internal and external network systems and servers
Microsoft Office Professional	11	$415.00	$4,565.00 [a]	To be installed on all computer systems
Encase Forensic 6.0	5	$3,600.00	$18,000.00 [b]	Analysis tools for the digital investigator to be installed on IW and FREDDIE units
Encase Introductory Training	5	$3,325.00	$16,625.00 [b]	Formal training in Encase
HSFI Certification Option	5	$250.00	$1,250.00 [b]	While not 100% necessary, this option better prepares investigators to act as expert witness. If purchased separately, would add, $3K per user.
Encase Intermediate Training	5	$2,495.00	$12,475.00 [c]	Formal training in Encase
Adobe Acrobat Professional	5	$498.00	$2,490.00 [c]	Creates secure and noneditable portable documents for reporting and presentation.
		Subtotal	$56,230.00	

[a] Purchasing (2011)
[b] InfoSec Institute (2011)
[c] Guidance Software (2011)

it will require training; it is highly recommend that each of the employees attend the introductory and intermediate classes for the product. The reasons for this include

- Each person will learn to perform tasks in a consistent manner.
- Procedures will be demonstrated by competent instructors.
- Trainees will learn how the application works, making them better candidates as expert witnesses, should the occasion arise.
- Learning proper case procedure will facilitate the capture, analysis, and presentation of evidence in a manner acceptable by the courts, should the necessity present itself.
- A formalized training program is likely to be more efficient, in that it provides incentive for the trainees to meet externally imposed deadlines.

- According to Bishop (1994), employees who receive on-the-job training in specialized fields realize an initial increase in productivity of 9.5%, whereas those who benefit from formal training see an increase of 16%.

The necessity of the Microsoft Office licenses should be self-evident. The organization already possesses a site license for this product. However, the cost of the software was included in Table 21.2 for comparative purposes. This is also true of the McAfee Total Protection. The Adobe Acrobat is a nonstandard purchase that will be necessary for this project. The ability to create portable documents with security enforced on the front end will be critical to this department.

Facilities Improvement

A dedicated digital forensic/discovery laboratory will be needed for maximum efficiency. It will not be sufficient to simply assign team members to existing cubicles and tell them to get started. Some elements of laboratory design unique to this environment include

- A secure network—disconnected from the corporate network—for forensic and investigative work
- Secure digital storage that is not accessible from the Internet or the internal corporate network
- An evidence storage room that is continuously monitored and accessible only to authorized personnel
- A work room that is suitable for disassembly and reassembly of computers, but that is not accessible by unauthorized personnel
- A work area that cannot be penetrated by external wireless network or cellular telephone signals (for small devices this can be a simple Faraday cage)

Since contracting costs vary so widely from one area to the next, it didn't seem logical to include any estimated or actual costs in this section. This would become a critical task for the project manager to either assume or to assign to the appropriate personnel.

MAINTAINING THE ORGANIZATION

Before the first floppy disk is searched, management must make sure that there are a number of policies in place. These must be clearly written out and in many cases signed by the people they affect. Other policies and procedures don't necessarily have to be documented, but when push comes to shove, it is always better to have things in writing. Among items that should be documented are

- Hiring practices
- Job descriptions
- Investigatory practices
- Evidence handling procedures
- Reporting templates and procedures
- Certification and training policies (including maintenance)
- Organizational chart
- Employee policy handbook

All of these documents should be freely available to anyone with a need to know. That certainly includes those impacted by a specific document, and it also includes any regulatory agencies that may occasionally drop in for a quick compliance check. A signed policy statement is the organization's best defense against the claim, "But you never told me that was the way we did things!"

There are certain services that are essential to keeping the organization flowing smoothly. In a corporate environment, things like accounting services and human resources are handled by other departments in the organization. This is likely to be the situation in a law enforcement agency as well. However, in a private enterprise, they must be factored into the equation separately. Smaller organizations are likely to outsource accounting services, and possibly even HR. Both require skills that are not mutually inclusive with those of the forensic investigator.

What it boils down to is that, as with any other business entity, a variety of disciplines are involved in order to be successful. In their effort to define a specific management model for a forensic organization, Grobler and Louwrens (2006) identify several critical skills that must be present for a digital forensic operation to enjoy a long-term existence:

- Corporate governance
- Policy
- Legal\Ethical
- Personnel
- Technology

While it is certainly possible that one individual can possess more than one of these skills, it is a rare person indeed who can claim all six of them.

GOVERNANCE

Grobler and Louwrens tell us there are two factors of corporate governance, strategic and operational. In their efforts to maintain a scholarly approach to their study, I think they missed a critical third component of governance—that of creating and maintaining a corporate culture. Therefore, I am going add that factor to the discussion.

Every business entity needs to have a strategic focus. A mission is identified, and the methods by which that mission will be accomplished are clearly defined. Any business that lacks a focus is a business that is swimming upstream from the moment of its birth. Executive management has to have a precise understanding of the core competencies that exist within the organization. Taking on roles or responsibilities for which competencies do not exist will lead to failure.

Once the competencies are identified and evaluated, a solid set of processes and procedures can be developed that serve as a model of how each case handled by the organization will be managed. That is the function of operational governance. "Making it up as you go" works in the movies. It rarely leads to success in the real world. The approach to operational governance is likely to vary greatly from one organization to another. In a corporate environment where the focus is on internal investigations and e-discovery, the focus is likely to be on patching holes as they are discovered. A security breach costs money, and a quick and confidential resolution is likely to be the first priority. Catching the bad guy and serving justice are secondary. In law enforcement, these goals are completely reversed. The professional forensics agency must be able to shift focus from one priority to another, depending on where the assignment originates.

Operational governance leads directly into the next segment of this discussion. A solid and well-defined set of policies defines the focus of operational governance. Without them, the organization drops back into making it up as they go.

POLICY

Probably the aspect of any job that elicits the most complaints is all those rules. Then again, where would we be without them? Real archaeologists have thousands of rules to follow. Where they dig, how they dig, what they can do with what they dig up, how they analyze . . . it goes on and on. And as much fun as a football game without rules might be, determining the winner by pinning a medal on the last man standing flies in the face of sportsmanship. In order to present evidence in a fair and unbiased manner, there are several areas of policy that the organization needs to address.

Hiring

Identify the key positions that must be filled. This is completely dependent on the types of work the organization will take on, the overall budget, and the focus of where those cases will end up. For each position, write a detailed job description identifying the type of skills required. Criminal investigation requires a different skill set than e-discovery response. A person with a solid background in civil litigation can certainly make the move into criminal investigation, but not without a degree of cross-training. There are psychological considerations as well. There are those who cannot handle continual exposure to graphic pornography. If a position involves stressful or strongly distasteful activities, applicants should be warned well in advanced. During the hiring process, a good screening procedure can eliminate candidates who are clearly unsuitable. For existing employees, the job description acts as a foundation for what each person will be expected to do in the course of their employment.

Training

Everybody who successfully navigates the hiring process will have demonstrated that they have the minimum education and experience to perform the tasks for which they were hired. However, the world and technology moves on. If the staff doesn't keep up, then neither will the business. Most certifications require periodic renewal, which requires attending refresher courses. Your organization needs to have a policy that defines the ongoing training requirements for each position. The policy also needs to specify how such training will be scheduled and who will be paying for it. The organization's annual budget needs to have a pool of funds from which it can draw for providing the essential training.

Accepting Assignments

It doesn't seem as if there should be any hard and fast rules for the types of assignments your team takes on. Lack of such a policy can lead to disaster. If you already know you don't have any people trained in searching iPads, it wouldn't be a good idea to accept a commercial assignment involving several hundred of them. However, it isn't just the technology that must be considered. Volume and speed are critical conditions to take into consideration. One person isn't going to be able to take on a hundred hard disks in any reasonable period of time. An assignment that must be completed in a very short time must be studied carefully. Do you have the resources to do it well? If you can't do it well, don't do it at all. A good assignment policy will define several criteria. These include the types of assignments (criminal vs. civil or discovery, etc.) that will be accepted, the policy of the organization regarding rush assignments, what personnel can be used for specific assignments, and the types of digital information that can be examined.

Procedure

Procedural policy can get very complicated if you let it. Here is an area to be as general as possible while still being specific. It is possible to break procedure down into two categories, first response and investigation management. A generalized set of procedures should be written for each category. For example, it would be a good idea to have a set of guidelines that help decide when live response is preferred over hardware seizure followed by a search. Certain practices should be defined and itemized in the procedure. Do you photograph every "crime scene"? For a criminal investigation, this should be standard procedure, but how much does it help in an e-discovery response? What tools will be used for which procedures should be clearly defined. While there is certainly a time and place for using unconventional methods, the conditions that lead to such a practice should be a matter of policy. Methods and approach to case documentation must also be clearly defined.

Evidence Handling

Law enforcement agencies are very familiar with the strict guidelines established by the Federal Rules of Evidence. Every step that is taken during a criminal investigation must conform. Even a minor misstep can result in evidence being rejected by the court. Whether a private enterprise should follow such strict guidelines is a matter of governance. Does the organization have a vested interest in bringing internal investigations before the court? If so, then it is in the best interest of everyone involved if the evidence handling policy is as strict as that required by law enforcement. For a corporate entity, it could come down to a matter of considering each case by its independent merits. Before touching anything, decide on how much damage can be done if the case does wind up in court. And then be prepared for surprises. The evidence handling policy should define how materials are collected, how they are packaged and transported, how they are stored, and how chain of custody is maintained. This is a policy that must be strictly enforced.

Reporting

Reporting is relatively straightforward. Each person who works within the confines of an investigation should have general guidelines regarding case documentation. In Chapter 17, "Case Management and Report Writing," this subject was covered in detail. In addition to what must be reported, it is necessary to define when it must be reported. What is the deadline from the end of a case to the due date for final documentation? Obviously, larger cases require more documentation, and therefore more time to prepare it.

Data Retention

What happens to data created during the investigatory process once the case is closed? There are several answers to that question, depending on what regulatory oversight is involved. This is an area where legal counsel should be sought. In addition to storing original data, it might be wise to consider how that data will be read several years from now. There is one case in which I am involved that, although I was not around when it was initiated, has been going on for many years. All of the original forensic images continue to be retained in a secure location on the corporate SAN. Throughout the course of a lengthy investigation, followed by an equally lengthy litigation process, it is now going into appeal. Even after the courts have their final say, it will be necessary to hold onto the data for at least seven more years in order to remain within regulatory compliance. One of the pieces of original optical media is so old that there is no longer a device on the market that can read the disk. Therefore, we are also retaining a drive that can read it.

How evidentiary materials will be retained is also a matter for consideration. In the example used in the previous paragraph, the data is stored in two separate locations. The forensic images are on the SAN, as mentioned, while the original media that were collected are stored in an evidence locker. When the time comes, it will be necessary to destroy the information. In criminal cases, the court will order the dispensation of materials. In civil matters, it will be a matter of either an agreement between parties or a court order.

Records of cases that are not evidentiary material are likely to fall under different guidelines. These fall under the category of business records. As such, their retention will be covered under rules defined for the specific type of document. Tax records have one set of guidelines, while payment records have another. Several different organizations have compiled lists of document types along with how long each should be retained. While there is not 100% agreement among all the recommendations, there is general consensus for certain types of records. Table 21.3 is a compilation of recommendations from several government agencies.

LEGAL/ETHICAL

There is no point in trying to pretend that legal and ethical issues are one and the same. Truly understanding the law is the domain of the lawyer. However, to be successful, the digital investigator needs to have a rudimentary understanding of

Table 21.3   Document Retention Recommendations

Record Type	Retention Period
Article of incorporation	Permanent
Bylaws	Permanent
Contracts and agreements	Permanent
Personnel records	5 years from termination date
Tax returns	Varies from 3 to 7 years, depending on status
Sale and use tax returns	Permanent
Payroll tax returns	4 years
Pension and profit sharing records	Permanent
Mortgage and note agreements	7 years
Accident reports	6 years
Fire and safety inspection reports	6 years
Accident reports	6 years
Settled insurance claims	4 years

the laws affecting the profession. That is why this book has three chapters regarding legal issues. This is not just a responsibility of management. Every employee needs to consider the legal ramifications of every action they take.

Ethical issues require a completely different mindset. If you refer back to the previous chapter on licensing and certification, you will recall that several of the certification programs required that the candidate sign off on a code of ethics. This is but one of the latest efforts of industry players to create a mantra of ethical behavior that will cocoon the industry with an aura of respectability. Nelson et al. (2005) call for a national standard of ethics for the digital forensic industry. While this sounds good on paper, the concept begs the question, who will write these standards? A philosopher is likely to arrive at a different set of standards than a lawyer or a banker. Central to everything is a simple premise. Honesty and integrity are standards that everyone in the industry should bear, regardless of how heavy they might be.

PERSONNEL

As was mentioned earlier in the chapter, one person is unlikely to possess all of the skills and talents required to successfully complete an investigation. When building an organization, you are building a team. Education and training are critical elements in selecting members for that team. Equally critical are personal attributes, such as patience, intuitiveness, and even humor. Never underestimate the value of a cohesive unit. Music lovers all know the stories of their favorite bands who split up because the members could no longer get along.

A digital forensics unit may consist of a single team or it may be several teams, each tasked with specific responsibilities. Regardless of the organizational makeup, in any team, there should be a single team leader. This person is the one who assigns responsibilities and interfaces with clients. In this regard, clients can either be external customers who come to the organization for its services, or they may be various departments within the organization. In a corporate entity, the division manager would be the team leader and would liaison between the unit and other management staff within the organization.

Such a unit as this will require several specialists. The person who is an expert cell phone analyst may be mediocre at hard disk investigation. Network specialists require a completely different skill set than either of these. And people who can do a thorough analysis of a memory image are hard to find. One specialist who is all too frequently overlooked is the person who is responsible for tracking evidence from beginning to end. If it is assumed that each person who handles evidence will be equally responsible for maintaining an accurate chain of custody log, then it can also be assumed that when the chain is broken nobody will be responsible. Regardless of the size of the team, only one person should be responsible for evidence handling. A large organization might have multiple evidence technicians, but if so, there needs to be yet another policy written. That policy should describe the steps to be taken to assure that all evidence technicians adhere to the same rigid procedures.

Occasionally, it may become necessary to outsource certain skills. A small organization that typically concentrates on hard disk acquisition will not be prepared when a case suddenly turns to the Internet. It is very bad policy to bid out each outsourced assignment and pick the lowest bidder. For outsourcing to be successful, there has to be a working relationship between the two organizations. Consider it essential to have a contract in place to define terms and conditions. For each assignment that the contractor takes on, there needs to be a separate statement of work, work order, and purchase order in place. A security agreement that defines how personally identifiable information (**PII**) is handled is a necessity when dealing with federally regulated industries such as banking, health, and education. All contracts and agreements need to be periodically reviewed and modified as needed. Regulations change.

TECHNOLOGY

The technology of this industry has been the focus of this book. However, there is an art to managing technology, just like there is for managing people.

There are a few critical issues to be integrated into a technology management program:

- What technology should we use?
- Is there a solid support infrastructure for each piece of technology?
- How should we handle the testing of products (and upgrades)?
- What will be the decision process for adding new technology?
- What sort of change control should we incorporate to manage and track changes to applications?

What Technology Should We Use?

Simply buying a bunch expensive equipment and software and turning the team loose on it won't be sufficient. Every new addition adds an element of training, a window for error, and additional potential for obsolescence. That last item is something that frequently gets lost in the excitement of acquiring a new toy. But the successful manager always considers what will happen if the company that manufactures and supports a critical element in workflow suddenly goes belly-up. What will be the costs of migrating the entire organization over to a different product that will perform the same functions?

Deciding on brands and levels of product require a great deal of research. There are several different forensic suites from which to choose and numerous hardware options. Together these all represent a significant financial investment, and most likely an equally significant investment in time and effort. Installation, testing, and training all take time and cost money. You only want to do it once. In researching the different software suites, you are going to discover that some products are very strong in one aspect of the investigation process—such as hard disk analysis—and weak in others—such as telephone analysis. If the plan is to cover all bases, will it make sense to purchase multiple suites? Many organizations do just that. However, keep in mind that this decision will also impact your personnel. It's hard enough to go through the certification for one product. Do you want the same person to go through it again for another product, or is it better to have dedicated personnel for each one?

Is There a Solid Support Infrastructure for Each Piece of Technology?

The need for excellent support cannot be overstated. Software runs on computers, and computers are notoriously fickle. Most software suites require that support contracts be renewed periodically. Make sure these commitments are kept up. Everything will work perfectly until the biggest case of your career lands in your lap. About a third of the way through your first hard-disk acquisition for the Big Event, your copy of Forensic Disk Copier 3.7 reports a "File Not Found" error or the Massively Powerful Forensic Investigation Unit suddenly blue-screens. Who do you call? The sign of really bad technical support is when, after three hours on hold, the person who finally answers says, "It can't be our software. It has to be the computer system." And then hangs up. Good support staff does not hesitate to consider all possibilities and, when necessary, work with other vendors to resolve problems. You know you have good support when the staff of one company willingly works with the support staff of a competitor to resolve an issue.

How Should We Handle the Testing of Products?

Every new piece of software or hardware that is added to the technology infrastructure must be put through a standardized test procedure before it is allowed into the production environment. Larger organizations have test labs set up just for this purpose. Earlier in the book, I mentioned the importance of having test images just for this purpose. If you know exactly what hidden files, deleted files, malicious software, and other nefarious codes exist on the system, then you know when the new piece of software fails to find it. More importantly, if cross-examined on the witness stand about your test procedures, you can confidently answer the opposing counsel's questions. Only after each new product has been submitted to a consistent testing script, using known data sets, should that product be introduced into production.

The same process applies to upgrades and patches. Anybody who has worked with computers and software for any length of time is fully aware that an "upgrade" is not always an improvement. Review any new upgrades and patches critically, applying the age-old philosophy that "if it ain't broke, don't fix it." Don't upgrade software unless the upgrade addresses a known issue or adds a new feature that is relevant or critical to your workflow. If a new patch only exists because it fixes a flaw in the FireWire interface—and you don't own a single FireWire device—why do you care? Don't install it. Because if you do install it, and don't go through the process of testing the code change, you open the door for somebody else to claim that your failure to do so is a possible source for errors in your results.

What Will Be the Decision Process for Adding New Technology?

Adding new technology as time goes on requires a good deal of thought and analysis if it represents a significant alteration in work flow or capability. Picking up an extra write-blocker is no big deal. The rules above still apply—test, test, and then test again before you use it—but no major hurdles need to be overcome. Taking on something that changes the way you work requires deeper study. You can't simply decide you want to suddenly have the ability to start acquiring and analyzing cell phone data. Not only is there a significant investment in hardware and software, but there are personnel issues to resolve. Do you have anyone who possesses the skill set necessary for this latest endeavor, or do you have to go out and hire someone new? What impact is the acquisition going to have on your annual budget? Will the resources be used with sufficient frequency to justify the cost and effort? It is in the organization's best interest for someone to conduct a thorough study before you wave the checkered flag.

What Sort of Change Control Should We Incorporate?

Change control is a critical aspect of management that often gets overlooked by smaller organizations. Federally regulated organizations are quite familiar with the concept, because it is one of the things that are mandated in many situations. There are two aspects of change control that are necessary. Changes to the way your business works are treated differently in some regards than changes you make to the technological infrastructure. Both are equally critical.

Business Change Control   Business changes are those that affect work flow, the way employees are hired or evaluated, or the way the organization decides which cases to accept and which to refuse. These are just three examples. The list could go on forever. Making changes of this nature require planning. Larger organizations have a change control process that is documented and followed for virtually every modification made to the way it conducts business. It generally starts with someone identifying a need or a problem and then follows a series of events to conclusion. If this series of events is clearly documented and then carefully followed, fewer problems are encountered. The process borrows a lot from the field of project management. For a change to be made, there has to be a clearly defined reason to make the change and equally well-defined penalties for not making it.

You need to understand the current process. Know the purpose for that process and why it exists. Record this information in a change request form. Next, find out what the reasons are for requesting a change in the current process. What is wrong with the status quo, and how will the proposed change make things better? This is part two of your change request. Now, identify all the options for addressing the need or fixing the problem. There is generally more than one solution to any problem. Be certain that all viable options have been considered before committing to anything. Document what those options were, and identify the reasons one solution was accepted and all others were rejected.

If all these questions lead to the answer, "We must change," then work with internal staff and (if applicable) outside vendors to put together a detailed plan of action. Here is where a skilled project manager becomes a valuable asset. This plan must include testing procedures and scripts, migration into production, and fall-back scenarios in case of disaster. Never assume that all will go as well as the sales executive promises it will. Installation, testing, migration, and roll-back plans are now documented as part of the change control process.

During the process of making the change, document each step taken. Identify individuals involved in specific tasks, and record the time and date that the change occurred. Table 21.4 is an example of what information should be recorded in a standard business change request.

Software Change Control Adding new software should be documented any time the change has a potential impact on the outcome of an investigation. In other

Table 21.4 Sample Business Change Request

Information	Description
Date of Request:	Date on which the request was initiated
Change Requestor:	Person making the request
Brief Description of Change:	Process that is being added or changed
Reason for Change:	Reason why this is necessary or desirable
Type of Change:	Modification, addition, removal, etc. of a process
Estimated Cost of Change:	How much it will cost
Estimated Time for Completion:	How long it will take
Cost Center to Charge:	Who will pay for it
Date Approved:	Date it got the go-ahead
Project Status:	Change identified as a project or a work request
Assigned to Change:	Who will be implementing the change
Test Group:	Who will test the change
Date Implemented:	Date the change will be migrated to production
Actual Cost:	Final tally of money spent
Actual Time for Completion:	Actual time it took to implement
Comments:	Any supplemental information that might be of interest in the event of an audit or other challenge
Attachments:	Attached documents related to the change, including RFQs, POs, test scripts, test results, etc.

words, if you add a new version of Microsoft Office, you probably won't need to document the changes. If you add new forensics software, upgrade computer or network operating systems, or change core business applications, it is definitely in your best interest to document the changes. As with all other additions, new software must be tested. Therefore, install it into your test environment and give it the usual workout. Then when everyone is satisfied that it performs its job satisfactorily, move it into production.

The same holds true of software upgrades. As mentioned earlier in the chapter, don't be upgrading simply because there is a new version out. Examine each upgrade or patch to see if it is needed, and then decide whether or not to proceed. A similar documentation process to the one used in a business change request should be used for every software addition, upgrade, or patch that involves network operating systems or core business applications. Some fields to be added to Table 21.4 would be version number, patch number, and release dates for each.

GENERATING REVENUE

Whether the organization is for-profit, nonprofit, or an internal division to a larger corporation, in order to survive, it must maintain a continuing stream of revenue. When the revenue stops, so does the organization. Without revenue, salaries won't be paid, the electricity and heat will be shut off, and the whole thing comes skidding to a stop. Where that revenue comes from is entirely dependent upon the type of organization. For-profit organizations must find clients willing to pay fees for its services. Nonprofits may depend on a combination of fees and external funding, such as grants or other government funding. The corporate division is entirely dependent on the mercies of executive management to continue funding the department. Since it is highly unlikely that a corporate forensic division is generating any revenue, it is a cost center and not a source of revenue. It is beholden upon the department manager to continue justifying each year's budget.

FOR-PROFIT ORGANIZATIONS

The skills and infrastructure that make for a decent digital forensics organization can be put to use in a variety of ways. There is the obvious service of providing investigation services for clients who are involved in legal matters. This can include working as an expert witness for either side, collecting digital artifacts that will convince a court of the veracity of that side's claims. For the most part, this will involve civil actions. However, in very small communities, it is not uncommon for law enforcement agencies to outsource certain forensic services to qualified organizations. Each agency will have its requirements for becoming a vendor for forensic services.

A lucrative source of revenue is the provision of electronic discovery services. This presupposes that the organization has properly trained personnel who understand the legal and regulatory issues that apply to specific types of clients. There is an entire chapter in this book specific to that subject. There is also a significant investment in specialized software and massive amounts of storage for each case undertaken.

Data recovery is a service that can provide a certain amount of revenue. This is not quite as significant as other sources, but is one that should be offered. There is a bit more chance involved here, as your organization will often have no control over the media where the lost data is stored.

Network intrusion analysis and penetration testing are two other services that can be offered by the company. Smaller organizations don't have the tools or the capabilities to handle network intrusions internally. And penetration testing should always be performed by a third party. As with e-discovery, taking on these assignments requires that your organization is equipped and staffed appropriately.

For any job accepted, your organization assumes the mantel of agency for the client. A contract that clearly defines the responsibilities of the client as well as those of your organization is signed by both sides. The contract needs to specify payment terms, including hourly or per-job rates being charged and a payment schedule for remitting payments due. Clear definitions of liability are critical. What risks does the organization assume on behalf of the client? This becomes particularly important any time the courts are involved, whether the case is civil or criminal in nature.

NONPROFIT ORGANIZATIONS

To start with, it should be clear that the term "nonprofit" does not mean that the firm doesn't charge a fee for its services. Nor does it mean that it doesn't charge more for those services than what it costs to perform them. A nonprofit simply collects surplus revenues and uses them for pursuing its stated goal.

With this in mind, it is easy to apply everything from the previous section to the nonprofit. It can perform any of the aforementioned services for the same level of fees. It simply does not distribute surplus funds to owners or shareholders. If the organization meets federal standards, it may be exempt from income tax.

Two other ways of funding a nonprofit are through charitable donations and through grants. Collecting donations for a digital forensics entity may be a bit of a challenge, but it certainly is not out of the realm of the imagination. It's a matter of finding people with sufficient disposable income and an avid interest in what you are doing. Former beneficiaries of your services are always a good place to start.

Grants are available to forensics organizations in several places as well. Law enforcement agencies are generally funded under a variety of block grants. A block grant is generally issued by the state or federal government and is intended to cover general expenses. Some of this money can be used to fund a forensics department. Shortly after the financial crisis of 2008, the U.S. Government also started issuing stimulus grants. Some of these grants were administered by the Department of Homeland Security, while others are general grants for local government agencies.

Not all grants are targeted exclusively at law enforcement. Several educational institutions have been funded to establish forensic centers with the two-fold intent of establishing academic programs in digital forensics and to provide assistance to local government entities that do not have sufficient funding to support their own departments. The University of Wisconsin in Platteville received such a grant, as did Purdue University. To find sources of such grants, check with the National Institute of Justice and on the federal government's grants.gov Web site.

CORPORATE DEPARTMENTS

Retaining funding in the corporate arena is possibly the biggest challenge of all. Most companies review every department's budget annually to determine how much funding it will receive for the following year. During that review, the division manager asks for about twice as much as she needs and the Budget Committee gives it about half. However, it is up to the division manager to provide justification for those funds. A forensic division is not a profit center in the vast majority of cases.

If a department isn't making more money than it is spending, then it somehow has to demonstrate that it is saving the corporation more money than it is costing. There must be a positive advantage/risk ratio or the department will be cancelled. There are several ways to justify the existence of such a department. The implementation of an internal e-discovery/forensics division with properly trained personnel will reduce the organization's reliance on third-party services in situations where current staff is not up to the task. Eliminating third-party access to private or privileged information significantly reduces the organization's exposure to threat. More importantly, the risks of noncompliance or unsatisfactory responses to e-discovery demands resulting from reliance on improperly trained personnel will be significantly reduced.

A dollar value can be applied to the services provided by an internal organization. A close estimate of actual costs can be obtained by looking at the company's past history of incident response, reviewing the volumes and types of information stored, and then getting quotes from third-party vendors for their services in this regard. While these are not "real" charges that the company pays, they do have the advantage of making the value of the department apparent to executive management.

In addition to the aforementioned advantages, Rowlingson (2004) notes that when an organization makes the effort to create a forensic department, the effort acts as a deterrent to internal fraud. It demonstrates a commitment by executive management to take internal security very seriously. It will only take one or two successful adventures by the new division for awareness of the organization's new abilities to permeate the corporation.

ORGANIZATIONAL CERTIFICATION

In the previous chapter, a great deal was said on the merits of individual certifications. There are also certification programs for organizations. The American Society of Crime Laboratory Directors/Laboratory Crediting Board (ASCLD/LAB) is an organization founded by the Scientific Working Group on Digital Evidence in 1998. The program is an offshoot of a program that has existed since 1982 that has certified laboratories that study physical forensic evidence.

In order to achieve ASCLD/LAB certification, the organization must demonstrate that it meets several criteria:

- Qualified personnel
- Demonstrably scientific procedure
- Strict levels of quality control
- Continued proficiency testing of personnel by outside parties

While these sound like relatively benign criteria, the definitions of these standards fill several hundred pages in ASCLD/LAB's accreditation manual. Demonstrating the qualifications of personnel is not simply a matter of submitting curriculum vitae. Each individual must pass competency examinations specified by ASCLD/LAB. The results of those tests must be submitted as part of the certification process. The organization won't even consider a lab that doesn't meet the Industry Standards Organization's (ISO) 17025:1999 standards.

ISO 17025:1999 includes supplemental requirements to meet international standards as well as U.S. government standards. They specify testing and calibration standards that a laboratory has to meet in order to qualify. Additionally, it defines minimum conditions that a facility must meet. To meet these standards, the physical facility is inspected and evaluated for its physical security, evidence storage and handling capabilities, and capacity.

ASCLD/LAB measures competency levels in multiple areas. A lab that does not focus on a particular area will not be tested in that discipline. Nor will it be allowed to practice it once certification is awarded. Doing so will get the certification suspended until the lab is recertified to include its new discipline. Following are the areas of investigation at the time of this writing:

- **Computer forensics:** Examination of digital evidence extracted from computers and computer networks
- **Multimedia evidence:** Evidence extracted from audio, magnetic media, film, and digital video
- **Image analysis:** Forensic analysis of digital images
- **Forensic audio:** Forensic analysis of voice and other forms of digital audio
- **Video analysis:** Forensic analysis of digital video files

Once a lab has achieved certification, it must undergo an annual conformance inspection. This will be scheduled, and your organization will have the opportunity to prepare for the visit. If during any one of these inspections, it is determined that standards have deteriorated below the minimum threshold, the certification can be suspended or even revoked.

What is the advantage of going to the trouble and expense of obtaining this piece of paper? The value of institutional certification has been a topic of discussion for many years. In 2003, the International Association of Arson Investigators posed the question of how we were supposed to put our faith in the practitioners of a science that few people understand (IAAI 2003). When two "expert witnesses" disagree on not just the conclusion but the actual results of the examination, there is good reason for laypeople—such as the members of the jury—to have reasonable doubt. Admittedly the object of their concern was physical evidence and not digital, but the core concept remains the same. A lab that has earned ASCLD/LAB certification is much more difficult to challenge. Everything about personnel, facilities, and workflow has been thoroughly examined and vetted by a knowledgeable team.

Therefore, for the law enforcement facility, the advantages of certification are relatively obvious. How does it benefit the private sector lab? ASCLD/LAB certification is not limited to labs run by law enforcement agencies. For the organization performing investigations for profit, the advantages are easier to see. When shopping around for third-party services that are critical to a client's legal well-being, the ASCLD/LAB certification is a sign that the services being paid for will be effectively delivered. The vice president of sales will find it to be an excellent promotional tidbit. Perhaps more importantly, the fact that the facility and all of its employees passed muster for ASCLD is very likely to lead to greater success in providing the support that leads to winning cases for the home team when they reach court. Even better is the fact that solidly documented and irrefutable evidence can keep clients out of court to begin with.

CHAPTER REVIEW

1. What are some advantages to having your organization build an in-house facility for performing digital forensic investigations? Are there any disadvantages?

2. Differentiate between one-time startup costs and recurring costs. Can you think of any one-time costs that will occasionally have to be repeated?

3. List at least three different policies that a diligent organization must create, publish, and enforce for its employees to follow. (There are far more than just three—be creative.)

4. What are some services that even a full-service organization may occasionally have to outsource? What risks does your organization assume when outsourcing services to another organization?

5. How can an in-house forensic department justify its value if it does not provide services on a for-hire basis? What can it use in place of actual revenue to demonstrate value?

CHAPTER EXERCISES

1. Write a brief policy, three to four paragraphs, that defines an employee's responsibility to securing information in the organization.

2. Write a job description for your evidence handling technician, based on everything you've learned in the previous chapters, as well as what is covered in this chapter regarding policies and management procedure.

REFERENCES

Bishop, J. H. 1994. "The impact of previous training on productivity and wages." In *Training and the private sector: International comparisons*, edited by L. Lynch, 172–174. Chicago: University of Chicago Press.

BK Forensics. 2011. Twister Box. www.bkforensics.com/Twister_box.html (accessed September 18, 2011).

Cetina, I., and N. Mihail. 2007. Evaluation of the risk and of the opportunities in launching new banking services. *Theoretical and Applied Economics* 9(514): 47–52.

Cost Central. 2011. McAfee USB Encrypted BIO. www.costcentral.com/proddetail/McAfee_Encrypted_USB_ Bio/USBBI0216GBMFA/11067579/pricegrabber/ (accessed September 21, 2011).

Dell, Inc. 2011. Desktops and workstation computers for business. www.dell.com/us/business/p/desktops-n-workstations?~ck=mn (accessed September 18, 2011).

Digital Intelligence. 2011. Freddie. www.digitalintelligence.com/products/freddie/ (accessed September 18, 2011).

Grobler, C., and B. Louwrens. 2006. *Digital forensics: A multi-dimensional discipline.* http://icsa.cs.up.ac.za/issa/2006/Proceedings/Research/62_Paper.pdf (accessed April 19, 2012).

Guidance Software. 2011. Course offerings. www.guidancesoftware.com/computer-forensics-training-courses.htm (accessed September 27, 2011).

IAAI. 1994. Is your lab giving you proper results? *Fire and Arson Investigator* 45(2):39.

InfoSec Institute. 2011. Sales department. Electronic Mail received September 28, 2011.

Kerzner, H. 2004. *Advanced project management: Best practices on implementation, 2nd ed.* Hoboken, NJ: John Wiley & Sons.

Nelson B., A. Phillips, F. Enfinger, and C. Steuart. 2005. *Guide to computer forensics and investigations, Second Edition.* Toronto: Thompson Publishing.

New Egg Electronics. 2011. www.newegg.com (accessed September 28, 2011).

Purchasing. Personal interview with purchasing department of bank under study, September 18, 2011.

Rowlingson, R. 2004. A ten-step process for forensic readiness. *The International Journal of Digital Evidence* (Winter):2.

WiebeTech. 2011. Wiebetech: Forensic Field Kits. www.wiebetech.com/products/forensicffk.php (accessed September 18, 2011).

Wiles, J., and A. Reyes 2007. *The best damn cybercrime and digital forensics book period.* Burlington, MA: Syngress Publishing.

CHAPTER REVIEW ANSWERS

This section contains answers for the review questions at the end of each chapter. Notice that it does not include those for Chapter Exercises. The Chapter Exercises were designed in such a manner that each person performing the exercise is likely to get different results than another person doing the same exercise. Expecting anything other than that would be akin to expecting every forensic investigation to uncover exactly the same data. Your instructor can assist you in determining how well you did in the exercises.

CHAPTER 1

1. Answers should include several areas of concern. Different file formats use different cluster sizes, which in turn lead to varying potentials for the amount of slack space. Also, each file system has its own way of dealing with file deletion. How files are tracked in the file system is important as well.

2. Looking for various text strings on the disk can help locate the folders and files that host those strings. Utilities such as GREP and strings allow you to find strings such as "Priscilla" or "Georgia." Also, a search for industry-specific terms or common phases used in pornographic literature can help.

3. When a file is deleted, the data is not immediately erased from the surface of the drive. Until that disk space is reused, the data can be recovered.

4. Slack space is unused data bits in a cluster. Unallocated space is any drive space not specifically assigned to a file. Either space can potentially hold residual data from files that were once store in those locations.

5. Data carving is the practice of extracting files from unallocated space. It works by finding a common file header and copying all data between the header and the end-of-file marking used by the type of file identified in the header.

CHAPTER 2

1. The First Amendment protects a citizen's right of free speech. A Web site operator can sue to protect sources of information and prevent the seizure of files as part of their "freedom of the press" liberties. The Fourth Amendment protects us all from unreasonable search and seizure. This is the constitutional right most frequently invoked. The Fifth Amendment prohibits the government from forcing a person to incriminate their own self. Giving up passwords and allowing access to encrypted information is frequently cited as a violation of the Fifth Amendment.

2. Constitutional protections only apply to government activities or those authorized by the government. A private citizen does not violate a person's constitutional rights even if the search performed is illegal. There may be civil issues involved, but not constitutional issues.

3. When the owner of the nightclub contracts with another entity to perform services, the owner assumes responsibility for the entity's behavior while in the owner's employ. The courts consider that the nightclub owner is obligated to know what goes on within the confines of the business. The building owner, on the other hand, is merely leasing residency rights to the nightclub owner. The lessor is not expected to monitor the behavior of the lessee.

4. Hearsay is the act of relaying something that you heard, and not something that you saw. There is no way of confirming the veracity of a rumor. So if you testify that Johnnie told you he saw Jimmy rob the liquor store, you are relying on hearsay evidence. If you testify that you *saw* Jimmy rob the liquor store, you are giving eyewitness testimony. An expert witness, on the other hand, is being asked to give an expert opinion based on what he or she is able to observe about the events that occurred. An expert witness is not expected to have been present at the scene, but is expected to be able to provide an analysis of evidence collected at the scene.

5. Trick question. The Constitution does not guarantee a right to privacy. That is why there has been so much legislation passed that protects an individual's privacy in a variety of circumstances.

CHAPTER 3

1. If you have been ordered to appear in court and present evidence or give testimony, you are responding to a subpoena.

2. A subpoena can be *quashed* if the recipient can demonstrate that the terms of the subpoena are unreasonable and impose undue hardship in order to comply.

3. A closed container receives special treatment in the eyes of the law. If a container is closed, the courts make the assumption that the owner has a reasonable expectation of privacy. A computer system is considered to be like a sealed box containing file folders. You have to "open" the box (by starting it up, logging in, and searching the folders) to get to the enclosed information. A computer or any other sealed box can be confiscated incident to arrest. But in order to search the files, a warrant must be obtained.

4. Particularity comes in the form of "particularity of place" and "particularity of items to be seized." Both must be met to fulfill the terms of a warrant. The warrant must state exactly where the search will occur and what evidence is being sought. Therefore, a warrant ordering the search and seizure of all computer devices at 1 Main Street owned by Billy Bob Smith would be considered valid. If the executor of the warrant seizes a computer from Billy Bob's car, that is an unconstitutional seizure, because the car was not specified in the warrant.

5. A sneak and peek warrant allows the executor to perform the actions specified by the warrant and then notify the suspect after the fact.

CHAPTER 4

1. The Privacy Act of 1974 specified what kind of information could be collected by government agencies, how that information could be used, and who had the right to view it. It added protections to individuals by setting up a process by which the individual had the right to view records and request that errors be corrected. Any organization collecting and maintaining private information was responsible for insuring the reliability of information they disseminated.

2. Financial data, medical information, and educational information all are maintained by organizations and/or agencies that were not necessarily covered under the Privacy and Electronic Communications Act. By passing separate legislation, the laws became more granular in regards to the type of information they protected and the rights that individuals had to safeguard their information.

3. There are a couple of significant differences between civil litigation and criminal prosecution. The most significant difference lies in whether or not the individuals involved enjoy constitutional protection. Two nongovernment entities duking it out over a patent infringement case will only be protected by acts of legislation and not constitutional enforcement. The second difference is that civil litigation is covered under the Federal Rules of Civil Procedure, while a criminal investigation is covered under the Federal Rules of Evidence. There are different rules regarding what information is allowable, how information can be obtained, and whether or not certain information is protected by law.

4. HIPPA covers the health and insurance industries. FERPA covers educational institutions. Each piece of legislation defines how information can be shared by the entities covered and what the rules for obtaining that information are.

5. Attorney/client privileges protect communications between a person and his lawyer. Such communications cannot be entered as evidence in court. The same applies to doctor/patient privileges. Work/product dictates that certain documents that are prepared in anticipation of legal action can be protected from a discovery motion. Lastly, intellectual property *may* be protected if ordered so by the court. Additionally, pretrial negotiations may limit exposure to intellectual property.

CHAPTER 5

1. The three elements of admissibility are *relevance, authenticity,* and *competence.* The information presented must be directly related to the case, it must be proven to be accurate and untainted, and it must prove to be unrestrained by statutory or constitutional limitations. Any piece of evidence that cannot meet all three of these requirements will be suppressed.

2. The *exclusionary rule* relates to the previous question. If evidence cannot meet all three elements of admissibility, it must be excluded from proceedings. If the evidence presented to the court is determined to be inadmissible,

and it is excluded, the judge may issue an adverse ruling against the party that presented the evidence.

3. Under the plain view doctrine, if during the course of a legal search, evidence that is not defined in the original warrant is found in a place clearly visible to the naked eye and is easily identifiable as evidence, then it can be legally collected and used. When searching for files on a computer, it is very common to find files that suggest that another crime other than the one under investigation has been committed. If these files are found during a legal search, they can be included as evidence. To start a completely different search without a warrant, based on finding the first file, would *not* be legal, and the subsequent files found are likely to be excluded.

4. As discussed in the previous chapter, a warrant must define precisely what is being sought and where the investigators are allowed to search. If the particularity requirements are not fulfilled, then the exclusionary rule kicks in and the evidence is suppressed.

5. Any search performed by a private citizen is not covered by the Constitution. This includes actions by vigilante groups. The search may be illegal in other regards, but it is not unconstitutional.

CHAPTER 6

1. Locard states that everything that touches a crime scene leaves something behind and that everything that leaves a crime scene takes something with it. All digital information leaves some sort of footprint behind. Deleted files leave behind information in the file system or the registry. Rootkits that run generally have some entry in the registry that they use to launch them. Remote connections can potentially leave behind logs of those connections.

2. Class characteristics of a house would include such information as what type of architecture it represents (Victorian, Tudor, Colonial, etc.) or whether it is a duplex or a single-family home. Individual characteristics would include what color it is, how much land it sits on, whether it is a tiled or shingled roof, what kind of porch it has, and so forth.

3. A digital document has metadata that may include information such as who the original author is, who edited it, creation and modification dates, and so forth. It also has associated system information tied to it, such as file system metadata, registry details, and so forth. The physical document can be examined for fingerprints, it can possibly retain DNA from people who

handled the document, or it can be studied to see if there are any unique characteristics that link it to a specific printer.

4. A lot can happen during the transportation of evidence. It can get lost or stolen. The package may pass through a heavy magnetic field, corrupting its contents. Or a cell phone not properly protected might have its contents altered remotely by someone dialing in. The chain of custody should define how the item was transported. If there is no accountability for the item during transport, the chain of custody can be challenged.

5. The Faraday box blocks electromagnetic radiation. Blocking incoming signals prevents a communications device from making a connection with a device seized as evidence. Nobody can call in and activate a logic bomb that wipes the contents before you have a chance to examine it.

CHAPTER 7

1. There is a high potential that material of evidentiary value can be found in RAM, in temporary files, and in log files that are constantly overwritten. Other information, such as routing tables, are rewritten constantly. The order of volatility suggests what sequence to take when capturing data from a suspect machine.

2. Items that can always be found in RAM include running processes, open ports, and routing tables. It shows what user is logged in at the time of capture. Potentially there could be passwords stored in plain text in RAM if used recently.

3. Some memory capture tools capture memory cache addresses from devices such as hard disks and controller cards in addition to live RAM. This is stored as part of the memory file.

4. The footprint is a term for how much space a running process takes in memory. If an executable file requires 104KB to run, then it has a 104KB footprint. Running the utilities required to capture RAM requires that the executable be run on the host, so its footprint exists in host memory and not the investigator's machine. In order to make room for the executable, the target OS may move information of evidentiary value from live memory to the swap file.

5. Write-protection devices prevent the process of capturing the forensic image from making any changes to the device being captured. Conventional OS processes, such as Copy or Move, will make changes to the file system and to the metadata of the files themselves. This is not acceptable when making a forensic image.

CHAPTER 8

1. The file system controls how files are stored on the hard disk, what metadata is used to identify files, and how those files are indexed. Additionally, different operating systems take unique approaches to deleting files. Therefore, the target OS not only determines the likelihood of recovering data, it dictates the methods and tools that you use in your approach.

2. Any tool that compares file hashes to the KFF database, such as The Sleuth Kit or any of the other suites, can help identify known pornographic files. String search tools, such as strings or GREP, can let you do keyword searches for specific names of people or states. In order to locate deleted files, a data carving utility can locate header and EOF markers for known file formats.

3. Most file systems do not wipe data from the hard disk when the user elects to erase a file. Instead, the space is merely reallocated for future use. The raw data continues to exist on the surface of the medium.

4. Slack space is disk area that is part of an allocated cluster or partition that cannot be used because the file system cannot directly address it for new data. In file slack, this is because the cluster is occupied by a file that does not use the entire cluster. The space it doesn't use is slack. In a partition, it is space that exists between multiple partitions on a disk. Unallocated space is space that is available to the file system but not yet assigned to a specific file—or no longer assigned to a file, in the case of a deleted file. Just because this space isn't addressed by a file system does not mean that it can't hold data.

5. Utilities that can directly access disk space can copy unallocated space as a file. Additionally, a disk image is a single file that holds the entire contents of the target disk, including unallocated space. Either way, data carving utilities can be used to rebuild files or disk editors can be used to copy data from unallocated space into a file that can be read by the system.

CHAPTER 9

1. The three forms of metadata are *system metadata, substantive metadata,* and *embedded metadata.* System metadata is part of the OS file system and tells you when a file was created and on what clusters it was located. Even after a file is completely wiped, the MFT files keep a record of that entry for a long time—until such point as the file system needs to purge records to make room for new entries. MAC data is derived from this source. Substantive metadata and embedded metadata are usually created by the application that

generates the file. From this information you can track version histories, user IDs of people who edited the document, and even conflicts in MAC information.

2. There really isn't much of a difference between headers and magic numbers. Both are useful in identifying what kind of file follows. A key difference is that magic numbers are generally a fixed length, whereas file headers vary widely in length.

3. MAC information is easily modified by the user. Many utilities can be downloaded off the Internet for this purpose. Additionally, a large number of file system activities, such as Copy and Move, alter MAC information in different ways. Investigators should always take care to corroborate MAC information in a file in other ways, such as system logs.

4. Word stores both substantive and embedded metadata. This includes information about the user who created the file and any user who edited it. You can see when a file was last saved or when it was last printed. If the "last printed" date falls before the Create date on the file, you know that the MAC data has been modified somewhere along the line. If other user information exists in the substantive metadata, then you know that the possibility exists that the file was modified, copied, or printed.

5. The list of temporary files isn't quite infinite, but it is certainly very long. The critical ones include autosave files, automatic backups, temporary Internet files, history files, and cache files created by applications. Many times, a document that was deleted leaves behind autosaves or backup files. These can be used to show what the contents of the file were at the time the backup was made. Such information proves that the document existed and what type of information it contained. It also may prove whether or not the document was edited somewhere along the line.

CHAPTER 10

1. The standard headers present in any e-mail message, regardless of client, are TO, FROM, SUBJECT, and DATE. While the content to be expected of any one of these headers should be self-explanatory, the problem is that there are numerous utilities that can falsify any of this information. The TO data can be harvested from e-mail servers and Web sites and autofilled into the header field. Virtually any mass-mailing software application allows the originator to fill the FROM field with any data that is desired. The subject is

a good search field, but if the subject line says RE: Your Resume and the contents of the e-mail are all about male-enhancement drugs, it isn't of much use. The DATE field, as in the FROM field, can be made to say anything the sender wishes.

2. Every e-mail contains information about every relay server it encountered. So even if the originating IP address is forged, the first SMTP server to relay it will most likely be authentic. This at least gives you the IP of the ISP.

3. Today's e-mail clients store much more than just messages. They contain address books, store the attachments that accompanied the original messages, and hold a lot of information about e-mail traffic. Additionally, there might be calendars and notes utilities built into the client that can provide a great deal of information. To extract this information, you need to know first of all where the files are held and what their default names are. Second, you need to have a utility that can extract and analyze these files unless you can mount the **information store** on a machine with the same client.

4. **Precision** is the ratio of true positives to false positives in a search. A search that yields 40 false positives for every 100 "hits" on a search only has a precision ratio of 60%. **Recall** is the percentage of actual documents retrieved, compared to the number that actually exists. The latter is very difficult to measure. If 100 documents related to the "Barney's Friends" search are turned up, yet 200 actual documents exist, you have a recall rate of 50%.

5. Nslookup will resolve a host name to an IP address, or vice versa. WHOIS will tell you a great deal of information about any machine or IP address registered in its database.

CHAPTER 11

1. Cookies store information about a Web site that has been visited through a particular browser. If the cookie exists, then the site was visited. It is true that the site may have been visited inadvertently, as through a redirect (pop-up) or clicking on a link by accident. But the site was visited.

2. The VisitType field tells you if a site was reached by a redirect.

3. A common defense for people who have been discovered with contraband on their machine is, "I had no idea that was there!" Unless the prosecution can prove otherwise, there remains a reasonable doubt. A site may show up in their browser history as a result of a redirect, or a guest in their home may have used their machine for nefarious purposes. By showing that a person

took a specific activity against a file, such as moving it, copying it, or deleting it, then there is evidence that the person knew the file was there to begin with.

4. Pop-up bombs occur when a user visits a Web site, which then instantly redirects the browser to multiple sites that the person probably has never even heard of. If a person under investigation actually was the victim of a pop-up bomb, it could appear that he or she visited a number of questionable sites during a single browser session.

5. Server log files will track a user's session from the beginning, when they first log on, until the moment they log off. These files can tell you what sites they logged onto, how long they were on each site, and how many levels deep into a Web site they browsed. Times and dates of each event are logged, so server logs can be used to generate a time line. They also log authentication failures. If a person is trying to hack into a site or a remote machine, it will appear as multiple authentication failures.

CHAPTER 12

1. Without knowing a specific time frame in which to search for evidence, network forensics makes the needle even smaller in a much larger haystack. Network logs can only get so large before they are overwritten. Most cautious network administrators schedule routine archival of log files so that the information is saved before it is overwritten. Knowing when an event occurred greatly reduces the complexity of the search. It can also limit the number of users who can be considered suspects. A user who was in his fishing boat drowning worms was probably not guilty of hacking the payroll files. Unless his laptop has a cellular connection.

2. A keylogger collects every strike of every key into a file. While it is not super-easy to analyze, it is not overly complicated either. A user who types a password into the system while a keylogger was enabled has just told you the password.

3. Standard mode filters out any packets not intended for the IP address configured onto the interface. Promiscuous mode processes everything, whether intended for that address or not.

4. A node-to-node communication will let you analyze traffic between two specific hosts, whereas node-to-any analyzes all traffic from a particular node, regardless of its target. Node-to-node allows you to analyze specific conversations, whereas node-to-any allows you to analyze patterns, habits, and so forth.

5. Router and switch information can corroborate information found in other sources. For example, the MAC data from a file might indicate that it was created on May 3 at 9:03:22AM. If the suspect is being investigated for pilfering information and you can demonstrate that this file existed on a secure location and that the user was logged on at that time, you corroborate that the file was moved at that time. Connection logs tell you what network connections were made from that user's host device during that time frame, so you can demonstrate that a network connection to the secure file was made during that time frame. While circumstantial, it is still convincing evidence that the suspect indeed copied the file from that location.

CHAPTER 13

1. The three basic structures of cloud computing are Software as a Service (SaaS), Platform as a Service (PaaS), and Infrastructure as a Service (IaaS). SaaS is like installing a complex application on a computer, except that the computer is really a Web interface and all of the processing, filing, and indexing are done by the vendor. IaaS steps up to the level where an entire organization's network exists remotely. Regardless of where an employee is located, they can log into the cloud network and work as if they were at a desk at work, with all applications at their disposal. PaaS is similar to IaaS, except that with PaaS, the organization has no control over how applications are installed onto their platform. The vendor chooses OS, programming language, and everything.

2. If a warrant only defines the computers owned by the suspect identified in the warrant, and that person employs cloud computing, then the warrant will allow you to seize all of their hardware, but the data and applications won't be on that hardware, so you have seized nothing of value. A warrant must be issued against the service provider, ordering them to turn over all virtual machines and data stores contracted by the suspect.

3. With virtualization, a single physical computer (or a cluster of networked servers acting as a single entity) hosts an application that allows a large number of "pretend" machines to be configured. Each one of these configured machines have their own I/O, their own storage, their own virtual network cards, and their own computer names. These virtual machines can be servers, or they can be workstations. They can even be virtual switches and virtual routers, creating virtual networks. In a forensic investigation, only the machines identified in a warrant or subpoena may be targeted. Other machines that exist on the same server must be ignored.

4. A document imaging system stores all of the actual documents in large cabinet files with archaic names. The master database files and the index files tell the application how to locate actual documents and pages within documents. Without them a CAB file is very difficult to break down.

5. Virtual machines exist as "instances" on a server. That instance can be copied as an image file the same way a disk from a regular computer can be imaged. Once that image has been captured, it is analyzed the same as any other disk image.

CHAPTER 14

1. Triangulation is a process of calculating the location of a signal source by measuring the distance and direction from three separate known locations to the source of a signal. Draw a line from those three locations, and where the lines intersect, that is the source of the signal. Now an investigator knows where the device is (or was) at the time of transmission.

2. A PIN is a personal identification number. Therefore, a PIN number is a personal identification number number, which is grammatically incorrect, so you should never call it a "PIN number." The PIN is used as an authentication device to increase the security on a telephone or a bank card. A user types her PIN to gain access to her phone. If she types it incorrectly a certain number of times, the device is locked and nobody can get in. PUK is the *PIN unlock key*, which is a separate code that allows a user to unlock a device that has been disabled by incorrectly typing in a PIN a certain number of times.

3. Since cell phones are by definition network devices, it is possible for someone with the right tools and expertise to connect to the phone remotely and wipe it clean to prevent a forensics team from uncovering evidence. By keeping the phone off the network, this possibility is greatly reduced.

4. Without a Faraday bag, a phone can be taken off the network by removing the SIM card. Some phones also have a feature called *airplane mode* that takes the device off the network so that it does not interfere with the communications devices on an aircraft.

5. Two sets of circumstances would automatically lead to cell phone confiscation without a warrant. The first of these is a seizure at the time of an arrest. Courts have repeatedly supported law enforcement's right to conduct search and seizure incident to arrest. The second is if the phone is in plain sight and it is evident from on the screen that the device was used in a suspicious manner.

CHAPTER 15

1. The forms of antiforensics are artifact destruction, data hiding, trail obfuscation, and attacks against forensic tools. Artifact destruction is the intentional deletion of files, erasure of information within files, or deletion of registry entries. Such activity constitutes antiforensics. Data hiding is finding obscure places to put information, such as in registry entries, using slack space or unallocated space for file storage, and alternate data streams. Trail obfuscation would include activities such as registry editing or log file editing or deletion. Attacks against forensic tools would include any activity that is intended to prevent an investigator's arsenal from detecting evidence or malicious activity.

2. In the registry, the *most recently used* (MRU) lists identify the last several files that were opened by a particular user or application. There is a large number of MRU entries in the registry, and the same event can be recorded in more than one. For example, a user has a file that appears in the KFF registry, but deletes it and subsequently uses a DoD wipe utility to permanently erase it. The fact that the MRU shows that file name as a recently opened file indicates that it once existed on the system and it may be possible from other registry entries to connect the file to a specific user. Additionally, applications that are uninstalled from a system do not necessary remove their hives from the registry. A hive in the registry for a known hacking tool can demonstrate that the program once existed, but was uninstalled.

3. Temporary files include automatic backup files, work files, and autosave files. There are also various log files generated by programs. Many times, a document that was deleted leaves behind autosaves or backup files. These can be used to show what the contents of the file were at the time the backup was made. Such information proves that the document existed and what type of information it contained. It also may prove whether or not the document was edited somewhere along the line.

4. Expandable String Value keys can store large amounts of text. Multistring value keys can store information such as telephone numbers or text.

5. An alternate data stream is a virtual link between two files. The host file is the one seen by the operating system. The alternate stream points to another file that exists inside of the host file, but is not actually a part of it. It exists as an attribute of the host file. Since the ADS file does not exist as part of the file system, it does not appear in Windows Explorer or any

other file system utility. The Streams utility from SysInternals detects alternate data streams.

CHAPTER 16

1. Rule 26f specifies that both parties in any civil action will meet prior to trial and discuss the nature of the claim. Efforts will be made to settle out of court, but if court action is inevitable, a discovery plan will be discussed and put into place. Any witnesses to be called will be identified and revealed to the other party.

2. As soon as there is any indication that litigation is on the horizon, a litigation hold should be issued. Anybody in the organization with access to relevant information should be advised and the IT staff should immediately be alerted to cease any automatic file purging related to document retention policies that might be in effect.

3. There are two clearly evident forms of spoliation. First, any destruction of a document that violates any statute would be considered spoliation, even if there isn't pending litigation. Second, any data destroyed in the face of pending litigation can be considered spoliation even if it occurs prior to a litigation hold order. If opposing counsel can demonstrate that the spoiling party knew they were about to be sued and got rid of all the incriminating evidence in advance, the court can find them guilty of spoliation.

4. Near-line data is any information that can be readily accessed through existing systems, even if not directly connected to a system being searched. This is in contrast to online data that exists on the system. Online data would include information stored on the hard drive. Near-line data is information that is easily accessed but not stored on the computer. This would include media such as CD-ROMs, flash drives, and external hard disks. Inaccessible data is information that can only be extracted through specialized processes, such as deleted files and encrypted tape backup files. Offline storage is that middle ground where the data is easy enough to get, but in a location that might provide challenges. This would include Internet locations (cloud storage, etc.), SAN or NAS volumes, and so forth.

5. The review of data requires that numerous individuals (most of them highly paid individuals such as lawyers and accountants) go over evidence one file at a time and identify which ones are evidence and which ones are protected. While most of the other processes are somewhat automated, this step is completely manual and very time consuming.

CHAPTER 17

1. The preparation phase contains a variety of elements, not all of which are case specific. Preparation includes assembling and training your team, installing and configuring your hardware and software, testing tools, and generating policies. Having the right personnel, hardware, and software determines your overall capabilities. In terms of specific cases, preparation would include gathering the necessary tools for the assignment, having sufficient fresh media for storing images, and having the necessary items for transporting evidentiary materials. Making sure that you have the right people fully available for the duration of the job is a critical aspect of preparation

2. Treat triage just as you would if it were a battlefield. Determine as quickly as possible if any of the threats would have an impact on someone's health or life. This sounds exaggerated, but in fact, if you are dealing with medical records, that may be more realistic than you suppose. Next, decide if there are any actions that must be taken to protect data or infrastructure. Personal and financial data must be secured.

3. Crime scene preservation would include securing and protecting any devices or media that could contain evidence. Don't let anything "get away," either through malfeasance or negligence. Survey the scene to determine if there is anything of value that is not readily apparent to the naked eye and be VERY careful that you do not trample on evidence that other teams might need for their aspect of an investigation. Document everything you see, everything you touch, everything you examine, and everything you take. Photograph everything and take careful notes. Search the area carefully for hidden evidence (such as CDs, flash drives, and so forth). Lastly, try to reconstruct what happened.

4. Evidence handling is crucial to any investigation. If opposing counsel can demonstrate that there was even a miniscule possibility that evidence could have been tampered with, corrupted, or altered in any way, they can have that evidence disallowed. The chain of custody is a critical document for demonstrating that evidence was properly cared for as long as it was in your possession.

5. The final report will contain copies of all documents requesting the investigation, copies of authorizations to proceed, warrants, and subpoenas. Inventories of all items touched by the team must be provided, along with a chain of custody report that includes each of those items. All case logs and

notes generated by the team are included. All photographs made throughout the investigation, and lastly, the conclusions made by the investigation, must be provided.

CHAPTER 18

1. Abstraction layers represent the varying layers of complexity that code assumes as it moves from one level of the system down to the final processor core. What starts out as a complex human-readable language is broken down, level by level, until it can eventually be represented by a long series of on-off switches. Forensic tools take advantage of abstraction layers to find raw data at the hardware level and bring it back to the humanly readable level. A lossless layer makes no changes whatsoever to data as it moves from one layer to the next. A lossy layer does a degree of interpretation as it moves up or down the chain.

2. The four standards are accuracy, verification capability, consistency, and usability. Without accuracy and consistency, a tool is totally useless. You cannot trust the results. Without verification capability, you can't really tell if you have accuracy or consistency, so the tool continues to be totally useless. Lack of usability doesn't make it totally useless. It simply means you need someone with a huge amount of training to use it.

3. Event viewer is a system level log generator that collects several different logs. The three most critical to the investigator are the System, Application, and Security logs. From these logs, you can tell when a particular user was logged onto the machine. You can see failed authentication attempts, and you can track the number of times data was copied to removable storage. Additionally, you can see when an application was installed or uninstalled from the system.

4. Virtually all of the commercial forensic suites have already been tested for accuracy and reliability. Since they are readily available to anyone who has the money to buy them, their verification capacity cannot readily be challenged. Also, all of them provide some level of training, ranging from free support to paid formal classroom sessions. This greatly enhances the usability rating for a commercial suite. Add the fact that most of them have been tested by NIST, and there is a lot on the plus side to buying a commercial suite.

5. Unless you use a write-protect device or can demonstrate that you write-protected the device through a software setting, you cannot demonstrate beyond a shadow of a doubt that critical data on the system was not overwritten.

CHAPTER 19

1. A basic system, at the very minimum, requires a system board, a CPU, RAM, a video adapter (which may be integrated onto the system board), and an enclosure. A keyboard and mouse are necessary to control the computer. A forensic workstation needs all of the above, but with more horsepower. It needs as much processor power as you can throw at it, and as much RAM as you can install. It also needs substantially more sophisticated I/O. Write-protect devices are needed for memory cards, hard disks, and so forth. Hot-swap bays for hard disks aren't required, but they certainly make life easier to live for the analyst.

2. The amount of onboard L1 and L2 cache greatly affect speed. A significant performance boost is gained by increasing the speed and width of the front side bus.

3. Since the system board dictates what kind of memory is supported, the memory sticks must be chosen based on what that board supports. In the event that a board supports either error correction code memory or not, it should be remembered that ECC tends to slightly degrade performance. The highest bus speed that the chosen CPU and board support should be selected. If multichannel RAM is supported, then as many channels as possible, using as much memory per channel as possible, should be configured.

4. Hot-swap bays allow a user to add and remove hard disks on the fly without shutting down the system. Since a forensic analyst is always looking at different disk drives, this is a valuable addition.

5. 32-bit operating systems do not support as much RAM as do 64-bit systems. Additionally, because twice as much data is transferred on each clock cycle of the CPU, 64-bit systems perform faster. However, a 64-bit OS requires a 64-bit processor, chipset, and so forth. So installing a 64-bit OS onto a 32-bit system won't work. You can install a 32-bit OS onto a 64-bit system with no problem. If you need a 32-bit OS for any reason, it would be good to config-ure a 64-bit system to dual-boot with a 32-bit system on a 64-bit machine.

CHAPTER 20

1. The three areas that should be covered by a digital forensics exam include admissibility of evidence, standards and certifications, and analysis and preser-vation. Certification programs can be either vendor neutral or vendor specific.

2. GIAC offers the Certified Forensic Examiner and the Certified Forensic Analyst certifications. The GCFE is considered the "entry-level" exam and is targeted at people who are new to the field. The GCFA requires significantly more expertise in order to pass and is targeted at the seasoned professional

3. Hard skills are generally technical in nature. Fine-tuned skills, such as an ability to analyze memory, an advanced knowledge of operating system structure, and so forth, are considered hard skills. Soft skills are often the ones that a person develops throughout life. Such skills would include an ability to communicate well, good observation skills, and such.

4. The ENCE is the Guidance Certified Examiner certification. It tests a candidate's ability to use Encase software in a general forensic examination. The ENCEP is the Certified eDiscovery Practitioner. As the name implies, it is targeted at those whose primary job entails fulfilling discovery motions in legal cases.

5. Every state has its own set of regulations that dictate whether a license to practice digital forensics is required. Some do not have any such requirement at all. Of those that do, some of them make the licensing requirement part of their overall requirements for licensing private investigators. Some states require that you pass exams; some do not. To find out what your state's requirements are, contact your state's attorney general's office and ask for guidance.

CHAPTER 21

1. Building an in-house forensics department has several advantages. For one thing, it gives you complete control over the process. You control your own security, and you pick your own people. It is not necessary to entrust sensitive and potentially damaging information to outside parties. On the other hand, the costs can be prohibitive for many smaller organizations.

2. For the most part, "one-time" costs are the expenses you incur in the process of creating a new business or department. Such expenses would include real estate development, building improvements, equipment purchases, and so forth. Recurring costs are those that that must be paid out on a regular basis. Salaries, rent, loan payments, insurance premiums, and so forth all qualify as recurring costs. However, some of the one-time costs are really one time. Computer systems will require regular upgrades, and it is likely that training costs will reappear from time to time.

3. There should be a policy manual that defines employee expectations. Hiring policies and training policies would fall into this category. Procedurally, there should be strict policies defined for data retention, naming standards, and documentation procedures.

4. Most organizations will not be able to justify maintaining a professional level of service and training for every form of digital investigation that exists. Occasionally, it might be necessary to go outside the organization for things like extracting data from fried hard disks, legal consultations, or specific forms of data acquisition. For example, not everyone will have a telephone analyst or a skilled memory analyst. It is a good idea to know where to hire those services out when necessary.

5. One way to show the value of an in-house department is to "bill" other departments for services based on net value. That way you're moving the cost basis from one department to another without cash actually changing hands. At the end of the year, you prepare an annual report showing what your services would have cost the organization had they been outsourced.

SAMPLE FORMS

The following are examples of forms you might use when conducting an investigation. The warrant sample was provided by the U.S. District Court of Vermont and is in the public domain. Other forms have been provided by other legal organizations and appear with their permission.

SAMPLE SEARCH WARRANT

AO 93 (Rev. 12/09) Search and Seizure Warrant

UNITED STATES DISTRICT COURT
for the

In the Matter of the Search of   )
(Briefly describe the property to be searched   )
or identify the person by name and address)   )   Case No.
)
)
)

SEARCH AND SEIZURE WARRANT

To: Any authorized law enforcement officer

An application by a federal law enforcement officer or an attorney for the government requests the search of the following person or property located in the _____ District of _____
(identify the person or describe the property to be searched and give its location):

The person or property to be searched, described above, is believed to conceal *(identify the person or describe the property to be seized)*:

I find that the affidavit(s), or any recorded testimony, establish probable cause to search and seize the person or property.

YOU ARE COMMANDED to execute this warrant on or before _____
                                                                    (not to exceed 14 days)

☐ in the daytime 6:00 a.m. to 10 p.m.   ☐ at any time in the day or night as I find reasonable cause has been established.

Unless delayed notice is authorized below, you must give a copy of the warrant and a receipt for the property taken to the person from whom, or from whose premises, the property was taken, or leave the copy and receipt at the place where the property was taken.

The officer executing this warrant, or an officer present during the execution of the warrant, must prepare an inventory as required by law and promptly return this warrant and inventory to United States Magistrate Judge

_____ .
                    (name)

☐ I find that immediate notification may have an adverse result listed in 18 U.S.C. § 2705 (except for delay of trial), and authorize the officer executing this warrant to delay notice to the person who, or whose property, will be searched or seized *(check the appropriate box)* ☐ for _____ days *(not to exceed 30)*.
                                     ☐ until, the facts justifying, the later specific date of _____ .

Date and time issued: _____   _____
                                                                    Judge's signature

City and state: _____   _____
                                                              Printed name and title

SAMPLE SUBPOENA

AO 88B (Rev. 06/09) Subpoena to Produce Documents, Information, or Objects or to Permit Inspection of Premises in a Civil Action

UNITED STATES DISTRICT COURT
for the

	)	
_____	)	
Plaintiff	)	
v.	)	Civil Action No.
	)	
_____	)	(If the action is pending in another district, state where:
Defendant	)	
	)	)

**SUBPOENA TO PRODUCE DOCUMENTS, INFORMATION, OR OBJECTS
OR TO PERMIT INSPECTION OF PREMISES IN A CIVIL ACTION**

To:

☐ *Production:* **YOU ARE COMMANDED** to produce at the time, date, and place set forth below the following documents, electronically stored information, or objects, and permit their inspection, copying, testing, or sampling of the material:

Place:	Date and Time:

☐ *Inspection of Premises:* **YOU ARE COMMANDED** to permit entry onto the designated premises, land, or other property possessed or controlled by you at the time, date, and location set forth below, so that the requesting party may inspect, measure, survey, photograph, test, or sample the property or any designated object or operation on it.

Place:	Date and Time:

The provisions of Fed. R. Civ. P. 45(c), relating to your protection as a person subject to a subpoena, and Rule 45 (d) and (e), relating to your duty to respond to this subpoena and the potential consequences of not doing so, are attached.

Date: _____

CLERK OF COURT		
	OR	
_____		_____
Signature of Clerk or Deputy Clerk		*Attorney's signature*

The name, address, e-mail, and telephone number of the attorney representing *(name of party)* _____
_____ , who issues or requests this subpoena, are:

SAMPLE CASE LOG

Independent Forensic Examiners, LTD

22 Liability Driven
Sometown, Vermont 05999
(802) 555-2851
Date: _____

Digital Forensic Examiner Processing Log

Examiner:	
Internal Case Number:	
External Case Number:	
Requesting Agency:	
Requesting Officer:	
Person Hours Engaged:	

Case Received:	Date:		Time:	
Case Approved:	Date:		Time:	
Report Completed:	Date:		Time:	
Case Completed:	Date:		Time:	

System Information

Device	Serial Number	F/W ver.	Sys. Date	Sys. Time	Act. Date	Act. Time	CPU	RAM	OS

BOOT ORDER:
BASE CONFIGURATION:

Media Information

Type	Capacity	Brand	Model	S/N	Interface	Obtained from

Activity Log: Note date and time of each activity. Describe in detail tools and procedures used in each procedure, along with the purpose of the procedure.

SAMPLE CHAIN OF CUSTODY

Chain of Custody Record

Report To:
Name:
Address:

Phone: Fax:
PO#:

IFE Information:

Case ID:
Initiated by:

INDEPENDENT FORENSIC EXAMINERS LTD.
14 LIABILITY DRIVE
ANYTOWN, USA 02999

Warrant #	Issued by:	te of Acquisti	Project or Subject Reference	Primary Investigator	Billing Code

Subject Information
Name
Street Address
City
State

Evidence Information		Collected			Purpose	ID	Returned			Actions Taken
Evidence ID	Evidence Description	Date	Time	by:		Presented	Time	Date	Reason	

HARD
INDEPENDENT FORENSISC EXAMINERS LTD
14 LIABILITY DRIVEN
ANYTOWN, USA 02999
CASE:_____

PHYSICAL DISK INFORMATION

EVIDENCE ID:		INVESTIGATOR ID:	
MANUFACTURER:		RATED CAPACITY:	
MAKE:		VOLUME LABEL:	
MODEL:		NO. PARTITIONS:	
SERIAL NUMBER:		PARTITION LABEL 1:	
FIRMWARE VERSION:		PARTITION LABEL 2:	
NO. CYLINDERS:		PARTITION LABEL 3:	
NO. SECTORS:		JUMPER SETTINGS:	

FORENSIC IMAGING DATA

DATE INITIATED:		DATE COMPLETED:	
IMAGE CREATED:		WRITE BLOCKER USED:	
IMAGING SOFTWARE USED:		FORENSIC IMAGE ID:	
HASH OF ORIGINAL:		WORKING COPY ID:	
HASH OF FORENSIC IMAGE:		MEDIA USED FOR IMAGE:	
HASH OF WORKING COPY:		MEDIA USED FOR COPY:	
NO. CYLINDERS:		WORKING LOG FILENAME:	
NO. SECTORS:		EVIDENCE STORAGE:	

PROVIDE LEGIBLE PHOTOGRAPHS OF PHYSICAL DISK

DRIVE TOP DIGITAL FILE NAME:	
DRIVE BOTTOM DIGITAL FILE NAME:	
DRIVE I/O DIGITAL FILE NAME:	

GLOSSARY

Accessible Data: In a search for information during the process of *discovery*, accessible data is that information that resides on easily read drives or network locations.

Actual Authority: A tangible demonstration of the right to act as an agent for a principle. A power of attorney gives a person actual authority of another person's affairs.

Admissible or Admissibility: The ability of evidence or testimony to be entered into consideration in a court of law. Generally, this is based on the factors of relevance, credibility, and competence.

Affidavit: A written statement of facts, created under oath, by the person affirming that the facts took place exactly as reported. An affidavit must be administered by a person who has been granted the authority to do so by appropriate government agencies.

After Hours Warrant: A specific order issued by a judge that allows agents of the government to execute the order during times of the day that are not generally considered normal hours for the action.

Agent of the Government: Any person, whether directly employed by a government entity or not, who is acting on behalf of such an entity is considered to be an agent of the government.

Alternate Data Stream: A file attribute that exists in the Microsoft NTFS file system that redirects the file to other data on the system. That data may be another file, or it may be data that is concealed within the file.

Antiforensics: Concentrated efforts to prevent or hinder an investigator from finding information on a system.

Apparent Authority: A reasonable appearance of either being an agent for a principle or having the power to act on behalf of a principle, whether such authority exists or not. An example would be a person who drives up in a service van with the logo of the local electric company and says she is here to read the meter. The resident allows her to enter because she appears to have the authority to do so.

Audit: To keep a detailed record of certain events as configured into the agent that is monitoring the events.

Authenticate: To verify that a user is who she says she is. Typing in a user name and password is a method that network services use to authenticate a user.

Bates Numbering: A process of applying a unique identification number to each document extracted during the *discovery* process.

Boolean: A type of search or data type that includes only two possible values. The name is after the inventor of binary algebra, George Boole.

Breadth: The scope of a warrant must define the probable cause upon which the writ was executed. Evidentiary materials found that are not relevant to the defined probable cause are beyond the "breadth" of the order.

Case Log: A detailed record of every task completed, every action taken, and every piece of evidence analyzed in the course of an investigation.

Chain of Custody: A document that identifies every place that a piece of evidence has occupied, every person who has handled that evidence, and any actions that were taken against it. Chain of custody records the actual time and date of each event.

Civil Action: A court trial in which one party is accusing another party of some form of wrongdoing. The *defendant* in a civil action does not face jail time or pay a fine, but if found guilty, may be expected to pay the *plaintiff* damages in the amount stated in the judgment.

Closed Container: Under U.S. jurisprudence, any opaque object that can be used to store objects that is shut at the time of inspection is considered to be a closed container. Such an object is not subject to search without a warrant, even if reasonable cause has presented the opportunity to search surrounding premises.

CLSID: Content Class Identifier. A data field in a file structure, directly following the header, that specifies the type of data that is stored within the file.

Cluster: A grouping of *sectors* that provides the smallest unit of data readable by a file system after the disk has been formatted.

Clusters: Two or more *sectors* on a hard disk that act as the smallest data unit read by the disk control.

Competent or Competence: Any evidence or testimony that is neither *prejudicial* or limited by statutory or constitutional constraints. In other words, the information will not unfairly sway a judge or jury's opinion without there being any basis of fact, nor will the introduction of the information violate anyone's constitutional rights or any existing law.

Covert Data: Data that is intentionally concealed on a system or media device for the express purpose of preventing others from finding it.

Credible or Credibility: Evidence or testimony that is easily believed without stretching reason

Criminal Action: A court trial in which one or more parties is accused of violating a law and faces penalties that may include incarceration, fines, or even capital punishment.

Curriculum Vitae: A document, similar to a résumé, that presents the pertinent facts about a person's education, experience, and any other qualifications that render that person suitable for a particular endeavor.

Dark Data: Information intentionally hidden or accidentally lost that exists on a system.

Data Carving: A method of extracting files in their entirety from unallocated space by identifying the file header and end-of-file marker, and then copying everything between those two points into a new file.

Defendant: In a criminal or civil action, the person who is accused of wrongdoing is the defendant.

Discovery: A legal process under which each party involved in litigation provides the other party with all evidence or documentation that it intends to use in presenting its case. Failure to adequately respond to a discovery order can result in significant penalties being imposed by the court.

Exculpatory: Any evidence or testimony that deflects blame from a specific individual.

Expert Witness: A person endowed with specialized training or unique knowledge who is called upon to state an opinion, based on technical information that may be difficult for the average person to comprehend.

Federal Rules of Evidence: A document adopted by the U.S. Supreme Court that defines exactly how evidence may be obtained, what makes it admissible, and how it may be presented in a court of law.

Forensic: Belonging to, used in, or suitable to courts of judicature or public discussion and debate.

FQDN: Fully Qualified Domain Name. The name and domain level (separated by a dot) for a specific Web site on the Internet. MWGRAVES.COM is the FQDN of the author's Web site.

Hash: A mathematical representation of a specific data repository. Many hash algorithms exist.

Hearsay: Any statement that is made outside of the proceedings by any party who was not under oath at the time the statement was made and that is not the personal knowledge of the person giving the testimony.

Host Protected Area: A partition on a hard disk, hidden by the computer manufacturer, where BIOS and device configuration information is stored.

IMAP: Internet Message Access Protocol. A more advanced protocol for receiving and opening email messages, IMAP allows users to use offline storage for incoming messages and allows multiple people to administer the same mailbox.

Inaccessible Data: In a search for information during the process of *discovery*, accessible data is that information that resides in locations that will require considerable effort to extract the information.

Incriminating: Any evidence or testimony that indicates the guilt of a subject in regard to a specific crime.

Inculpatory: Any evidence or testimony that directs blame to a specific individual.

Information Store: A file or collection of files used by an e-mail client to store messages, notes, calendar events, and other pieces of information the client is capable of collecting.

Internal Investigation: An inquiry made by an organization that is kept within the organization. Evidence extracted is not intended for presentation in a court of law.

Kernel Mode: A processing environment that allows full access to all aspects of the system.

Keylogger: A piece of software or hardware that intercepts each and every keystroke generated on the target computer.

Litigation: Any action brought before a court of law with the intent of enforcing a particular right or agreement. Generally speaking, litigation is a civil court action as opposed to a criminal action.

Litigation Hold: An order issued during the discovery process that instructs the recipient to cease and desist all destruction of documents, either physical or digital, until the proceedings have been completed. Another term for a *preservation order.*

Log File: A detailed record of every event that has occurred over a period of time in an application or a database or on a device.

Lossless: A form of data compression that restores a file precisely to its original state when uncompressed.

Lossy: A form of data compression that is unable to restore a file precisely to its original state when uncompressed.

MAC: Modify, Access, Create. These are file attributes that identify specific times and dates that each of the nominative actions occurred.

Mail Delivery Agent: A software package that sorts out incoming messages and delivers them to the correct mailbox on a mail server.

Mail Transport Agent: A software package that is responsible for moving an e-mail message from source to destination.

Mail User Agent: The software interface (or client) that allows users to send and receive email.

MD5: Message Digest, version 5. A cryptographic hashing algorithm that assigns a numerical value to a specific data repository.

Metadata: Literally speaking, metadata is information about information. A metadata file in the OS provides information about how data is stored and retrieved within the file system. Document metadata is a collection of hidden fields within the document that provides information about the document.

MIME: Multipurpose Internet Mail Extension. A file packaging standard used by e-mail messages that defines message format.

Netstat: A TCP-IP utility that identifies all network connects currently active on a network interface.

No Knock Warrant: A specific order issued by a judge that allows agents of the government to enter private property without knocking or without identifying themselves. Such a warrant is issued when there is reasonable expectation that valuable evidence will be destroyed before the executors of the warrant can secure the scene.

NSLookup: A command-line TCP-IP utility that can identify a URL by its IP address.

Null Cipher: A message-encoding technique that hides a secret message within a seemingly innocuous piece of text. The message is extracted by applying a pre-defined template to the carrier message, thereby extracting only the words in the text file relevant to the encoded message.

Offset: A method of obtaining an absolute address of a particular bit in memory, based on how many bits away from the base address the bit is located.

Ostensible Authority: Another term for *apparent authority*.

Parse: To analyze an object down to its most basic structure. To parse a file is to identify specific elements within the file, including elements not seen by the average user, such as metadata fields. A search engine parses a phrase typed in by a user by searching each individual word within the phrase as well as the phrase in its entirety.

Particularity: Warrants or subpoenas issued by the courts must be very specific in who is being targeted by the search, what is being sought, and where the evidence being sought is likely to be located. This degree of specificity defines particularity.

Partition: A logical division of a hard disk drive (or other storage medium) that divides a single device into multiple volumes.

PII: Personally identifiable information. When considering security and privacy issues, the information that is unique to a particular individual is considered sacrosanct. This is the PII that is most jealously protected.

Plain View Doctrine: A rule that states that evidence that is discovered by an agent of the government during the normal course of an arrest or interrogation, which is discovered because it existed out in the open where anyone could see it, can be seized without a warrant.

Plaintiff: In a criminal or civil action, the person who files the initial complaint is the plaintiff.

POP3: Post Office Protocol, version 3. It is a protocol that allows e-mail clients to receive and open messages.

Prejudiced or Prejudicial: Likely to sway the opinion of the average person without there being a factual foundation for the information, statement, or evidence that is being presented.

Preservation Order: A writ issued by a court ordering that no documents or other evidence be destroyed from that point forward.

Privileged Information: Any form of information that is protected from discovery during litigation. Such information includes doctor-patient communications, lawyer-client communications, or confessions made to a religious authority.

Probable Cause: A reasonable belief that an action is justified, based on circumstances or factual information that a "prudent person" would be led to believe merited such actions.

Promiscuous Mode: An operating method used by a network interface card that forces it to accept and process every packet that it receives from the network. The default configuration is to filter packets by IP or MAC address and only process packets for the device on which it is installed.

Protective Order: A writ issued by the court that prohibits the recipient from performing certain actions specific to document discovery. Generally, protective orders prohibit the disclosure of certain types of information, but they can also prohibit an unreasonable discovery request. On a physical level, protective orders are issued to put a stop to abusive behavior between two people.

Proxy: On behalf of. A proxy server is a machine that interfaces with the Internet on behalf of all the other computers on the proxy's network.

Rainbow Tables: A collection of hash values of every character in every character set. Password-cracking software compares hash values found in the tables to those on the system, looking for possible passwords.

Reasonable Expectation of Privacy: Any set of conditions that a prudent person would consider inappropriate for sharing with the general public. Anything that a person intentionally and with foreknowledge exposes to public view is excluded from such an expectation.

Redact: To intentionally render certain information in a file or document unreadable.

Relevant or Relevance: Evidence or testimony that is relevant is both *material* and *probative*. It directly relates to the case being presented (material), and it will provide some form of information that will allow the court to better perceive the truth (probative).

Scheme: In Internet terms, the scheme is the type of protocol used to access a particular resource on the Internet.

Scope: A definition of what work is expected to be completed in the course of an investigation, taking into consideration what is allowed under the terms of the legal authorizations allowing the investigation.

Search: Any examination of a person's body, residence, possessions, or any other aspect of that person's being that any reasonable person would consider private.

Sector: A unit of storage on a magnetic or optical disk. Whereas data consists of individual bits, the hard disk controller reads the platter in larger units. The sector is the smallest logical collection of bytes read by the hard disk. On earlier hard disks, the sector consisted of 512 bytes. The "super sector" used in the Advanced Disk Format is 4KB.

Seizure: The acquisition or confiscation of any items found in the process of a search.

Sessionize: To break a complex network capture down to only the packets exchanged between devices during a single established communications event.

SHA256 or SHA512: Secure Hash Algorithm (256-bit or 512-bit). A cryptographic hashing algorithm that assigns a numerical value to a specific data repository.

SIM: Subscriber Identity Module. A small chip on a cellular telephone that stores information about the user and that user's account with the service provider.

Slack Space: Space remaining in a cluster or partition that cannot be used, even though it does not contain data.

Sneak and Peek Warrant: A specific order issued by a judge that allows agents of the government to enter a private area or to monitor activities of an individual without that person's knowledge.

Spoliation: The intentional destruction of data or evidence in an effort to prevent it from being used in a hostile manner. Generally, spoliation occurs when data is destroyed in defiance of a *preservation order*. However, courts have also found that destruction of information in anticipation of litigation constitutes spoliation.

SQUID: A Linux-based *proxy* server.

Stakeholder: Any person, organization, or other entity that has a vested interested in the outcome of a project or investigation.

Steganography: The art of concealing messages or data inside other data. Music files are often used to carry image files in a fashion that, without specific software, is undetectable to most users.

Streams: A Microsoft utility for finding *alternate data streams*.

Subpoena: An order directing a person or entity to appear in court on a certain date and/or to produce specific documents relevant to a legal issue.

Subpoena Duces Tecum: A writ ordering a person or an agent of an organization to appear before a court that identifies specific documents or other forms of evidence that must be presented at the time of appearance as defined by the order .

Taint Team: A group of individuals assigned by a court to oversee the discovery process in order to prevent *privileged information* from being inadvertently being disclosed during discovery.

Testimony: A statement made by a witness, plaintiff, or defendant that is made under oath and that presents that person's understanding of the facts relevant to a case.

Timeline: A logical representation of all events that occurred, in the order in which they occurred, that are related to a specific incident or case.

Timestamp: A hidden field in a file or event log that identifies the exact time and date that a particular event occurred.

Triangulation: A method of locating a device transmitting a signal within a very large area, with a small margin of error, by taking three known coordinates and measuring the distance from each point to the source of the signal. When lines are drawn between the three coordinates, the device can be located where the lines converge.

Unallocated Space: Clusters on a hard disk that have not be "claimed" by a file in the file system. Deleted files become unallocated space without actually erasing the data. Therefore, unallocated space is a prime resource for locating deleted data.

URL: Uniform Resource Locator. A user-friendly (sort of) name for any particular Web site or file that can be accessed on the Internet.

User Mode: A processing environment within an operating system that offers relatively low privilege levels. Certain processes and commands are not allowed.

Warrant: An official order, issued by a person with sufficient authority, that approves a specific act. Warrants can be issued for the arrest of a person or for the search of a person or premises.

Warrens: Unconventional locations on a computer that are not generally used for storing data, but that, through special software or techniques, can be used for hiding data.

WHOIS: A TCP-IP service that returns critical data about a Web site based on its IP address.

INDEX

Safari
Books Online

FREE
Online Edition

Your purchase of *Digital Archaeology* includes access to a free online edition for 45 days through the Safari Books Online subscription service. Nearly every Addison-Wesley Professional book is available online through Safari Books Online, along with thousands of books and videos from publishers such as Cisco Press, Exam Cram, IBM Press, O'Reilly Media, Prentice Hall, Que, Sams, and VMware Press.

Safari Books Online is a digital library providing searchable, on-demand access to thousands of technology, digital media, and professional development books and videos from leading publishers. With one monthly or yearly subscription price, you get unlimited access to learning tools and information on topics including mobile app and software development, tips and tricks on using your favorite gadgets, networking, project management, graphic design, and much more.

Activate your FREE Online Edition at
informit.com/safarifree

STEP 1: Enter the coupon code: XIUAXAA.

STEP 2: New Safari users, complete the brief registration form.
Safari subscribers, just log in.

If you have difficulty registering on Safari or accessing the online edition,
please e-mail customer-service@safaribooksonline.com